MW00789076

Alabamians in BLUE

CONFLICTING WORLDS

New Dimensions of the American Civil War

T. MICHAEL PARRISH, Series Editor

Alabamians in BLUE

FREEDMEN, UNIONISTS, AND
THE CIVIL WAR IN THE COTTON STATE

Christopher M. Rein

LOUISIANA STATE UNIVERSITY PRESS

BATON ROUGE

Published by Louisiana State University Press

Copyright © 2019 by Louisiana State University Press

All rights reserved

Manufactured in the United States of America

First printing

DESIGNER: Mandy McDonald Scallan

TYPEFACE: Whitman

PRINTER AND BINDER: Sheridan Books

Library of Congress Cataloging-in-Publication Data

Names: Rein, Christopher M., author.

Title: Alabamians in blue : freedmen, unionists, and the Civil War in the Cotton State / Chris Rein.

Other titles: Conflicting worlds.

Description: Baton Rouge : Louisiana State University Press, [2019] | Series: Conflicting worlds : new dimensions of the American Civil War | Includes bibliographical references and index.

Identifiers: LCCN 2018037601| ISBN 978-0-8071-7066-3 (cloth : alk. paper) | ISBN 978-0-8071-7128-8 (epub) | ISBN 978-0-8071-7127-1 (pdf)

Subjects: LCSH: Alabama—History—Civil War, 1861–1865. | Unionists (United States Civil War)—Alabama. | Freedmen—Alabama—History—19th century.

Classification: LCC E551 .R45 2019 | DDC 973.7/461—dc23

LC record available at https://lccn.loc.gov/2018037601

For my mother,
Marilyn McWhorter Rein: Educator, Mentor, Alabamian

So far the men have done all that could be expected. Now that we are located and have an opportunity to be soldiers, let us be the best of soldiers. We are all new hands together but must all learn and I hope and trust that you will do all you can.

—CAPT. SANFORD TRAMEL
commander, Company L, First Alabama Cavalry

Sanford Tramel
1ST Ala Cav

Contents

Acknowledgments

When a young graduate student, whose background in history was admittedly poor, approached Dr. William Cooper in the autumn of 1999 and asked him to direct an MA thesis on Unionist military service in the Trans-Mississippi West, he very easily could have declined. Dr. Cooper most graciously did not, and his skillful direction, along with that of committee members Charles Royster and Stan Hilton, enabled me to complete that project and, almost twenty years later, inspired this one. Dr. William Freehling's work on "Anti-Confederate Southerners" gave this work its theoretical framework, and Dr. Margaret Storey's work on Alabama's Unionists was an enormous aid in completing it. The late Glenda McWhirter Todd and Ryan Dupree, respectively, have published on and maintain a website dedicated to the First Alabama Cavalry, creating some tremendous resources. Chris McIlwain's and Michael W. Fitzgerald's recent work on the state has been immensely helpful as well. Last but not least, Dr. Ken Noe of Auburn University provided much encouragement and helped place the work.

Iowa

    Archivists at a number of facilities gave generously of their time to provide assistance and prepare essential resources, especially Ellen Bridenstine at the State Historical Society of Iowa, whose efforts facilitated my use of the Grenville Dodge Papers, and Becki Plunkett, who assisted with gathering images from the same collection. Tom Parson at the Corinth Battlefield Unit of the Shiloh National Military Park shared his considerable expertise on the park and the units raised and stationed there, and provided access to the site's excellent resources. Archivists at the Birmingham Public Library, the Newberry Library, the University of Michigan, the Lincoln Memorial Library in Springfield, and the National Archives in Washington, DC all provided essential assistance. The voters and taxpayers of Jackson County, Missouri, are to be commended for establishing and maintaining the Midwest Genealogy Center branch of the Mid-Continent Public Library, which has an amazing, and accessible, collection of published local history resources, including enough focused on Alabama to rival many libraries within the Yellowhammer state. At LSU Press, the many efforts of series editor T. Michael Parrish, Editor in Chief Rand Dotson, and editor Gary Von Euer, as well as the anonymous reviewers who all contributed to making this a much better work than it otherwise would have been, are greatly appreciated. Thanks also to Drs. John Edward Grenier and Mark L. Bradley, who graciously reviewed early drafts of chapters, and Eric Burke and Matt White, copanelists at the 2018 Society of Civil War Historians Conference in Pittsburgh, for very helpful tips on several unidentified resources. All remaining errors of fact and interpretation are, of course, my own.

Colleagues at the Air Force Academy, the Air Command and Staff College, and the Army University Press provided support and encouragement. At US-AFA, Jeanne Heidler graciously lent her considerable expertise on the period, and gave me the opportunity to teach the History Department's courses on the American South and the Civil War, and Visiting Professor Juliet Walker (a long-lost cousin!) allowed me to audit her course on African American history. I'm grateful for the support and encouragement at ACSC of Drs. John Reese, John Terino, Seb Lukasik, Paul Springer, Kenny Johnson, Mike Weaver, and Joel Bius. At AUP, Don Wright has been an excellent director, mentor, and colleague, Ken Gott a model supervisor, and Joe Bailey a supportive colleague.

On a more personal level, my family has provided me critical indulgences as I pursued my many passions. My wife Beth and daughters Krista, Maddie, Ally, and Jossie have all sacrificed much while I worked on this project. Without their efforts, understanding, and love, writing this book would not have been even remotely possible. From an early age, my father, Charles Richard Rein, and mother, Marilyn McWhorter Rein, have been steadfast supporters, mentors, sounding boards, and friends. My mother's unconditional love and sage advice sustains me as much now as it ever has. For my high school senior trip, when friends were headed to Florida or Mexico, at my request she took me to Vicksburg to tour the battlefield. I enjoyed that trip more than I could have any other, and remember it well to this day. Her interest in and passion for the history of her native state and region, and the war years when her own ancestors endured much suffering, fear, dislocation, and loss, have been duly transmitted to the next generation. It is to her, with much love and deep gratitude, that this work is dedicated.

Alabamians
in BLUE

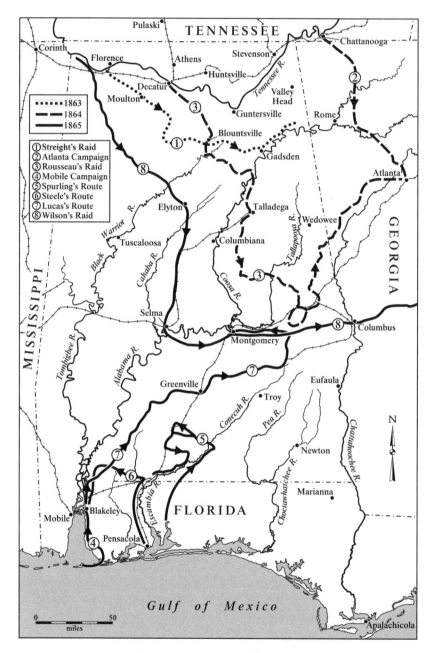

Principal Union Campaigns in Alabama, 1863–1865
Map by Mary Lee Eggart.

Introduction

Between 1862 and 1866, roughly 7,500 black and white Alabamians demonstrated their opposition to the so-called Confederate States of America by actively opposing it as soldiers in the Union army.[1] Their stated reasons for doing so were diverse, ranging from a desire to end the institution of slavery to ideological and political beliefs, or simply as a way of keeping themselves and their families alive during the crisis. Statistically, they represent only an infinitesimal portion of the nearly one million people living in Alabama in 1860, but militarily, they had an effect out of proportion to their numbers. Their efforts, by creating and supporting internal disruptions within the state, and denying their critically needed support to the cause of secession and disunion, helped to fatally undermine Confederate efforts. Most significantly, and in a junction of the "internalist" and "externalist" explanations for the defeat of the Confederacy, they magnified the power of the Union army by providing critical, if often unacknowledged, intelligence of Confederate dispositions and intentions and by protecting Union armies in the field from the efforts of Confederate raiders intent upon disrupting vital supply lines.[2] Though small in numbers, they helped Federal authorities regain control over Confederate-occupied areas and freed up manpower essential for conducting decisive conventional military operations.

Throughout 1864, regiments composed of black and white Alabamians fought battles, often unsuccessfully, that kept Confederate general Nathan Bedford Forrest away from railroads in Tennessee upon which Union general William Tecumseh Sherman depended for the successful prosecution of the Atlanta campaign and a buildup of supplies that enabled the "March to the Sea." These units successfully frustrated Forrest's efforts in the region, challenging the myth of the cavalry commander's effective leadership, as organizations largely comprised of freedmen and Unionists prevented the famed and

often overrated cavalryman from interfering with far more important operations. These actions were not undertaken by isolated units of either African
American, Northern, or Southern Unionist regiments, but by a cosmopolitan
force comprised of all three, in a well-coordinated strategy that exposed Forrest's shortcomings as a military commander.[3]

Black and white Alabamians wearing blue uniforms accompanied Sherman
on his decisive operation, which proved conclusively to the Confederacy that
their cause was doomed, led to the final destruction of the Confederate forces
in the western theater, and arguably ended the war four short months later.
The First Alabama Cavalry, a regiment of white Alabama Unionists, formed
Sherman's headquarters guard on his march through Georgia, and companies
of US Colored Troops (USCT), including the 110th and 111th US Colored Infantry (USCI), which were originally organized as the Third and Fourth Regiments of Alabama Infantry, African Descent, provided pioneer and teamster
services, preparing the roads and driving the wagons that sustained the force,
while other companies of these regiments still in northern Alabama absorbed
Forrest's ineffectual blows. In the southern part of the state, the First Florida
Cavalry Regiment, composed of a large number of Unionists from Alabama,
and additional USCT regiments, including the Eighty-Second and Eighty-Sixth
USCI, containing a number of freedmen who had escaped from bondage in
Alabama, challenged Confederate control of the Gulf Coast and eventually
contributed to the liberation of Mobile. Thus, the service of these "Alabamians
in Blue," or, as William Freehling has dubbed them, "Anti-Confederate Southerners," provided more than a visible and significant symbol of internal opposition to the Confederacy; they helped redeem their state from the dominion
of traitors.[4]

Freehling argues that white anti-Confederates, largely from the upper
South, helped secure the border states, while black anti-Confederates, mostly
from the Deep South, held the Mississippi Valley. Both groups are in evidence
in Alabama, but they often exchanged roles; the state's black troops also participated in combat while its white troops often performed garrison duty protecting vital railroads which, as William Thomas points out, became the focus
of the war.[5] White Alabamians, largely from the Hill Country, aided Federal
efforts to control the Confederacy's northern border, while black Alabamians
helped secure this area against Confederate raiders, or, at least, to occupy their
efforts before they could seriously disrupt important operations such as the

Atlanta campaign. Thus, the "disproportionally black army of occupation freed the disproportionally white army of conquest to move on" to the east, enabling the liberating armies to conduct further operations.[6] This division of labor was heavily influenced by the racial, often racist beliefs of the times, not least by Sherman himself, but provides an irrefutable example of biracial cooperation to achieve significant social change.

To date, these groups have received scant but increasing attention from historians. In her seminal work *Loyalty and Loss,* Margaret Storey has expertly and productively explored Unionist sentiment from Alabama, and this work has benefited tremendously from her efforts. Storey's work focuses more on the Unionist home front, though it includes some coverage of military service, perhaps the most ardent demonstration of the depth of Union sentiment.[7] As George Rable has pointed out, Storey's focus on Unionists on the home front, and its compelling story of suffering and loss, leaves some questions unanswered about its significance.[8] Similarly, Barton Myers's excellent recent volume on biracial Unionism in North Carolina, *Rebels Against the Confederacy,* covers the importance of Federal outposts in providing a place of refuge and employment for the persecuted Unionist communities, but largely omits any mention of what happened after black and white Unionists reached safety within Union lines. It is hoped that this work, by privileging tangible service that helped defeat the Confederacy, will provide essential context. The only scholarly work on the First Alabama, Stanley Hoole's *Alabama Tories,* dates from the war's centennial and derisively refers to the unit's soldiers as "Tories."[9] Kenneth Noe's edited volume *The Yellowhammer War,* a comprehensive effort to mark the war's sesquicentennial in the state, includes valuable information from Terry Seip on the First Alabama Cavalry's commander, Col. George Spencer, but lacks essays on either the black or Unionist military experience, and does not fully explore the war's environmental causes and effects.[10] Sadly, the experiences of the state's thousands of black soldiers remain undocumented in the literature outside of one slim volume.[11]

Far too often, narratives of USCT service, which have proliferated in the last quarter-century, have treated their subjects in some isolation from the larger context of the war.[12] Given their exclusion from earlier histories, this was probably appropriate, but historians must now reintegrate their experiences back into the larger narrative. Black and white Alabamians in the Union army did not fight in separate wars. They fought in the same war, often in the same battles, lived in refugee and "contraband" camps in the same "garrison towns," and fought, bled, suffered, and died supporting the same cause. Their service in largely segregated units does not undermine these simple truths. They were united by the same goals, and their efforts, under the guise of an active and interventionist Federal government, resulted in significant change and ushered in an important, but too brief, period of biracial political cooperation within the state. Today, this same triumvirate of massive black resistance, smaller numbers of native whites in support, and an activist Federal government, successfully replicated one hundred years later during the civil rights era, holds promise for sparking continued social progress and progressive change in Alabama.

If the services of Alabama's anti-Confederates have largely escaped scholarly attention, it was not due to a lack of sources. The American Civil War remains one of the best-documented in the nation's history, and the exploits of this group have been hiding in plain sight.[13] The War Department's records, including the 128-volume *The War of the Rebellion,* more commonly known as the Official Records, and other resources on military units and posts in Record Group 94 of the National Archives contain a detailed accounting of the recruitment and service of these soldiers, and the department's vast bureaucracy includes records of individual soldiers, units, and organizations, such as the Bureau of Colored Troops, involved in recruiting and employment. Members of Alabama's Union regiments left at least two publicly available diaries and published three memoirs, three from the First Alabama Cavalry, one from the First Florida Cavalry and one by an officer in the 111th USCI, which unfortunately skews coverage toward the white regiments.[14] The records of the Southern Claims Commission highlight connections between soldiers and the home front before, during, and after their service. As the government only accepted liability for depredations by US troops, and because these forces, except for brief raids, remained confined largely to the Tennessee River valley during the war, the claims records skew heavily to this region of the state, where most of the USCT soldiers lived before the war, and to the Hill Country to the south that provided the bulk of the white Union soldiers.[15] This is beneficial for units raised in this region, especially the First Alabama Cavalry, but conceals evidence of loyalty in the Alabama River valley and the Wiregrass region, which did not see Union forces until after the end of hostilities, if at all. Significantly, the entire SCC process serves to highlight the continuing struggle to recover resources lost during the war.

Most importantly, the turn toward social history, including new approaches by historians working on slavery, poorer communities, and the environment, has added rich detail. While often posited as a false dichotomy
between the "old," often referred to derisively as "drums and bugles" military
history, and the "new," or "war and society" approach, the best work continues
to blend these methods, enhancing our comprehension of military operations
and campaigns by understanding the societies that raised and equipped armies
and what they hoped to accomplish with them.[16] This volume benefits from
the new work by historians working in social, cultural, and especially environmental history to better understand why and how Alabama's Union troops
fought. Economic collapse, and the inability to coax a living from Alabama's
otherwise generous environment, both sparked and helped resolve the strife
within the state between 1861 and 1865.

Historians have recently emphasized the violent nature of the guerrilla
warfare behind the lines, often triggered by environmental factors, and as
Storey's work clearly demonstrates, northern Alabama offers a compelling
case study for the importance of this violent and brutal conflict.[17] Indeed, the
tide of recent scholarship on guerrilla aspects of the Civil War, perhaps influenced by events in America's contemporary excursions in Iraq and Afghanistan, makes pushing back against it a difficult task. But in reemphasizing the
conventional campaigns that ultimately led to the Confederate surrender and
ended the conventional war, I argue for the continuing relevance and importance of military operations in warfare. With some important exceptions, the
formal declaration of war unleashed the worst of the guerrilla violence and
largely ended it in 1865. But rather than set up another false dichotomy between the relative importance of one or the other, it might be most useful to
consider the conflict a "hybrid war," where conventional and unconventional
campaigns proceeded simultaneously, not unlike many of the United States'
post–Civil War conflicts.[18] The resistance offered by Alabama Unionists in
1861 and 1862 led to a brutal counterinsurgency campaign by state troops and
home guardsmen that drove Unionists into Federal lines. There, their stories
contributing to a "hardening" of the war that fueled the guerrilla violence
behind Confederate lines throughout the war, further undermining the rebellion. These combined internal and external pressures eventually crushed the
Confederacy.

Environmentally, Alabama is both a unique, yet also a typical southern
state, spanning from the Appalachian foothills to the sandy shores of the Gulf

Coast. Alabama's fertile creek and river valleys, fed with minerals from a decaying mountain range and watered by some of the heaviest downpours in the nation, sustained first an indigenous population and later a robust system of slave-based agriculture in both the Alabama and Tennessee River valleys. But the upcountry regions, especially in the north-central portion of the state and in the southeastern Wiregrass, provided less hospitable lands for agriculture.[19] Excluded from most of the benefits of plantation society, hardscrabble whites in these areas, including the "Free State of Winston," resisted Confederate control in a manner similar to other Appalachian and "pine barrens" communities in neighboring states, as in Mississippi's "Free State of Jones."[20] Slaves in the productive river valleys daily watched the product of their own labor being stolen by their masters, reinforcing the importance of control over the means of production, whether that included natural resources, industry, or simple human labor. Enslaved people throughout the antebellum period sought access to their share of the incredible profits being produced in their midst, either by securing permission to hire their time, purchasing their freedom, or escaping the region altogether. This struggle is as surely rooted in environmental causes as any other.

In addition to helping drive African American population centers and white political affiliation, the environment also determined, to an extent, the conduct of combat within the state's borders. The flat, east-west Tennessee River valley proved to be the best route for a rail linkage across the Confederacy, hosting the Memphis & Charleston Railroad which first led Union forces to the state. At the same time, Mobile's magnificent natural harbor sheltered blockade-runners and attracted a large Federal force to its shores, although only late in the war after other, seemingly more pressing campaigns in Texas and Louisiana. Finally, the rich mineral deposits of coal, iron ore, and limestone, which eventually made Birmingham the "Pittsburgh of the South," likewise generated both Confederate iron furnaces and Union raiders sent to destroy them. But the state's dense ridge-and-valley geography, with its limited settlement and poor resources, served as a barrier to movement on a north-south axis and repeatedly frustrated Union efforts, succumbing only in the last days of the war.

Environmental approaches to studying the Civil War have been especially fruitful, and the volume of literature on environmental aspects of the Civil War continues to expand.[21] Environmental factors figure prominently in the service of Alabama's Federal units, as recruitment was highest in areas where the agricultural system collapsed first, whether under pressure from invading armies, guerrilla raiders, or chronic drought. Freedmen and Unionists faced with starvation willingly relocated themselves through what Stephen Ash has characterized as a "no-man's-land" to Federal lines, where military service and labor offered support for themselves and their families and protection from the increasing disorder and violence on the home front.[22] By understanding the local natural, built, and cultural environment, Alabama's Union soldiers were able to magnify the effectiveness of Federal forces, gradually levering Confederate armies away from the essential resources they needed to sustain the rebellion, including food, raw materials, transportation networks and, especially, manpower. I find the Civil War within Alabama fits exceptionally well within a larger framework of a "struggle for resources," beginning with the state's first inhabitants, continuing among the early settlers and, arguably, enduring to this day.[23] While not minimizing the powerful ideological causes that scholars have identified in motivating military service, this work hopes to illuminate the more practical considerations that lay at the root of those ideological attachments. While historians generally agree that Civil War soldiers "seldom fought for money," they often did fight, as Russell Johnson and others have successfully argued, for the society that offered the best prospects for their continued economic success.[24]

While incorporating these various themes, the book is still organized chronologically. Chapter 1 makes the case for viewing the state's early history as a contest for resources, both militarily and politically, focusing on the state's history from prehistoric times through the secession crisis. Chapter 2 covers the war's first two years, highlighting environmental aspects that spurred enlistment and the guerrilla violence that led to freedmen and refugees gathering in "garrison towns." The following three chapters each cover the three most important years for Alabama's Union soldiers, 1863, 1864, and 1865, highlighting recruiting, employment, and demobilization, respectively, with environmental factors and the struggle for resources deeply interwoven. With the first Union units recruited in late 1862, the following year was the first full campaign season in which Alabama's Union soldiers participated in major actions, contributing to Union successes at Vicksburg and Chattanooga. The pivotal year was 1864, with the success of the Atlanta campaign guaranteeing Lincoln's reelection and the continuation of the war effort, as well as the destruction of the Confederate economy and the isolation of Robert E. Lee's army in Virginia. The war finally came to the heart of Alabama in 1865, with the destruction of her nascent war economy, and after the Confederate surrender, Alabama's Union soldiers garrisoned strategic points within the state, including Mobile and Huntsville, and were part of the first contingents of Federal troops to enter the state capital of Montgomery. Unfortunately, the army quickly mustered these units out of service, removing them from Federal control and denying freedpeople and Unionists their protection, contributing to the cycle of violence that led first to Congressional or Radical Reconstruction and then to Redemption. Following Chapter 5, a brief epilogue covers life in post-Reconstruction Alabama.

For over a century, a single, deeply flawed volume dominated the historiography of Alabama's experiences during the Civil War and Reconstruction. Since publication of Walter Fleming's magisterial, and horribly biased *Civil War and Reconstruction in Alabama* in 1905, no single work has attempted to capture the state's wartime experiences.[25] Perhaps the finest example of the Dunning school's mischaracterization of Reconstruction as a "failed experiment," Fleming's work, long discredited and overturned by professional historians, still haunts the shelves of far too many of Alabama's public libraries.[26] Among its many flaws, the volume devotes but one of its eight-hundred-plus pages to Union troops from Alabama. As late as 1950, Robert Reid of Tuskegee Institute wrote, "Contemporary historians still rely heavily on Fleming's *Civil War and Reconstruction in Alabama*. . . . It is high time for some industrious historian who is capable of examining this period of Alabama history dispassionately to correct the misconceptions and mistakes of Fleming."[27]

Fortunately, several historians have recently taken up Reid's injunction. In addition to Storey's excellent work on Alabama's Unionists, Chris McIlwain's recent *Civil War Alabama* and *1865 Alabama* expertly trace Alabama's political climate during the war, as "fire-eating" secessionists attempted to hold off "reconstructionists" who sought reunion, ideally with the institution of slavery intact.[28] Michael W. Fitzgerald's *Reconstruction in Alabama* picks up the narrative with his excellent recent study of that period in the state, representing a lifetime of effort.[29] Joseph Danielson found a fertile field for reexamining the evolution of Federal occupation policy in Alabama's Tennessee River valley, and both Anthony Carey's and David Williams's studies of slave communities have continued an impressive volume of work on the antebellum and wartime black experience.[30] Kenneth Noe's edited volume highlighting the war's sesquicentennial explored many of these same aspects, including some of the leaders of Alabama's Union regiments and its wartime Unionist communities on the home front.[31] It seems, by accretion, historians have tackled every part of Fleming's work except the war itself.

This work seeks to recenter the narrative of the Civil War in Alabama. Rather than focusing on events in the Black Belt in general and Montgomery in particular, it moves into the Wiregrass of southeastern Alabama and the dark, secluded hollows of the Hill Country, to the slave cabins and quarters of plantations in the Tennessee and Chattahoochee River valleys. Rather than trace the path of Alabama's Confederate soldiers in Virginia and Tennessee, it tells the story of the Civil War in Alabama through the eyes of its Union regiments, often exiled from their former homes, but facilitating campaigns from Union footholds just outside the state's borders, at places such as Corinth, Mississippi; Pulaski, Tennessee; Rome, Georgia; and Pensacola, Florida, where Alabama's Union regiments supported Federal efforts to reestablish control over Alabama's considerable natural resources.

At the outset, this project began with three simple questions: First, who were the Alabamians in blue, in terms of their communities and social groups? Second, why did they choose to join the Union army and fight against the Confederacy, and what factors drove this decision? And third, what did they accomplish? Did their efforts have any significant effect on the war? What about for themselves personally? Did they benefit from their service, or was it yet another sacrifice laid upon the altar of freedom? These are complex questions, with necessarily complex answers. Those who eventually joined the Union army were indeed a diverse group, from very different locales and situations, with a variety of motivations. Some joined to avoid persecution or starvation. Some joined because they happened to be close enough to army camps at a time when the army desperately needed additional manpower. But collectively, they made important contributions to the eventual Union victory. After the war, many were persecuted for their loyalty by unrepentant Confederates, either driven from their homes and forced to live in exile, or murdered in cold blood, continuing the legacy of the wartime years.

Throughout recorded history, armies have mobilized indigenous allies to assist expeditionary forces. The British became especially adept at this, either on the Indian subcontinent or in the North American woods, and sustained their global empire for centuries with this incorporated labor. The US Army continued this tradition, recruiting Indian allies and scouts on the Great

Plains during the Indian Wars, and in its various wars for empire at the end of the nineteenth century. Arguably, it continues today. Indigenous forces, such as the Anti-Confederate Southerners in Alabama, provided more than additional manpower. Their knowledge of the physical and cultural terrain, connections to communities either in the "no-man's land" between the lines or in Confederate-held territory, and ability to successfully exploit these to keep informed the talented and aggressive commanders—most notably Sherman and Grant—in command of the Federal armies in the western theater, made a substantial contribution to the success of Union arms in what Earl Hess has convincingly argued was the decisive theater.[32] While the Army of the Potomac provided an effective "base of fire" against Lee's Army of Northern Virginia, the western armies, as the "maneuver element," strategically outflanked the Confederate position.

While they received pay and subsistence during their time in service (though until 1864, black troops received only $7 per month, instead of the $13 allowed for whites), many suffered debilitating injuries or death while in uniform. Those who survived sometimes earned pensions, if they could prove their disabilities were service-related, but a lack of documentation or testimony from witnesses resulted in many denied claims. Still, these men were willing to accept these risks, in exchange for security for themselves and, in many cases, for their families too, as well as access to food and shelter that would enable them to survive. This is not to say that Unionists were motivated purely by practical considerations; for many, the source of their material need was persecution as a result of their ideological attachment to the Union and its promise of freedom. Indeed, both sides of the war showed a strong preference for material considerations in choosing their alignment in the sectional struggle. But the efforts of Alabama's freedmen and Unionists, seconding those of troops from the Northern states, brought about significant, if unsecured, social and political change within their home state. Thus, their efforts and cooperation serve as a model for the ongoing effort to reshape Alabama's postwar society.

CHAPTER 1

Alabama's Contests for Resources,
Settlement to Secession

I n many respects, the American Civil War was a war for life-sustaining resources. Southern planters started the war to preserve their unique system of slave-based agriculture, which brought them great profits but would ruin them financially if it were ever overturned. For the Union, the war ensured that all of the nation's resources, both above and below the Mason-Dixon Line, but also in the expanding West, remained under a single, united government and not subject to partition until it resembled a balkanized Europe. But for Southern Anti-Confederates, as William Freehling has labeled them, the war brought more immediate and life-threatening effects. For the over four million slaves, the war presented an opportunity to escape an inhumane system of bondage, where a slave's life mattered only if it could generate a profit for his or her master, and was therefore an opportunity to control that most important natural resource, the product of human labor. Poor rations, unhealthy climates, a lack of medical care, exposure to the elements, and brutal punishments, including execution, meant that the slave lacked guaranteed access to the most essential resources to ensure his or her own survival. For Southern Unionists, especially in the Alabama backcountry, the war quickly approached a similar war for survival. Before the war, they had been able to coax a living from an otherwise plentiful environment. But conscription agents, taxes-in-kind, and wanton destruction and persecution by secessionist neighbors quickly placed the Unionist in a similar situation with regard to control over resources necessary for survival. When the opportunity presented itself, both sought to save their lives, and those of their families, as well as to better their condition and gain some measure of revenge on their persecutors with service in the Union army. Thus, the American Civil War on the Alabama frontier became, as are almost all wars, a contest for resources.

The landscape that these factions fought to control represents one of the most ecologically diverse and resource-rich on the North American continent. The area that eventually became the state of Alabama was once covered by a vast sea that deposited sediments unevenly across its floor. Over time, these sediments compressed into the sandstone and limestone that today's residents of the northern half of the state can quickly recognize in rocky outcroppings, and chalks found in the western part of the state. Worn by erosion and constant rainfall, the sandstone and limestone easily weathered into deep ridges and formed large caves and even sinkholes. As the prehistoric oceans receded, the area became a coastal environment, with rich and dense vegetation composting and compressing into the coal veins still found not far from the surface in the middle of the state, and oil and gas fields, primarily along the western border with Mississippi. Across the center of the state, igneous and metamorphic rock predominates in the Piedmont region, further contributing to the state's rich diversity of minerals, including hematite in the future iron-producing region, and even copper and gold in the northeast. Though earthquakes are now rare, except in areas of intensive oil and gas exploration, ancient fault lines brought this rock to the surface, and further tectonic shifts thrust the overlying sandstone into regular ridges running northeast to southwest, and a broad plateau that spans the northern third of the state. Over time, ample rains washed these rocks south onto the sandy coastal plains, and in the shallower gradient, the heavier elements settled while only the lightest, smallest fragments, often pale quartzes, made their way to the coast, where they provided the Florida Panhandle with pure white sands and what some promoters claim are the "world's most beautiful beaches" along the "Emerald Coast." The various folds and pockets within the earth harbor massive aquifers, constantly recharged by the region's heavy rainfall. Mobile, along the Gulf Coast, records some of the highest rainfall totals in the nation, as frequent deluges top an average of sixty inches per year.

The humid subtropical climate makes precipitation, usually in the form of rain, but rarely during the brief winters as sleet or snow, a constant almost year-round. Frontal passage in early spring can bring heavy rain and tornadoes in "Dixie Alley," especially in the state's northwest, and hurricanes are not uncommon in late summer along the coast. Though severe drought is possible, most years feature sufficient rainfall and lengthy growing seasons that make extracting a living from the land an uncomplicated enterprise. For example, corn planted after the last frost in the Alabama River valley near present-day

Montgomery can top six feet before the beginning of summer, and a 250-day growing season enables double-cropping in areas where soil nutrients can support it. But the heavy rainfall also leaches nutrients from poorer soils, leading to rapid soil exhaustion outside of the riparian corridors.[1]

The frequent rain supplies a complex network of rivers that enables the state to rank first in the nation in navigable stream-miles.[2] Waterways generally run north to south, with one important exception. The Tennessee River, after rising in the foothills of southwestern Virginia, enters Alabama at its northeastern corner, but blocked from continuing on its southwesterly path by the massive uplift of Sand Mountain, turns first to the west, collecting the Elk River and then, inexplicably, back north again, leaving the state at its northwestern corner before falling into the deep valley of the Ohio River in western Kentucky. In the nineteenth century, the river was navigable as far as Muscle Shoals near Florence, and again above them to Chattanooga. In the 1930s, the Tennessee Valley Authority built three massive main-stem hydroelectric dams on the river, inundating rich bottomlands but easing navigation and spurring rural electrification. High on the aptly named Sand Mountain, the headwaters of the Black Warrior River rise a short distance from the Tennessee River near Guntersville and wind their way southwest, collecting further contributions from the Locust and Mulberry Forks before flowing into the Tombigbee River near modern Demopolis. From there, the combined streams head due south toward Mobile.

To the east of the Black Warrior River's headwaters, northern Georgia contributes both the Coosa and Tallapoosa Rivers to northeastern Alabama, the latter in a narrow and the former in a wider valley that angle southwest toward a junction just north of Montgomery. Now named the Alabama, the river runs more west than south for almost a hundred miles, collecting the waters of the Cahaba River, which rises near Birmingham and admirably fills the gap between the Alabama and Tombigbee drainages, before also turning south for the Gulf. Fifty miles above Mobile, the two streams begin an uneasy courtship, trading offerings in a quarter-million acre swamp known formally as the Mobile-Tensaw Delta (after the two rivers' newly assumed names), forming a dense wetland of tremendous biodiversity. But the marriage remains unconsummated, and both rivers travel under their assumed names to Mobile Bay, a fifteen-by-thirty-mile inundation of the lower delta that eventually opens onto the broad Gulf.

South and east of the Alabama River valley, four more streams drain the state's southeastern section. Along the eastern border, the Chattahoochee

River, also rising in the Appalachian foothills of north Georgia, flows south to its junction with the Flint River at the point where Alabama, Florida, and Georgia meet, with the ancient junction now submerged under the waters of Lake Seminole behind Jim Woodruff Dam. There they become the Apalachicola, which winds its way south another hundred miles, reaching the Gulf near its namesake village. Between Apalachicola and Mobile, three other river systems provide northwest Florida with fine anchorages: the Choctawhatchee/ Pea River system, which ends near Destin and Fort Walton Beach; the Conecuh/Escambia and Yellow Rivers, which form the twin arms of Pensacola Bay; and the Perdido River, which separates Alabama from Florida and empties into Perdido Bay. The frequent rainfall makes the streams regular and predictable, allowing each to carve a well-defined valley, with shallow gradients in the south and steeper sides in the north. The rivers also carry heavy sediment loads, depositing rich minerals below the "fall line" that marks the boundary between the Piedmont and the Coastal Plain and leaves a broad swath of fertile soil, known as the "Black Belt," stretching from the Georgia border south of Columbus clockwise up the Tombigbee River valley, Extensive agriculture in this region makes it visible from space to the naked eye, as the lighter-colored fields stand in contrast to the darker forests. The region originally took its name from the rich, dark, alluvial soils, but the dense collection of slave-based cotton plantations before the war make the name an accurate demographic descriptor as well.

The state's geology facilitates subdivision into five physiographic regions.[3] Below the fall line, the coastal plain generally features poor, sandy soils ideally suited for the Pine Barrens that dominate the region. The Black Belt, the extreme northern section of the coastal plain, is the exception, and the differences in soils led to readily identifiable cultural differences in the first half-century of statehood. The northern half of the state features greater ecological diversity, beginning with the Highland Rim north of the Tennessee River valley. Immediately south and west of that river sits the end of the Cumberland Plateau, or the "Hill Country" of north-central Alabama. To the southeast, the "Ridge and Valley" region resembles that of central Pennsylvania, with the sharp ridges funneling traffic in a northeast to southwest direction. Indeed, the rich iron ore deposits made Birmingham, for a while, the "Pittsburgh of the South." In the absence of gaps, which are few, it can be easier to travel fifty miles along the valley floor than five miles over the intervening

ridge to the next valley, which served to funnel early settlement to the southwest, moving upcountry Scots-Irish settlers into the Deep South. Most river
valleys, including that of the Cahaba, are narrow, but the Coosa is wider, enabling larger-scale agriculture and even slave-based plantations to flourish.
Between the Ridge and Valley Region and the Coastal Plain sit the Piedmont
Uplands of east-central Alabama, where mountains, such as Mount Cheaha,
the state's highest point, can reach over 2,400 feet in elevation. That region's
principal river, the Tallapoosa, occupies a narrower valley, limiting agricultural development for most of its length.

All five regions generally boast an impressive growth of trees, with decid-
uous oaks, hickories, maples, and tulip trees, a relative of the magnolia, dom-
inating to the north while pines, especially the stately and massive longleaf,
predominated in the sandier soils to the south. In the southeast, prairies of
dense *Aristida stricta* gave the region the moniker of the "Wiregrass," while the
Black Belt's rich soil sports dense groves of stubby cedars in places where natural fires have been unable to perform their cleansing function. River bottoms,
especially in the southern part of the state, support mixed forests of massive
cypress, tupelo, gum, and sycamore, well adapted to the waterlogged environment. The dense growth of vegetation supports large populations of mammals,
especially the *Odocoileus virginianus*, or white-tailed deer, which became an
important resource for food and clothing for Native inhabitants. Once Europeans discovered the better pliability of the thinner and softer textures of
deerskins, compared to cowskins, the hides became highly valued in Europe
for book bindings and gloves, making deer hides a valuable trade commodity
for indigenous peoples.[4] Other mammals, from bears to rabbits to squirrels,
fattened themselves on the dense growth and ample mast, and found their way
into the diets of both Indian hunters and larger predators, such as panthers
and wolves. Birds were especially plentiful, including the now extinct Carolina
parakeet and passenger pigeon, as well as the ubiquitous eastern wild turkey.
In the fall and winter, waterfowl are plentiful, including ducks, geese, and
sandhill cranes, and waterways abound in fish and shellfish, including mussels
in the inland rivers and oysters in the brackish coastal bays.

Natural food sources included wild fruits, especially blackberries, per-
simmons, and muscadines, which still dot many Alabama hillsides, as well
as nuts, including the hickory and native pecan.[5] Once cleared of timber, either through girdling or fire, fields yielded profuse growths of domesticated

maize, beans, and squash. Pumpkin vines grew several inches a day and rapidly crowded out competing weeds with their broad leaves. Sweet potatoes, first domesticated in Mesoamerica, spread north and became an important tuber. The best farming lands and densest game populations were in the river valleys, making these sites highly desirable for later human activities, such as hunting and fishing, and hosting the first towns and later cities.

When the first *Homo sapiens* crossed the Bering Land Bridge from Asia over 10,000 years ago, they found a region untouched by human habitation. As the ice sheets had receded during an earlier period of global warming, large mammals, known as megafauna, moved north onto emerging grasslands in the center of the continent. The availability of large game pulled humans down into the continent, and they eventually spread through Central America to the tip of South America. Continuous hunting pressure likely drove many species to extinction, including camels, mammoths, and giant ground sloths, with only the American bison and pronghorn antelope surviving as representatives of their species.[6] Human populations expanded eastward as well, filling the interior of the North American continent. Though these people were nomadic hunter-gatherers, they apparently developed attachments to certain areas, essential for life-giving resources, and defended them against the encroachment of other hunter-gatherers. In his seminal work, *War Before Civilization*, Lawrence Keeley reports excavating prehistoric sites near San Francisco with "many burials of unequivocal homicide victims," and "skeletons with embedded projectile points" that demonstrated an astonishingly high rate of homicide.[7]

In "rediscovering" the violent ways of our human ancestors, Keeley postulates three possibilities that might have driven ancient societies into conflict. There are certainly cultural explanations, as some societies are more "warlike" than others, and all societies, including our own, but especially early Native American ones, confer prestige and elevated status on warriors, making them both preferred mates and leaders. However, the root causes frequently point to resource scarcity or, at least, a desire for greater abundance. Keeley found that conflict increased during droughts in the American Southwest, with nomadic raiders "especially active during dry years."[8] And the status and prestige conferred on warriors, while an important aspect of culture, stems from the willingness of these individuals to defend their societies, or actively raid other societies, in order to gain or preserve access to life-giving resources, be they water, hunting lands, or areas with other food resources. In many respects, Keeley finds an inverse relationship between a society's size and its susceptibility to disaster or famine, with smaller communities lacking the resources to survive even minor disruptions, making them more likely to enter into conflict while larger societies enjoyed a more diverse, and resilient, resource base, and their sheer size often deterred potential adversaries.[9] Keeley's analysis is an accurate description of many Indian societies at the time of European contact.

In order to protect themselves against raiders, societies began constructing crude fortifications to protect villages. Evidence of native fortifications is widespread during the early contact period, most notably with the destruction of the Narragansetts in the Great Swamp Fight of 1675. Indeed, from first contact, the European explorers of what would become Alabama found evidence of fortifications among the current inhabitants of the region. In perhaps the most significant and devastating encounter, between Hernando DeSoto's expedition and the native inhabitants of the Southeast, the Spaniards attacked the fortified village of Mabila somewhere near Selma, with great loss to themselves and even greater loss to the poorly armed defenders.[10] The village's principal chieftain, "Tascaluza," anglicized today as "Tuscaloosa" or "Black Warrior," is the source of both the translated name of that stream and the town situated along its banks. Given the prior decades of contact between Spanish explorers and their African slaves along the coast, and native societies, it is interesting to speculate on Tuscaloosa's provenance. As he is described as being over a foot taller than the conquistadors, and well built, it is entirely possible that the first Africans to arrive in Alabama came not as bound captives, but, once assimilated into native societies, as proud and effective warriors. The adjective "black" is often dropped from the river's name, making it the slightly less threatening and more socially acceptable "Warrior River."

DeSoto's expedition, and indeed, all European colonization of the Americas, can be easily characterized as a war for resources. In order to maintain their growing empires in Europe, which provided not only wealth to kings but eventually tax revenues to their parliaments, European leaders needed colonies and markets to fuel their militaries. Spain's conquest of the New World came largely out of a successful search for mineral wealth, as the gold and silver specie of the Americas sustained the kingdom for centuries. Imperial rivals, including Great Britain and France, sought New World empires of their own, either to fuel their own wealth or, at the very least, to limit that of their competitors. Unable to conquer New Spain, English pirates instead concentrated their efforts on raiding the treasure fleets that carried the wealth annually across the Atlantic. While Jamestown is most often depicted as an entrepreneurial venture, it grew out of English efforts to establish raiding bases for privateers along the eastern coast of North America.

But the first Europeans to sustain colonies in what later became Alabama were neither English nor Spanish, but French. After establishing New France in the St. Lawrence River valley of modern Canada, French explorers and *coureurs du bois* expanded through the western river network, eventually arriving at the "Father of Waters," the Mississippi River, and followed it to the Gulf. Anxious to protect the mouth of what they hoped would become a continental empire, later expeditions sailing directly from France searched in vain for the mouth of the great river. After a failed attempt at colonization in Texas in 1688, the French finally founded their Louisiana colony at Biloxi in 1698, but moved the capital to the deepwater port of New Orleans in 1718. The French saw the advantages of maintaining flank protection for their Louisiana colony, establishing settlements to the west and north in the Mississippi River valley, and to the east in the Alabama River valley. From the fortified city of Mobile, founded in 1702, traders moved north along the Alabama and Tombigbee Rivers, establishing first Fort Toulouse, near Montgomery, at the confluence of the Coosa and Tallapoosa, in 1717, and later Fort Tombecbe near Demopolis, in 1736, near where the Black Warrior and Tombigbee Rivers joined, in order to control trade in that important drainage. The French force that traveled higher up the Tombigbee to the newly christened Fort Choiseul included forty-five black soldiers commanded by a free black named Simon.[11]

In the interior, pathogens from the Old World carried by DeSoto's expeditions and other refugees from Spanish Florida devastated the aboriginal inhabitants of the interior. Under constant demographic pressure, captives became an increasingly valuable commodity, to replace lost labor and ensure the vitality of Indian communities. Along the eastern seaboard, new colonies in the Carolinas, especially Charleston, established in 1670, developed an insatiable demand for labor, first enslaving the local native peoples in a genocidal campaign, but eventually reaching farther into the interior, making captives provided by powerful inland confederacies, especially the Creek and Cherokee nations, an essential resource. But these captives proved equally unable to withstand the brutal disease regime, and eventually English colonizers resorted to imported African slaves, who at least had some exposure to Old World diseases and might have acquired immunity.[12] Historians believe that the coalescence of the Creek and Cherokee nations into powerful Confederacies was largely a response to increasing pressure from European colonizers as well as the imperative to replace a population under constant assault from disease.[13] Paul Kelton has identified the symbiotic nature of war and disease, arguing that, among the Cherokees, the constant warfare exacerbated the effects of disease, as native populations constantly devoted resources to warfare and had life-sustaining activities disrupted by it, becoming far more susceptible to Old World diseases, especially smallpox, than they otherwise might have been.[14] But the pattern of slave-raiding and slave-trading reveals the critical importance of human labor as a necessary resource for survival in early America.[15]

To supply labor for the New Empire in the Mississippi River valley, the French likewise resorted to African chattel slavery, importing the first slaves to Alabama to augment the inadequate labor of the French settlers. In 1721, the appropriately named ship *Africane* dropped anchor at Mobile with a cargo of 120 Senegalese slaves, less than half the original cargo due to brutal conditions and high mortality on the middle passage across the Atlantic.[16] Hundreds more followed on each ship, beginning a new life in bondage in Alabama. In the following quarter-century, slavers transported over 6,000 Africans to Alabama, firmly establishing a slave society along the banks of the state's principal river system. Thus, African slaves had been working to build the society that would become Alabama almost a full century before statehood. Though the French *Code Noir* was, in some respects, less restrictive than later regulations, preventing the separation of families and mandating religious instruction, the system still appropriated labor without compensation, enabling slaveholders to triumph in the struggle for control of labor.[17]

But French domination of the Alabama coast and interior did not survive the unending struggle for resources. In 1763, after the decisive Seven Years,' or French and Indian, War, control of what became Alabama passed from France to Great Britain, while Spain assumed control of Spanish Louisiana as compensation for the loss of Florida.[18] In 1780, Spanish governor Bernardo de Galvez regained Mobile and the following year took Pensacola, reestablishing Spanish control over West Florida. Galvez's force was a polyglot of Spanish soldiers, French Acadians mustered into the Louisiana militia, and a company of free blacks from New Orleans.[19] From the older French city of Mobile, the Spanish pushed upriver, building an outpost at St. Stephens, which eventually became the territorial capital. But British traders from Charleston had already made deep inroads in the interior, intermarrying with the Creek and Cherokee Confederacies and attracting these powerful nations into their trading orbit.

During this time, the Anglo-American naturalist William Bartram made a historic foray into Alabama's interior, describing both the natural environment and the existing state of Indian societies, including the frequent conflict between them.[20] Of the Muscogees, or Creeks, the principal tribal inhabitants at the time of European settlement, Bartram eloquently reported their successes in both warfare and incorporation of conquered tribes. He reported their origins as

> from the west, beyond the Mississippi, their original native country. On this long journey they suffered great and innumerable difficulties, encountering and vanquishing numerous and valiant tribes of Indians, who opposed and retarded their march. Having crossed the river, still pushing eastward, they were obliged to make a stand, and fortify themselves in this place, as their only remaining hope, being to the last degree persecuted and weakened by their surrounding foes. Having formed for themselves this retreat, and driven off the inhabitants by degrees, they recovered their spirits, and again faced their enemies, when they came off victorious in a memorable and decisive battle. They afterwards gradually subdued their surrounding enemies, strengthening themselves by taking into confederacy the vanquished tribes . . . they never ceased war against the numerous and potent bands of Indians, who then surrounded and cramped the English plantations, as the Savannas, Ogeeches, Wapoos, Santees, Yamasees, Utinas, Icosans, Paticas, and others, until they had extirpated them.[21]

Another eighteenth-century visitor, trader James Adair, described the situation in neighboring nations with similar emphasis. According to Leah Rawls Atkins, "Adair reported that war was important to Cherokee society, and the taking of scalps was considered a brave deed. Cherokee mothers taught their small boys to avenge insults and to endure hunger and pain without complaint."[22] Bartram's and Adair's records clearly demonstrate the vital importance of warfare, not just as a ritual or cultural act, but as a necessity for the survival of native societies on the southeastern frontier.

Throughout his travels Bartram had frequent interaction with the principal tribes of the Southeast, meeting a war party of British-allied Seminoles, off to "fight their enemies the Chactaws," who historically allied with French Louisiana. Combat was an unavoidable consequence, "as the principal object of this expedition was hunting on the plentiful borders of the Chactaws."[23] Central Alabama formed something of an early "no-man's-land," with territories claimed by the Creek, Cherokee, Choctaw, and Chickasaw all meeting in the west-central part of the state, making it into a battleground as well as a de facto wildlife refuge, as hunting parties were just as likely to expend their arrows and powder on rival tribes as they were on game. But this was not the future state's last experience as a border region between warring factions.

The days of Indian Wars over Alabama's rich resources were numbered, as the consequences of the American Revolution gave the new United States title to the land as far west as the Mississippi River and removed the restraints the British had put in place to prevent expensive wars between land-hungry Anglo-American colonists and the native societies. With the American victory, settlers pushed first into the Tennessee River valley in North Alabama, arriving near Huntsville as early as 1805, eight short years after the formal organization of the Mississippi Territory. The future state's native inhabitants, the Creek, Cherokee, Choctaw, and Chickasaw Nations, were by now under pressure on three fronts, as the Louisiana Purchase in 1803 spurred American settlement in the lower Mississippi Valley. With immigration increasing in the Tennessee Valley to the north, and to the east in Georgia, Indian inhabitants found themselves compressed on all sides. When European warfare again spilled over onto the North American continent, in the War of 1812, some Creeks sought aid from Spanish West Florida, the only border largely free from crushing settlement pressures, in order to resist encroachment. But other factions, including many Creeks from the lower towns along the Chattahoochee and Flint Rivers, had already embarked on the path toward assimilation and could see no benefit from resisting what appeared to be inevitable. As a result, when the latest war for resources erupted at Burnt Corn Creek in 1813, the once powerful Creek Nation was too weak and divided to resist the land-hungry Americans.

The Creek War of 1813–1814 resulted in the US conquest of much Creek-held territory and led directly to the formation of the Alabama Territory in 1817 and statehood in 1819. The war erupted largely over concerns about increased traffic through Creek lands on the newly built Federal Road, connecting New Orleans with the eastern seaboard and cutting diagonally across southern Alabama, roughly parallel to the path of modern Interstate 65.[24] Some Lower Creeks, located along the route, welcomed the improved communications and increased commerce, and were likely to benefit from it, but many "Red Stick" Creeks from the upper towns along the Coosa and Tallapoosa Rivers feared additional pressures on their life-giving natural resources. War erupted on July 27, 1813, when a party of militia ambushed a band of Red Sticks returning from Spanish Pensacola, where they had traded for ammunition. Despite being pushed back, the militiamen succeeded in destroying the newly acquired shot and power, but were unable to prevent a reprisal that inflamed the Southeast.

In retaliation for the provocation at Burnt Corn Creek, a force estimated at seven hundred warriors attacked Fort Mims, near Bay Minette, where some four hundred settlers and slaves had fortified themselves against an expected outbreak of hostilities. On August 30, 1813, after skillfully breaking into the fortification, the Creeks killed many of those inside, taking about one hundred captives. The brazen attack and the high loss of life mobilized national sentiment for war against the Creeks. The ensuing struggle ultimately dispossessed the Creeks of most of their holdings in Alabama, while the commander of the American forces, Gen. Andrew Jackson, later as president, became the architect of their removal from the remaining reservation to what is now Oklahoma. Thus, the conflict over land, begun at Burnt Corn Creek and violently continued at Fort Mims, resulted in the most significant shift in human habitation in Alabama's history.[25]

Jackson's campaign against the Creek Nation was a model of effectiveness. After securing the cooperation of both Cherokees and sympathetic Creeks, who believed that they would remain in Jackson's good graces if they betrayed the hostile portion of their nation, Jackson formed the Tennessee and Kentucky militias, marched south from Tennessee, and routed Red Stick factions at Tallushatchee, Talladega, and Hillabee. After wintering over at Fort Strother at the Ten Islands Ford on the Coosa River near Ragland, and receiving reinforcements in the form of a full regiment of six hundred army regulars, Jackson resumed his march toward the Horseshoe Bend of the Tallapoosa, near present-day Dadeville, where an estimated seven hundred Red Sticks had fortified themselves inside a U-shaped bend in the river, blocking the only land access with a strong barricade. On the morning of March 27, after sending his Indian allies to block any escape across the river, Jackson assaulted and overran the barricade and slaughtered the Red Sticks, ripping the heart out of Creek resistance.[26] Two of Jackson's soldiers in this engagement were Tennesseans Henry and Jack Looney, whose nephew, Bill Looney, later played a prominent role in recruiting for the First Alabama Cavalry.[27]

On April 9, Jackson met with Creek representatives at Fort Jackson, on the site of the old French Fort Toulouse, just upriver from Montgomery. The resulting treaty forced the Creeks, whether allied or opposed in the war, to cede most of their holdings in central and southern Alabama, compressing the nation between the Coosa and Ocmulgee Rivers and severing access to Spanish Florida. Twenty years later, President Jackson orchestrated the forced removal of the remaining Creeks from these lands, resulting in a "Trail of Tears" all the way to Oklahoma. In the struggle for control of Alabama's immense natural resources, the native inhabitants had been unable to resist the superior forces marshaled from outside the state's borders. The Treaty of Fort Jackson threw open some 21 million acres to settlement, and Americans, primarily from Virginia, Georgia, and the Carolinas, and consumed with "Alabama Fever," rushed into the territory. The population expanded so quickly that, three years later, the US Congress split the Mississippi Territory vertically, roughly along the 88° longitude line, officially establishing the eastern portion as the Alabama Territory in 1817. Two years later, on December 14, 1819, Alabama joined the Union as the twenty-second state, satisfying southern politicians who wanted to see two states carved and formally admitted from the Mississippi Territory, doubling representation from the area in the US Senate.[28]

The new state constitution foreshadowed economic aspects of the coming struggle in Alabama, with few qualifications for voting in the frequent elections, a healthy skepticism of "interests," especially banks, and apportionment based on actual voters only instead of the Federal "three-fifths" model, thus limiting the influence of the slave districts in state politics.[29] Born in battle or, at the very least, in massacres, Alabama's statehood was the direct result of a struggle between Anglo-American and Indian peoples for control of a productive landscape. The rapid immigration and allocation of rich agricultural lands, and the pattern of settlement and development that followed, defined the state's economy, population, and culture for the next forty years.

The "land rush" to Alabama after the Creek Cession opened another contest for resources in Alabama, but one that favored those with existing wealth, European ancestry, and the ability to manipulate the existing social and legal systems to their advantage. Again, the main prize was land, but the essential resource to make the land productive was labor, and those who already owned slaves, or who had the financial resources necessary to purchase them, quickly gained the upper hand in this contest, resulting in a highly profitable slave-based agricultural system, focused primarily on producing cotton to fuel first Britain's, but later New England's burgeoning textile mills. Those who had the means to select and purchase the same rich bottomlands where Bartram had described Creeks living a life of relative plenty moved to the top of the social order, and reinvested their earnings in more land and more slaves, creating fabulous wealth. Their competitors, men and women of limited means, could either squat on Federal land, hoping to purchase it later— though often at a markup from speculators who had secured legal title—or remove to less profitable lands in the upcountry.[30] Many of them knew well the limited utility of these parcels, as they had already exhausted their farms in the Georgia and Carolina upcountry, and did the same to their new lands in Alabama before moving on to Mississippi or Texas. Unable to participate in this bonanza, slaves nevertheless created the overwhelming majority of the wealth that came to define Alabama, all through their uncompensated labor. The product of their work went to fuel lives of relative opulence for wealthy plantation owners, circulated in the local economy to sustain yeomen who provided services to the planters, or found its way into the public treasury, where it was used to fund limited improvements, primarily focused on moving the lucrative cotton crop to market. Over the next forty years, Alabama saw fortunes made and lost, as the state filled, rapidly at first, but unevenly, until the antebellum cotton and slave society faced its existential crisis.[31]

The "Alabama Fever" that gripped southerners from the coastal colonies who had fought in the Revolutionary War against Britain, as well as the innumerable Indian Wars on the frontier, quickly subsided as settlers pushed even farther west. Agriculture in the North and South Carolina Piedmont, while lucrative in the first few years of cultivation, quickly exhausted the soil of nutrients, placing expansionary pressures on the new republic. This, coupled with an ideological impulse that linked land ownership with republican virtue, prompted many to push the frontier westward. Absent new lands for settlement, farmers suffered declining yields, and parcels that might somehow be made to support them could not provide a sufficient inheritance to sustain their many children. As Leah Rawls Atkins notes, these backcountry "yeoman farmers of Alabama whose lives were stories of survival and endurance and whose contributions to Alabama history were far greater than traditional accounts have stated," were essential to the rapid peopling of the state.[32] An estimated population below 10,000 in 1810 had swelled to 127,000 by 1820 and 200,000 more followed in the next decade.[33]

Their journeys into the state were far from easy. The primitive road network led to only a few locales and quickly broke down under heavy use. Immigrants often had to blaze their own trail, including fording swift streams and crossing broad swamps or climbing steep ridges. One author has collected an early account of travel along the Federal Road under the title of *The Very Worst Road*, which describes both the thoroughfare itself and the conditions along the route.[34] Tavern keepers had difficulty maintaining their stocks during the rush and accordingly charged high prices for staples. Disease spread, as the water holes in the upcountry and slow moving streams became polluted, but failed to drain away the pestilence. For many, just getting to Alabama in the early nineteenth century was an ordeal.

Once the migrants were settled, or squatting, on some favored piece of land, the real task of survival began. The first order of business was to begin "clearing the thickets," the title of another social history of antebellum Alabama.[35] In addition to building some rudimentary shelter, usually of rough-hewn logs, farmers put in a crop, almost always corn, to have something to eat. This they supplemented with wild game from the still-teeming forests and fish from the streams. The lucky few had cows, but many herded swine, which grazed freely in the forests and where their feral offspring thrive to this day. Early settlers often traded what few possessions they had hauled through the wilderness for food from those who had come before, hoping to recover their losses from the next crop of immigrants. As Leah Rawls Atkins points out, they might eventually reach some level of comfort and stability, but they "owned no slaves and had little chance of acquiring any. They would not gain vast lands or build grand mansions or accumulate the wealth that brought prestige and power."[36] Tensions between these upcountry yeomen and the wealthy planters played out in early Alabama politics, as the state struggled to define just who the government would serve. Atkins notes that these would become the central questions in Alabama politics, highly relevant both then and still today, as "campaigns against wealth and aristocracy created statewide power bases, touching a responsive chord in the hearts of common people. Crusades against vested interests and corporate monopolies rallied the little man to the cause. What was the proper role of influence and wealth? Should the minority of wealthy planters and bankers control the engine of government for their own purposes?"[37]

One immigrant's letter to his family still back in Georgia provides testimony to these settlers' assessment of their new homes. On October 14, 1838, David McWhorter wrote to his brother John, still back in LaFayette in extreme northwestern Georgia, from his new home near Womack, in Wilcox County, Alabama. David reported, "I am still injoying the blessings of God in helth and my children injoys a reasonable portion of helth this yeare," but admitted that his locale near Pine Apple did not have the most healthful climate. He wrote, "I like Alabama tolerable well at this time except the helth of it that is the particular objection I have to it." Rather than improve his own land, the new immigrant worked for an established farmer and reported, "the spearet of farming is verry high crops of corn is tolerable good but coton is not so good as has been made upon account of its been so dry all the latter part of summer and fall[.] I am making a tolerabel crop of corn and cotton I shal make 14 or 15 hundred bushels of corn and 25 or 26 bales of cotton weighing from 4 to five hundred pounds."

Despite the agricultural success, McWhorter missed the absence of an established Presbyterian Church, "sose that I can bring my children up under the eye of the church," and asked his brother to look for a place for him back in Georgia, as "contentment is better than riches and helth better than fortune."[38]

McWhorter's experience in the Piney Hills of Wilcox County differed markedly from that of planters in the Alabama and Tennessee River valleys. Endowed with wealth, they quickly accumulated vast acreages of the best lands. Working initially as absentee landowners, they eventually relocated to be nearer their empires, creating new centers of wealth in places such as Eufaula, Demopolis, Marion, Selma, and the largest, Montgomery. With rich bottomlands, ample sunshine and rainfall, and access to Mobile's slave markets, plantations sprouted quickly along the Alabama and Tombigbee River valleys, with new inventions, such as the steamboat, facilitating the shipment of slaves up the river and cotton back down. The Black Belt, girdling the state's waist, became the center of wealth and political power in the state, though planters in the Tennessee Valley who guarded the interests of their region provided an effective opposition party. Politically, many of these planters gravitated toward the Whig platform, but the bulk of the state's voters remained Jacksonian Democrats, especially after President Jackson orchestrated Creek removal, opening up more lands for settlement on the last vestiges of the Creek reservation between the Tallapoosa and Chattahoochee Rivers, briefly reversing the generally east-to-west flow of settlement in the state.

The key to the tremendous wealth acquired in growing cotton was the institution of slavery. From less than 3,000 in 1810, the slave population expanded to over 40,000 by 1820 and almost 120,000 by 1830.[39] It tripled again in the next thirty years. Limiting the international slave trade after 1808 had little impact on the institution's growth. In addition to the natural increase, the interstate slave trade brought fresh shipments from the upper South, which by then had a surplus of labor, either by ship to Mobile or in coffles chained together for the arduous trek through the backcountry. While only a comparative few could afford slaves, their demand was insatiable and prices increased steadily. As good capitalists, many planters assiduously reinvested their profits in more human capital. While the rich seemed to get richer, except in the periodic downturns, such as the Panic of 1837, the yeomanry only seemed to get by. While some did make the jump into the planter class, many others risked falling back on a par with the poor white "mudsills," as the result of some calamity, untimely death, or natural disaster. But slaves themselves were excluded from any possible share of this bonanza. While an extremely small number of free blacks, especially around Mobile, where vestiges of the French system remained, did hold slaves and benefited from the institution, the overwhelming majority lived for decades at the bare subsistence level, a fact worth remembering when observing the poverty of Birmingham, Mobile, and Montgomery's modern African American communities.

By the 1840s, the first generation of upcountry farmers began to exhaust their soils, and the exodus continued to Texas and points west. But the rich soils of the Black Belt largely retained their fertility, especially when large landowners could afford to rotate fields, allowing some land to lie fallow each year and recharge itself. In the growing abolitionist community in the free states to the north, the planters perceived a new threat to their wealth and prosperity, and their control over uncompensated labor, that they believed threatened their way of life. To meet this threat, they began to mobilize politically, seeking first a common cause with their fellow citizens, then with those in the other slave states to present a united front dedicated to the preservation of their "peculiar institution."

The state of Alabama was but a year old when the issue of admitting Missouri as a slave state consumed national politics. As such, the Missouri Compromise, which brought Missouri, along with Maine, as a free state, into the Union but forbade further slave states north of the 36°30′ line of latitude, attracted little attention in still sparsely populated Alabama. But national politics eventually intruded in the state. Alabama had been admitted in 1819 largely to counter Illinois's statehood in 1818, maintaining the precarious balance of slave and free states. When sectional conflict again threatened to sever the nation in 1850, Alabamians were well aware of and fully engaged in the debates, leading to sharp animosities between the "slavocracy" and those who eventually wore the Union blue. Where communities stood on the sectional strife, and how strongly, accurately forecast which areas sent soldiers into the Union army during the Civil War.

During the time between statehood and the new debate over slavery in the territories, the institution of slavery witnessed a massive expansion within the state. The appropriated labor was a critical resource for slave owners and promoters hoping to advance the state, but represented a fundamental conflict over the control of resources. While abolitionists and proslavery advocates debated the institution's merits on moral grounds, it was economics that underlay the entire issue. The ability to extract a person's labor, in exchange for only the basic necessities of life, including rudimentary shelter, minimal clothing, and inadequate subsistence, represented an economic windfall for planters, and one they would fight to protect. At the same time, control of this resource, their own labor, increasingly motivated slaves to escape the peculiar institution in order to make a better life for themselves and their families. While the harsh and brutal treatment of slaves, including whippings, beatings, and even executions, played a large role in motivating slaves to strike back against their master and the institution, violence also proved an effective way to deter resistance and, in the constant conflict over the control of a man's labor, white southerners who controlled the economic, social, and legal systems in the state could easily extract an immense amount of uncompensated labor that generated tremendous wealth. And they guarded carefully against any potential threats, internal or external, to the society they had established and the resources they controlled.

Alabama sent several units of volunteers to Mexico in 1847 to support that conflict, which was as naked a land grab as has ever occurred in history. While both regions of the country saw the merits of territorial expansion, southerners especially would benefit from slavery's continued extension. For states in the upper South, new slave territories in Texas and potentially further west ensured a continued market for their excess slaves, while slave owners in the lower South could be assured of new slave states entering the Union, with fellow legislators friendly to the institution and its protections. That much of the newly acquired territory was unsuited for large-scale agriculture did not seem to matter; already enterprising businessmen were finding a ready application of slave labor in industrial pursuits. Imperial power in the Americas had successfully used slave labor for centuries in the mines of the New World, and there is no reason to expect that entrepreneurs would ignore this source of cheap labor in extracting the great mineral wealth of the newly conquered territories. In his gin factory in the model factory town of Prattville, near Montgomery, northern industrialist Daniel Pratt was already using slave labor to produce the cotton gins that had done so much to fuel the growth of slave-produced cotton agriculture.[40]

But northern expansionists also wanted to spread their program of free soil and free labor into the West, and did not want to compete with wealthy slave owners who would surely have sufficient capital to outbid them for the most productive bottomland and secure claims to the wealthiest mining regions. Excluding slavery from the territories, therefore, became an important part of guaranteeing their access to the resources they needed to survive and thrive. This motivated a Pennsylvania congressman, David Wilmot, to introduce his "Wilmot Proviso" in 1848, stipulating that slavery be banned in any territory ceded by Mexico, in order to ensure a continued outlet for unfettered expansion through homesteading and the construction of a transcontinental railroad to help spur development. It was this core issue, as much as any other, that sparked the Crisis of 1850, when California, in the midst of a gold rush begun in 1849, applied for admission to the Union as a single, free state.

Alabamians had fought in Mexico, both to defend their country and especially a fellow slave state, Texas, from perceived aggression, as well as to extend the territory available for the expansion of slavery. The state had already filled its most productive farmland, along the Alabama, Tennessee, and Chattahoochee River valleys, forcing new settlers to scratch out a living in the remote mountain valleys or piney scrublands of the southeastern quarter of the state. At the same time, an active underground railroad, operating primarily on the axis of the Tennessee River, which led north to Ohio and was used in reverse by invading Federal armies in 1862, led slaveholders to demand a strengthened Fugitive Slave Act in order to secure the return of what they deemed their property. At Hillsboro, Ohio, John Mathews Nelson operated one "station." Later, Nelson's grandson, Joseph Kibler Nelson, helped recruit one of Alabama's black regiments.[41] Already, African Americans, by striking for freedom, were influencing the national debate, at the very least, by making it possible for free-state advocates to offer a potential concession to the slave states in the form of a strengthened Fugitive Slave Law, in order to secure passage of the remainder of their agenda.

The state's most significant contribution to the national debate came in the form of the "Alabama Platform," a series of radical proposals by William Lowndes Yancey, a Georgia-born slave owner with strong ties to South Carolina who relocated to Cahaba, Alabama, in 1838. Yancey became one of the most notorious "fire-eaters," a group of demagogues who brooked no dissent with slavery and who rose to increasing prominence on the national stage in its defense. Yancey suffered severe financial losses, both in the Panic of 1837 and in an episode in which a neighbor or disgruntled overseer poisoned a well used by his slaves, causing further financial losses. Thus, Yancey came to view any threat to his slaves in particular, and to slavery in general, as a threat to his ability to survive and live as he felt he should (he had no occupation other than being a planter and politicking, though the latter pursuit enabled him to succeed as a newspaperman). Relocating to Wetumpka, he became a leading voice of the "Eufaula Regency," which gradually came to control Alabama politics and worked the system largely to the benefit of planters in the state's Black Belt.

Yancey's "Alabama Platform" was perhaps the most extreme entry into the series of possible resolutions of the Crisis of 1850. It demanded, not only that the territory north of 36°30′ be opened to slavery, but that *all* territory not already organized into states be open to slavery as well. This was the genesis of northern Democrat Stephen Douglas's fateful 1854 Kansas Nebraska Act, which opened those two territories north of the demarcation line to "popular sovereignty," leading to the violence and bloodshed that became known as "Bleeding Kansas."

While Yancey's radical platform was too extreme for the nation in 1848, and most of his proposals led to defeat and frustration for their sponsor, they did energize debate within the state, though historians have overgeneralized the competing factions within Alabama state politics. North Alabama, generally considered to be the poor farmers of the Hill Country and north-leaning planters, or, at least, those hailing from the upper South in the Tennessee Valley, appears as a strongly Democratic element, appreciating both Jackson's Indian removal, which opened up lands for settlement, and his alleged focus on the common people, though Jackson himself considered himself to be part of the southern aristocracy. South Alabama was more Whiggish in outlook, as wealthy planters supported improvements, especially in Mobile's harbor and along the Alabama River, that could spur development and aid in getting their valuable cotton to market. But there are subtle nuances to this broad generalization. Planters in the Tennessee Valley, especially in the thriving cotton town of Huntsville, could be as ardent secessionists as those to the south, and wealthy interests in the Tennessee Valley could be Whigs and Unionists. Similarly, the poor farmers of the Wiregrass in the south resembled politically the Hill Country, while wealthy planters in Montgomery remade the Democratic Party into a sectional, proslavery organ and provided such effective leadership that they eventually split the party into northern and southern wings. Thus, in the short decade before secession, politicians representing both sections of the state enjoyed electoral success, but the broad generalization of "North vs. South" endures, as representatives of the sections were not often on the same side.

The presidential election year of 1852 witnessed two significant events that hardened the institution of slavery within Alabama's borders. In March, the runaway success of Harriet Beecher Stowe's *Uncle Tom's Cabin* began to unite northern opposition to slavery and contributed to the siege mentality within Alabama. But Alabama slaveholders had already responded to the perceived threat by using their control of the legal system to implement additional proscriptions on slaves. While the new laws were ostensibly designed to reduce the possibility of deadly insurrections, the economic motives behind them were only thinly concealed. Ultimately, they were intended to ensure slave owners' access to the vital resource of uncompensated labor and further ensure that slaves had no opportunity to assert any control over their economic well-being. Section 1005 specifically prevented slaves from hiring themselves out, preventing the accumulation of capital that might someday be used to purchase their freedom. Section 1018, which stated, "No slave can own property," goes directly to the heart of separating slaves from resources. It reaffirmed prohibitions on slaves owning any property, again depriving them of the right to accumulate any resources that could be used to sustain life, either during any economic downturn or during a potential escape attempt. And Section 1012, which stated, "No slave can keep or carry a gun, powder, shot, club or other weapon," ensured that slaves would not have the means to dispute the laws nor protect any property.[42]

To eliminate any "corrupting" influence, the new code required any free blacks that had entered the state since 1832 to leave within thirty days, or be sentenced to hard labor in the penitentiary. Free blacks were not allowed to associate with slaves (1035, 1042–1044) nor provide them with passes (1038). The code was clearly intended to eliminate the possible example of slaves who had earned their freedom, and control over their own labor, and who might, by their example, encourage other slaves to do the same. And all of these laws were enforced by a vigorous system of patrols, essentially making non-slave owners liable, with their time and their livestock, to support their institution. The system stipulated, "All white male owners of slaves, below the age of sixty years, and all other free white persons, between the ages of eighteen and forty-five years, who are not disabled by sickness or bodily infirmity, except commissioned officers in the militia, and persons exempt by law from the performance of militia duty, are subject to perform patrol duty."[43] Those who failed to perform the prescribed duty were liable to be fined. Not content to appropriate the labor of their slaves, the wealthy plantation owners likewise appropriated the time and labor of their less-wealthy neighbors to assist in regulating their slaves, an issue sure to cause resentment among those who lacked the resources to successfully compete with their neighbors.

Slave owners needed the new patrols, specifically intended to catch runaways and return them to their owners, because slaves were increasingly striking for their own freedom. While the likelihood of successfully completing a journey on foot of the almost four hundred miles from the Black Belt to the Ohio River was small, the availability of new forms of transportation increased the odds. Rail connections offered the potential for hiding away on trains, or "passing," for lighter-skinned slaves, and riding the rails to freedom, as Frederick Douglass did.[44] Slaves might also take advantage of steamboats to reach either coastal ports, where they might be able to stow away or book passage as a free black on oceangoing vessels, or travel north directly down the Tennessee River. Every runaway that safely reached the North threatened to undermine the slave system, and increasing difficulty in enforcing the Fugitive Slave Law meant that successful attempts were more likely to be permanent.

In 1848, a Democrat from Michigan, Lewis Cass, narrowly defeated Zachary Taylor, a slave-owning Whig from Louisiana, in Alabama although Taylor prevailed nationally and won the White House. The demise of the Whig Party nationally, and its replacement first by the weak "Know-Nothing" Party and then the sectional Republican Party, freed Democrats to eventually split into moderate and radical wings, with fire-eaters from Montgomery leading the latter while Jacksonian Democrats in rural areas, along with former Whigs, occupied the former. But the 1851 gubernatorial election offered no evidence of this eventual schism, as the Virginia-born Tuscaloosa moderate Henry Watkins Collier won reelection virtually unopposed. In the 1852 presidential election, Franklin Pierce, a Democrat from New Hampshire who provided reassurances for slave owners, easily defeated the Virginia Whig and hero of the War with Mexico, Winfield Scott. In Alabama, Whigs still maintained their strength in the Black Belt but lost two counties, Lowndes and Barbour, in the Alabama and Chattahoochee River valleys, respectively, to Georgia's George Troup, a Yancey supporter running on a strong proslavery platform. While Pierce enjoyed dominant support statewide, the Hill Country and Wiregrass provided his highest margins. The term-limited Collier's successor in the governor's office, John Winston, also hailed from North Alabama and significantly refused to use state funds to finance improvements, especially railroads, during his time in office from 1853 to 1857, in an acknowledgment that small farmers did not want their government using their hard-earned tax dollars to support corporate interests.[45] But legislators more sympathetic to improvements overrode most of the governor's vetoes. Winston easily bested his Whig and Union Democrat opponents, losing only two Black Belt counties to the former and two Hill Country counties to the latter in 1853, but had a closer contest in 1855 against united opposition in the American or "Know-Nothing" Party. In that race, Winston lost badly in former Whig strongholds around Mobile and in the Alabama and Tennessee valleys, but enjoyed strong support in the Hill Country and Wiregrass.[46] State politics in the 1850s provides clear evidence of the political leanings of each section and subregion of the state, which eventually fueled much of the opposition to both secession and the Confederate war effort.[47]

In early 1854, an ambitious Illinois senator, Stephen Douglas, threatened to undermine the carefully crafted truce of 1850. In a sop to southern slaveholders, especially those across the Mississippi River in Missouri, Douglas proposed and aggressively forwarded legislation that would open the remainder of the Louisiana Purchase, most notably the area north of the 36°30′ line where slavery had been barred, to the possibility of organizing as new slave states under Douglas's concept of "popular sovereignty," or the idea that a territory's voters should be free to decide whether or not slavery would be permitted. Missourians, who by now had filled nearly the full length of the Missouri River valley with large plantations stretching to the Kansas border, feared that allowing Kansas to organize and enter as a free state presented an existential threat to the institution in Missouri. Already slaves, aided in some cases by sympathetic conductors on the "underground railroad" through Kansas, were helping other slaves escape to free states. Douglas's Act, while easing the concerns of slaveholders, threatened the carefully laid balance of slave and free states and infuriated many "free soil" northerners, who hoped to see the Kansas and Nebraska territories thrown open to homesteading once the indigenous populations had been removed. For Alabama slaveholders, settling Kansas, or at least supporting those Missourians who had crossed the border with their slaves, offered an opportunity to play an active part in the struggle for the all-important resource of arable land.[48]

In late 1855, a South Carolina–born slave owner from Eufaula, Jefferson Buford, organized an expedition of over four hundred men, many from Alabama, who might settle in Kansas and add their names to the voter lists in the hotly contested republic. In early April of 1856, the first "settlers" left Montgomery by steamboat, arriving in Kansas the following month. While Kansas's proslavery faction desired their ballots, it had more immediate needs for their guns, and accordingly enrolled them in the state militia, adding strong reinforcements at the height of the period known as "Bleeding Kansas." Many of Buford's men took part in the sack of the Free State town of Lawrence in 1856, an act that sparked John Brown's retaliatory murder of proslavery settlers on

Pottawatomie Creek later that year. While few of Buford's men remained in Kansas, they returned with an appreciation of the use of force and violence against abolitionists which they easily transferred to Unionist Alabamians during the Civil War.[49]

In the presidential election that fall, Democrats nominated a Pennsylvanian, James Buchanan, whom supporters deemed "safe" on slavery, proving yet again, and not for the last time, that Alabama's voters cared more about a candidate's public pronouncements than his specific background or geographical origin. When the newly formed Republican Party nominated John C. Frémont, with strong abolitionist support, and the American Party, or Know-Nothings, attempted to resuscitate the political career of the former Whig Millard Fillmore, the two parties split the anti-Democrat voters, handing Buchanan an easy victory. Feeling that their interests would once again be preserved in the executive mansion, and through his appointments to the Supreme Court, which the Dred Scott decision seemed to confirm, slave-owning Alabamians felt vindicated in their efforts. But Frémont's strong showing in New England and the upper Midwest portended a momentous conflict in four years. Within the state, Buchanan's strongest support came from the Hill Country of North Alabama, where five counties, including Winston, gave him over 90 percent of their vote, demonstrating the enduring strength of Jacksonian Democrats in that region of the state.[50] In contrast, Fillmore carried seven Black Belt counties, formerly the preserve of Alabama's Whigs, and the port county of Mobile, which had seen an influx of immigrants, especially from Ireland, in the preceding decade and likely responded to the Know-Nothings' xenophobia.

While slavery was certainly an important issue nationally in 1856, the results within Alabama provide better support for explaining the election within the framework of a "struggle for resources." Poor farmers from Alabama's Hill Country still viewed the pro-development Whigs, and their successors, as a threat to their economic independence and livelihood. They had no desire to be used as slave catchers and saw no benefit to using their hard-earned dollars as handouts for railroad companies, which would surely avoid the rugged hills of North Alabama in favor of the more gentle gradients, not to mention larger potential revenues from hauling cotton to market in the more densely populated river valleys. Indeed, this remained the case as long as Alabama had an economy based on agriculture instead of industry. It was not until 1872 that a railroad finally traversed the state from north to south, unlocking the rich mineral deposits of the Hill Country.[51]

In the 1857 gubernatorial election another South Carolina–born but moderate Democrat, Andrew Moore, from Perry County in the state's Black Belt, easily won an uncontested race, signaling the demise of the Whig Party in Alabama. But all was not well for the Democrats, as Moore drew an ardent secessionist as a challenger in the 1859 race, William F. Samford, whose son eventually held the office at the turn of the century. It is surprising that the governor, who eventually committed treason by taking his state out of the union, could be challenged just a year before as being insufficiently sound on the slavery question. Most likely the strength of this challenge, and John Brown's attempted uprising at Harper's Ferry just a few months after his re-election (Alabama held gubernatorial elections in August at that time), accounted for Moore's change of heart.[52]

As Frémont's strong showing in 1856 foreshadowed, the new Republican Party continued to gain strength and prompted stronger reactions south of the Mason-Dixon Line. While social movements certainly provided the bulk of the support for each side, leaders disproportionately influenced events. In the South, fire-eaters, most notably William Yancey, worked to ensure protections for slavery that eventually undermined the Democratic Party, fracturing a coalition that had held sectional strife at bay for over forty years. At the same time, an eloquent Illinois lawyer gave voice to frustrated Free-Soilers and abolitionists, allowing them to find common ground for a sectional agenda that had national implications.

Springfield lawyer Abraham Lincoln's rise to prominence was largely unheralded, and the "Great Emancipator's" views on slavery and black citizenship morphed during his meteoric lifetime. But whatever reservations Lincoln held about black equality, he clearly recognized the fundamental inconsistency within slavery—depriving a man or woman of the fruits of their labor. In the late summer of 1858, Lincoln and Stephen Douglas held a series of well-publicized debates across Illinois. Douglas's support remained in the state's southern counties, where many recent immigrants hailed from slave states, especially Kentucky, across the Ohio River. Lincoln's base was in the northern counties and the bustling metropolis of Chicago, where many residents had ties to New England and the "Burned-over" district of upstate New York, where abolitionists and advocates of greater rights and protections for women garnered support from religious organizations. In a debate at Quincy, Illinois, on October 13, 1858, Lincoln responded to Douglas's charges that he supported racial equality. He said, "I agree with Judge Douglas that he (a black man) is not my equal in many respects, certainly not in color—perhaps not in intellectual and moral endowments; but in the right to eat the bread without leave of anybody else which his own hand earns, he is my equal and the equal of Judge Douglas, and the equal of every other man."[53]

Lincoln's clear appreciation of the threat slavery's extension posed to the nation, coupled with an eloquence born of a simple upbringing, endeared him to both his party in the North and eventually to many Unionists in the upper South. Many agreed with the Kentucky-born Lincoln that the southern radicals posed an existential threat to the nation, not to mention their own security and prosperity, and did not find the Republican Party's views on slavery personally threatening to them. His election was certainly insufficient reason to tear the nation apart. But southern opponents vilified Lincoln and his party, leading to a disastrous schism within the national Democratic Party. In this effort, Alabamians, most notably William Lowndes Yancey, played a prominent role.

As secessionists gained the upper hand within Alabama's state Democratic Party, they ensured that their slate of delegates to the national nominating convention in Charleston, South Carolina insisted upon inclusion of Yancey's old "Alabama Platform" in the national party program. But Yancey and his fellow southerners lacked control of the party, thanks in part to continued growth in northern Democratic strongholds, and, when the platform went down to defeat, Yancey symbolically led Alabama's delegation out of the convention, an act repeated almost one hundred years later by "Dixiecrats" in 1948. When other southern states followed, the national party lacked a quorum and was unable to nominate a candidate. At a subsequent convention, in the border-state city of Baltimore, Douglas earned a majority from a convention featuring replacement, as well as more moderate delegates from many southern states, while the secessionists held a rump convention in Richmond and nominated Kentuckian John C. Breckinridge as their candidate. Unable to stomach either of those two men, a new party, styling themselves the "Constitutional Unionists," who insisted on both the permanence of the Federal union as well as the protections for slavery guaranteed in the constitution, placed Tennessean John Bell's name on the ballot. Secessionists loudly threatened to dismember the Union if Lincoln prevailed in the election.

Alabama's electoral returns for 1860 offer a clear approximation of sentiment in the state on the eve of the Civil War. There is a strong correlation between a lack of support for Breckinridge, who easily carried the state, and counties that eventually sent large numbers of white soldiers into the Union army. With Lincoln not even appearing on the ballot, Breckinridge won a majority of the state's counties, but his margins were smallest in the Black Belt counties that had traditionally supported Whigs. But northern Democrat Stephen Douglas carried five Alabama counties, including four in the Tennessee River valley centered on Huntsville, as well as Mobile, and had a strong showing in the Hill Country. One of the Douglas voters was Thomas Nation, a slave-owning Unionist born in East Tennessee but then living in Blount County. He later reported, "I had worked a long time and had got a little property, and I felt that it would all go up if there was a rebellion and I was in favor of the principles of the old government and I could not see where there had been any cause for a rebellion or a separation. I told my neighbors that if they got up a rebellion the country would be ruined and that if it would end or prevent a war they could take my negroes."[54] Voters in five counties, most notably Baldwin, Butler, and Covington, along the state's southern border with Florida, rejected the Democratic Party altogether and joined voters in the three Florida Panhandle counties across the state line in throwing their support behind Bell, who also carried the border states of Tennessee, Kentucky, and Virginia, suggesting support for secession was lukewarm at best in that region.[55] But Lincoln prevailed nationally—and likely would have against a united Democratic Party, if they had agreed on a candidate—sending apoplectic slave owners into fits of secession.

Alabama's unique geography and rich natural resources have made the state a site of conflict throughout its recorded history. While native societies struggled to secure life-giving resources, including both hunting lands and captives to rebuild their declining populations after contact, they were unable to resist white encroachment that dispossessed them of all their holdings in Alabama in just a few decades. But as white settlers poured into the newly opened lands, the patterns of settlement created distinctive cultures and competing economic systems that left deep divisions in the state's electorate. The decade preceding the election of 1860 witnessed significant changes in Alabama. Politically, the state's competing parties underwent a drastic transformation, as the Whig support in the centers of commerce collapsed along with the national party, while Democrats who had traditionally protected the interests of the freeholders in less-prosperous areas found their party in the hands of radical, fire-eating defenders of slavery. Economically, the state took the first steps toward an industrial market economy, as entrepreneurs such as Daniel Pratt constructed model factory towns that presaged the textile industry's near takeover of many rural areas in the postwar years. The first railroads began linking the state's still lucrative, slave-produced cotton centers to wider markets, and the improved transportation network and population pressures pushed cotton farmers into the sandy and mountainous preserves of subsistence farmers. As Leah Rawls Atkins found, in the future Unionist preserves of "Blount, Walker, Winston and Covington counties the increase (in cotton production) topped 300 percent, indicating that farmers in these regions were moving into a market economy with cash-crop production."[56] In a world where everything seemed to be changing at the same time, many white Alabamians sought to hold on to one constant, the flag and the Union of states that they had known since birth, and which had used its collective power, often with their active support, to wrest their future homes from its aboriginal inhabitants. At the same time, many black Alabamians embraced the onrushing chaos as a harbinger of the long-awaited exodus that promised deliverance from bondage and a new life in a promised land. Eventually, members of both of these groups, who likely felt few common bonds or shared interests, found themselves caught up in the same struggle, to defeat the architects of secession and defenders of slavery and support the "old government" against the injustices and usurpations of the new.

CHAPTER 2

Low Ebb

Confederate Mobilization and Resistance, 1861–1862

F ollowing President Lincoln's election, the communities that provided soldiers for Alabama's Union regiments largely adopted a "wait and see" approach, as their rebellious and deluded neighbors embarked on a course of insurrection, treason, destruction, and ruin. North Alabama's Unionist community sent antisecession delegates to the extralegal convention meeting in Montgomery in the first week of 1861, but they were unable to prevent the passage of an ordinance of secession. But their efforts, along with those of representatives from the Wiregrass counties and other sections, did impress upon the fire-eaters the depth of antisecession sentiment in their sections of the state. Alabama's black communities, undoubtedly aware of the political debates about their future, monitored developments both in person and through the efforts of sympathetic whites or literate blacks, but as failed revolts in the summer of 1861 demonstrated, the time was not yet right for a mass strike for freedom.[1] After Confederate Secretary of War Leroy Pope Walker, a Huntsville resident, ordered troops to fire on Fort Sumter in Charleston Harbor, President Lincoln issued a call for 75,000 volunteers to defend the Union and restore order. But these troops would first have to penetrate deep into the South before the oppressed Unionists and bondsmen could demonstrate their loyalty by taking up arms for their country.

Just as the returns of the 1860 presidential election mirror later white Union enlistment, the selection of delegates and arguments against secession also hewed closely to the Alabama counties that eventually provided the bulk of the state's Federal troops. Indeed, the oppression of their selected representatives, including the imprisonment of Winston County delegate Christopher Sheats, provided some of the impetus to armed resistance, as Alabama's state government indicated its willingness to cast aside the rule of law in coercing Unionists to express fealty to the extralegal government now occupying the state house in Montgomery. Through an orchestrated campaign of coercion, arrest, imprisonment, and eventually murder, Alabama's Confederate officials repeatedly demonstrated, despite the lenient punishment that they themselves later received for their treason against the Federal government, that they would tolerate no dissent within the state's borders. These actions unleashed a period of guerrilla warfare behind Confederate lines that undercut support for both Unionist communities and the newborn Confederacy. By harassing and economically devastating Unionists and brutally repressing slave dissenters, the white, slave-owning aristocracy guaranteed that Alabama's Anti-Confederate Southerners spent a long, tortuous year before Federal authority came to their rescue and provided opportunities for relief.

In response to secessionist agitation, Alabama's governor, Andrew Moore, agreed to issue a call for a convention to meet in Montgomery after the first of the year to discuss Lincoln's election and overtures to secession being entertained in other states, especially in radical South Carolina, the birthplace of many of Alabama's fire-eaters. It is not clear why the existing state legislature, duly elected by the people and already empanelled in Montgomery, was inadequate for this momentous task, but this body, composed of the best men in the state, had been elected before the mad rush to secession and therefore, in the minds of the rebels, might be insufficiently motivated to attempt to sever the bonds between the state and the country.[2] A new body, elected in the heat of the moment, would surely contain the most ardent secessionists, and a majority of the men elected would be sufficiently motivated to support, or at least, not to actively resist their efforts. Of course, the preference of Alabama's 400,000 slaves, denied the ability to weigh in on their future at the ballot box, a cause sufficient to foment revolution among their masters' forebears eighty years earlier, had no say in the matter at all.[3] But Alabama's Unionist community rose to the challenge and sent delegates to the rump convention who argued eloquently for the folly of secession and the certainty of war, destruction, and ruin. The strength and depth of their feeling led the secessionists to refuse to submit the ordinance of secession to a popular referendum, fearing defeat at the hands of the people who would actually have to make the sacrifices and bear the burdens of war. Thus, the legitimacy of Alabama's so-called Confederate government had already been

Cahoun Co.

called into question by the state's dissenters long before the first sparks of war.[4]

12-1860

Nevertheless, in a special election held on Christmas Eve, 1860, in which each county sent delegates to meet in Montgomery during the first week of the new year, Unionists attempted to save their fellow citizens, and their state, from the perils and destruction of civil war. The results mirrored those of the presidential election the previous month, though turnout lagged, in part due to cold and rainy weather that kept rural voters from traveling to the polls. Still, every county in the northern part of the state, with the exception of Calhoun, clustered as it was along the Coosa River valley and containing a higher percentage of slave owners than its neighbors, sent "cooperationist" delegates to the convention, who either in earnest or as a tactic to forestall the "immediate secessionists," insisted upon cooperation with other Southern states before entertaining secession. All of South Alabama sent secessionist candidates, with the exception of Conecuh County, along the Florida border, which contained a small percentage of slave owners, demonstrating southeastern Alabama's concerns about the rebellion and treason being openly discussed in the state capital. The cooperationist platform opposed secession on the grounds that Alabama, small and poor as it was, was incapable of operation or even self-preservation as an independent republic, and therefore should delay secession until the state could be assured of "cooperation" with neighboring states.[5] It is clear that many adherents to this position saw it as a way to maintain the Union without antagonizing their "immediate" secessionist counterparts, who wanted to strike while the iron was hot and realized that any delay in securing cooperation might allow the secessionist ardor to cool and more rational desires to prevail. Undoubtedly, many "cooperationists" were staunch, "unconditional" Unionists who would not countenance secession under any circumstances, including cooperation with other states, as their refusal to sign the ordinance suggests. But they sought to persuade the "immediate" secessionists by adopting a less threatening and polarizing position. Of course, the secessionist response was to label their opponents "submissionists," attempting to smear them with the stain of "black Lincolnite" Republicanism in the public eye.[6] To forestall this, many "cooperationists" did make arguments in favor of increased protections for slavery, and many wealthier Unionists did, in fact, own slaves. But it is debatable whether they agreed on the dire threat to the institution or merely

Cahoun N -Stovall

Cahoun Co, pg.5 footnote 42 = Stovall

offered these additional protections for the peculiar institution simply to pla- *Convention*
cate the secessionists and forestall disunion.[7]   *Jan '61*

The convention opened on January 7, 1861, with debates and committees
discussing secession's risks and merits. For the most part, the fire-eaters allowed the "cooperationists" to have their say, confident that they had the votes
for the passage of an ordinance, and that their colleagues, having done all that
was necessary to placate their voters and preserve their "honor," would then
submit to the inevitable and sign the declaration, maintaining the fiction of
unanimous support for the insurrection. In some respects, the tactic back-
fired, as Unionists, awakened to the perilous course before them and, encouraged by the support of their peers, argued eloquently for the preservation of
the Union and the folly of rebellion.   *Counties*

Given that men born in Walker, Morgan, Marion, Fayette, Franklin, and
Winston Counties led the state in enlistees in the First Alabama Cavalry, it
should come as no surprise that men from those counties led the "cooperationist" charge in Montgomery. Indeed, many of those same counties provided
the largest majorities for "cooperationist" delegates, with Walker, Franklin,
and Madison leading the way (see Table 1). Two counties, DeKalb and Winston, did not record any secessionist votes, while Lawrence County's returns
have been lost to history. It should be noted that the standing of a particular
county could be swayed by an individual candidate, and might not accurately
represent the depth of antisecessionist sentiment, as in Madison County,
where Huntsvillians undoubtedly placed great reliance in the cooperationist
former senator Jeremiah Clemens.

Aware of the large minority opposed to immediate secession, noted
fire-eater William Lowndes Yancey took to the convention floor in an attempt
to coerce the opposition. In an effort to reassure the secessionists, as well as
intimidate his opponents, he charged, "Men, who shall, after the passage of
this Ordinance, dissolving the union of Alabama with the other States of this
Confederacy, dare array themselves against the State, will then become the
enemies of the State. There is a law of Treason, defining treason against the
State; and, these who shall dare oppose the action of Alabama, when she as-
sumes her independence of the Union, will become traitors—rebels against
its authority, and will be dealt with as such."[8]

Madison County's Nicholas Davis presciently responded to Yancey's charge
that North Alabamians must submit or be charged as traitors. He argued, "If it

Walker Co.   Franklin Co.
Marion
Fayette   Winston Co.

43

1st Al. Cav ?.

TABLE 1. "Cooperationist" Percentages in December 24 Election of Delegates
to Secession Convention and Enlistees in 1st Alabama Cavalry

County	Cooperationist %	1 AL Cav. Enlistees
Lawrence	Unknown	24
Winston	100	33
DeKalb	100	9
Walker	84.8	90
Franklin	79.8	33
Madison	78.6	25
Marion	75.7	83
Marshall	73.5	29
Fayette	72	54
Limestone	71.1	12
Lauderdale	70.3	17
Tuscaloosa	63.9	15
Tallapoosa	62.1	4
Blount	61.5	32
St. Clair	60.5	16
Coosa	55.6	5
Jackson	55.2	18
Morgan	54.7	86
Talladega	54.2	1
Randolph	54	15
Jefferson	54	22
Conecuh	51.1	0
Cherokee	50.5	16

NOTE: The majority of delegates from every county except Coosa and Talladega voted in opposition to the ordinance. Adapted from Hoole, *Alabama Tories*, 9, 13, 16.

? Calhoun Co may not have sent a delegate. "cooperation" "delegates"
See pg. 42.

should turn out that the popular vote is against the Act of Secession, should it pass, I tell you, sir, that I believe it will and ought to be resisted. The minority of the people of this State ought not to control the majority." He continued,

> We must be dealt with as public enemies. But yesterday, sir, this Convention condemned this doctrine. With one voice, you declared against it, and expressed your determination to meet such an invasion of your rights as it ought to be met, with arms in your hands. It will be asserted as readily against a tyrant at home as abroad; as readily by the people of my section against usurpation and outrage here, as elsewhere. And when compelled to take this course, they will cheerfully, no doubt, assume all the responsibility that follows the act.

Davis closed the day's proceedings with the following, prescient warning, directed specifically at Yancey:

> I seek no quarrel with the gentleman from Montgomery, or his friends. Towards him personally, I entertain none other than the kindest feeling. But I tell him that should he engage in that enterprise, he will not be allowed to boast the character of an invader. Coming at the head of any force which he can muster, aided and assisted by the Executive of this State, we will meet him at the foot of our mountains, and there with his own selected weapons, hand to hand, and face to face, settle the question of the sovereignty of the people.[9]

The following day, an amendment offered by Jeremiah Clemens, also of Madison County, to submit the referendum to the people, lost narrowly, with forty-five in favor and fifty-four opposed. Thus denied the opportunity to weigh in personally on their fate, the Unionists of North Alabama followed through on their charge to meet Yancey's minions, armed, at the foot of their mountains. James Clark, of Lawrence County, after providing an eloquent argument against immediate secession as the death knell of slavery, likewise accurately predicted a future where "Alabama, having assumed the untried responsibilities of separate secession, shall find herself torn, convulsed and rent in twain by the dissensions of her own people. Shall the martial roll of the warlike drum ever be heard reverberating through the deep ravines of the

Sand Mountains, calling the clansmen of the hills against our brothers of the South?"[10] Though Clark walked back his comments the following day, lest he "be guilty of inciting hostile divisions between different sections of the State, and thus enkindle the flames of civil war throughout the borders of Alabama," his predictions had already been made, and were, in time, fulfilled.[11]

When the convention finally voted on January 9, the immediate secessionists prevailed in a close vote, with fifty-four in favor and forty-six against. Believing the matter settled, the secessionists now began to pressure the opposition into signing, in order to create the illusion of unanimity, an effort that continued for the next century in the texts and treatises of adherents to the "Lost Cause." Fifteen cooperationists did defect, making the result a more respectable sixty-nine to thirty-one in the secessionists' eyes, but those who refused to submit quickly attracted the ire of the disunionists.[12] According to Wesley Thompson, whose thinly sourced *A Free State of Winston* cited fictional accounts penned by the author, Winston County's delegate Christopher Sheats refused to sign the ordinance of secession, despite extreme pressure, before his enemies dragged him from the hall and deposited him in a local jail for several days, without charges.[13] If this account is true, Sheats's treatment explains the indignation that residents of Winston County felt toward their fellow Alabamians, especially the "Montgomery faction," now fomenting a Civil War that threatened their very livelihood. Sheats did return to Winston Country, where he began working to defend Unionists and their communities from the new power forming in Montgomery, leading to an insurgency in several northern counties. If his opponents thought his treatment in Montgomery served as an effective warning and left him suitably chastened and resigned to rebellion, they were sorely mistaken. Sheats became one of North Alabama's most vocal opponents to the so-called Confederacy, and an active and ardent recruiter of soldiers for the First Alabama Cavalry, while his constituents were "highly incensed over the treatment he had received at the hands of the Rebels."[14]

In response to the convention, residents of Winston County's 5th Beat met on February 7 at J. W. Allen's store and adopted seven resolutions, later printed in the March 1 *Moulton Democrat*. They indicated their opposition to the governor in calling the convention and found fault with its decisions, stating clearly, "we disapprove of the States going out of the Union, for we think it is uncalled for."[15] Similar meetings occurred in Limestone and Franklin Counties, with the attendees in Franklin particularly incensed that the Confederate

Constitution had been ratified without consulting the people, unlike the US Constitution seventy years earlier.[16] A number of former Unionists bent to the popular will and attempted to work with the new, seemingly inevitable regime, but many others remained just as adamantly opposed to it.[17]

The day before the war began, Winston County resident John Bell wrote   Bel his brother Henry, who resided across the state line in Choctaw County, Mississippi, that everyone in his area was a Unionist and "for linkern [Lincoln]."[18] The boys' father wrote Henry a week later, distressed to learn that his son supported the Confederacy. He believed his son had been duped by slaveholders who wanted to "git you pupt [pumped] up and go to fight for there infurnal negroes and after you done there fightin you may kiss there hine parts for o [all] they care." Sadly, Henry reported both his father and his brother as disloyal and forwarded their letters to Governor Moore in Montgomery, where the letters remain today.

Even before the convention met, secessionists succeeded in convincing Governor Moore to seize the Federal military installations within the state's borders, hoping to precipitate a crisis that would strengthen their cause. At the very least, an inept response by the Buchanan administration allowed the Federal arsenal at Mount Vernon, along with the masonry forts protecting Mobile Bay, to fall easily and bloodlessly into the state's hands. This act of treason, if not armed insurrection, was intended to stiffen the resolve of wavering delegates who received assurances that the rebels were serious about their work. Ironically, efforts a year earlier by John Brown and his coconspirators to seize a Federal arsenal and arm a rebellion had been deemed a dire threat to the safety and security of the republic. Now, a year later, those who expressed outrage at Brown's actions prepared to duplicate his efforts.

On January 4, Capt. Jesse L. Reno commanded the Federal arsenal at Mount Vernon. A year later at South Mountain, Maryland, Reno lost his life accidentally at the hands of his own troops, in an incident eerily similar to the one that claimed "Stonewall" Jackson's life the following spring, and residents of the territory of Nevada named a city in his honor. But in 1861 the Mexican War hero and his seventeen men found themselves surprised by four companies of militia from Mobile. Later that day, he reported, "I did not make, nor could I have made any resistance, as they had scaled the walls and taken possession before I knew anything about the movement. The governor has demanded all the public property, and his men now have entire possession of

47

the arsenal."[19] This act, as much as any other, marks the beginning of the Civil War in Alabama, as armed insurrectionists seized Federal property and first raised their weapons against agents of the Federal government.

Moore attempted to justify his actions by claiming that he fully expected the convention to vote for secession, and by seizing the arsenal, he "deemed it my duty to take every precautionary step to make the secession of the State peaceful, and prevent detriment to her people." As four long, bloody, and destructive years of war attested, Moore utterly failed to discharge the great responsibility entrusted to him by the citizens of Alabama. While no blood was shed in seizing the national property, it was used to supply and sustain a bloody insurrection and civil war. Moore facetiously claimed, "the purpose with which my order was given and has been executed was to avoid and not provoke hostilities between the State and Federal Government." While Moore may have prevented any clash for control of the forts guarding Mobile Bay in January 1861, their liberation in 1864 cost many more casualties than Captain Reno and his seventeen men could ever hope to inflict.

Having secured the forts defending the primary harbor in his own state, Governor Moore next turned his attention to those in neighboring Pensacola, which remained in Federal hands. Since the days before statehood, Pensacola had remained a potential threat to the security of South Alabama. When it was still part of Spanish, and later British West Florida, the port provided entry for naval forces bearing arms for hostile inhabitants of the interior. The British trading firm of Panton and Leslie, led by loyalist exiles from the Revolution, reaped record profits exchanging British arms and manufactured goods for Creek and Seminole deer pelts from the interior, prompting an unauthorized foray by Andrew Jackson to evict the threat.[20] A half-century later, this threat remained, prompting Moore to write on January 8 to William Brooks, the Secession Convention's elected president, relating concerns from Florida's governor about the weakness of his state's forces and his requests for aid from Alabama. Moore, worried about the potential for Federal reinforcement, opined, "I need not suggest the danger to Florida and Alabama that must result from permitting a strong force to get possession of these forts." Indeed, the forces in Florida never captured Fort Pickens, guarding the entrance to Pensacola Bay, even with the help of Alabama troops or others from across the South. Moore's correspondence reveals a conspiracy, both to predetermine the result of the convention and to hasten events along a path that would result in armed conflict, ideally to push those who were wavering into the traitors' camp. Following his inauguration in March, Lincoln's administration paid as much attention to events at Fort Pickens as to those at Fort Sumter, believing the Confederacy's first blows were even more likely to fall at the Florida fort.[21]

Events on the Gulf Coast occupied the attention of much of southeastern Alabama. Residents of the cotton-producing region along the Chattahoochee River worried about the security of the port of Apalachicola, much as citizens of the Midwest who depended on the Mississippi River's uninterrupted flow through New Orleans to access global markets cast wary eyes toward that city. In early March, H. E. Owens, a convention delegate from Henry County, relayed the concerns of Gen. A. C. Gordon, who reported that cotton was accumulating in that port, and "unless some of our companies are sent to Apalachicola it will be burned up and our cotton taken if war should be declared. . . . Alabama will suffer more than Florida if that place should fall into the hands of the enemy." Thus, the potential for a Federal incursion from Pensacola, coupled with a closing of commerce on the Apalachicola River, prompted secessionists to view with great concern any potential threat of disloyalty to the Confederacy in Alabama's Wiregrass and adjacent regions of Northwest Florida.[22]

But Unionists in the interior already maintained communications with Federal forces on the coast. On March 18, prior to the opening of hostilities, the Confederate commander at Pensacola reported that "the commanding general learns with surprise and regret that some of our citizens are engaged in the business of furnishing supplies of fuel, water and provisions to the armed vessels of the United States now occupying a threatening position off this harbor. That no misunderstanding may exist on this subject, it is announced to all concerned that this traffic is strictly forbidden."[23] Thus, the Confederate commander, Gen. Braxton Bragg, attempted to outlaw an important source of income to the people of northwest Florida and southern Alabama—the supply of provisions and goods to the military base at Pensacola. This edict threatened the economic livelihood and engendered little support for the newly established Confederacy from the local population, who knew the Confederacy could not maintain a large naval establishment that would require their goods and services.

By May, after the declaration of war in April, the vulnerability of the Florida coast became an even larger concern. On May 10, George Ward wrote from Montgomery to the Confederate secretary of war proposing a scheme of defense of the Florida coast. He felt this was essential for the security of the interior because "If the plantations belonging to our Gulf Coast are ravaged or deserted, to avoid the plunder of negroes (not to speak of insurrection), the capacity of the country to contribute to the war is at an end."[24] Ward was particularly concerned with both St. Joseph and St. Andrew's Bays, as "both afford the means of penetrating into Florida, Alabama and Georgia."

On May 22, the Troy, Alabama, *Independent American* reported arrests at Pensacola by the "Alabama Mounted Rifles," raised in Wilcox County. It relayed that "a man by the name of Antony . . . had been charged with provisioning and communicating with the fleet off the harbor," while another man "had also been arrested for attempting to inform the commander of Fort Pickens of the vessels" in Pensacola's harbor.[25] Two months later, the renamed Troy *Advocate and American* reported that the response to the earlier incidents had apparently been insufficient, as "at a public meeting of the citizens of Pensacola, it was resolved to form an association to ferret out spies and require each member to subscribe" to an oath pledging allegiance to the Confederacy. These were the first steps in suppressing any insurgency—to ferret out the loyal and disloyal. The oath read, "I will endeavor to discover and will report any and every unfaithful person of whom I may obtain reliable intelligence." As Matthew Clavin has demonstrated, the city of Pensacola, and the surrounding area of Northwest Florida and South Alabama, remained a haven of discontent and resistance that placed it at odds with those currently in power in the region.[26]

The presence of an anti-Confederate population, whether white or black, to aid, support, or guide any excursion from the coast imperiled the Black Belt plantations just over a hundred miles inland. By September, the first inklings of such a population appeared in Union correspondence emanating from Fort Pickens. On September 10, Colonel Brown, commanding the post, reported that nine men, purporting to be Confederate marines, deserted to Fort Pickens with their boat and equipment. At the same time, two lumberjacks from near Milton reported that there were "many Union men in this country," but found "the expression of Union sentiments to be dangerous."[27]

George Ward's concerns about a slave insurrection in the Chattahoochee Valley were not unfounded. While Alabama had not seen a major insurrection during the antebellum period, at least not anything to rival the Stono, Gabriel's, or Nat Turner's rebellions, with a population of over 400,000 slaves, the concerns were never far from white Alabamians' minds. In his diary, Moores-ville native and future Confederate officer Daniel Hundley reported that sus-picious slave owners uncovered evidence of a conspiracy in Limestone County in May and June of 1861. He recorded "startling news of a most hellish insur-rectionary plot among the slaves. . . . It seems that the negroes have concluded that Lincoln is going to free them all, and they are everywhere making prepa-rations to aid him when he makes his appearance." The plot apparently had biracial origins, as investigators determined that "Peter Mudd, Andrew Green and Nicholas Moore, slaves, and one or two free negroes, aided by base white men are the leaders of the proposed servile insurrection." Similar concerns emerged elsewhere in the state. David Williams found that "during the late spring and early summer of 1861 a rebellion hysteria swept through southwest Georgia. Especially worried were slaveholders in the large plantation districts along the Chattahoochee and Flint Rivers."[28] Similarly, "There were more uprisings in the Alabama black belt counties of Montgomery, Autauga, and Marengo. They collectively involved hundreds of slaves."[29] The *Montgomery Advertiser* alleged, "They look for aid from Lincoln and the northern people."[30] Individual acts of resistance increased as well, as one slave stabbed an overseer to death rather than submit to a whipping.[31] As with many allegations of ser-vile insurrection, the normal rules of collecting evidence and due process did not apply. Vigilance committees executed several men without trial, primar-ily as a lesson to others who might consider striking for their own freedom. Hundley's assessment was absolutely correct—slaves were planning their lib-eration, and, while Lincoln himself did not make an appearance in Alabama's Tennessee River valley during the war, the first elements of his blue-clad army arrived in less than a year, and they received a rousing welcome from Lime-stone County's enslaved population.[32]

Slaves in Alabama's Tennessee Valley were not alone in monitoring events and making plans to strike for freedom. As Winthrop Jordan found in Natchez, Mississippi, slaves remained aware of the civil insurrection in their midst and made their own plans to separate from their unjust masters. But evidence of these insurrections, and their brutal repression, have been largely missing in the historical record. Jordan required detailed detective work to uncover ev-idence of the Natchez plan and, given similar efforts around Huntsville, it is not unreasonable to expect that slaves throughout Alabama planned additional efforts. On May 25, the *Abbeville United South,* in Henry County, reprinted a story from the *Cassville* (Georgia) *Standard,* across the state line, which reported the hanging of a slave accused of "planning and endeavoring to incite an insurrection." This plot was also a biracial affair, as "a white man by the name of Underwood was implicated in the plot. He is now in jail, committed on a charge of treason." The irony of accusing others of treason obviously escaped the editors of the *Standard,* who opined, "our citizens cannot be too vigilant in watching the action of the negroes and mean white men."[33] While the majority of Alabama's slaves remained far from Union lines in the Alabama River valley, those on the state's borders, including the Chattahoochee Valley around Abbeville, soon had better opportunities to strike for freedom.[34]

Unionists often shared their knowledge of events and their expectations with their slaves. In her investigation of testimony before the Southern Claims Commission, Margaret Storey found the following statement of Nelson Irwin, a slave of Unionist William Irwin: "He took us in his room and shut the door, and told us that he expected we would be free, but for us to make ourselves comfortable at home and he would let us know when the time came." Richard Mosely, a future soldier in the Forty-Eighth US Colored Infantry, added his testimony to Irwin's claim.[35] Slaves in Russell County had become so attuned to the political discourse that they attracted increased attention from white officials, who eventually barred them from attending political rallies.[36] After the war, Henry Hall of Tuscaloosa testified, "At the beginning of the rebellion I sympathized with the Union cause, my sympathies were all with the Union cause. I was then a slave and was afraid to express myself openly, but I talked away [to] the colored people."[37] In Tuscaloosa, a group of slaves led by carpenter Dudley Smith met surreptitiously with loyal whites to learn of the war's progress, recognizing that their common cause trumped any racial divide.[38] This threat of insurrection added further fuel to efforts to violently suppress disloyalty to the Confederate cause.

Judge William Winston of Valley Head went even further, according to John Gordon, Winston's enslaved coach driver. "Just as soon as the war broke out he told us colored people that we were just as free as he was." Gordon added,

> In 1861 he told me that I would be free, and for to remain at home that
> I might as well catch my freedom at home as anywhere. He told me

that as I had been his old loyal servant and would stay with him as long as he had bread he would divide with me, but if at any time I wanted to go, that he would do the best he could for me when I concluded to go.

Gordon also testified that Winston "would come out to our quarters at night and set and talk to us and tell us that the union army was advancing pretty fast towards us and he would tell us how the union army was whipping the Rebels. When he would get a paper he would bring it down and read it to us." It is difficult to reconcile Winston's reported generosity and honesty with slaveholding, but if Gordon's testimony is accurate, it speaks to the strength of the connection between freedmen and Unionists.[39]

Governor Moore's concerns about the security of military installations within and near Alabama's borders took on a new urgency when placed alongside reports of disloyalty to the Confederacy that peppered officials in Montgomery. On February 3, Jeremiah Clemens, having compromised his integrity by signing the ordinance, wrote his fellow townsman Leroy Pope Walker, warning that that the people in the Tennessee Valley were not yet resigned to secession. Clemens falsely believed that this resistance would decline with time. He reported, "There is still much discontent here at the passage of the ordinance of secession, but it is growing weaker daily, and, unless something is done to stir it up anew will soon die away. Last week Yancey was burned in effigy in Limestone (County), but I suppose it was rather a frolic of the 'b'hoys' than a manifestation of serious feeling on the part of the older citizens."[40] As with his decision to support the Confederacy, Clemens was also mistaken about the depth of the intense feelings and opposition to the extralegal government in Montgomery, as subsequent events clearly demonstrated.

After the war, staunch Unionists across North Alabama recorded their reactions to secession for posterity. Of Braxton Dunlavey, a Winston County Unionist who sent three sons into the Union army, a character witness later recalled, "After the secession of the State, he was so troubled that there was many nights that he could not sleep because he felt like the government was ruined and that he was ruined." He also "had no use for the Confederacy or its friends," and was "the bitterest man against the Rebels you ever saw."[41] A character witness for Green Haley, later the president of the Union League in Haleyville, claimed, "from the deep of his heart, he had prayed that the earth might open and swallow up the Confederacy and its supporters."[42] William

Hyde later recalled hearing Andrew McCullars say, "the war was uncalled for and he thought the South had no right to go into war. He called it a rich man's war and a poor man's fight, and said he was opposed to the war." In retaliation, "The Rebels fed on him as much as possible."[43] Buckner Walker's opposition extended through the war to the postwar period. He claimed, "I adhered to the Union cause from beginning to the end of the rebellion and I am square out Republican; never have nor never will if I know it, vote with the secession and Ku Klux Democracy."[44] Judge Winston of Valley Head in DeKalb County, though a slaveholder, had been a Unionist delegate to the Secession Convention and later "claimed that the object of the secessionist was to form an aristocratic government and that the government would be represented by slave holders, and that it was very probable that they would legislate in such a manner as not to allow any one to vote except slave owners, that laboring men and men of small property would be disenfranchised."[45] Zachariah White went a step farther, giving speeches across northern Alabama, including in Holly Grove and Jasper, on the dangers of secession, despite threats of injury or death. He frequently claimed that he would gladly have his head cut off or be shot through with a cannonball if it would save the Union. Benjamin Curtis reportedly heard White say, "secession was wrong, it was uncalled for, and would ruin the best government the sun and heaven ever shown its ray upon." A. J. Taylor heard White say, "the war was gotten up by the rotten hearted secession party and he hated them so bitterly."[46]

While sporadic reports of a "disloyal" (meaning Unionist) population filtered in from across the state, events paled in comparison to the outright revolt in northern Alabama's Hill Country. Incensed over the treatment of their representative, Christopher Sheats in Montgomery, and appalled at not being allowed to exercise their vote on either the ordinance of secession or the ratification of the Confederate Constitution, residents of several Hill Country counties began to band together for their own protection. Documentation is thin, due in part to the danger of committing names and events to paper, but also because word apparently traveled through an informal grapevine typical of close-knit rural areas. According to Thompson, after the outbreak of hostilities, Hill Country residents began to meet regularly to discuss how to protect their own interests.

On June 1, a small group apparently met in Houston, then the county seat of Winston County, in hopes of planning an even larger meeting to build solidarity with fellow Unionists in surrounding counties. The larger gathering would take place on the national holiday, July 4, at Looney's Tavern, owned by Bill Looney.[47] The proprietor was a staunch Unionist who recruited for the First Alabama Cavalry, and his son, Anderson Looney, was one of the first enlistees in the regiment and served throughout the war, rising in rank to first sergeant.[48] Attendees at the June meeting agreed to send riders to neighboring Lawrence, Blount, Marshall, Walker, Fayette, Franklin, and Madison Counties, spreading word of the gathering. In this, they were largely successful, as accounts estimated that as many as three thousand Unionists from as far away as Tennessee attended the meeting.[49] Though details of the event are unclear, speakers affirmed that, if Alabama had the right to secede from the Union, then individual counties also had the right to secede from Alabama and retain their allegiance to the old flag. While evidence of Winston County ever having done so is unsubstantiated, efforts were already under way to form a new state of "Nickajack" along the Alabama-Tennessee border, just as loyalists eventually carved West Virginia from Virginia, and some counties, most notably Jones County, Mississippi, did issue formal secession declarations from their states.[50]

Word of the large gathering eventually leaked out of the region, traveling as far as Governor Moore's office in Montgomery. On July 16, a citizen wrote from Blount County that "a very considerable number of the inhabitants of the counties in Winston, Marion and Morgan are disaffected towards the Confederate government and are actually raising and equipping themselves to sustain the old government of the United States."[51] Rebels pleaded with Moore to break up the Hill Country Unionists, but eventually took matters into their own hands. Secessionist landlords expelled renters suspected of retaining their loyalty to the Union from their farms, many with crops still in the ground, forfeiting almost a full year's worth of labor and improvements. And prosecession store owners refused to serve or extend credit to Unionist neighbors, while mills refused to grind their corn and secessionists intimidated those who did serve Unionists.[52] Unionist Nathan Montgomery reported that he "ground corn at the mill he had in charge at that time for the wives and families of Union soldiers who were in the Union army toll free and aided and assisted them all he could on the sly," but was repeatedly threatened for doing so at his mill near Jasper.[53] Throughout the war, those who tried to ameliorate the suffering of Unionists likewise attracted the ire of rebel authorities. Thomas Sawyer of Blount County reported that he was twice arrested and jailed in Blountsville for "feeding the wives and children of men who were in the Union army."[54] While the first battles were still far from the state's borders, some Alabamians were already experiencing scarcity and want. When persecuted residents petitioned for relief, they were told to "get it from their Yankee friends." Many eventually did, and Thompson believes this persecution "might have been a factor in causing some of the hill people to join up with the Yankees." Kinship networks largely ameliorated suffering during the first summer of war, but some families became refugees or headed north. But many others remained, biding their time and watching events anxiously.[55]

The actions to control dissent in Pensacola and the Hill Country coalesced in August of 1861 into the Confederate "Alien Enemies Act" and the "Sequestration Act." The former permitted expulsion of anyone over the age of fourteen who refused to swear allegiance to the so-called Confederacy. The latter authorized the seizure of anyone declared an "enemy alien," a term broadly defined and revealing the true intent behind the legislation. Courts across the state could seize the property of suspected Unionists with only the flimsiest burden of proof, leading to what some Unionists referred to as the "shut mouth time," when expressing loyalty to the United States could result in economic devastation and the loss of their homes.[56] Thus, the Civil War transformed Alabama into a direct war for resources, as the state, in the hands of secessionists, used the legal system to appropriate the property of its neighbors, and then used some of it to support the rebellion against the national government. These two laws, and their rigorous enforcement, did as much to destroy Unionist communities as any other, both spurring an exodus of refugees and reducing subsistence for those who remained. It also inspired hatred and a desire for revenge among those who were willing and capable of bearing arms against the Confederacy.[57] Jonathan Barton, later a sergeant in the First Alabama Cavalry, reported of Andrew Ingle, "In the early part of the war he raised a Union company for home protection and when things got too strong against him, he advised us to go to the Union army."[58] In June 1861, Robert Bell wrote his brother Henry, a Confederate living in Mississippi, that he was "a heap freader of the disunions with their helish principals than I am of lincon." Sadly, Robert Bell's concerns were well justified, but he was willing to "Dy before I will take an oath to support the Southern confedersa."[59]

By the fall of 1861, the state slowly awakened to the reality that the war would be a long one and require greater sacrifice than many had believed, despite cooperationist delegates' predictions of a long and bloody war to oppose the South's secession. In his impassioned plea to his fellow delegates, James Clark of Lawrence County argued that secession would surely mean war, as "The annals of all time furnish but few, if any, instances of a people changing their allegiance by a bloodless revolution."[60] But to reassure supporters of secession, South Carolina senator James Chestnut had promised to drink all the blood spilled in the war, a task already made impossible by the sanguine battles at Bull Run in Virginia and Wilson Creek in Missouri. There would be a war, and it would not be a short one. And before it was over, much of Alabama was ruined and all of her slaves freed, as Alabamians fought one another in a bloody civil war, waged between armies arrayed on battlefields and between partisans in forested thickets, just as North Alabama's cooperationist delegates had predicted.

A Confederate officer attempting to organize a regiment at Camp Kewburn in Greene County, on the state's western border, during the winter of 1861–1862 wrote the Confederate secretary of war, Judah Benjamin, of his concerns about Unionists in the area. He claimed to have received word of over eight hundred "avowed Union men," who, he feared, might attempt to liberate prisoners, including fellow Unionists then imprisoned in Tuscaloosa. Though the officer could have been exaggerating the situation in order to expedite the organization of his unit and the shipment of badly needed weapons, the reports likely bore some truth, as loyal Alabamians were by now armed and organized, and ready to defend themselves against the assaults and usurpations of their neighbors.

The second year of the war was a pivotal one for Alabama's freedmen and Unionists who eventually donned the Union blue. The Confederate military collapse in Kentucky and Tennessee opened Alabama to penetration by Union armies operating along two of the three most vulnerable corridors, the Tennessee River valley and the rail lines that entered the state at several points. Only the coast, blocked by the forts defending Mobile Bay, remained secure, but the easy passage of the forts defending New Orleans and the capture of that city in April demonstrated that Mobile's security might not be assured for long. As Union armies entered the state, they set in motion a chain of events that led Alabama's slaves through the transition from "contraband of war" to impressed labor for the army and, eventually, on the first day of the following year, into the category of "freedmen," and with it the opportunity for enlistment as soldiers. At the same time, a harsh drought raised the specter of famine across North Alabama, which, combined with both Confederate conscription and increasing levies by armies on both sides operating in and passing through the state, threatened the subsistence agriculture that both freedmen and Unionists relied on for survival. Faced with increasing levies and requisitions, and a near-total crop failure and other environmental disasters that left corn cribs and smokehouses empty before the first leaves had fallen from the trees, Alabama's dissenters faced the prospect of a starvation winter. Fortunately, the Federal gains in the spring, though rolled back in North Alabama, were secure enough to sustain garrison towns in the neighboring states of Mississippi and Tennessee. In both states, the first Alabamians in blue added their small contribution to the Union armies defending those threatened points and eventually worked toward the liberation of their home state.

At the beginning of 1862, the state of affairs in Alabama was far closer to what it had been before the declaration of war than to what it would be just a year later. Caught up in the enthusiasm of war, many secessionists had enlisted in the state regiments formed in the spring of 1861 and traveled by rail to threatened points in Virginia and Tennessee, and along the Florida coast. But except for this absence of manpower, the war was still far away, and few of those who had joined the rebel armies had seen any significant combat, leaving communities largely untouched by the severe losses that marked the later years of the war. Mobilization proceeded apace in the North, and especially the Midwest, and a strong Union army of midwesterners sat in northern Kentucky, poised to use the Ohio and Mississippi River valleys to project force deep into the western Confederacy. Initially, Southern armies had respected Kentucky's declaration of "neutrality" and sat in a defensive line across the northern boundary of Tennessee, but the positions along the Mississippi, Tennessee, and Cumberland Rivers could be easily flanked by Union forces using gunboats and transports to push past these defenses and well upriver, into the heart of the Confederacy. Aware of these vulnerabilities, in September of 1861 Confederate forces violated Kentucky's neutrality and entered the state, primarily to secure more defensible positions, especially Island No. 10 in the Mississippi, and the natural barrier of the Ohio River, in order to block the advance south. But Union forces responded in kind, preemptively moving their troops across the Ohio and into northern Kentucky, pushing Confederates back to their defenses along the Tennessee-Kentucky line. Fort Henry, on the Tennessee River, attempted to deny access farther south, but the fort was

Fort Henry
Feb 1862
Fort Donelson

poorly sited, leaving it inundated at high water and vulnerable to naval gun-
fire. On the Cumberland River, the more northerly of the two nearly parallel
streams curving clockwise from the Appalachians to the Ohio, Fort Donelson
enjoyed a high, commanding position and Confederates in Nashville felt secure behind its batteries.

But they had not figured on the energy and determination of a West Point
graduate and Mexican War veteran who, at the beginning of the war, had resigned his commission and was clerking in his father's leather goods store in
Galena, Illinois. Ulysses S. Grant rose to command the Union forces holding
Paducah, Kentucky, from which point he could move up either the Tennessee or Cumberland Rivers, forcing the Confederate defenders to divide their
forces between the two forts. Grant chose the easier objective first, and on
February 6, forced the evacuation of Fort Henry, opening the Tennessee River
to traffic as far as the railroad bridge at Florence, Alabama. Retracing his steps
to the Ohio, Grant's amphibious force then moved up the Cumberland River
where, in a week-long campaign, his combined force captured Fort Donelson,
leaving the river open to Nashville. When Confederates evacuated that city
on February 25, Union forces held both their first Southern state capital and
a rail line pointed like a dagger south toward Alabama. Already, gunboats had
moved up the Tennessee River as far as Florence, Alabama, forcing the rebel
defenders to evacuate that point on February 8, but the Muscle Shoals just
upstream blocked further progress.

Ky
Perry
Fort Henry
F Florence
← Perry's Letters
Fort Donelson

Attempting to salvage these losses, Confederate forces from across the
Deep South, including the garrisons of New Orleans and Pensacola, gathered
under Gen. Albert Sidney Johnston at the vital rail center of Corinth, the in-
tersection of the Memphis & Charleston and Mobile & Ohio Railroads. They
marched north during the first week of April to attack Grant's army, camped
between Pittsburg Landing, on the west bank of the Tennessee and a small
church named Shiloh. According to Judge George Washington Lane of Huntsville, the Confederate defenders of Tennessee transited North Alabama en
route to Corinth and "levied contributions as they passed through," which,
when combined with a poor harvest in 1861, in which the "grain crop was very
short . . . made the supplies less than usual."[61] In part to justify his inaction
later in the summer, Gen. Don Carlos Buell made the following assessment:

Corinth

> The demand upon the surplus provisions of Tennessee had been in-
> creased by the rebellion, which cut off the supply from the Northwest,

and by the armies, rebel and Union, which during the winter and spring of 1862 fed upon the country to a considerable extent. North Alabama particularly was left in a condition to need the necessaries of life, instead of affording subsistence for an army.[62]

The bloody, two-day Battle of Shiloh on April 6–7 inflicted thousands of casualties on each army, draining the Confederate manpower pool and contributing to the Confederate Congress's decision to implement the first draft in American history on April 12th, the first anniversary of the attack on Fort Sumter. The legislation, known as the Conscription Act, required all males between ages eighteen and thirty-five, unless specifically exempted by their occupation in war industries, to join the rebel army. Later modifications excluded anyone who owned twenty or more slaves, ostensibly to help prevent slave rebellions but in reality a clear demonstration that the elite of the slavocracy enjoyed a different set of rules.

For Unionists, the passage of the Conscription Act represented a significant turning point. As historian Margaret Storey points out, before it, dissenters could simply ignore recruiting efforts and appeals to serve a cause they disagreed with, with no greater harm than insults and charges of cowardice, including those directed by Confederate troops toward future First Alabama trooper John R. Phillips.[63] But after the Conscription Act, loyalists became "outlaws," in violation of the Confederate government's orders and subject to arrest and confinement, or worse.[64] Confederate authorities arrested and jailed Christopher Sheats, and a mob beat and disfigured Jeremiah Clemens for encouraging others to defy the draft.[65] Conscription agents, who now scoured the Confederate interior, resorted to increasingly severe means in their attempts to coerce service, and the Alabama hills suffered immensely as a result of their well-deserved reputation for Unionism. On April 21, Confederate general Bushrod Johnson wrote from Columbus, Mississippi: "The northern counties of Alabama, you know, are full of Tories. There has been a convention recently held in the corner of Winston, Fayette and Marion Counties, Alabama, in which the people resolved to remain neutral; which simply means that they will join the enemy when they occupy the country."[66] The report likely referred to a meeting near Natural Bridge, where Unionists vowed to resist conscription and do all they could to undermine the efforts of its agents. Conscription agents, and military forces supporting them, swept the

Margaret Storey

Phillips'
Bio-
Diary

Winston, Fayette, Marion Co.
60

Meeting at Natural Bridge *

Hill Country for recruits. A Confederate prisoner taken in a skirmish at Russellville on July 3 admitted "that their special business was to burn cotton and arrest certain Union men and take them South."[67] By mid-1862, these actions had generated a nascent guerrilla war in the Alabama backcountry.

After many Unionists resorted to "lying out" in the woods, home guards targeted families and loved ones who, they correctly assumed, were providing shelter and provisions to their fathers, husbands, brothers, and sons who concealed themselves in the woods.[68] This coercion increasingly included the appropriation of vital resources, from protection from the elements, such as clothing and bed coverings, to the houses themselves, which they frequently put to the torch.[69] In addition, Confederate agents, home guards, and civil law enforcement officers levied "taxes-in-kind," usually in the form of foodstuffs and forage, to sustain their armies in the field. But subsistence farmers in Alabama's mountain valleys relied on the meager supplies of corn and ham to get them through the winter, and needed forage for their draft animals in order to put a crop in the following spring, and the loss of male labor made farming a more difficult undertaking. Short of supplies, many families found their ability to support those "lying out" undercut by food shortages, which was precisely what the Confederate agents intended.[70] With food and forage stolen or requisitioned, and draft animals confiscated, Unionists faced the threat of starvation if they remained in their homes behind Confederate lines. Though many were able to survive through the war, especially in areas where they constituted a majority and could therefore rely on one another for support, many isolated or minority areas saw an exodus of refugees fleeing the burgeoning guerrilla war for Union lines. Faced with these circumstances, some sought to exchange the one resource they still controlled, their labor, for provisions for themselves and their families. As James Baggett observed, "For most if not all—and they realized it—their food and clothing would be better in the Union army than at home or in the Confederate army," if they were caught by conscription agents.[71] While some civilian occupations, such as driving wagons, cutting wood, and shoeing horses were available in the Union towns, the greatest need was for military manpower.[72]

Those lines moved much closer with the arrival of Maj. Gen. Ormsby Mitchel's division of Federal troops in Huntsville on April 11. Marching south from Nashville, Mitchel's troops entered the Tennessee Valley, initiating a chain of events that led directly to both black and white Alabamians serving

blk +
wt

in the Union army. Mitchel's initial objective was to secure the Memphis &
Charleston Railroad, a vital artery across the middle of the Confederacy. After an overnight forced march from Fayetteville, Tennessee, to Huntsville, his
blue-clad infantrymen captured fifteen locomotives and dozens of rail cars at
the Memphis & Charleston shops, as well as two hundred Confederates. With
a secure supply base in Huntsville, Mitchel's troops could supply flank protection for an advance by the victors of Shiloh down the Mobile & Ohio Railroad
from Corinth, or for a lateral move along the Memphis & Charleston to Chattanooga before turning southeast for Atlanta. On April 12, his troops moved
to Decatur, where the Memphis & Charleston joined the Nashville & Decatur
and then crossed the intact railroad bridge to the south bank of the Tennessee. On their arrival, they were greeted by 150 "stout, honest, dusky" men
who helped clear the failed Confederate incendiaries and roadblocks from the
bridge.[73] By April 13 they were outside Tuscumbia and entered that town the
next day. Forces sent east held the line as far as Stevenson, and eventually
Bridgeport, where the railroad crossed back to the south back of the Tennessee
before proceeding on to Chattanooga. Mitchel's 7,000 troops now occupied a
substantial portion of the vital rail artery, but holding the exposed section of
railroad proved difficult. Along a 120-mile front, Mitchel had ample infantry
but only one depleted regiment of cavalry, severely restricting his mobility.
For the time being, his control of the railroad gave him some mobility, but
increased pressure on the line itself, in the form of bushwhackers laying ambushes or destroying culverts, diminished the line's utility. Just two weeks after
seizing the vital bridge at Decatur, Federal forces had to burn it to prevent any
rebel forces from gaining the north side of the river. With the arrival of Union
forces, Confederates in North Alabama easily transitioned from counterinsur-
gents oppressing loyalists to guerrillas waging their own insurgency against
the Union army.

As Joseph Danielson has conclusively demonstrated, secessionists in northern Alabama were not yet ready to accept Federal liberation of their part of the
state.[74] Almost from the start, Mitchel found his columns harassed by rebels in
and out of uniform. His troops termed their opposition "bushwhackers" due
to their habit of taking potshots at trains while concealed in the dense underbrush of late spring. A month of constant skirmishing saw incursions against
Bridgeport on April 23 and Tuscumbia, at the opposite end of his section of
the line, the very next day. On April 28, just outside Huntsville, a small de-

tachment of the Tenth Wisconsin Infantry held off an attack on the Paint Rock Bridge. And in early May, a strong force of Confederate cavalry raided Athens leading to one of the more notorious reprisals of the war, and a seminal event in the Union shift from a conciliatory policy to what historian Mark Grimsley has described as "hard war."[75]

On May 2, Col. John Turchin, born Ivan Vasilyevich Turchaninov in the Donbas region of Russia, posted one of his brigade's four infantry regiments, the Eighteenth Ohio, in the town of Athens.[76] The town was in the center of a productive agricultural region and was home to many wealthy planters and slave owners, but by virtue of being in North Alabama, hosted a number of Unionists as well. Union troops had passed through the town several times during their first three weeks in the valley and had generally maintained cordial relations. Mitchel had received "a deputation of citizens from Athens who express strong attachment to the government," and soldiers and townspeople maintained cordial, if frosty relations as the Eighteenth pitched their tents around the town.[77] But on the morning of May 1, the relationship irrevocably changed. A battalion of the Confederacy's First Louisiana Cavalry, under Col. John Scott, charged into town at daybreak, surprising and overrunning the Ohio regiment's pickets. Believing he was outnumbered, Col. Timothy Stanley rallied his troops and evacuated the town in the direction of Huntsville, where he hoped the rest of Turchin's brigade could rescue him. As they left the town, troops reported that some townspeople jeered them while cheering for Jeff Davis and the Confederacy, and at least two citizens grabbed their firearms and joined the Confederates in the pursuit.[78]

At the same time, General Mitchel left Huntsville for Athens by rail and was saved from riding into the town, and capture, by a freedman who stopped the train and warned him. Mitchel's train made it back across the bridge at Limestone Creek, near Mooresville, but a heavier train loaded with 25,000 rations that Stanley had ordered out before evacuating Athens was not as lucky. When it reached the bridge, the stringers sawn in two by Confederate guerrillas gave way, wrecking the locomotive and setting the train on fire. According to later testimony, two Union soldiers aboard the train burned to death while the guerrillas, who had hidden to watch the results of their handiwork, restrained two slaves who attempted to save the soldiers. Upon returning to Huntsville, Mitchel immediately ordered out a relief column and Turchin's brigade took up the march, but he had to detrain at Madison Station due to the break in the rails, and was still nine miles from Athens when darkness overtook him, forcing him to camp for the night. Meanwhile, Scott's troopers returned to Athens, where the townspeople treated them to dinner.

Turchin had his command back in motion before dawn and arrived in Athens shortly after sunrise. His cavalry had preceded him and pushed the Confederates out of the town, but Scott reformed his command to contest the advance, until the infantry's arrival convinced him to retire. Meanwhile, the soldiers of the Eighteenth returned to their camp but found their belongings missing, especially their knapsacks, which contained personal items and spare clothing. Many resolved to make up their losses from the well-stocked stores in town, and looted several. Undoubtedly, the same occurred in private homes as Turchin, finding the Eighteenth Ohio's tents confiscated or stolen, ordered his soldiers quartered in the town. But the treatment of Athens paled in comparison to other towns later in the war. There was no wholesale looting, no buildings were burned and, unlike Lawrence, Kansas, where William Quantrill murdered 150 citizens a year later, not a single person in Athens was harmed, though a slave owner later alleged that soldiers raped one of her slaves, a charge that was never proven.

But this event provided a public relations coup for the Confederacy, and from it arose "The Sack of Athens," complete with the name of Greece's most noble city-state and a "Yankee horde" led by no less than a Russian Cossack. In his history of the war, historian Walter Fleming traded in many of these images:

> Athens was a wealthy place, intensely southern in feeling, and on that account was most heartily disliked by the Federals. Here, for two hours, Turchin retired to his tent and gave over the town to the soldiers to be sacked after the old European custom. Revolting outrages were committed. Robberies were common where Turchin commanded. His Russian ideas of the rules of war were probably responsible for his conduct. Buell characterized it as "a case of undisputed atrocity." For this Athens affair Turchin was court-martialed and sentenced to be dismissed from the service.[79]

But the resulting court-martial, held in Athens (hardly an unbiased venue) in mid-July, turned into a referendum on the conduct of the war. Turchin, representing himself after his counsel failed to arrive in time, asked to challenge the loyalty of his accusers but was prevented by the presiding officer of the courts-martial, future president James Garfield, from doing so. Many of the witnesses were Confederate sympathizers, a fact that became clear when Turchin cross-examined the "postmaster" and asked him which government he served.[80] Other witnesses refused to answer questions about their loyalty to avoid self-incrimination. In an eloquent defense, Turchin lamented protecting the property of secessionists while bushwhackers and guerrillas daily raided Federal supplies and killed Federal soldiers by shooting into trains. In the end, the court convicted Turchin of dereliction of duty, which he was certainly guilty of by failing to maintain discipline, but President Lincoln had his conviction and dismissal set aside, and Congress approved Mitchel's recommendation for Turchin's promotion to brigadier general, reinstating him in the army. He went on to become a successful field general who further distinguished himself at the Battle of Chickamauga.

Hidden within the testimony of Turchin's accusers, and in the military communications emanating from the court's convening authority, Gen. Don Carlos Buell, himself a former slaveholder, are concerns about how the Union army was already reordering Southern society, and how Alabama's black residents had already pushed themselves to the forefront of the debate.[81] By providing information to Union forces, they earned their protection. And with the army's protection, Southern slave owners lost control over their charges, both physically and socially, as freedmen and women began to interact with Union soldiers in ways that had been impossible in Southern society. When officers sympathetic to slaveholders, such as Buell, ordered camps searched for runaways, other officers with abolitionist sympathies refused to grant them permission and barred entry to the search parties. When he arrived in Huntsville with his Army of the Ohio in June, Buell reported a visit to the camp of the First Michigan Artillery in search of a former slave of a Mr. Patton, a resident of Huntsville, possibly the future governor Robert Patton. "My attention was attracted to the negro by the suit he had on of a new and handsome uniform of the artillery company." Capt. Cyrus O. Loomis, commanding the battery, refused to hand over the freedman, stating that "General Mitchel had set the negro free, and had asserted positively that he should serve no man again. . . . Captain Loomis said the slave had given valuable information to General Mitchel," and, in Buell's presence, ordered his new soldier to return

1862

to camp, which he did. This unidentified freedman may have been the very first Alabamian to don the Union blue.[82]

Actions such as Buell's had a decided effect upon slave morale. After the war Ben Turner, a slave from Selma who later earned election to the US House of Representatives, testified, "When the war broke out of course my sympathies were for freedom, and when Gen. McClellan captured some negroes along his lines, and sent them back to their masters, I did not know how to decide. But when Mr. Lincoln issued his Emancipation Proclamation, then I was for the federals; until then I was wavering. I was waiting to see which side would give me my freedom." Turner's testimony, taken well after the war, was either a measured swipe at his Democratic political opponents or an affirmation that freedom and the ability to keep the products of their own labor (which Turner accumulated a considerable amount of after purchasing his freedom during the war) lay at the root of black Unionism.[83]

When Union armies left liberated territory, they often, but not always, took their charges with them. When a division of his army crossed the Tennessee River in June, Buell ordered Gen. Alexander McCook to see that "all unauthorized persons are expelled from your command and prevented from crossing with it. By these are meant fugitive slaves and all other hangers-on, white or black, who have not some legitimate connection with the service."[84] While Buell's actions were certainly correct militarily, in order to speed the division's crossing, and were repeated by General Sherman two years later when his army crossed a river in Georgia on its "March to the Sea," they also left the newly liberated slaves to the tender mercies of the Confederate cavalry and bushwhackers trailing the army, who were far too happy to reprise their former duties of slave catchers. Indeed, Buell's refusal to offer protection to slave informants, and his active assistance to slave catchers, resulted in several slaves being hung near Tuscumbia.[85] Other officers also treated freedmen cruelly, with one Union division commander having a slave whipped near Jackson's Ferry, and soldiers sometimes played cruel tricks on naïve slaves who had come to help them.[86]

For many slaves, the arrival of the Union army fulfilled a biblical prophecy of an "exodus," and slave communities, already aware of the war's outbreak and significance, immediately took steps to ensure that Federal forces prevailed. Blacks in the Tennessee Valley proved from the start to be one of Mitchel's most reliable sources of information about Confederate activities. On one occasion he reported, "The negroes are our only friends, and in two instances I owe my own safety to their faithfulness."[87] Mitchel was duly concerned about his safety—in May, Confederate cavalry captured a relief column near Pulaski, including his son, and in August bushwhackers ambushed and fatally wounded Brig. Gen. Robert L. McCook as he rode, indisposed, in his ambulance.

Mitchel had organized an effective network of black informants, reporting, "with the aid of the negroes in watching the river I feel myself sufficiently strong to defy the enemy." He also took steps to begin employing his black informants in various occupations, aware of "the absolute necessity of protecting slaves who furnish us valuable information."[88] Mitchel even reported his efforts directly to Secretary of War Edwin Stanton, perhaps an indicator of the difficulties plaguing the Federal communications network so early in the war. Stanton approved of Mitchel's actions, wiring, "The assistance of slaves is an element of military strength which, under proper regulations you are fully justified in employing for your security and the success of your operations," demonstrating that slaves' contributions and Mitchel's efforts were receiving attention at the highest levels of the government. Often, slaves identified disloyal men, but were frequently the only witnesses, prompting Mitchel to wire Stanton, "Am I to convict on the testimony of blacks?"[89] This uncertainty highlighted an issue that plagued postwar efforts to guarantee civil rights. But many freedmen had other employment in mind. In June a black military company acquired Enfield rifled muskets and began drilling openly in the streets of Huntsville, to the horror of the town's white residents. But at this point in the war, armed military service was still a step too far in Northern Alabama, and the provost marshal disarmed the company.[90] When Federal forces evacuated Huntsville in September, many former slaves who had freed themselves followed their liberators into Tennessee, eventually taking up residence in the contraband camps around Nashville.[91]

For those who remained, the breakdown in the Confederate agricultural system threatened their survival as well. As Douglas Hurt has demonstrated, most cotton production depended on monocultural plantations that were not self-sufficient in food. Rather than diversify their operations and give valuable cotton acreage over to less remunerative subsistence crops, planters found it easier to use a portion of their substantial profits from the sale of their crop to purchase the minimal rations they issued to their slaves. As a result, much of Alabama depended on the import of foodstuffs from the upper South and

Midwest, especially wheat from the Old Northwest and hogs from Tennessee. As Judge Lane explained to a commission investigating events in the state during the summer of 1862, the war had closed off trade with the Northwest, and the loss of Tennessee cut off supplies of bacon. While southerners could, and in some places did, switch to cereal production for the 1862 growing season, these crops would not ripen until the fall. And the intervening summer saw both record requisitions by invading armies and a severe drought that caused many crops to fail, especially in the Tennessee Valley, home to most of the freedmen who eventually served in Alabama's USCT regiments. As a result, they too felt food shortages and, as the weather finally cooled, faced the prospect of entering a winter with insufficient food stores, and masters who, despite their rhetoric, became less and less interested in their slaves' welfare.

With farms and fields stripped by the armies of both sides, many plantation owners could no longer afford to feed their charges, and despite postwar myths of familial loyalty, simply turned their slaves out. According to one Confederate refugee, Elizabeth Meriwether, who had fled occupied Memphis for less-accessible Tuscaloosa, "every day negroes were leaving in batches in search of the Yankee army, which always welcomed them, [and] gave them rations." The deluded mistress believed, "It was not that the negroes *wanted* to leave their former white masters, it was because they were *hungry*." When shortages came, masters quickly broke their ties with their bondsmen. Meriwether continued, "the white Masters would urge their negroes to run off to the Yankee army—it left more food for the white men and women."[92] Levi Coffin corroborated this version of event in his memoirs when he recorded, "Many of the slaveholders fled farther South, taking their able-bodied slaves with them, and leaving the women and children, aged and sick ones, to take care of themselves. In many cases there was nothing for this helpless class to live upon. The two vast armies that had swept over the country had consumed all the provisions, and the poor slaves were left in a suffering condition."[93]

Thus, environmental factors, coupled with the proximity of Union camps and the decreasing effectiveness of slave patrols, led many slaves to embark on the perilous journey to freedom, often leaving behind loved ones and the only lives they had ever known. They traded this for an uncertain future in a "contraband camp," subject to the goodwill of a fickle army that, while promising employment and freedom, repeatedly demonstrated that military concerns came before those of freedmen and refugees, picking up and moving on a moment's notice if the military situation required it. Indeed, this is exactly what happened in September 1862, when a Confederate offensive required the forces garrisoning Huntsville to remove to Nashville, bringing a long column of freedmen and Unionists north to the fortified city. By one estimate, over 10,000 freedpeople left with the Union army, and many of the USCT regiments recruited from the Nashville contraband camps likely contained a large number of Alabamians.[94]

For those that remained, their actions had already put into motion events that changed the course and conduct of the war. Slaves whose liberators were close at hand began to exert themselves against their masters and, mostly, mistresses, much to their consternation. Huntsville resident Mary Chadick was already performing many of the tasks, including cooking and cleaning, formerly performed by her domestic slaves.[95] As a result of events in Nashville and elsewhere in the liberated South, and in the absence of a coherent policy on freedpeople, on July 17, Congress passed the Second Confiscation Act, which, among other things, directed "that every person who shall hereafter commit the crime of treason against the United States, and shall be adjudged guilty thereof, shall suffer death, and all his slaves, if any, shall be declared and made free."[96] Perhaps just as significant, Section 11 stated, "the President of the United States is authorized to employ as many persons of African descent as he may deem necessary and proper for the suppression of this rebellion, and for this purpose he may organize and use them in such manner as he may judge best for the public welfare," which, while not specifically stating it, left open the path to black enlistment in the Union army. Already enterprising officers had enlisted soldiers in the First Kansas Colored Infantry Regiment at Fort Leavenworth, though without official sanction, and three regiments of the Louisiana Native Guards were drilling in their home state.[97]

On September 22, the president went a step further, declaring all slaves in areas still under rebellion to be free as of January 1, 1863. Ironically, while the Emancipation Proclamation legally freed all the slaves in Alabama, by virtue of the army's withdrawal, most remained in bondage until 1865. However, it did not legally free those who had evacuated to Tennessee, as Nashville and its environs remained under Union control. But the document did clear up any ambiguity in the Second Confiscation Act. It unequivocally stated, "such persons of suitable condition, will be received into the armed service of the United States to garrison forts, positions, stations, and other places."[98] Though it did not specifically mention fighting, combat was an essential element of "garrisoning forts," and Alabamians enlisted under this authority increasingly saw combat in the field.

As a result of the Confederate Conscription Act issued in April, and attempts to enforce it in the months that followed, armed conflict erupted between Confederate authorities and home guards on the one hand and Union resisters on the other. While a precise chronology of the various ambushes, raids, and reprisals is beyond the scope of this work, largely because these various small-scale but almost continual episodes of violence did not attract the same attention in the documentary record as the larger campaigns between fielded forces, there are sufficient references in the record to piece together the impact. Most are found within the letters and correspondence of state officials, such as Governors Shorter and Watts, who fielded repeated requests for additional forces in the Unionist enclaves, and then forwarded their complaints to Confederate authorities in Richmond, who continued to strip the state of military manpower. By the following November, Confederate general Braxton Bragg reported, "I hear very bad accounts from our friends (citizens) in North Mississippi. Many declare their preference for Yankee military rule to the terrors of the mob now around them; they plead for discipline and beg for men who will shoot marauders, if necessary, in their protection."[99]

Another source is the documentation in the Southern Claims Commission of relatives captured and murdered while in Confederate control, including that of "Wash" Curtis, a Unionist, by conscription agents on June 8, 1862, and furtive references to Unionist attempts to band together to meet fire with fire.[100] The chief band of oppressors in the Hill Country came from Confederate general Philip D. Roddey's command, or companies initially organized by Confederate authorities but who later went "rogue" and fought their own war beyond Confederate or state control. The one that receives the most mention in the SCC claims is that of Capt. Dan Whatley, originally organized as Company B of the Tenth Alabama Cavalry but a unit that seems to have operated with increasing autonomy as the war progressed.[101] At one point, Green Haley organized a group of twenty-eight men to ambush Whatley's company, but the attack miscarried.[102] Andrew Ingle likewise organized a "Union company for home protection," and Thomas Martin stood accused of organizing a raid on the jail in Jasper in 1865 in which a combined force of furloughed Union soldiers and Unionist guerrillas raided the jail, driving off the guards and freeing

Unionist prisoners, including Martin's son.[103] While individual Union soldiers from Alabama-raised units often participated in these skirmishes, the accounts did not always make their way into the official records, leaving a narrative of the war skewed toward convention battles that, as Dan Sutherland and others have successfully argued, obscures the true nature of the internecine violence in the region.[104] But while the guerrilla violence typified the experience of the war for many Alabamians, especially in the hills of the northern part of the state, successful resolution by one side or the other would have had little impact on the course of the larger war, which both unleashed the brutal and horrific violence and then largely, though not entirely, quelled it at the end of the war.

Due to the by-now widespread guerrilla conflict, the situation in the Unionist counties of North Alabama had deteriorated so badly by midsummer that large groups of Unionists came down from the hills and attempted to cross the southern part of the Tennessee Valley in order to reach Union lines across the river. The first to successfully complete the journey were fortunate to reach a sympathetic ear in Decatur, in the form of Col. Abel Streight of the Fifty-First Indiana Infantry. On July 16, Streight reported:

> While in command at Decatur there were several small parties of loyal Alabamians who came into our lines begging me to give them protection and a chance to defend the flag of our country. The tale of suffering and misery as told by each as they arrived was in itself a lamentable history of the deplorable condition of the Union people of the South. . . . About this time (10th instant) I was informed by a courier that there was a party of about 40 men some 5 or 6 miles towards the mountains trying to come to us and about the same number of the enemy's cavalry were between them and Decatur trying to intercept and capture them.[105]

After mustering the forty men into his depleted regiment, on July 10, Streight requested permission to take a column south, across the rebel-infested valley to the base of Sand Mountain, in order to bring in even more Unionists from the Hill Country. He secured guides from among the loyal men who promised to lead the expedition to their friends, and marched to Davis Gap on July 12, his progress slowed on account of "it being very hot in the middle of the day," but he still reached a Mr. Menter's by evening, where he found that his advance guard of sixteen troopers from the Fourth Ohio Cavalry had been surprised and scattered, eventually returning safely to Decatur. After camping overnight and collecting 150 more recruits, Streight returned the next day toward Decatur but found his advance contested by Confederate cavalry, who threatened but refused to engage. After returning, Streight reported,

> I wish to say a word relative to the condition of these people. They are mostly poor, though many of them are, or rather were, in comfortable circumstances. They outnumber nearly three to one the secessionists in portions of Morgan, Blount, Winston, Marion, Walker, Fayette and Jefferson Counties; but situated as they are; surrounded by a most relentless foe, mostly unarmed and destitute of ammunition, they are persecuted in every conceivable way, yet up to this time most of them have kept out of the way sufficiently to avoid being dragged off by the gangs that infest the country for the purpose of plunder and enforcing the provisions of the rebel conscription act. Their horses and cattle are driven off in vast numbers. Every public road is patrolled by guerrilla bands, and the Union men have been compelled to seek protection in the fastness of the mountain wilderness. They cannot hold out much longer. This state of things here has so disturbed them that but very little attention has been paid to farming, consequently many of them are now destitute of food of their own and are living off their more fortunate neighbors.[106]

Streight was confident that he could raise a regiment from the loyal men of the mountains and implored his superiors to come to their aid: "Never did people stand in greater need of protection. They have battled manfully against the most unscrupulous foe that civilized warfare has ever witnessed. They have been shut out from all communication with anybody but their enemies for a year and a half, and yet they stand firm and true."[107]

The Fifty-First Indiana's regimental chaplain added his observations on the plight of the Unionists:

> When squalid poverty stared them in the face and depression was ensuing, caused by their being driven from home to seek a place of

safety in the mountains, in caverns, and dens, they opened their eyes to gaze upon the painful site of liberty gone, constitution prostrated, home gone, and with it quietude and honor. To escape despotism and these heartless ruffians, men left their homes and fled to the mountains. Some made for the Union army, coming through the mountain pathways for twenty, forty, sixty, and some even ninety miles, having a complete line of friends to help them extending from Decatur to near Montgomery—the best underground railroad ever heard of or ever established.[108]

Allen Smith, a sixty-eight-year-old farmer and blacksmith from Winston County, led a group of men over the mountains to enlist and became a sergeant in one of the new companies. One son rode with him while another stayed behind at his home near Warrior and assisted others.[109] In one instance, Ms. Anna Campbell of Morgan County, "not in good health, and fifty-five years old, had ridden a poor old horse over the mountains, tracing the mountain pathways through the gorges and around the precipices, sixty-four miles, counting the distance to and from her friends, and had made the trip in thirty hours," to lead twenty recruits into the Union camp. These vital networks were often biracial affairs, with blacks and whites helping one another to reach Union lines.[110]

The chaplain also recalled a speech that Chris Sheats gave to the assembled men of both sections of the country. He described the Unionist as "a young man of fine promise" who

makes a splendid speech. He declared to his downtrodden countrymen that the time had come for them to act, and act they must, either in an army they had no sympathy with, and in a cause for which they could have no reasonable hope of success—must thus fight an enemy they loved and for a cause they hated; or, on the other hand, join the army of the United States, fight in a cause they loved it, among their friends, contend against a foe of God and man and woman, one they hated, and one that must be put down before peace, quietude and prosperity could again prevail. He advised them to join the army and be men, and fight the Southern Confederacy to hell and back again. Said he, "To-morrow morning I am going to the Union army. I am going to expose this fiendish villany [sic] before the world. They shall hear from me. I have slept in the mountains, in caves and caverns, till I am become musty; my health and manhood are failing me. I will stay here no longer till I am enabled to dwell in quiet and home."[111]

But Sheats did not remain long behind Union lines, returning often to the mountains to recruit for the Union army, and was caught and imprisoned by Confederates on several occasions for his efforts and beliefs.[112]

Organizing the loyal Alabamians into combat formations proved less difficult than the journey to reach Union lines. While many Union regiments, especially those that fought and suffered severe losses at Shiloh, sought to replenish their manpower, the loyalists evidently preferred to organize their own unit, likely to preserve the wartime precedent of being able to choose their own officers. But Union officials attempted to dissuade this course, arguing on July 10:

> The recruits from Alabama had better join regiments now in service. . . . It would be difficult for them to organize companies and regiments of their own—no Governor to aid them, no clothing, arms or equipments to give them, and no officers to assist them. They would not get pay until they were organized and would probably fail. By joining any old regiment their pay commences at once; they come under officers who know how to provide and take care of them and no difficulty arises. Tell them to enlist as recruits in any of our regiments and assist them to do so in any way required.[113]

While some took this advice and enlisted in Northern regiments, many of the Alabamians persisted, and on July 18 Special Orders No. 106, issued from Huntsville, directed, "The volunteers from Alabama will be organized into companies, under the direction of Capt. H. C. Bankhead, who will enroll and muster them into the United States service in accordance with the laws and orders on the subject. Company officers will be selected from among the men. . . . All Alabama men desiring to enlist and now traveling with any of the regiments of this command will be sent to or left at this place."[114] Three days later, confirmation arrived from the War Department, granting Buell the authority to "organize and muster into service such number of Alabamians in companies and regiments as you may deem expedient for the service."[115] The authority to organize was a significant hurdle, but many others had to be cleared as well. On August 8, the quartermaster at Huntsville wired the Federal depot at Nashville, "Requisitions have been forwarded for a complete supply of Enfield rifles and accouterments for the companies (180 men) of the Alabama volunteers. Direct the ordnance officer to forward them without delay."[116]

The requisition for infantry equipment envisioned using the loyal men as foot soldiers, but the dearth of Union cavalry in protecting vulnerable supply lines was already becoming apparent. As early as May 15, Mitchel acknowledged that, in his efforts to "hunt down and destroy" Confederate raiders on the north side of the river, he was "hopelessly deficient in cavalry."[117] He later reiterated, "If guerrilla warfare is to be waged, I must have a large force of cavalry," complaining that his current force was less than five hundred men.[118] When Buell arrived, Mitchel made his needs known, arguing on June 18, "there are small bands of cavalry hovering around us almost everywhere, and we have no cavalry to destroy them."[119] Buell echoed these complaints repeatedly, wiring Secretary of War Stanton in July, "I cannot err in repeating to you the urgent importance of a large cavalry force in this district."[120] This shortage led to the Alabama unit eventually being mustered in as a cavalry command.

Mounted attacks on the railroad continued through the summer. On July 25, rebels overran a detachment guarding a railroad bridge at Courtland, which was then in use running supplies received from riverboats in Tuscumbia to Huntsville. The Tennessee River was impassible over Muscle Shoals, and low water from the deepening drought threatened to keep the boats from Tuscumbia. Mitchel now depended on the rail link running south from Nashville, but Confederates had burned the bridge over the Elk River during their retreat, necessitating a forty-mile-long detour by wagons, which slowed the rate of delivery of supplies and decreased the quantity that could be delivered. In response to a Confederate raid by Nathan Bedford Forrest on Murfreesboro on July 13th that cut the Nashville & Chattanooga Railroad for almost three weeks, Buell put his troops on half rations, but soldiers were unlikely to meekly accept a 50% cut in their caloric intake. They made up for the deficiency with increased levies on the local population, either through purchases or confiscation. Col. John Beatty of the Third Ohio wrote, "the bread and meat we fail to get from the loyal states are made good to us from the smokehouses and granaries of the disloyal. Our boys find Alabama hams better than Uncle Sam's side meat and fresh bread better than hard crackers. So that every time this dashing cavalryman destroys a provision train, their hearts are gladdened."[121] Every bite that a soldier consumed from resources obtained from the local population was one less that would be available during the coming winter, and Forrest's raid, while successful, did not force an immediate Union evacuation of North Alabama and only increased the levies on the Southern population.

Foraging occurred across the Tennessee Valley, as residents recalled that "Gen. Mitchel's troops swept the valley clean." Near Florence, soldiers confiscated wagons and mules, then "loaded the wagons with hams and cured bacon and corn." One Union soldier predicted that the shortage would be so severe that farmers would have to plant only corn the following year, and that "corn will be king instead of cotton."[122] Indeed, on a reconnaissance of the region later that year, Gen. William Rosecrans reported that the "Tennessee Valley for 70 miles long and from 5 to 7 wide is one immense corn field."[123] But cultivating corn required stock to plow the ground, and the Federal armies had a voracious appetite for horse and mule flesh. William Collins, from Somerville in Morgan County, testified that he and Henry Slaughter, a slave who hired his time, "rented land on the river and he and I were going to farming and the Yankees taking his stock broke us up."[124]

During the summer of 1862, northern Alabama became the seat of the war in the western theater. After the victorious army at Shiloh pushed Beauregard's Confederates out of Corinth, Buell's entire Army of the Ohio, over 40,000 men, marched slowly across northern Alabama toward Chattanooga. Throughout that time the army suffered serious logistics shortages, as supply lines that initially stretched up the Tennessee River to Eastport, Mississippi, had to be rerouted to Nashville and then down the Alabama & Tennessee Railroad. By midsummer, Buell wrote, "We are using about 500 wagons, managing with great difficulty to subsist our animals mainly on the country, already nearly exhausted of supplies."[125] On July 16, he explained, "We only eat about 75 tons a day . . . the country here cannot supply the flour." By August his commissary officers were buying up every barrel of flour they could find, including over 1,000 barrels as far away as Manchester, Tennessee.[126] Confederate raiders frustrated efforts to put the Nashville & Chattanooga Railroad in service to its junction with the Memphis & Charleston at Stevenson, which would then allow supplies to reach Huntsville on that road, and the first trains did not arrive over that route until the beginning of August.

As Buell's column moved west to east across North Alabama, his commissary officers found out firsthand how difficult it would be to forage off the country. While this could reflect Confederate efforts to move supplies out of the path of the oncoming army, a Union officer later testified, "the country through which the troops were marching was totally stripped of its resources by the enemy."[127] Another commissary officer testified, "the country was entirely bare of resources and near our lines of march, both of forage and subsistence."[128] A Federal expedition toward Confederate-occupied Guntersville in late July resulted in the shelling and destruction of "about ten buildings, including the warehouse, filled with forage and commissary stores," which would have to be replaced from the surrounding countryside.[129] And the evacuation of Bridgeport in August resulted in the loss of still more commissary stores, demonstrating war's incredible destructiveness.[130]

While Union forces moved slowly across the state north of the Tennessee River, Beauregard's army, now under the command of Braxton Bragg, paralleled their course south of the river. Before leaving Corinth, Maj. Gen. Henry Halleck reported, "he stripped the whole country south of here of food, and many of the inhabitants are in a starving condition," which helps explain the considerable number of loyal Mississippians who enlisted in the Alabama units at Corinth the following winter.[131] In September, a foraging party from the Eighteenth Missouri (US) "learned that foraging the countryside west of Iuka was one poor way to put a banquet together, for the Confederates had stripped the local farms." The group "finally collected four ears of fresh corn and four pods of blackeyed peas. When they finally got back to camp one of the boys gave them a leg from a goose 'with the hair and flipper' still on it."[132] Most of Bragg's infantry moved by rail from Tupelo down the Mobile & Ohio Railroad to Mobile, then across Mobile Bay by boat and up other railroads through Montgomery and Atlanta to Chattanooga, but Bragg sent his cavalry and artillery overland through North Alabama. Mitchel reported on June 15, "We learn from citizens on the other side that large bodies of the enemy are passing almost daily en route for Chattanooga."[133] Union officials speculated that this movement's "object would be to stop our communication with the Union men of Winston and adjoining counties, who have recently been joining our ranks."[134] Commissary officer Capt. Joseph Slocum reported, "We had nearly exhausted the whole country in the way of supplies," and reports came in from across the Tennessee that "on the south side of the river they were suffering for the substantials of life."[135] Spies reported that the Confederates were "feeding stock on green corn" in Chattanooga, stripping the 1862 harvest even before it ripened.[136] Once there, Union forces reported that the persecution of loyal men continued. McCook wrote, "They are driving up cattle and conscripts and bring out and shoot Union men."[137] The focus on "meat on the hoof" extended to the Union army, and when Federal forces evacuated Huntsville at the end of August, Buell ordered Colonel Lytle to "seize all cattle fit for beef and drive them" ahead of him, to which Lytle responded that he was "driving 400 head of horses and cattle."[138]

On August 22, as he prepared to leave Huntsville and pursue Bragg's army into Kentucky, Buell wrote Col. William B. Stokes, a former US representative from Tennessee and the current commander of the First Middle Tennessee (later Fifth Tennessee) Cavalry, US, "It is a matter of the greatest importance that I should have a few scouts to use, particularly as couriers, who understand thoroughly the country." Buell wanted twenty such men sent to his headquarters, removed that day from Huntsville to Decherd, Tennessee, promising, "They will receive liberal extra pay and should be reliable, prudent and courageous."[139] When Federal forces evacuated Huntsville, the two companies of Alabamians headed north to Nashville, and on September 24, Special Orders No. 155 transferred them to Stokes's command, where they would become Companies D and E of the First Middle Tennessee Cavalry.[140] The transfer enabled them to receive pay and equipment immediately, as part of an existing unit, but also retain their identity, in service under another loyal southerner who understood their situation. The two companies of Alabamians served with Stokes's regiment in Middle Tennessee for most of the next year, including at the Battle of Stones River, near Murfreesboro, from December 30 to January 3, 1863, before joining the First Alabama Cavalry in Corinth in the summer of 1863.[141]

By the time both armies finally moved into Tennessee and toward their fateful rendezvous at Perryville, Kentucky in October, there was little left to eat in the valley. With the continuing drought and resumption of the activities of Confederate tax collectors, there was also little prospect for loyalists to rebuild their stores before the coming winter.[142] Food stores were still adequate farther south in the Alabama River valley, but "Alabama's inadequate transportation system made it impossible to convey food to the northern hill country and Wiregrass where people were starving."[143] In later testimony, Buell recalled that "there was a great scarcity of the article of meat there," and "never to my recollection was there so great a scarcity" as there was in Huntsville in the summer of 1862.[144] It did not help that "hog cholera devastated herds in Mississippi and Alabama and anthrax struck in the latter state as well," exacerbating the meat shortage.[145] In the hills, Unionists supplied themselves with wild game, with one recruit arriving for muster with a freshly killed deer over his shoulders, and the squirrel and rabbit populations must have suffered fearfully.[146]

On August 29, Maj. Gen. William Rosecrans, then in command at Iuka, wrote to Grant's staff, "I have no doubt that the poverty and destitution of the mountaineers in Northern Alabama is such that we could raise a large force for border service . . . I think the measure should be promptly taken in hand, or the people will be driven by want into brigandage."[147] It is little wonder that, in the fall and early winter of 1862–1863, many other Alabamians, both white and black, did the same, hounded in their journey by Confederates who, like the guards of East Berlin a century later, refused to let their citizens pass from confinement to liberty. Out of this great exodus of contrabands and refugees to Corinth, the nearest remaining Federal post, Gen. Grenville M. Dodge provided these Alabamians with safety, sustenance, and an opportunity to strike back at their persecutors at the head of an avenging army.

CHAPTER 3

Exile in Corinth, 1863

The third year of the war proved to be a pivotal one for Alabamians who wore the Union blue. The presence of permanent Federal military outposts close to the state's borders, coupled with the continued attrition on the battlefield in massive campaigns along the eastern seaboard and in the Mississippi Valley, created the conditions for increased enrollment in Federal military forces. At the same time, forays into Alabama, often guided and aided by loyal Alabamians, both black and white, increased the level of destruction of the state's natural resources, complicating survival and accelerating the struggle for control of increasingly scarce resources, driving more freedmen and Unionists into Federal arms, in an ongoing cycle of destructiveness that only accelerated in the final years of the war. The year saw the first, abortive Federal cavalry raids deep into the state's interior, and the first serious efforts to restrict supplies and munitions from Alabama's forges and fields from reaching Confederate armies in the east and west. The military units established from loyal Alabamians in 1863 played important roles in the military campaigns in and around the state, and many of these same units helped to eventually restore the Stars and Stripes to flagstaffs in Montgomery at the war's end.

Following the failed Confederate invasion of Kentucky in the fall of 1862, concluding in the Battle of Perryville, Confederate forces attempted to salvage something from their efforts by recovering northern Alabama and portions of Middle Tennessee, especially the fertile Duck and Elk River valleys, which produced a substantial portion of the Confederacy's agricultural resources, including large numbers of horse and mules that could be appropriated for transportation by the army.[1] Unfortunately, the Union retrograde movement left northern Alabama as a no-man's-land between small Confederate forces charged with enforcing conscription and securing supplies, and Union forays

[handwritten marginalia: 1ST Ala Cav. 1863 / 1862 / Emancipation Proc.]

into the region designed to prevent that object. Local residents found themselves caught in the middle, forced to endure a recurring cycle of reprisals and suffering from appropriations from both sides, but primarily rebel forces. As a result, freedmen and Unionists evacuated to the nearest remaining Federal stronghold, the rail junction at Corinth, Mississippi, where the north-south Mobile & Ohio Railroad crossed the east-west Memphis & Charleston. Union forces had occupied the critical rail junction after the bloody Battle of Shiloh in the spring of 1862 and had held it against a rebel attack in early October, as it offered avenues of approach east into Alabama and south into Mississippi from the growing base at Memphis. In the autumn of 1862, Gen. Ulysses S. Grant embarked on his first, abortive assault on Vicksburg by heading south from Memphis. For one of the few times in the war, Confederate cavalry raids behind Grant's lines in northern Mississippi and western Tennessee forced Grant to turn back and eventually embark on a brilliant amphibious and overland campaign down the Mississippi in the spring of 1863, which resulted in Vicksburg's capitulation on July 4th. Union forces at Corinth were primarily responsible for supporting this effort, protecting Union-held territory and launching cavalry raids, including Benjamin Grierson's famous raid the length of Mississippi, in support of Grant's effort.

*[handwritten marginalia: 1st Ala *]*

But Union commanders at Corinth, primarily Brig. Gen. Grenville Dodge, had limited forces on hand to conduct their assigned mission. In addition, they found their lines overwhelmed by self-liberated freedmen and women who congregated in the city. On September 28, 1862, shortly after President Lincoln issued the Emancipation Proclamation, Dodge wrote, "Negroes are rushing in under the new proclamation; they will not even wait until 1st January. I do not know what we shall do with them; they crowd our camps, demoralize our army and unfit men for duty: my orders are stringent about them but hard to enforce."[2] When presented with the opportunity, he moved quickly to embrace the new Federal policy of arming these "contrabands," resulting in the formation of the first two Alabama Federal units composed of freedmen, the First Alabama Infantry, African Descent (later the Fifty-Fifth US Colored Infantry) and the First Alabama Siege Artillery Regiment, African Descent (later the Sixth USCT Heavy Artillery). White Unionists from northwest Alabama were also congregating in northeast Mississippi, lobbying Federal commanders to provide support for their families still behind enemy lines. As a result, the first companies of the First Alabama Cavalry, also formed at

[handwritten marginalia: Dodge / Blk Amer. / Emancip. Procl. Sept '62 / ⚑ / 1st Ala Inf Blk Amer / 1st Ala Cav]

at Corinth during this same time, conducted raids and recruiting forays back into their home state, most frequently along the line of the Memphis & Charleston, which led into the natural east-west corridor the Tennessee River provided across northern Alabama. Corinth could therefore be described as the birthplace of the "Alabamians in Blue," and the training conducted there and early operations launched from there proved instrumental in the units' future employment, foreshadowing the small but growing contribution Alabamians would make to the liberation of their own state.

Alabamians arriving in Corinth in late 1862 came from a variety of motives. Certainly some freedmen and Unionists came voluntarily, taking advantage of the opportunity to "self-emancipate" or to live again under the "old flag." Many others were forced—slaves could be confiscated as "contraband" in order to deny the Confederate economy their services, and Unionists were increasingly driven out of their strongholds in the mountains of northern Alabama by the ongoing guerrilla violence. As Margaret Storey has expertly detailed in her work on Alabama Unionists, these efforts drove white and black Alabamians closer together. Long skilled at meeting surreptitiously and maintaining informal networks through which critical information could pass, slaves became exemplars for persecuted Unionists attempting to evade Confederate conscription agents or to organize clandestine meetings to coordinate support. In many cases, slaves assisted Union men "lying out" from their homes to avoid the Confederate press gangs. In some cases, authorities hunted these men in the manner of slave patrols, even tracking men with dogs. In citing numerous instances of interracial cooperation in evading conscription agents and press gangs, and how this drove slaves and Unionists together, Storey notes, "In the prewar South, white men, unless heinous criminals, were never subjected to the humiliation and terror of being hunted with dogs. When white conscripts received such treatment during the war, there was no question in their minds, the minds of secessionist neighbors, or even in the minds of neighborhood slaves, that 'tories' were outcasts in Southern society."[3] Those who could escape often joined together for protection, or traveled surreptitiously along routes pioneered by underground railroaders.[4] Others waited, held captive in their own homes behind enemy lines. But for both freedmen and persecuted Unionists, liberation most often came in the form of the blue-clad soldier.

After taking command of the District of Corinth in late October 1862, and later the Second Division of the Sixteenth Army Corps, then assigned to

Corinth + Iuka Battles

† 1862

Grant
Dodge

Oct 3
1862 †

Blk Amer

#6

Jan 22

Ulysses S. Grant's Army of the Tennessee, Brig. Gen. Grenville Dodge found himself beset with requests from all quarters for information about the Confederate forces to the east. Union forces had fought two bloody battles, at Iuka on September 19 and at Corinth on October 3–4, increasing Grant's concern for his eastern flank as he embarked on the first stage of his campaign for Vicksburg.[5] During the latter battle, efforts of freedmen already gathering in Corinth to build a new defensive position, literally overnight, contributed substantially to the Union victory, and one veteran wrote, "I attribute much of our success at Corinth to the labours of the Black Men."[6] White Alabama Unionists were also seeking refuge in Corinth and likewise benefited from the freedmen's labors. In August, Henry Rikard, a native of Franklin County, traveled to Iuka, enlisted in the Sixty-Fourth Illinois Infantry, and fought with the regiment in the Battle of Corinth, where he was wounded.[7] On November 18, Grant asked Dodge to provide information from the east, as far as Florence, Alabama, especially if Confederate forces returning from the Kentucky campaign were crossing the river there. On November 22, he sent Dodge explicit instructions to send out "spies and scouts," something Dodge was already adept at doing dating from his time in Missouri during the first year of the war. On December 3, Dodge reported that a reliable scout had returned from Huntsville and that he "brought with him several refugees who live in that section of the country," who corroborated his scout's reports. On December 13, Dodge further reported that some 16,000 infantry were en route from Tennessee to reinforce Confederate general John Pemberton at Vicksburg, information "given by refugees from Alabama who arrived today from Walker County." North Alabama Unionists had by now given up hope that the Federal army would return to their section and instead sought refuge within Union lines. For some, including Christopher Tompkins of Franklin County, that meant a journey north to refuge in Illinois, but after a year he returned and enlisted in the First Alabama Cavalry.[8] For those Unionists still behind the lines, especially in Walker and Winston Counties, the nearest point under Federal control was Corinth, roughly eighty miles as the crow flies through the hilly, sparsely inhabited landscape.[9]

In late January 1863, Dodge described the atrocities and outrages committed on these North Alabama Unionists. He reported to his superiors at Memphis that he was "now feeding some one hundred of these families, who, with their women and children, some gray-haired old men, and even cripples on

80 miles Winston to Corinth

crutches, were driven out and made their way here, through the woods and by-ways, without food or shelter—all done for the simple reason they were Union men, or that they had brothers or relations in our army. The statements of these people are almost beyond belief, did we not have the evidence before us."[10] Dodge sought to balance the Confederate narrative of chivalry, arguing that "While all their leaders, from the President down are boasting of their carrying on this war in accordance with the laws that govern nations in such cases, and are charging upon our troops all kinds of depredations and outrages," in reality, rebels in Alabama were murdering, plundering, robbing, and burning the homes of loyal citizens. Dodge went on to list several by name, including two men hung in Hackleburg for being Unionists, several men and women shot in cold blood, and over thirty homes "burned over their heads." With no food or provisions, nor any way to provide for their refugee families, and a burning desire for revenge on their oppressors, these men formed the nucleus of the First Alabama Cavalry. One of these men was Dennis Cantrell, who joined Company D on February 4, 1863. After the war, he recalled, "I was threatened and hunted after, to be killed, night and day, by the Rebs in the year 1862 by Captain Lewis and Captain Mayfield that belonged to Rebel general Roddey's command. They also taken my gun and two horses worth at least $400. They were so tight after me on account of my Union principles that myself and son went and joined the U.S. Army."[11]

To combine Dodge's twin missions of collecting intelligence in northwest Alabama and providing for the Unionists in his midst, he elected to raise companies of cavalry that were intimately familiar with the country to the east and could be used to collect information there, and would also receive payment for their services, which would enable them to provide for their families. Officially authorized in December of 1862, the unit carried the name "First Alabama Cavalry," and eventually included twelve companies of one hundred men each in a full regiment. While a full-strength regiment might have over 1,000 men, many shrank to less than five hundred due to attrition over the course of the war, and it was only in exceptional circumstances that the First Alabama hit even this number. Men remained on detached service, scouting or recruiting, and stock shortages meant that many recruits remained without mounts for months. Dodge initially organized two companies of Alabama Cavalry, under the command of Capt. James C. Cameron, formerly of the Sixty-Fourth Illinois Infantry, which had enrolled a number of the first refugees, including

84

Henry Rikard. In the regiment's "Order No. 1," issued March 3, 1863, at Glen-dale, Mississippi, Cameron enjoined each man to put forth every effort to "make this a complete and efficient regiment, and it is hoped that every man will feel the importance of his position as an American soldier and endeavor to conduct himself in a manner worthy of the cause he has enlisted to de-fend."[12] Sadly, Cameron had just over a month to live, falling in action at Bear Creek, Alabama, on April 17, 1863.[13] On May 17, 1863, Dodge learned from the War Department that he was "authorized to fill up to a full Regiment the 1st Regt. of Ala. Cavalry," and begin to organize additional companies. The unit recruited throughout the summer and by September had nine full companies, with two more recruiting.[14] But Corinth was just one of what Stephen Ash has described as "garrison towns" on the Alabama frontier. Recruits also traveled to towns in Tennessee, especially Nashville, to enlist in loyal regiments raised for that state.[15]

Dodge later recalled that he "found the men and their families of great assistance in obtaining information. These mountain men were fearless and would take all chances, and I utilized many of them." The unit also filled a critical role between Dodge's intelligence network and the commander. He reported, "My method of having the spies communicate with me was to have them send their reports to some one of the family of a member of this reg-iment, then a member of the family (generally a woman) would come into my lines on the excuse of seeing their people who had joined the 1st Alabama cavalry and others who were refugees in Corinth and they would bring the reports to me."[16] In postwar testimony, Isaac Berry of Blountsville, Alabama, claimed to be "Chief of Scouts and spy for the army in North Alabama," and reported that he often visited the home of his father-in-law John Nesmith, the father of another First Alabama trooper, who Berry testified "harbored and fed me at his house" and gave him "all the information that I wanted in regard to the rebel movements." Nesmith also provided "information to offi-cers of the Union Army in aid of their movements and cause." Confederate home guards forced Nesmith to remove his daughter Virginia and her five children to within Federal lines on account of her husband's Federal mili-tary service, but they apparently never learned of his espionage activities.[17] Phoebe Bennett of Winston County, who had both a son-in-law and a grand-son in the Union army, "was an old lady, not suspected of doing anything to aid the Union cause by the Confederate soldiers. Consequently, she would do a great deal," including feeding and protecting furloughed soldiers of the First Alabama Cavalry.[18] William Dodd, who had two brothers in the First Alabama, later testified, "all the information I received from the rebels I carried and gave it to United States soldiers who were encamped near my residence, such as newspapers and other information." John Baughn of Company L, First Alabama Cavalry, corroborated Dodd's testimony, stating, "While myself and others were scouting and recruiting, [Dodd] would inform us where the Confederate cavalry was."[19] First Alabama trooper John R. Phillips recorded that Green Haley, namesake of Haleyville in Marion County, "lived on the public road and . . . was always watching out for the rebel cavalry and rebel conscripts [agents] and would give and send word to the Union boys and Union soldiers of the whereabouts of said cavalry."[20] As Stephen Ash has observed, this information became increasingly valuable in the campaign to suppress guerrillas that infested the Southern interior. "The occupiers had more success when they dispatched their forces not blindly, on random patrols, but on specific missions guided by hard intelligence. Here the use of detectives, secret agents, and informants proved valuable."[21] While unable to completely suppress guerrillas, conventional forces did keep the insurgents from inhibiting Federal military operations.

According to the unit's new commander, Col. George Spencer, "During the investment of Vicksburg by General Grant, we kept a large number of spies in the rear of Vicksburg, and daily furnished General Grant information concerning the movement of troops in Mississippi, outside of Vicksburg."[22] One of the spies, Alabama native Philip Henson, even traveled to Vicksburg with a friend, on the pretense of visiting the man's sons, and provided Dodge detailed information on the city's defenses, which Dodge dutifully relayed to Grant.[23] Armed with this information, Grant knew he could defeat Pemberton's army at the Battle of Champion Hill without having to worry about a large Confederate force gathering to his rear at Meridian.[24] After the war, William C. Oates, governor of Alabama from 1894 to 1896 and famous for his repeated charges on Joshua Chamberlain's Twentieth Maine on the slopes of the Little Round Top at Gettysburg, paid Grant the ultimate compliment when declining an invitation to a banquet held in Grant's honor. Oates wrote, "He either employed better means of ascertaining the strength of his immediate foe than any other general in the Union army, or knew it by intuition."[25] Given that Dodge was organizing the banquet, Oates likely included the comment as a subtle compliment to Dodge's efforts in keeping Grant informed. Historians agree, noting that Dodge's intelligence network was unmatched, "for scope or tenacity," in the Union army.[26]

During the first week of May 1863, a brigade of Confederate Alabamians fought as part of Robert E. Lee's Army of Northern Virginia at the Battle of Chancellorsville. The Confederate victory, often called Lee's greatest, though it cost him the services of his principal subordinate when his own troops accidentally but mortally wounded Gen. Thomas J. "Stonewall" Jackson, did little to change the outcome of the war, other than add thousands more to the butcher's bill and open a path to the north that led to a humbling defeat at Gettysburg two months later.[27] While troops of Cadmus Wilcox's Alabama Brigade lost almost five hundred irreplaceable men from their prebattle number of 2,000 in defending Salem Church in Lee's rear, their home state witnessed the first major raid deep into its interior. The raid failed to achieve its operational objective, cutting the Western & Atlantic Railroad at Rome, Georgia, but it was a harbinger of things to come, as Union forces increasingly entered the state in massive *chevauchees,* raids intended to deplete the country of resources that could be used to sustain troops, thereby preventing the state's use as a base of operations for Confederate forces and denying equipment, food, and transportation to Confederate armies in the field, all while demoralizing soldiers who received news of the Yankee depredations from families back home.[28]

The first two companies of Alabama Unionists raised in the summer of 1862 in the Tennessee Valley followed Buell's army back to Nashville when it abandoned the area in late August. Known then as Companies D and E of the First Middle Tennessee Cavalry, but eventually Companies I and K of the First Alabama Cavalry, the units were the first identifiable Alabama Union units to see combat, being actively engaged in the Battle of Stones River, near Murfreesboro, Tennessee.[29] The two Alabama companies continued to serve with the Tennessee regiment until detached for service with Col. Abel Streight in what became one of the more famous episodes in North Alabama's Civil War history. As Gen. William Rosecrans sought to maneuver Confederate general Braxton Bragg out of Middle Tennessee, forcing him to give up the rich Duck and Elk River valleys and the vital rail junction at Chattanooga, Union authorities sent Streight on a raid behind Confederate lines, hoping to sever Bragg's main railroad between Atlanta and Chattanooga near the vicinity of

[handwritten marginalia: May 1863]

[handwritten marginalia: 1862 Summer]

[handwritten marginalia: Cos D+E. of Tenn. I+K 1ˢᵗ Ala.]

[handwritten marginalia: Rome, Georgia]

[handwritten notes at bottom: Start Summer 1862]

[handwritten notes at bottom: Co. I+K]

[handwritten notes at bottom: Col. Abel Streight Ap 22? May 4, 1863 Northern Ala. Streights Raid - Ap 19? May 3, 1863]

Streight's Raid
Apr 19 → May 4, 1863

Rome, Georgia. In order to reach their destination, Streight's 1,800 blue-clad troopers first marched overland from Nashville to the Tennessee River, then traveled by steamboat up the river to Eastport, Mississippi, before debarking and mounting mules for the trip diagonally across the entire state of Alabama. The chosen path required transiting Sand Mountain at an angle, ensuring the expedition would spend much of its time behind enemy lines in difficult terrain, with limited forage available. As a result, Confederate forces eventually surrounded Streight's command and Forrest himself forced their surrender once their path to the railroad at Rome had been blocked by a second force guarding the bridge over the Oostanaula River and the Federals had exhausted their ammunition. Despite being captured, troopers of the two Alabama companies were quickly exchanged and were back in the saddle by mid-June, again supporting the Union campaign in Middle Tennessee, though many officers, including Colonel Streight, languished in Richmond's brutal Libby Prison. There they suffered from disease, malnutrition, and harsh treatment until Streight and four of his officers escaped on February 9, 1864, taking almost a month to reach Federal lines in Washington, DC.[30] In his long-delayed report of the raid, Streight wrote, "The balance of my officers, or nearly all of them, are still confined as prisoners or have died of disease, the result of long confinement, insufficient food, and cruel treatment at the hands of the enemy."[31] Most of Streight's men escaped a similar fate at the horrific Confederate prison at Andersonville, Georgia by being exchanged for Confederate prisoners, and most had returned to their regiment by mid-June. That same month the two Alabama companies of the First Middle Tennessee transferred to Corinth to help fill out the First Alabama, as Union commanders intended to deploy the regiment within its home state, where knowledge of the local physical and human terrain could be best employed. After being formally exchanged at Camp Chase, Ohio, the men traveled by boat to Louisville and Memphis before crossing northern Mississippi to Corinth.

Col. Abel Streight, of the Fifty-First Indiana Infantry, first proposed the raid through the Alabama Hill Country to Rome, Georgia, a remote and hopefully lightly defended point on the Western & Atlantic Railroad between Atlanta and Chattanooga. At one point, Streight's regiment contained an estimated four hundred Alabamians, recruited during the Union occupation of the Tennessee Valley the previous summer, most notably when Streight led his regiment onto Sand Mountain, enabling Unionists to flock to his colors,

POWs mid-June +

400 Alabamians via Tenn. Valley

but many of these men later transferred to the Alabama companies organized in Huntsville. With their knowledge of the local terrain, and Streight's recognition of both the potential for additional recruits for his command as well as the opportunity for advancement, the Union forces devised a complicated plan to place a brigade of mule-mounted infantry in the Confederate rear. The route maximized Streight's time in the Alabama hills, increasing the chances of contacting Unionists hiding out in the mountains, even if it added fatal miles to the march. A more easterly route, through southern Tennessee and the eastern Tennessee Valley, offered a more direct route to Bragg's rear, but was also better defended by Confederate cavalry under Forrest, then operating on Bragg's flank. As a result, Streight's command chose the longer route, first overland between the Cumberland and Tennessee Rivers, gathering additional stock along the way, and then up the Tennessee to Eastport, Mississippi, where they debarked and then marched diagonally across the state toward Rome. As the Union forces around Nashville suffered chronic shortages of horses and the chosen route was mountainous, Streight mounted his men and supplies on mules to enable them to cross the rugged terrain. In hindsight, it was a foolish idea—the mules were slow, balky, and afflicted with horse distemper, which caused many to give out along the way, and the men of Streight's provisional brigade, ultimately comprised of his own Fifty-First Indiana, as well as the Seventy-Third Indiana, the Third Ohio, and the Eightieth Illinois Infantry Regiments, had not been trained as either cavalrymen or muleskinners, further hindering their effectiveness. Streight planned to employ the command as mounted infantry if fighting became necessary, using the mules only for mobility, which enjoyed some success, as then men were never driven from the field when fighting dismounted.

Mule issue

In order to decrease the likelihood of Streight's "jackass cavalry," as the Confederates derisively described them, having to fight any engagements at all, Rosecrans asked his neighboring department commander, Maj. Gen. Stephen Hurlbut at Memphis, for the cooperation of Dodge's command at Corinth in launching the expedition. Ideally, Dodge would drive east from Corinth into northwestern Alabama, capturing the twin cities of Tuscumbia and Florence, on the south and north banks of the Tennessee, respectively, thereby drawing Confederate forces to his front and enabling Streight to slip south into the mountains undetected. Dodge's expedition became the most useful part of the entire operation, as he inflicted significant damage to Con-

Dodge @ Corinth

Dodge Command

federate forces and supplies in the area, which provided further protection to his area of responsibility in northeast Mississippi. Unfortunately, he pulled back from his raid just as Streight departed, allowing Confederate forces to disengage and pursue Streight into the mountains. Streight himself wrote, "I am convinced that had we been furnished at Nashville with 800 good horses, instead of poor, young mules, we would have been successful, in spite of all other drawbacks; or if General Dodge had succeeded in detaining Forrest one day longer, we would have been successful, even with our poor outfit."[32]

For his part, Dodge enthusiastically supported the venture, as it provided him an opportunity to secure his position from attack by pushing Confederate forces farther away from Corinth, especially as the Army of the Mississippi was about to lose a good portion of its most mobile force on a long cavalry raid from LaGrange, Tennessee, to Baton Rouge, Louisiana, traveling down the length of Mississippi from April 17 to May 2, 1863. "Grierson's Raid," named after Col. Benjamin Grierson, succeeded in disrupting the Confederate logistics network in eastern Mississippi and distracting the rebels from Grant's brilliant movements opposite Vicksburg, as the future president led his command downriver below the city, then crossed to high ground below the fortress and marched inland to Jackson, temporarily abandoning his supply lines. After pushing back Confederate forces at Jackson, he invested the garrison at Vicksburg, reestablished his supply lines on the river just north of the city, and eventually forced Gen. John Pemberton to surrender the city, hundreds of cannon, and over 30,000 men. Grierson's raid demonstrated what a well-mounted force of trained cavalrymen could do behind enemy lines and foreshadowed later raids into Alabama, especially Wilson's famous campaign in 1865 that destroyed Selma, captured Montgomery, and pushed Forrest out of the state.[33]

Unfortunately for Streight, such successes were still years away in Alabama. With Union cavalry, including the First Middle Tennessee (later Fifth Tennessee) regiment actively skirmishing and raiding the no-man's land between Rosecrans's and Bragg's armies, none could be spared for a risky raid in the enemy's rear. Accordingly, Streight began to assemble the 1,200 mules it would take to partially mount his 1,700-man provisional brigade from the area around Nashville, with the balance to be obtained en route. Unfortunately, the time of year conspired against his efforts to assemble the best stock possible. As the grass in Tennessee was just greening up in spring, Streight's animals were still recovering their strength after a winter of subsiding on

mules

less-nutritious forage that undoubtedly weakened their resistance to disease. Streight "discovered that the mules were nothing but poor, wild and unbroken colts, many of them but two years old and that a large number of them had the horse distemper; some 40 or 50 of the lot were too near dead to travel, and had to be left at the landing; 10 or 12 died before we started." By the time he left Tuscumbia, he had lost close to four hundred animals and, rather than increasing his number to mount the remainder of his command, was barely able to replace his losses. Only by securing an additional four hundred animals from Dodge's force was he able to depart on his expedition with his command fully, if poorly mounted.

Dodge, for his part, left Corinth on April 14 with a strong force of 4,000 infantry, 1,500 cavalry, and two batteries of artillery, and added another 2,000 men under Col. John Fuller en route. He expected to meet Streight at Eastport on April 16, but had to wait three days for him to arrive, as he had been detained both in getting his command from Nashville to its embarkation point on the Tennessee and when his transportation failed to arrive due to delays in loading forage and supplies destined for Dodge's command. Dodge detached his cavalry brigade, consisting of the Tenth Missouri and Fifteenth Illinois Cavalry regiments, plus the newly formed battalion of the First Alabama Cavalry and the Ninth Illinois Mounted Infantry, totaling 1,050 men under the command of Col. Florence Cornyn of the Tenth Missouri, to buy time while he waited for Streight to arrive. The Alabamians performed well on the expedition in their first test, leading Dodge to remark, "The fighting of the cavalry was excellent. The Tenth Missouri, Seventh Kansas, Fifteenth Illinois and First Alabama all did themselves credit; they invariably drove the enemy, no matter what their force."[34]

Screening for Dodge's command, the Alabamians saw their first action at King's Creek, near Tupelo, where Cornyn reported that he "found that the enemy had been repelled, and that the 1st Alabama Cavalry, under Captain Cameron, had started in pursuit."[35] Cornyn pressed on through Iuka on April 15, detaching the Alabamians to repair a bridge over Yellow Creek and guard a forage train sent to sustain him. They rejoined the command late in the evening of April 16 at Cook's farm, on the Memphis & Charleston Railroad. As Cornyn pressed on toward Alabama, he encountered small Confederate forces obstructing his advance. After a skirmish at a place named Buzzard's Roost, Cornyn found that his artillery had nearly exhausted the ammunition in their

Dodge
Apl4
1863
rl p 16

Apl5

A p 16

Iuka
Dodge
Cornyn
Yellow Creek

34.

caissons, and he sent two guns of the First Missouri Light Artillery to the rear of the column. Unfortunately, they fell well behind and became easy prey for Roddey's cavalry, which had been pushed by a detached Union column onto the road in the rear of Cornyn's force, and they gobbled up the lightly defended guns and their forty-man escort. As Dodge reported, "Colonel Cornyn, hearing firing in the rear, immediately fell back and, with the First Alabama Cavalry, charged the rebels and retook the artillery and caissons, with the exception of one gun, which the enemy succeeded in getting off with. The charge of the Alabamians with muskets only, and those not loaded, is creditable especially as they are all new recruits and poorly drilled. In this charge, Captain Cameron, the commanding officer of the Alabama cavalry, a deserving and much lamented officer, was killed."[36]

Cornyn's report, perhaps attempting to deflect blame for losing the guns in the first place, was less flattering, alleging that he "ordered a charge by the First Alabama Cavalry which, I am sorry to say, was not obeyed with the alacrity it should have been. After charging to within short musket range of the enemy, they halted for some cause I cannot account for, and the enemy escaped to the woods with one of the pieces and limber of the other, it having been previously thrown down the railroad excavation. Here Captain Cameron was killed." Cornyn was an experienced commander and was accustomed to commanding experienced troops, so it is not surprising that he expected greater "alacrity" form the partially trained recruits of his command. At the same time, he acknowledged the death of Capt. James Cameron, but claimed he could not "account" for the delay in the face of the enemy. Certainly, the loss of an esteemed and "much lamented" officer, as Dodge described him, could have this effect on even an experienced unit. Nevertheless, the Alabamians succeeded in enabling Cornyn to reclaim part of what had been lost due to his inattention, and the brigade proceeded in the direction of Tuscumbia, pushing the rebels opposing them toward Decatur.

In occupying the western portion of Alabama's Tennessee River valley, Dodge went to work stripping the area of resources used to sustain Confederates. He first destroyed over forty flatboats used to ferry elements of Confederate cavalry across the Tennessee between Florence and Tuscumbia, limiting the South's ability to shift units between the armies opposing Rosecrans and Grant. He then set to work on the valley's rich agricultural resources, claiming to have captured nine hundred horses and mules, and sixty bales of cotton, and destroyed 1,500,000 bushels of corn and 500,000 pounds of bacon, as well as six "flouring mills" and five tanyards, depriving the Confederacy of food, transportation, and leather equipment, and "keeping the whole command in meat for three weeks." Most importantly, he brought back with him to Corinth "some 1,500 negroes," severely crippling the valley's ability to produce more foodstuffs and providing a manpower pool for the recruitment of additional Federal units. These freedmen and women became residents of Corinth's growing "contraband camp," and many of the men became the nucleus of the First Alabama Infantry, African Descent, as well as the First Alabama Heavy Artillery Regiment, four companies of which garrisoned Corinth's defenses, simultaneously defending both the army's supply center that provided their employment and sustenance, and their families. Dodge boasted that he had "rendered useless the garden spot of Alabama for at least one year, besides inflicting a deserved chastisement upon a most unrelenting community of intense rebel sympathizers," but observed that his newly liberated charges were "the most motley and poorly-dressed crowd I ever saw."[37]

As Dodge returned to Corinth, Streight and his 1,500 blue-clad troopers embarked on their primary mission—a two-hundred-mile raid across rough terrain to cut Bragg's primary railroad in the vicinity of Rome, Georgia. Streight undoubtedly hoped to add soldiers to his command and inflict further damage on Alabama's ability to supply resources to the Confederacy. The plan envisioned an unopposed crossing, but Forrest's dogged pursuit and eventual capture of the entire command made the raid a tactical failure. But it also signaled the importance of local auxiliaries in the form of Alabama Unionists to guide the force, as the raiders came within twenty-five miles of their objective despite their poor mounts, and foreshadowed the potential for far more destructive raids by horse-mounted cavalry led by Maj. Gen. Lovell Rousseau in 1864 and, decisively, by Maj. Gen. James Wilson in 1865.

Despite the continued losses from disease and the two hundred animals lost in the debarkation stampede, Streight's command was almost fully mounted when he left Dodge's company late on the evening of April 26 for the week-long raid. In addition to two hundred mules, Dodge also provided six wagons for ammunition and rations, and enabled Streight to leave his sick men and animals behind, expediting the campaign as much as possible.[38] But 150 of Streight's 1,500 troopers still lacked animals, and a steady rain turned roads to quagmires, slowing the pace of the advance toward Moulton. Henry

Breidenthal, a sergeant in the Third Ohio, remembered the evening as "storming furiously, the rain coming down in a flood," and remarked that the command "made but five miles by daylight on account of the badness of the roads and depth of the streams swollen by the recent rains." Springtime is North Alabama's rainiest season and frontal passages can bring rains in excess of several inches, quickly elevating streams and liquefying the ground. Narrow valleys in the mountainous region amplify the effect, as hillsides can turn shallow brooks into torrents overnight.[39] The following April, a similar spring storm struck a Federal cavalry camp outside Nashville, where "the merciless wind uprooted trees and leveled all the tents, tearing some to shreds," and scattered the regimental papers of the Third Tennessee Cavalry (US).[40] Despite the weather, the command marched all day, reaching Russellville by mid-morning and Mount Hope by sunset, brushing aside light resistance. The expedition camped for the night, having covered over thirty road miles, but, by angling southeast, only put fifteen miles between themselves and the Confederates massed at Town Creek. Still, Streight halted his exhausted command for the night at Mount Hope before covering the remaining ten miles to Moulton during the day on April 28. Here Streight paused for only a brief evening rest before pushing on for Sand Mountain, which, it was hoped, would slow any pursuers. Dryer weather on the 29th enabled them to cover the thirty-five miles to Day's Gap, at the foot of Sand Mountain, where they again halted for the night, the command's last full night of rest during the entire campaign.

During the day on the 28th, a man Breidenthal described as a probate judge approached the command seeking the return of several slaves the raid had captured. During the discussion, "our guide, (of the First [Middle] Tennessee cavalry) came up and recognized in the old gentlemen one of the leading secesh of Lawrence County," and refused to take the old gentlemen's hand when he offered it. The judge "then appealed to our sympathies, saying that it was hard, very hard for him, in his old age, to be deprived of his all and turned adrift in the world; that he had done nothing to merit this misfortune." The guide challenged the man, saying that, despite his past support for Stephen Douglas, there was "no reason or apology now why you should, in your old age, prove recreant to those principles, and lend all your influence and devote your whole time and means to the interest of secession and the traitor Jeff Davis—that you should now compel Union men to enlist in the rebel army or be incarcerated in Moulton jail, as you have done." The judge claimed to have been an opponent of secession at the convention in Montgomery, with:

instructions to go out with the state; and although I was in favor of remaining in the Union, yet when the state went out, I went with her. Now would you not have done as I did? "No" was the emphatic answer. "Yes, but you are a young man and have no wife or family, and home associations to sacrifice, and you could go where you listed." "You are mistaken," was the quick, cutting retort; "I have a wife and two children and they are as dear to me as yours are to you, and I left them, and now you see me here. It is true you did give notice to the disaffected ones toward your pretended government to leave the state in forty days, yet when they took you at your offer, they were apprehended; and if they refused to enlist in the rebel army, they were thrown into prison. . ."

Here the scout listed several acquaintances that the judge "had placed in Moulton jail last spring, and left their families to suffer, and you will have to answer for it. This is but a small portion of the fearful retribution that will be meted out to you."[41] Upon reaching Moulton, the blue troopers liberated these prisoners from the Lawrence County jail.[42] Streight noted, "We were now in the midst of devoted Union people. Many of Captain Smith's men (Alabamians) were recruited near this place, and many were the happy greetings between them and their friends and relations."[43] When Breidenthal's unit ascended the Tennessee on steamboats, the command had passed "some two hundred Union refugees, consisting of men, women and children, with all their scanty effects piled upon the bank, all awaiting some friendly boat to transport them to the promised land of freedom . . . these persons have been driven from their homes in Alabama, Mississippi and East-Tennessee for opinion's sake, and compelled to take refuge from tyranny by fleeing from home and all the dear associations that gather around that hallowed spot."[44]

BlK Hmer
Af Amer

    In addition to the slaves whom the judge was seeking, that evening "scouts brought in ten or twelve wagon-loads of contraband women and children from our front, whom the rebels were running off South," intending to keep them from Dodge's command, and perhaps recoup their investment by selling them further south in the Black Belt. At the same time, Streight intercepted military supplies, including "a large number of wagons belonging to the enemy, laden with provisions, arms, tents, &c., which had been sent to the mountains to avoid us, but, luckily they fell into our hands." Unfortunately, Streight would later have to leave these "contrabands" to their fate at Blountsville, as he burned his remaining wagons to prevent their slowing his command.[45] Breidenthal recalled that the men surprised a Confederate supply detachment that morning, "in charge of some bacon intended for their army, but on perceiving our approach, they fled to the woods, leaving wagons, mules, negroes and their breakfast of corn-cakes, which I can testify disappeared in another direction . . . we captured several loads of good bacon and a number of good mules and horses. We retained the latter." Another detachment confiscated "several thousand pounds of bacon" and "considerable supplies at Stephenson's Springs, which was likewise destroyed."[46]

After a restful night, the command broke camp early on the 30th, hoping to ascend Day's Gap and begin crossing Sand Mountain. Though the command hoped it had put some distance between itself and the Confederate forces in the Tennessee Valley, they were still only thirty miles from the Confederates along the river, who, by now, were fully aware of the column's presence. After first racing back to Decatur, believing the column intended to outflank and capture him, Forrest began his pursuit late on the 28th and intercepted the command just as it ascended the gap. Streight's Unionist scouts lost ten videttes to the Confederates before effectively screening the column as the balky, braying mules climbed the 1,000 feet to the wide plateau above. Realizing that he would be closely pursued, Streight halted his well-rested command at the top of the pass and formed a line of battle, which Forrest's men impetuously charged. After breaking the charge and severely wounding Forrest's brother William in the process, the Union forces counterattacked and seized two of Forrest's cannon, which they carried off and added to their own. Again leaving the Alabamians of the First Middle Tennessee to screen the rear, the command marched eleven miles, crossed Crooked Creek, and formed another defensive line on Hog Mountain around sunset.

At Hog Mountain, Streight fought the second battle of the day, again holding his lines but yielding the field to the Confederates in order to continue his march, leaving the two captured guns, whose ammunition had been exhausted, spiked on the side of the road. That night the command covered another thirty miles, arriving in Blountsville at mid-morning, interrupting the town's May Day celebration. After a short rest to feed and water the animals, the men pressed on toward Gadsden, hoping to cross the several forks of the Black Warrior River and destroy the bridges behind them, buying some time. The men sustained themselves by foraging and, according to Breidenthal, were becoming "very particular about what we eat, now that the commissary is located all through the country, and we will not have any other meat but ham, for we sent one of our boys to get meat for the company, and he returned without any, saying that 'there was nothing in the smokehouse but shoulders and middlings.'"[47]

After a second consecutive all-night march, the command arrived at Black Creek, near Gadsden, the following morning. Here Streight's plans were frustrated by Confederate heroine Emma Samson, who directed Forrest to a little-used ford, enabling him to outflank the destroyed bridge and continue his pursuit. Samson's actions also signaled that the command had come down from Sand Mountain, leaving the Unionist-leaning area behind, and that the raiders were now in the Coosa River valley, where more residents were sympathetic to secession. The gray-clad troopers pressed Streight through Gadsden on May 2 but were unable to prevent the destruction of the government stores in that town, including "four thousand dollars' worth of good flour, five hundred stands of arms and the ferry-boat" over the Coosa River. Unfortunately, the now-unemployed ferry boat operator embarked on an all-night, fifty-mile ride to Rome and warned the residents there, earning him praise as a modern-day Paul Revere.

As Streight began his third consecutive day without rest, he admitted that "many of our animals and men were entirely worn out and unable to keep up with the column; consequently they fell behind the rear guard and were captured."[48] He intended to halt for the night at Blount's plantation, fifteen miles east of Gadsden, but Forrest again forced him to form a line of battle where many of the men fell asleep on the firing line. Again disengaging, the exhausted men began their third-straight night march without rest, stumbling through a cut-over area near the Round Mountain furnace in a search for a bridge over the Chattooga River. That night the men of Breidenthal's Third Ohio made the short march to the foundry and set fire to the buildings, "with the hearty cooperation of the negroes, who threw the first brands into their own sleeping-berths." The foundry had been producing pig iron for the Confederacy, sending it up the Coosa River valley to Rome, and the destruction was but the first for many of Alabama's iron mills. Throughout the war, the state produced more iron than all other Confederate states combined, more than 12,350 pounds.[49]

From Blount's plantation, Streight sent 250 of his best mounted men ahead to hold the bridge over the Coosa at Rome, but the riders found the town alerted and the bridge both well defended and primed for destruction. They returned to Streight and gave him this news the following morning. Believing it would be impossible to achieve his original objective, he sought terms from his pursuers. Forrest, for his part, offered generous terms, knowing that he was outnumbered and that his men, too, were greatly fatigued by the pursuit. He allegedly duped Streight into surrender by parading his small command repeatedly in Streight's sight, to make it appear larger than it was, and had couriers report periodically the presence of nonexistent commands, subterfuges he would repeat later in his career. Streight's 1,365 raiders kept their flags, sidearms and personal property, surrendering only their arms to their captors, though guards later violated these terms, robbing the prisoners and liberating their personal equipment. After imprisonment in Atlanta and rail transport to Richmond, the enlisted men returned to Federal control less than two weeks later, as paroles and prisoner exchanges were still the order of the day. For his part, Breidenthal was unimpressed with his impromptu tour of the Confederacy, observing a general scarcity of foodstuffs, including "but a small quantity of cornmeal in the station" at Dalton, Georgia, and describing the country around Richmond as "barren." He wrote, "Judging from what I have seen of the 'Sunny South,' there is not sufficient supplies in it to keep this miserable apology of a government six months longer from starvation." He could not have known that just a month prior, residents in Richmond had rioted for food, having nearly exhausted the previous years' supply months before the new harvest would be in, in a repetition of what early Native Americans knew as the "starving time."

But the almost one hundred officers found themselves confined in Richmond's notorious Libby Prison, having been accused of inciting a slave insurrection. Governor Shorter wanted the Alabamians tried and hung for their crime, but was unsuccessful in his efforts. Streight and several of his officers escaped from the prison through a tunnel in February 1864, reaching Washington after a harrowing overland journey when they were secreted and shepherded by slaves along the route. Those who remained suffered increasingly from disease and short rations; Capt. David Smith, the native Alabamian who commanded the loyal detachment of cavalrymen of the First Middle Tennessee, succumbed to pneumonia shortly after his release on April 18, 1865.[50] According to Bob Mackey, Streight's Raid was a tactical failure but a strategic

Corinth

Contraband Camp

success. It kept Forrest on the defensive and away from the forces moving toward Chattanooga and Vicksburg, and it unfitted his command for months, costing him over three hundred mounts killed by overwork and disease.[51]

Perry's Letters

The newly liberated freedmen who returned to Corinth with Dodge's command after their raid to Tuscumbia joined a growing "contraband camp" established to provide relief to the former slaves and assist the government with the financial burden of providing food and shelter for the community. The gathering of freedmen, by all accounts, thrived throughout 1863 and provided a glimpse at what postwar Reconstruction could have looked like, given a greater commitment from other branches of the Federal government besides the War Department. Unfortunately, the camp was always an adjunct to military enterprises, providing labor and foodstuffs to the military garrison of Corinth and collapsing completely when the seat of war moved on and Corinth's garrison evacuated to Memphis at the end of the year.[52] In the interim, the camp provided a fertile recruiting base for the emerging Federal program to enlist African American soldiers in the Union army, furnishing the nucleus for an infantry regiment that helped defend the Mississippi River valley and an artillery battalion that suffered one of the war's worst atrocities, with many of its soldiers murdered in cold blood after surrendering at Fort Pillow, Tennessee, the following year. But the Corinth Contraband Camp, and the two units raised there, provided a beacon to Alabamians still toiling under the yoke of slavery and garrisoned a military city that launched raids challenging Confederate control of northwest Alabama, northeast Mississippi, and western Tennessee.

Corinth

About the same time that Unionist refugees were gathering in Corinth, army officials realized that the growing number of "contrabands," or self-emancipated former slaves, required more formal assistance. Since capturing Corinth in April 1862 after the Battle of Shiloh, Federal troops employed former slaves as laborers, cooks, and washers, primarily in constructing the fortifications that saved the army during the Confederate assault in October. As the rebels vacated the area, more slaves left their masters and congregated around what looked to be a stable and enduring Federal post. The two railroads, the Memphis & Charleston and the Mobile & Ohio, certainly weren't going anywhere and looked to become even more important as Federal forces advanced farther south. At the same time, Confederate cavalry raids, such as the one by Forrest into west Tennessee in December 1862, suggested that Union forces would require a continued presence in the area. As a result, the number of freedmen and their families gathering in Corinth continued to grow in late 1862.

On November 14, General Grant issued orders for the formal establishment of "Contraband Camps" at Grand Junction, Tennessee.[53] General Dodge took this act as tacit permission to establish his own camp, initially under the direction of James M. Alexander, chaplain of the Sixty-Sixth Illinois Infantry. The war had brought a large number of midwesterners in blue coats to northeastern Mississippi, and many of these men held abolitionist sentiments and strong religious beliefs. As a result, men such as Alexander had little difficulty organizing relief for the camp's residents, both from fellow soldiers and from missionary and abolitionist groups. The latter were essential in providing educational services and religious instruction and foreshadowed the Freedmen's Bureau established formally later in the war. As superintendent, Alexander organized labor parties, both within the army camp and on local plantations, which provided a source of funds for relief and additional projects. Alexander's stewardship of funds later became the primary cause of his relief from his responsibilities of caring for and leading freedmen but, initially, he was an effective administrator who organized a camp that relieved the army of much of the burden and expense. The army also welcomed the religious influence, as destitute women in the camp had become a potential source of companionship for many soldiers, with the attendant risk of debilitating sexually transmitted diseases and lapses of discipline. Poor camp sanitation and discipline also threatened to spread communicable diseases, and the army benefited from a well-regulated camp whose residents had adequate food, shelter, and medical care, in addition to the demands of humanity that they care for their fellow man. But according to later testimony, military discipline was a primary motivator in the camp's organization, as the camp "gathered up the wandering, starved and demoralized element that was hanging on the skirts of our army and too often sapping its manly strength and pride."[54]

During the first months of 1863, the camp grew from a disorganized assemblage of cast-off army tents and crudely constructed shacks to a well-organized village, complete with square blocks, permanent houses, a church, gardens, and fields. In many respects, it became a model for other camps in the department, providing an example of how to organize space and labor, and provide security for freedpeople. By providing services to the nearby army encampment, residents of the camp could earn wages in exchange for cooking and cleaning and found a ready market for produce grown in individual or communal gardens. Before enlistment became an army priority, the camp benefited from labor provided by all ages and genders, but recruiting for the First Alabama, African Descent, deprived the camp of its most-able bodies. Freedmen drilling, mounting guard duty, or laboring in the military camp did not directly contribute to the accumulation of resources necessary for survival, but did draw a salary, though less than that of white troops, that could be used to purchase essentials. Accordingly, the army became, as military service has been throughout the nation's history, both a job and a path out of poverty for those willing to risk their lives, even though the primary threat to survival still came from disease rather than enemy action.[55] The army also realized the importance of adequately providing for the soldiers' families in the camps. An investigator looking into conditions in the camps reported, "If we take colored soldiers into our armies . . . we must take them under the obligation to take care of the families that would be otherwise left in want. When the enlisting colored soldiers are assured that the care of their families shall be the care of the government, that assurance must be made good. If we exact good faith from them, we must keep good faith with them."[56] Though Alexander, by most accounts, labored hard to meet this responsibility, many others fell well short.

Dodge's views on contrabands evolved gradually, and can be traced in official orders he issued at Corinth. On February 23, 1863, he ordered that "all able bodied negroes in the Garrison not regularly employed in Regiments, be taken and turned over" to the post's engineers, due to "the present state of the intrenchments."[57] Two weeks later, Dodge's assistant adjutant general, George Spencer, issued further guidance. "Fugitive Slaves may be employed in this District as Laborers in the Quarter Master's, Subsistence, and Engineer Departments . . . also, as Teamsters, as Company Cooks . . . as Officer's Servants (to be paid and rationed by the Officer employing them) and as Hospital Attendants and Nurses. They will be taken up on the Q. M. Rolls, paid and accounted for the same as all persons similarly employed."[58] This marked the beginning of the transition from "contraband of war" to uncompensated laborers to regular employees and, eventually, soldiers for the Federal government.

Recruiting for the First Alabama, A.D., came about as a direct result of the manpower shortage facing the Union army in the spring of 1863. The Emancipation Proclamation, effective January 1 in areas still under Confederate control, increased the flow of freedpeople to Federal garrisons, and the army enviously eyed the black manpower concentrating within their lines. The army had employed freed slaves as laborers and teamsters since first liberating Corinth in 1862, but the formal establishment of the US Colored Troops in early 1863 provided a formal process for black enlistment. For Dodge, this had the potential not only to increase the security of the posts he was responsible for, but also to free up more troops for future expeditions into Confederate-held territory. The April raid into Alabama had required him to call in troops from outlying posts to effectively garrison Corinth against Confederate cavalry in his absence. Posting even poorly trained African American troops behind breastworks alongside experienced troops under capable leadership increased the post's security and protected its stores. After a recruiting visit on May 15 by the adjutant general of the army, Lorenzo Thomas, officers selected from the northern regiments in Corinth began officially organizing the First Alabama Infantry, African Descent, eventually the Fifty-Fifth Regiment, United States Colored Infantry.[59] On June 12, the *Corinth Chanticleer* listed the officers and reported approvingly, "these men are all well qualified for their positions and, what is better than all, they are heart and soul in the cause."[60] When asked why he enlisted, one of the soldiers, teenager James Spikes, later recalled, "I didn't know no better. I thought I would be took care of." Regardless of how well taken care of he was, Spikes survived the war, mustering out in Baton Rouge in 1865 before settling in Pine Bluff, Arkansas, where he lived to at least ninety-one years of age.[61]

General Dodge recalled that the regiment's origins came from the "thousands of negroes which were a great burden to us," who followed him back to Corinth after his campaign into Alabama. Dodge initially stationed white soldiers as guards around the contraband camp, but white soldiers objected to the task and "there was a great deal of trouble in relation to it. Finally Chaplain Alexander came to me and said he believed if I would let him have the arms, he could organize two negro companies that would guard that camp much better than the white soldiers. I agreed to do this and, although I had absolutely no authority for doing so, I gave him the arms and he organized two companies of negroes, officering them with some sergeants from my command. That action caused a great deal of criticism but it worked admirably."[62] Alexander later described the regiment in a letter to Dodge as "a child of your own raising."[63] While the men were eager to defend their new homes, not all were physically prepared for the rigors of military service. The regiment's surgeon, John M. Eaton, found that "most bore indications of flogging, and he saw some with their Achilles tendons severed to prevent escape."[64] Others escaping from slavery suffered from malnutrition. Levi Coffin recalled, "The rebel army had taken away or destroyed the property of Union men in the South; the Federal army had done the same with the property of the rebels, and nothing remained for the poor slaves to live upon. The women and children, and the aged and feeble were often found on the ruined plantations suffering for the means of life."[65]

The first task the troops undertook was to construct a military barracks adjacent to the contraband camp, which was located over a mile outside of the fortifications around the city. In addition to protecting the camp itself, troops manned roadblocks leading into and out of the city. Corinth presented an unhealthy environment, as a result of both the battle the previous October, and the large number of troops that had been encamped around the city for over a year. In addition to a high incidence of disease, mostly caused by poor water, even Mother Nature seemed to conspire against the soldiers. On June 4, a "dreadful storm of rain and wind" blew through the camp, blowing down tents and uprooting trees, resulting in the death of two soldiers of the Tenth Missouri to falling timber.[66] Joseph Nelson of the Eighty-First Ohio and a half dozen colleagues narrowly escaped a small cabin before "a large oak tree standing fifteen feet south of it was torn up by the roots and fell on the cabin and smashed it."[67] Standing guard in the enervating heat against an enemy that never appeared could sap a soldier's strength and will, but the First Alabama, A.D., initially reported good discipline under Alexander. As the former chaplain and superintendent of the contraband camp, Alexander had little of the military training necessary to command large units in battle, but had time to learn and willing tutors from his old regiment among the staff officers he selected to assist him. The army also did not anticipate actually using black troops in combat except in an emergency, largely due to racist concerns about their reliability, and deemed it more important to have a commander sympathetic to the freedmen's cause rather than an experienced field officer in command.

Col. Moses Bane of the Fiftieth Illinois Infantry formally presented the new regiment with its colors on June 21, 1863, and cautioned the men that it must never be deserted, after which Rufus Campbell, a member of the color guard, "made his intentions as a solider abundantly clear."[68] Another correspondent reported the color-bearer's words as, "Why, theye's not much blood in a man any how and if he is not willing to give it for the freedom of his children and his friends, he does not deserve to be called a man."[69] Typically, the presentation of colors came from the local communities that raised Civil War units, but the presentation by fellow soldiers at Corinth was yet another demonstration that the army post was now the community's "home." Reports for Company A for July and August indicated, "The First Alabama Infantry Regiment now guards nearly one half of the lines around Corinth besides furnishing heavy interior guards. Our men are on duty every other day. The regiment does as much guard duty as any white brigade [usually four or more regiments] of old Regiments here. The Work Posts on the Hamburg, Glendale, Clear Creek and Danville roads are guarded entirely by colored soldiers under colored sergeants and yet not one member of the regiment has been known to desert from their posts, notwithstanding excellent opportunity . . . Company 'A' has always performed its full share of duty."[70] Company A had been organized as early as February specifically to guard the contraband camp, under the command of Capt. H. B. McCord, lately a sergeant in Alexander's old regiment, the Sixty-Sixth Illinois Infantry. On a visit to Corinth, Levi Coffin reported, "It was called the Alabama Regiment, because most of the men composing it were from that State. They were all able-bodied, and presented a fine appearance on dress parade. Their colonel told me that they were the most orderly and best behaved regiment in camp; it was the first time that their manhood had been recognized, and they were anxious to prove that they were worthy of the confidence reposed in them."[71]

The regiment saw its first action during a Confederate raid on the post's corral of lame and convalescent mules and horses on July 7.[72] According to an account published in the Cincinnati *Daily Gazette,*

> Colonel Alexander had his regiment in line, distributed ammunition and sent a company to re-enforce each of the picket posts in front. By this time, however, Colonel Cornyn's sweeping battalions were pouring out in the direction of the enemy, and the assistance of A.D.'s as the blacks are called was not required. One company of them, however was taken out. I met it returning—every man of them was singing the air of John Brown, with a full chorus upon the "Glory, glory hallelujah." The

only verse I heard was: "Yes we now are going a soldiering, yes we now are going a soldiering, We are bound to fight for the Union, As we go marching along."[73]

But the unit spent so much time on guard duty that it was difficult to properly train for its combat role. Colonel Alexander, intent upon seeing his regiment vindicate itself on the field of battle, remonstrated with his superiors for more opportunities for drill.[74] He also felt that black troops should be brigaded together, so that their commander would hold a rank superior to or commensurate with that of most post commanders, better enabling him to protect the troops from excessive guard duty. By the time of the Mobile campaign in 1865, black regiments were brigaded together, forming an entire division (three brigades) of the force that captured Alabama's port city.

Dodge attempted to recruit a second regiment of black infantrymen at Corinth, but the department commander, Maj. Gen. Stephen Hurlbut, ordered the regiment broken up, with the recruits transferred to Memphis to fill up an artillery regiment recruiting there to man the city's defenses. He also returned the new regiment's white officers to their old units, including Joseph Nelson, of the Eighty-First Ohio, who had been appointed a second lieutenant in one of the companies, but Nelson later reprised his role as a recruiter for a black regiment just a few months later in Pulaski, Tennessee.[75] Colonel Alexander felt that "the breaking up of 2(nd) Ala. was certainly very unjust," and "since these troops do so well I am much in favor of increasing them as fast as possible."[76] Commissions for officers of the new black regiments became a form of patronage for officers to dispense, and sometimes led to competition among commands. Dodge received solicitations from former associates asking for commissions, but selected the First Alabama's officers from the most qualified applicants from units already in Corinth.[77]

The First Alabama Siege Artillery, later the Sixth, and then Seventh Regiment of US Colored Heavy Artillery, before being renumbered the Eleventh US Colored Infantry, was the only other unit of black troops fully organized at Corinth. These men served the heavy field guns studding the defenses around the town. Eventually, recruiters raised a battalion of four companies, beginning with Company A in January 1863, followed by Company B in August and Companies C and D in October. The troops manned Battery Robinette and Battery Williams in the Corinth defenses, equipped with four eight-inch howitzers, two twenty-pound Parrott rifles, and 1,300 rounds of ammunition.[78] Though never tested, the men proved to be adept artillerymen and freed up more of Dodge's garrison for active patrolling.

Throughout the summer, the camp worked hard to train and equip soldiers and establish military discipline, but it suffered occasional lapses. The offenses ranged from the minor, such as a theft from the sutler's store, to the capital, including allegations of rape. The indiscipline was not limited to the regiment's black soldiers, as one of the white officers was likewise tried and dismissed from the service for various offenses, including misappropriation of funds amid allegations of an illicit affair with one of the camp's cooks, calling into question whether the freedpeople were corrupting the army or vice versa. But all incidents at least had recourse to a well-established system of military justice, which dealt swiftly, if sometimes severely, with the accused and granted them access to a fair trial, which could not always be hoped for behind Confederate lines.[79]

On August 9, Pvt. Harrison Anderson of Company H, a thirty-eight-year-old farmer born in Carroll County, Mississippi, and enlisted into the regiment the previous month, stood accused of breaking into the regimental sutler's store and taking a box of violin strings, a gold bracelet, and several breast pins. He was caught by a fellow member of the regiment, Pvt. Richard Smith of Company B, who was getting water from the well when he saw someone pulling a board off the sutler's store. According to Smith's sworn testimony, itself rare for a black man in Mississippi in 1863, he "told him to halt. He offered to pay me if I would let him go. I told him I could not." Anderson then tried to hide the evidence of his crime by throwing the items in the "privy" (latrine). Smith's testimony was sufficient to convict, and the court sentenced Anderson to five days of marching, two hours on and two hours off, with his head through a board on his shoulders, and a fine of $10, paid as a forfeiture of one-half month's pay for three months.

On the surface, it seems it would have been in Smith's best interest to simply let Anderson get away with the theft, especially if he promised to share the spoils with him. But Smith likely recognized the larger significance of the actions. A regiment that garnered a reputation for lawlessness and indiscipline risked all that the army was doing for freedpeople in Corinth, including providing provisions, shelter, and protection from a return to slavery. The regiment was the key to all of this, with its payroll, demand for civilian employment, support for families and security, an aspect of military service that remains true today.[80] Unable to sustain themselves on their former plantations in the western Tennessee Valley, due to either absentee masters or depredations from both sides, the former slaves now depended on the army, and the ample resources it alone could daily muster and dispense, in order to meet their needs for survival. In fact, the army's largesse became so significant, it began to tempt the officers of the regiment who were less dependent on the army for survival, to misappropriate a portion of these assets for their own gain, but on a much larger scale than anything Private Anderson could attempt.

Later that summer, controversy embroiled the regiment when Colonel Alexander and his adjutant, Lt. George Haskins, traded charges of impropriety in managing the contraband camp's now growing revenues. Haskins appeared to have filed charges first, forcing Alexander and his officers to defend the commanding officer's performance of his duties. In a letter signed by most of the company officers and noncommissioned officers in the unit, the group argued, "As drillmaster he has no superior in this department of Colored Troops. As a disciplinarian he is considered second to none. Exact, energetic, firm yet kind, his discipline is acknowledged and seen in every portion of the regiment."[81] Alexander asserted his innocence, claiming, "I never sold any rations drawn from the government," and "I can account for every cent coming into my hands," but admitted that he did redistribute military rations and clothing to the sick and naked in the camp. In an attempt to defend Alexander, or perhaps to impugn Haskins, his principal accuser, one of the regiment's officers later testified: "The said George Haskins, 1st Lt., Company C, 1st Alabama Infantry was found in an officer's quarters with no company other than a colored girl employed in the camp as a cook or servant with his (said Lt. Haskins) trousers unbuttoned and partially off his person in the act of stripping away from said colored girl as she (the said colored girl) occupied a bed or bunk and was in the act of pulling her clothes down over her lower extremities and all this in a manner making it quite evident to the spectator the he (the said Lt. Haskins) then and there had sexual intercourse with the colored girl," sometime between August 25 and September 21, 1863. Lieutenant Haskins's actions, if true, demonstrate the variable quality of leadership in USCT units, prejudicing military commanders against their use and raising questions about their reliability, limiting the opportunity for active operations. The allegations in the First Alabama, A.D., resulted in Alexander's dismissal the following year and an unsuccessful campaign to clear his name of wrongdoing. He later returned to Illinois but, according to one account, "deserted his most excellent Christian wife and five children, became a spiritualist, licentious and everything that was bad. The last I heard of him he was living in New Orleans. His name was stricken from the (church) roll."[82] Haskins was likewise dismissed, and the affair did little to reassure the army that the regiment could be ably led and administered.

Haskins's experience with formerly enslaved women who had survived lifetimes of sexual exploitation likely influenced his experiences. Women who had been exploited by their masters, and even by fellow slaves, were far less likely to view intercourse and prostitution as moral violations. While stationed near Corinth, Joseph Nelson revealed one of the particularly brutal aspects of the institution, when he reported, "At Pocahontas, we learned of one more of the beauties of slavery of which we had not previously thought. A resident here owned a large strong muscular negro whom he stood as men do a stallion, $100 to insure a live youngster to kick, yell, and suck. Slave women were brought to him and bred, that they might reproduce their kind."[83] While not having control over the product of their own labor was central to slaves' economic opposition to the institution, not having control over their own bodies, and indeed, lives, was even more fundamental.

In late September, the War Department finally issued guidance on both recruiting and the regulation of contraband camps. Special Orders No. 63, issued September 29, stipulated that:

> All male negroes, who after examination shall be found capable of bearing arms, will be organized into companies and regiments. All others, including men incapable of bearing arms, women and children, instead of being permitted to remain in camps in idleness, will be required to perform such labor as may be suited to their several conditions, in the several staff departments of the army, on plantations, leased or otherwise, within our lines, as wood choppers, or in any way that their labor can be made available.

The order made the Army's Quartermaster and Medical Departments responsible for issuing necessary supplies and required the payment of wages, subject to a 10 percent withholding for the care of the "sick and otherwise dependent." It also authorized volunteers in the camps, including missionaries and teachers, to receive rations, quarters, and transportation on government steamships and railroads. The camp at Corinth, where many of these measures were already in place, had provided a model for the system now extended across the South.[84]

Oct 1863

By October, the 893 men, now fully equipped with Enfield rifled muskets and who, according to their commander, "surpass our highest expectations," were at least well trained enough to conduct excursions away from the city's defenses. Dodge sent Company A to Pocahontas in western Tennessee to guard railroad bridges against Confederate raiders attempting to cut supply lines and distract Union forces from the siege of Chattanooga. He later bragged about his "fine negro troops" who did "the same duty as white troops."[85] Dodge had used his railroad experience to reconstruct many of the railroad bridges around Corinth and designed strong blockhouses to protect their defenders. His efforts in rehabilitating Southern rails attracted Grant's attention, who sent him east the following month to work on the railroads in southern Tennessee and northern Alabama, in order to increase the flow of supplies into the besieged garrison of Chattanooga, after Rosecrans's defeat at Chickamauga.[86]

While in Tennessee, Alexander demonstrated that he was not reluctant to discipline his troops when required, including using the harshest measures available to him as a military commander. On November 19, Alexander wrote that he had executed one of his soldiers, Pvt. Lawson Kemp of Company A, after a court-martial found him guilty of committing a rape upon a white woman near Pocahontas. Alexander felt the extreme punishment was justified because their harsh lives of servitude had inured his men to traditional forms of punishment. Alexander believed that "stopping pay and lying in the guard house is no punishment to these men."[87] The charge itself represented one of the oldest tools for white control of black populations in both the antebellum and Jim Crow era, as even allegations of rape aroused strong emotions and could be co-opted to strike fear into black communities and bring out lynch mobs. In reporting his actions, Alexander did not elaborate on the charges, but only made it clear that he had dealt swiftly with them.

That same month, six more companies sortied to Big Hill, Tennessee, to again guard railroad bridges along the Memphis & Charleston Railroad and remained there in December, just missing out on an attempt to capture Forrest's command on their latest raid into Tennessee. At Moscow, Tennessee, a sister regiment, the Second West Tennessee Infantry, African Descent (later the Sixty-First USCI) engaged Forrest's command at the bridge over the Wolf River and repelled an attack. The affair justified recruiting black soldiers to the department's commander, Maj. Gen. Stephen Hurlbut, who issued the following congratulations: "The recent affair at Moscow, Tennessee, has demonstrated the fact that colored troops properly disciplined and commanded can and will fight well," and the unit's "successful defence of the important position to which they had been assigned . . . vindicated the wisdom of the Government in elevating the rank and file of these regiments to the position of freedmen and soldiers."[88]

The more active times for Corinth's garrison were a signal of things to come—in early January 1864, the entire garrison, including the contraband camp and the First Alabama Infantry and Heavy Artillery Regiments, A.D., were all evacuated to Memphis, both to free up more troops for active campaigns and because the rail center had lost much of its importance, now that Federal forces held the vital junction at Chattanooga and were poised for a campaign into Georgia in the summer of 1864, which proved to be a more profitable path into the Confederacy than the line south from Corinth. With the Confederacy cut in two after the loss of Vicksburg in 1863, interior Mississippi lost much of its value and became host to raids and reprisals, most frequently pitting Forrest's Southern cavalrymen against Northern formations comprised, in part, of black soldiers, including the First Alabama, A.D., but denying Forrest any significant role in the far more important campaign unfolding in the mountains north of Atlanta.[89]

Events outside Alabama drove the next Federal foray into the state, accelerating the recruiting of Alabamians into the Union army and involving existing units in direct combat with their Confederate opponents. As the black Alabama troops drilled and stood guard in the Corinth heat, the growing First Alabama Cavalry continued to receive recruits who had either been driven from their homes in north-central Alabama(or)were Confederate deserters demoralized by the twin victories at Vicksburg and Gettysburg. Coupled with increasing supply shortages within the Confederacy, many of these men decided to throw in their lot with the opposition. Not all of those mustered were trustworthy, though. On June 1, Pvt. Alex Johnson enlisted in Company

[handwritten: Col. Spencer Sept 7 1863 ☆ to Dodge]

D but deserted on June 19. Less than a month later, Union troops captured a detachment of Confederates, including Johnson, after repeated instances of firing on pickets that suggested the Confederates were too familiar with the Union routine. Dodge ordered the man tried by court-martial and on July 23, after a receiving a guilty verdict, had the man publicly executed by a firing squad composed of eight men of the First Alabama Cavalry, to deter further instances of disloyalty and desertion.[90] Francis W. Dunn, one of the officers of the First Alabama, observed, "The scene was solemn but it did not seem to affect the soldiers that witnessed it. They are a careless set."[91] While inured to violence, as a result of their persecution at the hands of their secessionist neighbors, the men likely took the execution as well-deserved justice against one of their enemies rather than a caution against desertion. On September 7, the unit's commander, Col. George Spencer, reported that he had men recruiting in Fayette County and expected to have a company filled there in less than ten days. Spencer also wanted "to take my reg't. to Marion, Fayette and Winston Co's Ala. to recruit it," which led to the unit's first campaign and battle the following month.[92] On September 10, the regiment finally received "cavalry arms," preparing it for field service, with over 800 men enlisted by the end of the month.[93]

[handwritten margin notes: July 23 1863 firing squad; • Recruit; • ARM; • 1st Fight; Sept 7 1863 ☆; Sept 10 1863]

Grant's operations in central Mississippi continued to concern Confederate officials even after Vicksburg's fall. To the north in Tennessee, Rosecrans had finally launched his campaign for Chattanooga through Middle Tennessee, capturing that city in September and reopening supply lines through northern Alabama along the Tennessee River axis. These efforts led to a requirement for scouts with knowledge of the local area, especially in extreme northeastern Alabama, which sat on Rosecrans's right flank, and resulted in the recruitment of the First Alabama and Tennessee Vidette Cavalry from several organized bands of Unionists in the area.[94] One of these men was Anthony Barnes, of Valley Head, whose father was a native of North Carolina.[95] His neighbor William McNew also joined the unit, after lying out near Valley Head to avoid conscript agents, but finally traveled to Whiteside, Tennessee, and enlisted in the new command. John Bowman frequently fed McNew while he was lying out and often ferried Unionists and rebel deserters headed for Union lines across Little River in his canoe.[96] Bowman continued his efforts until the fall of 1864, when Federal forces took 250 bushels of corn, seventy-five bushels of sweet potatoes, thirty bushels of peas, fifteen head of hogs, twenty-five chickens, as

[handwritten: 92. Fayette Co / Marion Co. / Winston Co.]

[handwritten: ⧣ 92]

well as hay and fodder from his farm near Valley Head. With the farm cleaned out, there was little reason to stay, as Elijah McNew later testified, "after Sherman's men eat us up the old man [John Bowman] to get rid of the danger from the rebels and to get supplies left our neighborhood and moved to Bledsoe County, Tenn.," then well behind Union lines, where two of his sons, George and Madison, enlisted in the Sixth Tennessee Mounted Infantry (US).[97] Other Alabamians joined loyalist regiments from Tennessee during the fall of 1863, with the Twelfth Tennessee Cavalry recruiting sixty-six men in Decatur.[98]

On August 26, 1863, Union commanders reported from Stevenson, Alabama, that "A good many mountaineers are enlisting. About 20 joined the Fourth Indiana to-day and yesterday. Seventy-six partisans of Mr. Latham's company (are) waiting here to be mustered in."[99] A week later Rosecrans's chief of staff, the future president James A. Garfield, wired that now-Lieutenant Latham, "commanding the First Independent Company, Alabama Volunteer Cavalry, is ordered to report to the commanding officer at Stevenson, who is directed to furnish the company with arms as soon as possible." Once they had been furnished with horses, they were to be posted in the vicinity of Larkinsville and scout along the line of the Memphis & Charleston between Stevenson and Huntsville.[100] Rosecrans reported his successes to the War Department on September 11, 1863, noting, "We have organized and mustered into service under authority already received, several companies of loyal Alabamians, for twelve months service. Since the occupation of this country and East Tennessee, men are fast organizing and applying to be mustered."

This created a problem for Rosecrans, and he sought approval from the secretary of war himself, Edwin M. Stanton, to begin accepting loyalists and deserting conscripts from the Confederate army retreating before him. In suggesting that these men be given gainful employment, he wrote, "They cannot follow the avocations of peace nor have proper protection at home, and will soon be driven by causes founded in human nature to some course prejudicial to the public interests." While history is replete with examples of sending surrendered soldiers back to their homes to cause mischief, Rosecrans could also have been referring to baser "human nature," the need to gather resources necessary to survive. Pilfering, raiding, and reprisals in his rear area would only complicate logistical difficulties and sap manpower to guard his lengthening supply line, in what military strategists recognize as "strategic consumption," most notably demonstrated on Napoleon's disastrous invasion of Russia in 1812.[101] Instead, Rosecrans could muster the disaffected men into his own force, equip them and allow them to provide security in his rear area, without additional levies on his own manpower. For his part, Stanton immediately wired Rosecrans, "You are authorized to use your discretion in regard to the enlistment of deserters," and that he was further "authorized to organize regiments and companies from loyal citizens of the States in which your army may be operating."[102]

Unfortunately, simply mustering and equipping forces did not make them militarily effective. Less than a month later, guerrillas surprised Latham's command while it was guarding an important sawmill near Larkinsville. According to the Federal commander on the scene, they ran away disgracefully, abandoning government property, losing forty of their number captured. Fortunately relief arrived at the sawmill before the flames could do their work, and saved the facility. But a company of Alabama scouts guided Maj. Gen. O. O. Howard's corps of Hooker's relief column into Chattanooga, skirmishing with Confederates at the Battle of Wauhatchee. Two additional companies of Alabama scouts, under Captains Allen and Long, continued to provide intelligence around Chattanooga throughout the winter, scouting the surrounding valleys and keeping tabs on Confederate forces blocking the advance to Atlanta. But when the armies left for Atlanta, the unit lost the justification for its existence, and Federal authorities disbanded it in the summer of 1864.

In late 1863, the events around Chattanooga precipitated a transfer of troops from Grant's command to Rosecrans's, including an exchange of commanders that placed Grant at the head of Rosecrans's army and led to Grant bringing his most capable subordinate during the Vicksburg campaign, Gen. William Tecumseh Sherman, to southeastern Tennessee to eventually lead the campaign to Atlanta. Sherman's troops traveled by way of Corinth across northern Alabama, reopening a supply line along the Tennessee River line into Chattanooga and bringing Federal forces back to northern Alabama after a year's absence. In his march east from Corinth, Sherman overwhelmed the small Confederate cavalry units guarding northern Alabama, pushing them out of his way at Tuscumbia and Florence as Union gunboats ferried his command to the northern bank of the Tennessee River. This meant another expedition for Corinth's garrison, as Sherman requested additional cavalry forces familiar with the area to guide his advance, the beginning of an affiliation that led to Sherman selecting a company from the First Alabama to serve as his personal escort on his "March to the Sea."

For the time being, though, Dodge, and through him, Hurlbut, sought to retain the services of the regiment Dodge had raised at Corinth, telling the native Ohioan that Sherman could have the Fifth Ohio, "or any other cavalry at or near Corinth except Spencer's (Alabama) cavalry, which is designed for specific service."[103] As a demonstration of that special service, Hurlbut provided a broader description in a letter to Grant: "Colonel Spencer's regiment is wholly composed of refugees from Alabama. They have been in several engagements and behaved well. They are thoroughly acquainted with the country, well mounted and armed; have two light steel guns, take with them as volunteers 6 engineers who can either run or destroy railroads and steamers." With this highly specialized force, Hurlbut sought to assist Rosecrans's troops besieged in Chattanooga by disrupting the rail lines supplying Bragg's army arrayed against him, specifically the railroad between Montgomery and West Point, Georgia. On October 4, he ordered Spencer to take 650 trained men on a route through Jasper, the county seat of Walker County, and then strike the railroad at some point east of Montgomery. They were to avoid the main roads, to decrease the likelihood of interception, and were not to "interfere with private property further than is necessary for remounts and for sustenance to the command. All public works will be destroyed."[104] Aware of the possibility that Spencer, like Streight six months earlier, could be cut off behind enemy lines, Hurlbut advised him to look south to reach Union lines, as "the line of escape will probably be by Pensacola."

The regiment continued to recruit in order to rebuild its numbers and fill out additional companies. On September 28, Lieutenant Hornbeck, commanding Company K, reported, "Last night Lieutenant Tramel, of this regiment returned from Marion County, Alabama, where he went two weeks ago with only ten men to get recruits for this regiment. He brought in one hundred and ten recruits and eight prisoners, among them is a Lieutenant and a rebel mail." Hornbeck also reported that many of his men, who had been in Tennessee since the fall of 1862, were reunited with their families in Corinth, as "there are a great many refugees here living mostly in tents." He professed, "The Union people in North Alabama, in some quarters, are armed and organized, and hold their own against the bushwhackers. I learn there are several squads ready to come to this regiment and will be in here shortly. They have

[handwritten margin notes: TRamel / JR Phillips / Gabe]

raised good crops and have plenty of provisions, except salt and groceries. . . . They are very much like the loyal men of East Tennessee, and certainly deserve the sympathy and merit the help of all true patriots. Their Union sentiments have cost them something."[105] One Union soldier reported the arrival of a refugee who recounted that her husband had been "hung, holding up for the Union caus, [but] he Succeeded in killing three Rebels' before they took him [and] her brother is in the union army."[106] In addition to recruits, family members continued to arrive at the refuge in northeastern Mississippi. On *[handwritten: Aug 15]* August 15, Thomas Files's wife Martha left Winston County and joined her husband in Glendale. A witness later recalled, "the Rebs had driven his family from Alabama and his wife came to our camps at Glendale Mississippi and she fetched the mule with her and our regiment was very scarce of stock," leading to the mule joining the Union war effort as well.[107] Later that winter Hornbeck observed, "I feel like doing everything in my power to assist the loyal people of the South, and there is a great deal done for them in this regiment. . . . The holidays create quite a demand for salt and groceries, among the inhabitants and the only place where they can be obtained is at some post or camp."[108]

[handwritten margin note: TRamel + Phillips Diary]

One of the men who came in with Lieutenant Tramel was John R. Phillips, a North Carolina native who resided in Marion County at the beginning of the war. Years later Phillips wrote that, after his father's death, "Mother turned me over to a trusty negro who taught me to work. His name was Gabe. I loved him. He was a good religious negro and wanted me to do right. I would work with him through the day and many nights we would 'possum hunt. He slept in the kitchen and would skin his game at night. I would enjoy watching him." Phillips had managed to both avoid Confederate conscription and accumulate a substantial estate, which consisted of "seventy five head of cattle and the same number of hogs and four head of horses and mules. I had made a big corn crop and had about a thousand bushels of corn and plenty of fodder and hay," but this attracted the attention of Confederate troops, especially after inaccurate rumors spread of Phillips joining the Union army. After that, according to Phillips, Confederates "commenced robbing my family of the support I had left for them, they drove off my cattle and took my horses and mules, also my corn. They even went so far as to pour what meal my family had out in the floor and fill the sacks with meat. They even took their cups, saucers and plates, not leaving any thing for their sustenance."[109]

Phillips had to "lie out" for a while in Winston County, and attempted to

[handwritten at bottom: 115 John R. Phillips ☆ Diary B15 / TRamel A]

return home to bury his daughter, who had succumbed to illness, but was physically restrained by neighbors who knew rebel soldiers were guarding her grave in an attempt to capture him. But conscription agents eventually caught Phillips and forced him to join Roddey's cavalry, where he waited for a chance to escape and reach Union lines or desert. He returned home to find that the "Rebels had been robbing all the time until there was not much left to subsist on."[110] Finally, with a group of over one hundred others, Phillips reached Union lines and, after "eating a hearty meal," promptly enlisted in the First Alabama, swearing that the Confederates who had caused him and his family so much suffering, would never take him alive. Phillips's service record gives the date as October 21, 1863, and he served in the regiment until the end of the war.[111]

By now Dodge had appointed one of his associates from Iowa as the First Alabama's commander. George Spencer, a New York native who been a small-time businessman, minor elected official, failed land speculator, a "fifty-niner" in the gold fields of Colorado, where he founded the town of Breckenridge, and a sutler for a Nebraska regiment. His skill in keeping Dodge informed of Confederate movements before Iuka and Corinth earned him a commission as Dodge's assistant adjutant general in September 1862. But Spencer did not find a desk job to his liking and became an integral part of Dodge's intelligence-gathering network, which included frequent forays behind rebel lines, often accompanied by a flag of truce under the guise of negotiating prisoner exchanges. With the First Alabama Cavalry, Spencer had a ready-made unit for daring scouts and hard riding, keeping tabs on the enemy while bringing more soldiers into Federal lines. His biographer, Terry L. Seip, describes Spencer as a sharp man who could talk or bluff his way out of any tight spot.[112]

Under Spencer's leadership, the raid toward the Montgomery & West Point Railroad finally departed on October 19, but it turned back after only five days while still ten miles short of Jasper due to the rough country, heavy downpours, and jaded stock. On their return, the five hundred men encountered a far stronger Confederate force of two regiments, the Second Tennessee and Second Alabama Cavalry under Brig. Gen. Samuel Ferguson, of Forrest's command, which inflicted a serious defeat at Vincent's Crossroads, near Red Bay, Alabama, on October 26. Although the First Alabama troops formed a line of battle protected by their two artillery pieces, a Confederate charge pierced the

Vincent's Crossroads
Oct 26, 2022

lines and drove the Unionists from the field. Ferguson claimed that "The chase was kept up for some 10 miles through dense woods and over a mountainous country until dark. Their perfect knowledge and our ignorance of the country enabled most of them, however, to escape by separating into small squads and leaving the road." However, Ferguson's claim that "I have succeeded in effectually destroying the First Alabama Tory Regiment" was a bit premature, despite being repeated by Ferguson's superior, Gen. S. D. Lee, in his official report.

☆ Lee's Report

Despite their escape, the First Alabama still suffered heavily, losing the two artillery pieces, abandoned when they became mired in a stream, over fifty horses, sixty breech-loading carbines, and five company guidons. Orders issued shortly after the battle required additional training in dismounted fighting, as well as additional equipment needed to refit the unit for field duty.[113] The unit also tightened discipline, increased drill, and tried to separate soldiers from their families, directing that "all women must leave this camp at once; a man cannot do his duty as a soldier and keep house at the same time."[114] A relocation of the regiment's camp from Glendale, Mississippi, well east of Corinth, into Corinth proper evidently prompted the last comment, as Francis Dunn recorded in his diary that, "the refugees tumbled out of the [train] cars and began to cook. It looked more like an emigrant train than a regiment of soldiers."[115]

Dunn

This was John Phillips's first engagement with the unit, and he reported taking several positions on the firing line, but eventually being forced to fall back. In his words, "A little before sunset we came to a creek where the road seemed to give out. Here we found our artillery deserted and did not see any way of crossing the stream. The banks were from six to eight feet high and perpendicular. The Rebs were pressing us in the rear, charging us and shooting a continuous volley in the rear. Our men were shouting forward at every breath. I plunged my horse off a steep bank, into the creek and he commenced pawing and trying to go up on the opposite bank. I slid off of him in the water and assisted him all I could, and as he went up the bank I caught him by the tail and went out with him."[116] After three days of hiding in swamps and subsisting on a single ear of corn, Phillips and five companions, including one rebel who had fled during the engagement in hopes of reaching the Union lines, eventually returned to Corinth. The losses inhibited the regiment's effectiveness later in the month, when two hundred men, including Phillips, accompanying their brigade on a pursuit of rebel raiders into Tennessee, had to return to Corinth

Phillips at Vincents

Oct 19th:
o departed
• Turn back 5 days later Oct 24th
117

See pg 255

Jesperis near Double Springs Winston Co.

#113
14
#115
116

Spencer's Biographer = Terry & Seip

o 10 miles short of Jasper Ala Turn-back.

Vincent's CrossRoads

Like:
Lt.
James
Perry

B

as guards for captured prisoners due to the poor condition of their mounts. The campaign into Walker County and the escape from Ferguson's men had taken a toll on both men and horses.[117] But by mid-December, the regiment recovered its strength and reported 802 men present for duty. Further scouting in pursuit of the latest raid into Tennessee, cost six men, killed in a skirmish with Confederate forces near Jack's Creek, Tennessee on Christmas Eve.[118]

The losses at Vincent's Crossroads opened vacancies for officers in the regiment. Many of the unit's first officers had come from northern regiments stationed at Corinth who had more than two years of hard campaigning under their belts, including the battles at Shiloh and Corinth. One of these men was Capt. Philip Sternberg, a sergeant in the Sixty-Fourth Illinois who had been commissioned as an officer in Company B of the First Alabama Cavalry and was killed in action at Vincent's Crossroads, along with the company's first lieutenant, James Swift. Earlier, while on leave in Memphis, Swift had recruited a former messmate of his in the Fifteenth Illinois Cavalry, Francis W. (Frank) Tupper, of Minooka, Illinois, to fill the vacant position of second lieutenant in the company. Tupper had been serving as an army-detailed railroad clerk in Jackson, Tennessee, and renewed his acquaintance with Swift while returning from furlough in Memphis. After hearing nothing about his application for a commission in the First Alabama for months, Tupper finally learned in early November that his application had been approved, and he reported for duty at Camp Davies, five miles south of Corinth. But the loss of his good friend in combat during that time meant that "all the pleasure that I had anticipated was now gone as I had calculated very much on being with Swift."[119]

In the months that followed, Tupper gradually acquired the trappings of his new office, including equipment purchased in Memphis, and a black servant, named Benjamin Franklin, who roomed with Tupper in a twelve-foot-square log house. Tupper reported that, in exchange for shelter and sustenance, Franklin "takes care of the horses and mornings when I get up I find a good fire in the fireplace, my boots blacked, clothes brushed, a wash dish of water towel and soap ready. In fact, he is my man Friday, always on hand and always ready. He has been learning to read and he is now rejoicing in the possession of a new third reader that I bro't him from Memphis. Evenings when I have nothing to do I hear him read and it amuses me greatly."[120]

The return of Federal forces to northern Alabama permitted a resumption of enlistments of freedmen, and Federal commanders began to organize an-

Freedmen

Blk Amer.
Tenn
Pulaski

other Second Alabama Infantry, African Descent, this time at Pulaski, Tennessee, in November, again, largely from former slaves from the Tennessee Valley.
Dodge again received recommendations for officers for this new regiment. On
December 10, Col. Augustus Chetlain of the Twelfth Illinois offered his strongest endorsement for Sgt. Norton Campbell, who later commanded Company
F of the 110th. Chetlain urged Dodge to continue recruiting and believed "another reg't could be raised in this part of the country" and stated, "I would
very much like to see Capt. [Wallace] Campbell at the head of a regiment of
negroes."[121] Dodge complied immediately, issuing the order appointing Sgt.
Norton Campbell to command of Company F, Second Alabama Infantry, African Descent, the following day, and appointed Capt. Wallace Campbell, also
of the Twelfth Illinois, to command of the Second Alabama, A.D., on December 25, 1863.[122]

With Corinth almost one hundred miles from the heart of the valley, and
with many of the volunteer freedmen from the western half of the valley in
that city already, opening a second recruiting station in Pulaski, roughly thirty
miles from Huntsville and Decatur and much closer to the as-yet unexploited
central and eastern parts of the valley, promised to induce new recruits into
the ranks. The influx of recruits prompted the raising of a second regiment at
Pulaski, the Third Alabama Infantry, A.D. in January 1864. The Second, later
redesignated the 110th Infantry, USCT, and the Third, later the 111th Infantry,
USCT both played a vital role in protecting the Nashville and Decatur railway
from Confederate raiders and forays. Dodge's forces were busy reconstructing
the railroad and benefited from supervision by the future chief engineer of the
transcontinental railroad. With the Nashville & Chattanooga road suffering
heavy damage during the summer campaign season, the route south to Decatur and then east along the Memphis & Charleston line to Chattanooga proved
a promising route for supplies destined for the Federal forces in that city. Men
from both of the new USCT regiments actively guarded key bridges along the
route, and companies of both regiments eventually accompanied Sherman's
army in the 1864 Atlanta campaign, the March to the Sea, and the Carolinas
campaign in 1865.

1864

Joseph Nelson, formerly of the Eighty-First Ohio, helped recruit the Third
Alabama Infantry, A.D., at Pulaski, though he admitted it went against his nature. "To find a darky of the right age and say to him, 'Mount one of old Mas-
sa's best horses or mules and come with us,' was not exactly palatable to me,

although it was one of the right and proper ways of fighting a malignant rebellion, which started out to first tear down a good government, and build upon its ruins another with slavery as its 'chief corner-stone.'" Nelson modified his approach, instead meeting at the local mills where slaves brought in wheat from the surrounding area for the soldiers to grind into flour, with a healthy portion appropriated for the army's use. He reported, "They responded to this invitation. I explained the situation to them as I understood it, and found that they already saw it in the same way. Soon had 40 recruits for our company. Every one of them volunteered." But even here, the recruits performed one last drama for their erstwhile owners that helps explain reports of forced conscription of slaves. Nelson reported, "At their request, I went through the motion of 'Pressing,' too. Took a squad with me and ordered them to come along. They did not want the 'Old Missus' to think that they had voluntarily left her." Nelson gave his men the week of Christmas to spend with their families, but "on the last day of the old year they reported for duty, and we marched to Pulaski."[123]

In the southern part of Alabama, similar movements were afoot, with Pensacola playing the role of Corinth. As the only Federal outpost on the Gulf Coast between New Orleans and Key West, Pensacola was again fulfilling its role as the destination of choice for refugees, as Matthew Clavin's work has conclusively demonstrated.[124] Since the Spanish colonial period the city had served as a beacon for slaves in West Florida and South Alabama, promising the cover of an urban environment with maritime connections across the hemisphere. After Confederate forces had been unable to dislodge the Union garrison at Fort Pickens, Pensacola became a vital port for the Navy's Gulf Blockading Squadron, even after the fall of New Orleans, due to the latter city's location far up the winding and fast-flowing Mississippi River. As Federal forces reoccupied the Navy Yard and Fort Barrancas, freedmen and Unionists from the Alabama interior embarked on journeys down the well-worn paths along the Escambia, Conecuh, Pea, and Choctawhatchee Rivers toward the refuge on the coast. As early as July 1862, a Confederate soldier near Pensacola reported the capture of "two negroes here who were trying to get to the Yankees," including one who "ran away from a plantation near Montgomery."[125] By 1863, as life-sustaining resources evaporated in the wiregrass and sandy uplands, white Alabamians also found new opportunities for Federal service in Pensacola.

62

One of those making the perilous journey from central Alabama was Wade Richardson, a native of Troup County, Georgia, who had been raised near Tuskegee in a strict Universalist home opposed to slave-owning. Richardson and a colleague felt increasingly threatened by Confederate impressment gangs and resolved to journey to the Florida coast in hopes of joining the Union forces there. In a week-long ordeal, during which they begged and bluffed their way across South Alabama, the two teens sustained themselves by posing as paroled Confederate soldiers from Vicksburg, but for intelligence on home guard activities, they frequently "called on the darkies, who often supplemented the information with a bit of bread or a roasted potato or ear of corn."[126] After joining a party venturing to St. Andrew's Bay (now Panama City) to make salt, the men surreptitiously slipped away and headed west toward the mouth of Choctawhatchee Bay, where they hoped to make contact with Union gunboats patrolling the area. The two men wandered around lost for a while, during which time Richardson's traveling partner proposed that the men should "give ourselves up to the Confederates at Vernon, if we could find them, rather than perish in this wilderness."[127] After gnawing on green cornstalks and half-ripe watermelons for sustenance, they finally reached Point Washington at the head of the bay, where sympathetic residents gave them a meal and put them in touch with fishermen who could carry them down the bay. After assembling with a dozen other refugees, the men finally clambered aboard a Union gunboat where, according to Richardson, "there went up a shout from those (now) on board that I hope I shall never forget to my dying day; a shout of deliverance and joy that we had again assembled under the flag of the Union."[128] After reaching Pensacola, Richardson worked for a while as a laborer, surviving a yellow fever epidemic that ravaged the port in the fall of 1863 (the height of the season for that disease) "due to the care given me by an old auntie—a colored nurse, who had nursed yellow fever patients before . . . thanks to her, I survived." His traveling companion was not as lucky and succumbed to the disease.[129]

Richardson was not the only central Alabama Unionist persecuted by rebels. Alexander Bodiford headed a family of loyalists at Saville, near Luverne, in what was then part of Lowndes County but is now in Crenshaw County. Bodiford's son Isham hid in the woods despite being hunted by dogs. He later testified, "I lay out in the broom sedge fields many a cold night, and some of these were pretty bitter. One night Tom Coker and I were out together and my wife came and told us they were after us with about fifty dogs and we went on foot, twenty-eight miles before day and it was an awful cold rainy night." Despite his best efforts to avoid conscription, agents eventually captured Bodiford and forced him into the Seventeenth Alabama Infantry, but he claimed to have refused to shoot at Union soldiers and "fired in the air when I had to fire." While home on furlough in early 1865, Bodiford finally made his way to Pensacola. Ephraim Dorman, a native of Pike County and a postwar resident of Glenwood in Crenshaw County, also made it to Pensacola, enlisted in the Second Maine Cavalry, and served with the unit until the end of the war. Aaron Bodiford, Isham's brother, also sought refuge in Pensacola and cut shingles for a living on East Bay. Upon learning that a group of Confederate deserters wanted into Union lines, Aaron Bodiford took a boat to assist them but was captured, losing an arm to a gunshot wound in the process.[130] A claims adjustor for the Southern Claims Commission found, "There was a community of Union men in Crenshaw Co., small in number but decided in their sentiments."[131]

On October 29, 1863, Gen. Nathaniel Banks, commanding the Federal Department of the Gulf from New Orleans, sent Brig. Gen. Alexander Asboth, a Hungarian-born refugee of the failed Revolution of 1848, to Pensacola with reinforcements for the town's small garrison in hopes of supporting General Banks's anticipated campaign against Mobile the following year.[132] He directed Asboth, "It has been represented that a regiment of cavalry could easily be raised in that portion of Florida to the command of which you have been assigned. You are authorized to take immediate steps for the enlisting of such a regiment on your arrival at Pensacola," with orders to requisition "horses, equipment, arms and ammunition" should the attempt prove successful.[133] This effort became the genesis of the First Florida Cavalry, a six-company regiment composed primarily of West Floridians and South Alabamians. Indeed, the regiment could have been attributed to the state of Alabama, as 267 of the 658 men on the muster rolls were Alabama natives and many more were likely residents, given the large number of birthplaces in neighboring areas of Georgia and South Carolina where many Alabama migrants originated. Of those whose birthplaces can be determined, most of the Alabama-born were from the five southeastern-most counties in the state (Pike, Henry, Coffee, Dale, and Barbour) and those bordering Florida (Covington, Conecuh, and Baldwin).[134] Richardson claimed that "every fishing smack that ventured up the bay was sure to bring a cargo of refugees," and that "most of these men had suffered the ravages of war from the Confederates and were willing and eager to enter the United States army and help to recover their homes. There was a strong thirst for revenge among men whose housetops had been burned over the heads of their defenceless wives and children for the reason that they had joined the Union forces."[135]

In many cases, the desire to exact retribution on secessionists such as Columbus Holley who had persecuted runaway slaves and draft evaders alike, formed strong biracial bonds. In one episode in Dale County, Alabama, Holley's slaves conspired with a local deserter, John Ward, to kill Holley as he slept. The slaves carried Ward to Holley's bedroom window, where Ward fired the fatal round into Holley. They then carried him back to his horse, so that there would be no trail for the bloodhounds to follow, other than that made by the unarmed slaves. Their skill in plotting the man's demise meant the murder went unsolved for years, until Ward finally issued a deathbed confession. Ward led a band that may have included deserters, Unionists, and runaway slaves, as Governor Shorter complained of close cooperation among all three across the Wiregrass.[136]

In November, Asboth reported that, with the assistance of a shallow-draft steamer that could traverse the coastal rivers, he could "collect at once sufficient men for two Florida regiments, one white and the other colored." Refugees continued to reach Federal lines despite the efforts of Confederate cavalry screening the approaches to the city "with a view to prevent the white and black refugees concealed in the woods from joining the Union forces." Once these men had been mustered, Asboth hoped to use them as an investment, as it would "encourage and bring in the Union service many men from the interior neighboring country of South Alabama and West Florida, and would give me a better basis to start from against the Mobile, Pollard and Montgomery Railroad, which passes through the best cotton and corn lands of the State of Alabama, with large plantations, now almost exclusively engaged in raising corn for the Confederates."[137] From Pensacola, and eventually Mobile, the rich Black Belt of central Alabama could finally come within range of Federal *chevauchees,* denying vital resources to the armies arrayed on the roads to Atlanta and Richmond. According to Richardson, the regiment "proved themselves to be brave and valuable allies to our regular forces," largely because "every road, I had almost said every cowtrail of southern Alabama and Florida was known to some of our men."[138]

On December 5, after his first successful steamboat-mounted raid across Pensacola Bay, Asboth demonstrated the truth of his earlier assessment. He wrote, "Several contrabands, who succeeded in reaching our lines, were added to the Fourteenth Regiment, Corps d'Afrique," the exotic name given to the first black troops raised in Louisiana, a regiment of which had accompanied Asboth to Pensacola. It was later redesignated the Eighty-Sixth US Colored Infantry, and many of its men returned victoriously to Alabama, assaulting Confederate works during the siege of Mobile and being among the first Union units to see the Stars and Stripes raised again over the state capitol in Montgomery. As early as June of 1863, one former slave who had reached Pensacola and freedom volunteered to return to southern Alabama and led an additional thirty-one bondsmen to the city, and Federal authorities forwarded many of these men to Louisiana, where they enlisted in black regiments being raised there.[139] One freedman traveling on his own had gone to great lengths to reach Pensacola. "One of them came in with a heavy iron bar on his leg, wandering with it three weeks through woods and swamps." The men were augmented by white Unionists, as Asboth recorded. "Deserters are constantly coming in, taking the oath of allegiance. Fifteen young men have enlisted in my cavalry company. One officer of the Confederacy, Lieutenant Howard, reported also voluntarily with valuable information and took the oath."[140]

By the end of the month, the growing tide of men arriving at Pensacola made Asboth "daily more convinced that not only one but several regiments could be raised in Western Florida, by offering to all those who are anxious to enlist into the Union army proper assistance to come within our lines." The captain of a contracted boat crossing the bay to East Pass brought in "25 able-bodied men—all his schooner could take. They enlisted at once, and, in addition to those, 33 more, who have found their way through the rebel pickets, at the risk of their lives; of those 18 have enlisted in Company M, Fourteenth New York Cavalry, and 40 in the Florida regiment." Asboth expected the next foray would bring in an additional two hundred recruits. In addition to providing refuge and employment, Asboth also sought to partially compensate them for their losses, asking for the payment of a bounty for any men who would enlist for three years. He argued, "Considering the general destitution of the people here, it would be an act of humanity, as well as good policy, to grant advance payment of bounty." Due to growing manpower shortages, the following year the Union army offered bounties of up to $300 for men who would enlist or reenlist from three-year regiments raised in 1861, which led to an unfortunate epidemic of "bounty jumping" in some locales, where men enlisted and deserted from multiple units in a short period of time, leading the army to withhold payment until the end of the contracted term of service.[141]

As the calendar turned to 1864, four Alabama regiments, three black and one white, of all arms—infantry, cavalry, and artillery—had added the state's name to the list of Federal forces active in suppressing the rebellion, while yet another black regiment was organizing in southern Tennessee and a second white regiment, also comprised largely of Alabamians, prepared to do the same under Florida's banner. Each man enlisted in these units represented a double loss for Confederate authorities attempting to maintain control within the state and continue to produce sufficient agricultural resources to sustain both the population and the rebellion, as they did not serve in Confederate units and did not produce a crop to feed those who did. The bloody raids and reprisals of a sustained guerrilla war made large swaths of north-central Alabama uninhabitable, and labor shortages in the Tennessee Valley made Confederate control untenable, while food shortages and famine also stalked the Wiregrass. Without sufficient resources to feed their horses and victual their men, Confederate raiders under Forrest and others had been pushed back from Federal lines and were unable to effectively oppose Union campaigns against Vicksburg and Chattanooga. Despite gallant but futile efforts, including an attack through North Alabama to Nashville in 1864, they remained unable to do so in the year that followed, leading to the fall of Atlanta and a path of destruction carved, in a small part, by both black and white Alabamians in these new organizations under Sherman's command, across Georgia to the sea.

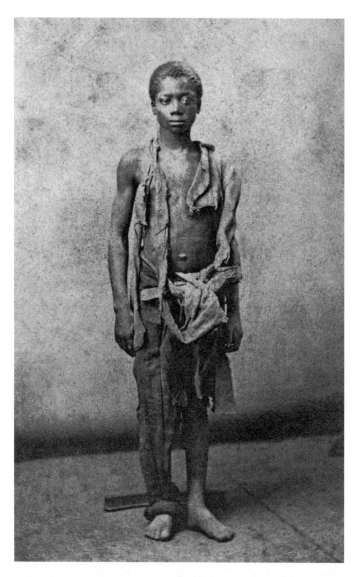

"Typical Slave Boy Surviving Civil War on Streets" (Armistead & White, Corinth, Miss., Library of Congress). This photograph demonstrates the condition of freedpeople arriving in Corinth during 1862 and 1863. He also represents Lt. Francis Tupper's servant Benjamin Franklin, who accompanied the First Alabama Cavalry on their campaigns.

Major General Grenville M. Dodge, Commander of the Sixteenth Army Corps, 1864 (Grenville M. Dodge Collection, State Historical Society of Iowa, Des Moines). Dodge has been called the "Father" of the Alabama regiments, having raised the First–Fourth Alabama Infantry, African Descent (55th, 110th, 111th, and 106th USCT) and the First Alabama Cavalry.

General Dodge's Staff (Howard & Hall, Corinth, Miss., Grenville M. Dodge Collection, State Historical Society of Iowa, Des Moines). Seated, from left to right, are Gen. Dodge, Maj. Stone, Lt. Col. Barnhill, Surgeon Marsh, and Capt. George Spencer. Standing, from left to right, are Capt. Barnes, Lt. Ozro Dodd, Capt. Carpenter, Capt. Wing, Lt. Hogan, Maj. Howard, Capt. Honeyhorn, Capt. Chenoworth, and Lt. Bailey. Spencer later served as the colonel of the First Alabama Cavalry, Dodd as the lieutenant colonel, Hogan as captain of Company G, and Bailey as first lieutenant of Company D. Spencer served as a senator from Alabama from 1868 through 1879.

"After Execution of Rebel Spy" (Armistead & White, Library of Congress). Pvt. Alex Johnson was a Confederate spy who joined the First Alabama Cavalry, deserted, and was later recaptured and executed at Corinth on July 23, 1863. The soldiers in the background are from the First Alabama Cavalry, and this is believed to be the only photograph of the regiment in the field.

Captain Phillip A. Sternberg of Co. B, First Alabama Cavalry Regiment (Howard & Hall, Corinth, Miss., Library of Congress). Sternberg is representative of the northern-born officers who helped recruit Unionist companies in the South and led them in combat. He was killed October 26, 1863, in the Battle of Vincent's Crossroads.

Vincent's CrossRoads.

Colonel James A. Alexander (Army Heritage and Education Center, Carlisle, PA). Col. Alexander commanded the First Alabama Infantry, African Descent (55th USCT) during its time in Corinth.

Railroad Bridge over the Elk River (Army Heritage and Education Center, Carlisle, PA). This bridge is typical of the type constructed on the Nashville and Decatur Railroad and guarded by soldiers of the 106th, 110th, and 111th USCT.

Johnsonville Camp of Tennessee Colored Battery (Library of Congress). Though not of an Alabama-raised unit, this photograph of the camp of Company A, Second U.S. Colored Light Artillery at Johnsonville, Tennessee, in 1864 is typical of USCT encampments and formed part of the depot area defended by USCT soldiers against Forrest's raiders on November 4–5, 1864.

CHAPTER 4

Defeating the Confederacy, 1864

T he period from January to December 1864 witnessed continued growth in the size and number of Alabama's Union forces, as two additional black regiments and one white regiment augmented the four regiments, three black and one white, raised in 1863. Although the evacuation of Corinth moved the initial refuge for freedmen and Unionists farther from the state's borders, and led indirectly to one of the war's most notorious massacres on the banks of the Mississippi, the Atlanta and Mobile campaigns, and the railroad lines that supported them, brought new and expanded posts and operations into Alabama. Supplementing the rail line from Nashville to Chattanooga, the reopened and repaired Alabama & Tennessee Railroad from Nashville to Decatur, continuing east to Chattanooga along the old Memphis & Charleston line, brought large numbers of Union forces back into Alabama's Tennessee Valley. It also created a new demand for military manpower to guard the railroad and its vulnerable bridges from Confederate raiders, resulting in the recruitment of the Third and Fourth Alabama Infantry, African Descent, which in late June were renumbered the 111th and 106th regiments, United States Colored Infantry, respectively.[1] A new base of operations, at Pulaski, Tennessee, under an old commander, now Maj. Gen. Grenville Dodge, provided employment opportunities for freedmen and Unionists escaping a collapsing agricultural system in the Tennessee Valley and in the hills farther south.

Extending the rail line from Chattanooga to Atlanta, in the rear of Sherman's victorious army, placed additional manpower levies on the Union ranks, resulting in the First Alabama Cavalry's relocation for most of the summer to Rome, Georgia, on the Western & Atlantic Railroad supplying Sherman's armies before Atlanta, but within easy recruiting range of many of eastern Alabama's Hill Country counties, swelling its ranks. The campaign for Atlanta, which this extensive infrastructure supported, eventually severed the state from the rest of the Confederacy, and Alabamians accompanied and, in the case of the First Alabama Cavalry, even led Sherman's famous "March to the Sea." An abortive Confederate attempt to recapture Nashville temporarily reclaimed the Tennessee River valley in the fall of 1864, but the decisive battle outside that city demonstrated the growing importance of African American troops, both in garrison and combat, and virtually destroyed the once-proud Confederate Army of Tennessee and left behind only Forrest's small cavalry force, which was inadequate for the defense of an entire state.[2] On the Gulf Coast, freedmen and Unionists operating from their Pensacola base expanded their operations inland, in conjunction with the campaign to seize Mobile and close the fine harbor there to commerce and blockade running. Again, Alabamians with knowledge of the local physical and cultural terrain provided key intelligence that facilitated the success of Union arms, while at the same time the army provided subsistence for those who could no longer survive on the land. By the end of the year, Alabama stood isolated from the rest of the Confederacy and loyal Alabamians, black and white, had played an important role across the state in the defeat of Confederate arms and the destruction of the resources that sustained them.

The Chattanooga campaign in late 1863 had shifted Union priorities in the western theater away from the Mississippi River valley and toward the increasingly vulnerable rail lines knitting together the eastern and western halves of the Confederacy. As Sherman and Grant moved their battle-hardened veterans from camps around Vicksburg into Chattanooga, in preparation for a drive southeast toward Atlanta, the once-vital rail hub of Corinth lost much of its justification for a massive Union base. After Sherman personally led a massive *chevauchee* from Vicksburg toward Meridian in February 1864, wrecking a major depot on the Mobile & Ohio, including track for thirty miles in both directions, Corinth stood isolated and unimportant alongside a growing manpower demand that threatened to undermine Union war aims for 1864. Exacerbating the crisis was the expiration of many veteran soldiers' three-year terms of enlistment. Those who had rushed to the colors after Fort Sumter were reaching the end of their time, and the War Department offered the inducement of a thirty-day furlough to any veterans who would reenlist for the duration. While many veteran units did largely reenlist, the furloughs placed additional demands on Union troop strength just as the important campaigns for 1864 got underway, including Grant's Overland campaign in Virginia, Sherman's Atlanta campaign, and Nathaniel P. Banks's Red River campaign. Accordingly, Federal commanders sought to economize on troop strength by abandoning superfluous posts and concentrating their forces only at decisive points.

Unfortunately, this perfectly sound military decision had dire consequences for the residents of the Corinth contraband and refugee camps. Throughout the summer of 1863, they had planted and harvested crops, sold their produce and their labor to the army, built more permanent quarters, and supported increasing military levees upon their able-bodied males. A Federal evacuation of Corinth would leave these hard-won gains subject to Confederate authorities, who would undoubtedly move into the vacuum and attempt to reinstall a society less conducive to the prosperity of freedmen and Unionists. Accordingly, most elected to abandon their hard-won gains and follow the army back to Memphis, which provided greater opportunities for employment and better security, as traffic along the Mississippi was still vital to the war effort. Fortunately, the movement came at the depth of the growing season, meaning no crops had to be abandoned in the fields, but Memphis had less land available for agricultural pursuits in the immediate vicinity of the military posts, and more refugees competing for relief. Despite the promising start, the residents of the Corinth contraband camp would never again enjoy the same level of prosperity they had in the summer of 1863.

The First Alabama Infantry, African Descent (later redesignated the Fifty-Fifth USCI), recruited in the camp, was still in excellent condition. On January 16, 1864, Col. James Alexander reported, "We have mastered every part of company and Bat.[tallion] drill," and bragged that "ours is the best regt. here, white or black." On January 1, the regiment reported a strength of 952 men, and remained healthy, with only four in the hospital, and not one fatality due to disease during the month of December. Discipline remained strong as well, with "not one man in the guard house or on arrest. Not a single officer or enlisted man has any charges against him." All thirty-nine commissioned officers were present for duty, and thirty-four of them were teetotalers, a fact which impressed the former chaplain. He also claimed, "Not a card is played in the Reg. neither is betting or gambling allowed by any one." The simple threat of confinement with a 120-pound ball and chain was sufficient to ensure good discipline, and the men were apparently "in the best of spirits and in good condition in every way. None desert." Alexander was particularly anxious to be under Dodge's command again, even offering the prize of a portrait of the general for the headquarters of the best-drilled and best-disciplined companies.[3]

For most of the families of the soldiers of the Alabama units, the move to Memphis went by rail and in conjunction with the military units their male family members served in. On January 12, Brig. Gen. John D. Stevenson, now commanding the District of Corinth, reported the evacuation was proceeding apace, even as Confederate raiders launched new forays into western Tennessee in an attempt to disrupt Union operations. Stevenson promised his commander, Maj. Gen. Stephen Hurlbut at Memphis, that he would "not be embarrassed by Colonel Mizner and command encumbering the road with trains of old shanties torn to pieces," but was concerned for the welfare of "at least 600 wives and children of federal soldiers that require to be cared for, and also about the same number or more contrabands." In order to provide security for the families and stores evacuated from Corinth, Stevenson had to call in his cavalry from the surrounding countryside, including the First Alabama. By January 23, Stevenson had dispatched one "immense train of refugees" to Memphis and had another ready to depart, and was busily destroying the works in and around Corinth.[4]

Lt. Francis Tupper of Company B reported that the three hundred mounted men of the First Alabama formed the rear guard of the column, and that the last he saw of Camp Davies, the regiment's former home, "the barracks and stable were in flames and burning handsomely." Corinth suffered the same fate, with the fortifications destroyed and "a good share of it was burned and I expect before the rear guard leaves it there won't be a building left that a rebel could find shelter in."[5] Tupper reported that his men performed the task of burning the city, "such were their orders, but it was a great pity, for it had been a home to them for a year and a half, but the order to burn it only made them laugh."[6] While the unit only set fire to government buildings, strong winds quickly spread the flames to nearby hotels and homes, virtually leveling the town.

During the evacuation, John R. Phillips, despite being one of many men in the regiment afflicted with an outbreak of measles, remembered an incident between the First Alabama Cavalry and "a regiment of negroes camped about a mile from our camp." According to Phillips, "Some of the boys who did not like the negroes any too well, for some cause got to shooting into their camp, and it almost terminated in a serious battle." Despite hailing from the same state and being engaged in the same cause, racial animosities still ran deep and were too difficult for some Southerners to put aside.[7]

Already General Dodge, then working on repairing the rail line at Pulaski, Tennessee, was asking for the return of the regiment he had raised and equipped. On January 12, he apprised Sherman of what intelligence he had gained about Confederate forces in the Tennessee Valley and suggested, "If we could make a lodgment at Decatur it would give an outlet to a large number of Union people who are seeking our lines and who would join our Alabama regiments, and if Colonel Spencer's First Alabama Cavalry could be ordered to me, it would form the nucleus that would soon give us another mounted regiment." On the 29th he reiterated, "The rebel conscription is driving to our lines a large number of union men, who furnish substitutes, and men who have always stood by us and kept out of the rebel army by taking to the mountains." To meet their immediate needs, Dodge levied assessments on wealthy secessionists in Giles County "for the support of Union refugees coming within the lines of this command."[8] Dodge initially received authority to recruit the Second Alabama Cavalry, and appointed postwar Reconstruction-era Governor William H. Smith to lead the recruiting effort, perhaps the genesis of his later title of "Colonel."[9] But the title remained honorific, as Smith proved unable to fill a second regiment with white Unionists before the department rescinded that permission a month later, though it did authorize Dodge to continue recruiting and muster them as infantry.[10] Most of these men filled vacancies in Northern regiments, and it took until April for the First Alabama Cavalry to reach Dodge's new post at Pulaski.

Dodge also began filling his three new black regiments with contrabands escaping bondage in war-torn northern Alabama and southern Tennessee. As early as November 1863, Dodge ordered "the negroes now employed with the Pioneer Corps of the 2nd Division, 16th Army Corps, will be mustered into service as Cos. A, B, & C, 2nd Ala. Inf'y Vols., A. D. and the officers of the Corps are hereby authorized to recruit persons of African Descent to fill the three companies to the maximum."[11] In early January, Lieutenant Nelson of the Third Alabama, A. D., marched his men to the Sulphur Branch trestle, then under construction, where they mustered in as Company B, before moving a few miles north to Mill Creek.[12] Dodge had continued recruiting and received complaints from planters around Pulaski that his recruiters were forcing freedmen into Federal service. On January 22, a "Mr. Neeley," then residing five miles from Columbia, Tennessee, on the Pulaski Pike, arrived at Dodge's headquarters complaining that a recruiting party under Sergeant Major Henry "by force took the last negro upon Mr. Neeley's place for the purpose of making him a soldier." Dodge's adjutant allegedly told the man that he could not see Dodge to discuss the matter and that "nothing would be done."[13] Dodge's actions apparently met with the War Department's approval, as Gen. Lorenzo Thomas wrote that he was "gratified to hear of your success in recruiting this class of troops."[14]

In late January, Dodge received word from Grant that he was very concerned about the security of the Union supply lines in Tennessee for the upcoming Atlanta campaign, and had organized a series of efforts to keep any potential raiders occupied. In addition to Sherman's raid from Vicksburg toward Meridian, Brig. Gen. William Sooy Smith was to leave Memphis on January 25 for Okolona, and Maj. Gen. John L. Logan was to cross the Tennessee River upstream of Dodge at Larkin's Ferry and march toward Rome, Georgia. Grant hoped that Dodge could "collect and organize at once, under a competent officer, all the mounted men possible of your command," to "hunt down and drive the enemy's cavalry now threatening our rail-roads in Middle Tennessee." He related, "From all these expeditions and threatening movements it is hoped much will be accomplished and especially in forcing the enemy back from within striking distance of our communications."[15] These operations dominated Union strategy in the Tennessee River valley for most of the 1864 campaign season, and Dodge's units of Alabamians played an important role.

Dodge had already sent eight full regiments of veterans and three artillery batteries home for their thirty-day furloughs, with seven more ready to depart, and was becoming very concerned about the security of the railroad, which had been completely repaired except for the Duck River bridge at Columbia. He worried that his "weak force will be discovered," with the result that "our heavy works on the railroad would be left exposed, unguarded and no doubt would be destroyed," and accelerated recruiting for his new USCT regiments to fill the void. By late March, Dodge ordered the Third and Fourth Alabama, A.D., forward to Athens, despite the fact that they were "just organizing" and "not armed."[16] By midsummer, soldiers held the fort in Athens while their families lived in a nearby contraband camp, but short rations meant "over 2,000 old men, women and children . . . desired a little aid 'till their crops, of which 2,000 acres were under cultivation, would come in."[17]

Officers also struggled to indoctrinate their new troops into the requirements of military service. Records from courts-martial during the period find soldiers convicted of crimes ranging from falling asleep on guard duty to conspiring with cotton thieves to steal cotton. Punishments ranged from confinement at hard labor in a military prison, to carrying a twenty-five pound sack across the parade ground for eight hours a day, to suspended sentences of being marched in front of their companies with their hands tied behind their backs. In suspending the latter sentence, the convening authority instructed:

> Officers of Colored troops are reminded that they are appointed to command an unfortunate, untutored and ignorant class of men, who have neither enjoyed the benefits of education, liberty of thought or action; they have had others do their thinking for them, whose constant study was to keep them in absolute ignorance and abject servitude. These negroes have been taught nothing but obedience and all that is needed to make them good and dutiful soldiers is rigid (not cruel and capricious) discipline, and proper instruction.[18]

Officers were reminded to read the Articles of War and appropriate regulations and explain them to their charges frequently.

As part of their obligations to their soldiers, USCT officers also looked after their families. Lieutenant Nelson of the 111th USCI reported that a "colored Sergeant from Decatur, Alabama, I think, came into camp one day with a letter from his Colonel to Colonel Lathrop asking him to send an escort 15 or 20 miles into the country for his family," and Nelson and twelve men set out to "bring in the Sergeant's wife and children and their bedding," which Nelson and his small command did. Along the way, they also captured a distiller illegally turning much-needed fodder into moonshine who turned out to be "a deserter from the Union Army." Nelson and others from the 111th frequently suffered harassment from guerrillas, but Nelson believed it was "chiefly to get the rations and blankets."[19]

By mid-April, Dodge's policy toward freedmen had shifted as a result of the overcrowded conditions in the contraband camps. On May 1, First Lt. J. W. Harris, superintendent of contrabands in Dodge's command, reported that there were 2,590 residents in the seven contraband camps in the area (situated as shown in Table 2), an increase of 1,327 over the previous month, despite forty deaths.

TABLE 2. Contraband Camps in the Tennessee Valley, April–May, 1864

County, State	Plantation	Number, May 1	Number, June 1
Giles, Tennessee (Pulaski)	Brown's	1,253	1,210
	Phillips's	697	896 (remainder of
	Reynolds's	205	Giles County
	Rivers's	80	combined)
	Alex Carter's	7	
	Thomas Jones's	5	
Limestone, AL (Athens)	Hobbs's	303	379

Harris was busily constructing quarters for his tenants, completing fifty houses during April, but most were still housed in "rail pens and sheds." There were 1,000 acres of cotton under cultivation, 200 acres of corn, and "three large gardens," but Harris had drawn and issued 35,778 rations during April, despite running the grist mill on the Brown plantation constantly. Freedmen on that place cut 22,400 board-feet of lumber, most for the Army's use, but pastured 100 "condemned" animals that might be either nursed back to health or slaughtered for food. The influx had depleted the account in the Post treasury from over $8,000 to barely $5,000, funds initially generated by freedmen picking, ginning, and baling the cotton on the Phillips and Reynolds plantations, and from a 10 percent tax on the woodcutter's wages.[20] In addition to establishing a new camp at Nashville, which would ease the logistical difficulty of shipping rations forward at the same time the army was attempting to build up supplies for Sherman's Atlanta campaign, Dodge also ordered a subordinate to "send in no more negro women and children than he can help, but encourage them to stay on the plantations; but to send us all the able-bodied men he can."[21] The measures were apparently effective, as Harris reported little increase in his numbers during the month of May, though he suffered another thirty deaths among his charges.[22]

In Memphis, the First Alabama Infantry, First Alabama Heavy Artillery, A. D., and the First Alabama Cavalry settled into garrison duty in their new home. At the time, the First Alabama Infantry, A. D., was brigaded with three other USCT regiments under their original commander, Col. James Alexander. Col. Robert Cowden, commanding a sister regiment, the First West Tennessee Infantry, A. D., raised largely at La Grange, Tennessee, vividly described the troops' arrival in Memphis:

> As it marched with steady step to the music of its own martial band through the streets of that once proud but now humbled city, the inhabitants thereof saw as they peered from the windows of their homes or stores, what they had never before seen and never expected to see— their own former slaves powerfully and lawfully armed for their overthrow, and led and commanded by those whom they considered their invaders. The sight must have burned into their very souls.[23]

Memphis remained an important commercial center and supported a thriving trade in confiscated cotton moving up and down the river, while disloyal citizens smuggled contraband goods to Confederate sympathizers in the surrounding countryside. Major General Hurlbut, commanding the city's garrison, attempted to maintain law and order within the city while at the same time protecting it against attacks from Confederate cavalry that roamed the countryside. Sherman demanded that Hurlbut cooperate with him against Forrest's forces and bases deep in the interior of Mississippi, resulting in several unsuccessful operations that failed to destroy the Confederate forces but did keep them away from Sherman's critical supply line through Tennessee to Chattanooga and eventually Atlanta. By garrisoning Memphis's defenses, and its outposts, most notably Fort Pickering, built atop the ruins of the French colonial Fort Assumption, the men of the future Fifty-Fifth USCI and Sixth USCHA freed up more of the Union army's manpower for field operations. By January 25, 1864, black troops comprised five of the Memphis garrison's eight regiments of Infantry, most of its artillery, and Southern whites made up both of the city's cavalry regiments, meaning that Memphis could be held at this point in the war largely by Anti-Confederate Southerners.[24]

The first foray against Confederate raiders in the interior of Mississippi, the failed attempt to cooperate with Sherman's raid on Meridian under Brigadier General Smith, is traditionally viewed as another of Forrest's "victories" at the Battle of Okolona on February 22. While Forrest did force Smith back to Memphis, he utterly failed to protect Meridian, which Sherman's troops leveled during a week-long occupation during February 14–20. In this time, Sherman's forces destroyed over one hundred miles of railroad, including over sixty bridges and all the rolling stock. The damage at Meridian prevented its use by large military forces for the rest of the war. Had Smith been able to join Sherman at Meridian, Sherman had hopes of sending him down the Mobile & Ohio Railroad to Mobile, but instead Sherman returned to Vicksburg as Smith retreated to Memphis. Thus, while Forrest had indeed repelled a cavalry raid through north Mississippi, he had also failed to prevent the Federals from achieving their objective of making central Mississippi largely untenable for large forces, removing any potential threat to Vicksburg and enabling forces from that garrison to participate in the Red River, Mobile, and Atlanta campaigns. Smith's men had been ordered out with only "small rations," consisting of coffee, tea, sugar, and salt. Tupper wrote, "The rest they will forage. I pity the country they pass through."[25]

The First Alabama Cavalry screened Smith's advance through Hernando and Germantown as far as the Coldwater River, but the poor condition of their mounts caused them to be left behind there. While on an earlier scout to Hernando, a party of the First Alabama learned of a dance being held at one of the local homes "in a wealthy neighborhood," and captured a number of Confederate officers who were there as guests. Lieutenant Tupper wrote, "Here were the elite of that part of the country, that is the kind we look after . . . twenty or twenty-five very handsome young ladies in evening party dress and some half-dozen men, several of whom were in Confederate uniform."[26] Upon learning that some of the folks back home presumed that he had taken a position in a "negro regiment," Tupper wrote that they were "grandly mistaken," but that the "1st Alabama Infantry from Corinth is a Negro Regiment and hearing of that regiment may have caused the mistake." Tupper asserted, "Our men are all southern men, 'whites,' they have little or no education, as there are no schools in this country that a poor man can send his children to. Every large town has its seminary or Private school but they are patronized by the wealthy cotton raisers and nigger traders. The majority of the officers of the Regt. are Northern men."[27]

March brought a quieter month but left the men restless. Tupper reported that his company had spent most of the month guarding woodcutters, which was "very dry business," and that "the boys don't like it either, as they have been out for eight miles and they can't find anything to eat to steal, and that is a bad fix for them to be in."[28] Rebels attacked Company H while across the river in Arkansas, guarding a working party that was taking up track on the Memphis & Little Rock Railroad for use elsewhere, resulting in the loss of twenty men.[29] This and the earlier operations in central Mississippi had further worn down the unit's horses, and on March 24, when finally ordered to join Dodge at Pulaski, the regiment's stock was in such poor condition that they had to travel by steamer up the Mississippi, Ohio, and Cumberland Rivers before moving by rail from Nashville to Decatur.[30]

Eager to strike back at his oppressors, and unable to be adequately supplied in Mississippi, Forrest planned a large raid into western Tennessee in late March, carrying him as far north as the banks of the Ohio at Paducah, Kentucky. Short of manpower, Hurlbut could do little other that strengthen his breastworks and send the few mobile forces he had—largely, loyal Tennessee regiments—to shadow the Confederate cavalry. Upon crossing into western Kentucky, the raiders entered into the District of Cairo, under the command of Brig. Gen. Mason Brayman, who had also seen his command stripped of excess forces to support the buildup in Chattanooga. In addition to his main post at Cairo and the naval base at Mound City, which supported most of the navy's inland fleet, he held the river ports of Paducah and Columbus, Kentucky, and an isolated garrison in the interior at Union City, Tennessee. Forrest reached Jackson, Tennessee, on March 23 and moved quickly to Union City, just below the Kentucky line, a rail junction garrisoned by Colonel Hawkins and the Union Seventh Tennessee Cavalry. The next day 1,500 of Forrest's troopers compelled Hawkins's 500 "Homegrown Yankees" to surrender, though Hawkins likely could have held out behind his well-prepared defenses until a relief column under Brayman arrived from Columbus. But Hawkins succumbed to Forrest's threats to show no quarter if the garrison resisted, and he and his men went into captivity.[31]

Forrest attempted to duplicate this success at Paducah on March 25 but found a more resolute commander, Col. Stephen Hicks, who led a mixed garrison comprised mainly of the Sixteenth Kentucky Cavalry and a regiment of black artillerymen known as the First Kentucky (later Eighth US Colored) Heavy Artillery, and three companies of the 122nd Illinois, who were the only men who had ever been under fire. Hicks evacuated the city into a strong fort and, supported by two gunboats in the river, held off several charges, inflicting heavy casualties in Forrest's command, with only minor losses. During a lull, Forrest again attempted to bluff the garrison into surrender, ominously threatening not to show any quarter if his demands were not accepted. Hicks wisely refused and continued to inflict heavy casualties on the attackers. After the battle, he wrote, "I have been one of those men who never had much confidence in colored troops fighting, but those doubts are now all removed, for they fought as bravely as any troops in the fort."[32] This was the first time Forrest and his men had met black troops on the battlefield and felt keenly their severe losses from a "mongrel" garrison of black and white Kentuckians. Before returning to Tennessee they attempted a similar bluff on the Federal garrison at Columbus, Kentucky, where Brig. Gen. Abraham Buford threatened, "Should you surrender, the negroes now in arms will be returned to their masters. Should I, however, be compelled to take the place, no quarter will be shown to the negro troops whatever; and the white troops will be treated as prisoners of war."[33] Here too, they were unsuccessful, and retreated south into Tennessee, seeking a weaker post, which they eventually found at Fort Pillow.

By now, Forrest's true intentions for his operations became clear. His efforts had not disrupted the buildup of men and supplies for Sherman's campaign, but they had helped to ameliorate his own supply condition. Shortly before attacking Fort Pillow, he wrote, "they have horses and supplies which we need."[34] While it is possible that his men needed these horses and supplies to continue operations in support of the war, it is just as likely that they needed them in order to supply their own immediate wants and needs for survival. Throughout 1864, Forrest's command became less about disrupting the Union war effort and more about picking off isolated garrisons from which he could resupply and sustain his own command, lending credence to the charge Bragg had leveled against Forrest the previous fall that "he is nothing more than a good raider."[35]

Built by Confederate forces in 1861 thirty-five miles upriver from Memphis, Fort Pillow stood on a high bluff at a commanding turn on the river, where the channel forced boat traffic close under its guns. Concerned that marauding bands of rebels could occupy the position and use it to attack Union shipping on the river, Hurlbut had garrisoned it with roughly three hundred men of the Thirteenth (later renumbered the Fourteenth) Tennessee Cavalry, a new regiment recruiting in the area from loyal west Tennesseans but only partially trained, and unequipped and not yet mustered. Concerned for the post's security after the attack on Union City, on March 28 Hurlbut ordered Maj. Lionel Booth of the Sixth US Colored (formerly First Alabama) Heavy Artillery to reinforce the post with two hundred of his own men and another forty men and two twelve-pound howitzers from the Second US Colored (formerly First West Tennessee) Light Artillery, a unit recruited in Memphis in 1863. In his orders, Hurlbut fatefully told Booth that he didn't think Forrest would try the river again, and that he would recall the men to Memphis when the threat had passed. Given the strong position on a high bluff over the river and protected in the rear by steep ravines, Booth reported of the post on April 3, "I think it perfectly safe."[36]

On April 12, two of Forrest's brigades under the command of Brig. Gen. James Chalmers emerged from the trees and drove Booth's pickets back toward the fort. The fort's defenders rushed to their arms and met the rebel attack with rifle and cannon fire, repelling repeated charges throughout the morning. At one point, Booth fell with a shot through the heart, which killed him instantly, and Maj. William F. Bradford of the Thirteenth Tennessee Cavalry assumed command of the post. After several attempts to take the fort by storm, Confederates sent forward a truce flag, again demanding surrender and threatening to show no quarter if refused. Ominously, during the cease-fire, Union forces witnessed rebel troops moving into positions close to the fort, in clear violation of the truce, thereby gaining positions which had been denied to them by brisk fire from the fort's defenders all morning. After Bradford, in Booth's name, refused to surrender, firing resumed and, in short order, Forrest's men used their newly won positions to storm the fort. At this point began what can only be described as a massacre, as the enraged rebels began shooting down the Federal forces, white and black alike, as they either ran from the fort toward gunboats in the river or after raising their hands in surrender.

Though later Confederate apologists and Forrest defenders attempted to hide the evidence, inquiries from a congressional investigation completed in the weeks afterward, to the most recent scholarship on the event, clearly prove that Forrest's men murdered over half the fort's garrison after it fell to the assault. While the attackers slaughtered more black Union soldiers than white, contemporary accounts suggest that it was the combination of Tennessee "Tories" who had both suffered from as well as committed retaliatory outrages on their neighbors, combined with the presence of black men in arms, that provoked the massacre. Forced by his inferior numbers to resort to bluffs to induce garrisons to surrender, Forrest also likely hoped to put some force behind his threats, in hopes of securing easier victories in the future. Though there is little evidence that he directly ordered the massacre, he also did little to prevent it, as the killing continued well after he arrived on the field, even into the night and the following morning. He must at least be held culpable for failing to restrain his men. He may also be guilty of indirectly ordering his troops not to take prisoners, black or white. A month before Fort Pillow, he had told his men, "Now boys, War means fight and fight means kill. What's the use of taking prisoners to eat up your rations?"[37] As Dudley Cornish observed, "It has been asserted again and again that Forrest did not order a massacre. He did not need to."[38]

Evidence of more sinister intentions came from his principal subordinate in the massacre. General Chalmers later reported that they had "taught the mongrel garrison of blacks and renegades a lesson long to be remembered." One eyewitness reported that "the rebels were very bitter against these loyal Tennesseans, terming them 'home-made Yankees,' and declaring they would give them no better treatment then they dealt out to the negro troops with whom they were fighting." Another recalled a Confederate saying, "You fight with the niggers and we will kill every last one of you." Even Forrest himself referred to Fort Pillow's garrison as "a motley herd of negroes, traitors and Yankees" in a congratulatory message to his troops. It is clear that, while Fort Pillow was primarily a massacre of black troops, the combination of black soldiers and Southern Unionists, the two groups Confederates hated most, played a significant role in spurring the atrocities. Slave insurrections had traditionally been punished by summary execution, and whites "inciting" slaves to rebel suffered equally serious sentences. Confederate soldiers viewed white officers in the black regiments as guilty of inciting insurrection, and especially loathed white Southerners, such as the soldiers of the Thirteenth Tennessee, for turning their backs on accepted social mores by fighting alongside the freedmen, thereby aiding the "insurrection." This coalition threatened to undermine Southern society and everything the Confederacy, and the elites who had spawned it, were fighting for, and thus it often met with the severest consequences possible.[39]

In addition to allowing the massacre to stain his reputation, Forrest also failed to divert or delay in any meaningful way the reinforcements destined for Sherman's army in Chattanooga. Though Brayman did briefly detain one division (Veatch's) for the abortive relief of Union City, it was back on its boats and en route after only a few days. Further, Forrest's efforts in western Tennessee, while fulfilling his goal of obtaining supplies from both the countryside and the garrisons at Union City and Fort Pillow, failed to disrupt Sherman's supply line through Middle Tennessee, which proved critical to the sustained combat of the Atlanta campaign from the beginning of May until the city fell in September. Indeed, Grant wrote of Forrest's operations along the Mississippi, "I hope Forrest will prolong his visit in that neighborhood."[40]

In Memphis, when Hurlbut learned that the fort was under attack, he immediately ordered the First Alabama, A. D., now the Fifty-Fifth USCI, to board steamboats and rush to relieve their beleaguered comrades in arms, many of whom had been recruited together from the contraband camp at Corinth. But before they could depart, further news arrived that the fort had fallen, and the men returned to their camps.[41] As news of the massacre trickled in, first from those who had visited the post after the battle and later from survivors returning to their commands from hospitals who had witnessed the atrocities firsthand, the black troops in Memphis seethed with a desire for revenge. According to Hurlbut, "I know very well that my colored regiments at Memphis, officers and men, will never give quarter (and) I have some very good colored regiments." They got their chance the following month in yet another expedition into Mississippi against Forrest at the resulting engagement at Brice's Cross Roads.[42]

Mindful of Forrest's efforts in Kentucky and western Tennessee in April, and what his troops could do if applied against Sherman's vulnerable supply line winding south from Louisville through Nashville and Chattanooga to the hills of north Georgia, Union officials sent another expedition from Memphis under Gen. Samuel Sturgis against the rebel raider's base in east-central Mississippi. Over 10,000 blue-coated cavalry troopers, infantrymen, and artillerists, including the Fifty-Fifth and Fifty-Ninth US Colored Infantry, left the city on June 1, the same day Forrest left Tupelo "for the purpose of destroying the railroad from Nashville and breaking up the lines of communications connecting that point with Sherman's army in Northern Georgia." Sturgis's expedition achieved its desired effect almost before it entered Mississippi, as, on June 3, Gen. S. D. Lee ordered Forrest to abandon his raid in order to meet the column moving from Memphis.[43] Confederate resources and assets in Tupelo paled in comparison to the importance of Sherman's campaign, but the

Confederate high command sacrificed an opportunity to inflict a strategic set-back in order to gain a tactical victory. Even that looked unlikely, as Sturgis's column outnumbered Forrest's men 3–1, resulting in Lee ordering reinforce-ments from Roddey's command in northern Alabama to unite with Forrest. Abandoning the northern portion of Alabama had a strategic effect as well, as it left the northern half of the state exposed to a devastating raid by a Union Kentuckian, Lovell Rousseau, which interrupted Johnston's communications into Atlanta at a critical time during the campaign.

Unlike Rousseau's hard-charging cavalrymen, Sturgis's force consisted pri-marily of infantry and was encumbered by a train of almost 250 wagons, as the area of northern Mississippi to be traversed had been raided and fought over for years until it came to resemble a desolate no-man's-land. Several sub-ordinate commanders commented on the difficult conditions. Col. Alexander Wilkin wrote, "Upon reaching Ripley the animals were much worn out for want of forage and the men were on less than half rations."[44] Col. William McMillen observed, "The line of march was through a country devastated by the war, and containing little or no forage, rendering it extremely difficult, and for the greater portion of the time impossible to maintain the animals in a serviceable condition."[45]

Having forced the Federals to bring their own forage in a lengthy supply train, nature doubled its impact by dropping heavy rains for the entire dura-tion of the march from Memphis to the intended point of intercept on the Mobile & Ohio Railroad at Guntown, turning the poor roads into quagmires and sapping the strength of men and horses struggling through the muck, with temperatures that ranged well into the 90s between showers. Altogether, it became a hellish advance and had as much to do with Sturgis's defeat as For-rest's impetuous cavalrymen. Sturgis complained that the rain had slowed his advance to a "snail's pace," allowing Forrest to concentrate his dispersed forces against him. Wilkin echoed his commander, saying, "Owing to the rain, bad condition of the roads, and the almost entire absence of forage for the animals caused our advance to be necessarily slow," and that "the weather being very warm, many men were obliged to fall out and all came into action more or less fatigued and distressed." McMillen reiterated, "The roads were narrow, lead-ing through dense forests and over streams rendered almost impassable by the heavy rains which fell daily."[46]

These difficulties fell especially hard on the two black regiments. Hurlbut's replacement in Memphis, Maj. Gen. Cadwallader Washburn, ordered Sturgis to "see that they have their proper position in march and take the advance in marching when it is their turn to do so," but Sturgis ignored the order, and the black units remained at the rear of the column, escorting the wagon trains for most of the advance.[47] According to the Fifty-Ninth's commander, Robert Cowden, "Progress was slow and difficult, owing to daily rains, swelled streams, and a stiff clay which the large train soon worked into an almost impassable slough. Thus the tiresome march continued daily."[48] Worse, the men were not even permitted to draw water from civilian resources, in a precursor to the segregated drinking fountains of the Jim Crow era. Col. Edward Bouton, commanding the brigade containing the two black regiments, testified, "Guards were placed at houses and prevented my colored soldiers from going in to get water from the wells and cisterns, from the time we left La Fayette Station until we arrived at Stubbs,' except it may be at a few poor peoples' places," demonstrating further how the color line blurred below class barriers.[49] Finally, on the day of the battle, the colored regiments had to "double-time" (run) from their position at the rear of the column to reach the fighting at the front. Colonel Bouton reported later that, as he rushed his men to the battlefield, "many of them double-quicked two or three miles," in thick wool uniforms, carrying heavy equipment, in the hottest part of a June afternoon in Mississippi.

In spite of these difficulties, the troops fought well, earning unanimous praise in preventing the retreat from becoming a rout. Arriving at Brice's Cross Roads after Forrest had defeated Sturgis's cavalry and infantry in detail, the Fifty-Fifth formed a line behind Tishomingo Creek, where McMillen ordered Maj. Edgar Lowe, commanding the regiment, to "hold this position until the troops then engaged should retire, when he could then bring up the rear."[50] Though immediately pressed, they held the line long enough for a second line to form in their rear along a ridge featuring a prominent white house. Falling back to the second line, with the Fifty-Ninth USCI and the guns of the Second US Colored Light Artillery, the black troops again bought time for the fleeing Union forces, until again flanked and forced to fall back. This they did at five separate positions, often double-timing until "many of the men were nearly exhausted," permitting the army to withdraw in good order from the field, but suffering heavy casualties for their efforts.[51]

Pvt. George Jenkins of the Fifty-Fifth recalled, years later, "I would turn &

shoot & then retreat. We were crossing a little opening in a kind of old field 200 or 300 yds from some woods, when as I turned a bullet struck me in the right hip and passed clean through & went into the left thigh. I fell like a dead man & fainted away."[52] Both Major Lowe and Colonel Cowden fell with serious wounds, but their men bore them from the battlefield. At one point, the Fifty-Ninth rallied and charged into the attacking Confederates, using their muskets as clubs to hide the fact that they were running low on ammunition. All night, the men struggled back through the bottoms of the Tallahatchie River, a distance of over twenty miles. Here many of the wagons and most of the artillery pieces had to be abandoned and destroyed, as the roads were in too bad of a condition to permit a second passing. Shortly after reaching Ripley, Forrest's mounted men again attacked the column, after resting after the battle and then riding, rather than walking, to Ripley. Again, Bouton formed his men to receive the attack, after the Union cavalry passed through his lines, and again the freedmen fought well until pushed from the field. Here disaster struck, as Confederate troops cut off the primary escape route, forcing the units to move cross-country. Except for one group of three hundred men, formations began to disintegrate, as weakened men exhausted from their exertions fell behind or darted into the underbrush to escape mounted cavalrymen. In two days, the beaten troops completed a retrograde march that had taken ten days on the outbound leg, and men continued to return to the lines for the rest of the month.[53]

Union commanders unanimously gave the brigade of USCT regiments credit for fighting well and protecting the army. Washburn pronounced, "The colored troops made for themselves on this occasion a brilliant record. Their gallant and soldierly bearing, and the zeal and persistence with which they fought, elicited the warmest encomiums from all officers of the command. Their claims to be considered as among the very best soldiers of our army can no longer, in my opinion, be seriously questioned."[54] Sturgis reported that, upon seeing that his command had been forced to fall back, he sent his aide to "place in position in a wood the first regiment of colored troops I could find. This was done, and it is well due to those troops to say here that they stood their ground well and rendered valuable aid."[55] McMillen, commanding the infantry on the ground, observed, "The colored regiment fought with a gallantry which commended them to the favor of their comrades in arms. I desire to bear testimony to their bravery and endurance . . . this checked the pursuit."[56] Wilkins reported, "At one time our rear was charged upon by about 150 of Buford's cavalry but they were repulsed by the negro troops . . . the imperturbable coolness and steadiness of the colored troops . . . kept them in check."[57] Sturgis's final report asserted, "The colored troops deserve great credit for the manner in which they stood to their work."[58]

But in postbattle correspondence, ostensibly over the exchange of prisoners, Washburn and Forrest broached another aspect of the Fifty-Fifth and Fifty-Ninth's fighting that escaped notice in the official reports. Just four days after the battle, Forrest wrote Washburn, "The recent battle of Tishomingo Creek was far more bloody than it would otherwise have been but for the fact that your men evidently expected to be slaughtered when captured, and both sides acted as though neither felt safe in surrendering, even when further resistance was useless."[59] Forrest claimed that this was because "it has been reported to me that all the negro troops stationed in Memphis took an oath on their knees, in the presence of Major General Hurlbut and other officers of your army to avenge Fort Pillow." Confederate troops claimed to have heard Union officers shouting, "Remember Fort Pillow" during the battle, and several black soldiers were found with those words written on paper pinned to their uniforms. Forrest facetiously, and falsely, claimed that, "in all my operations since the war began, I have conducted the war on civilized principles," but he now felt unnerved and wanted to know if his men could expect to be treated as prisoners of war or if they would be put to death on the battlefield by their former servants, one of the deepest fears of the antebellum period and one that could undoubtedly affect morale in Forrest's command.

Washburn correctly replied to Forrest's superior, Gen. S. D. Lee, that he had not issued any explicit instructions to his black troops regarding reprisals against Confederate prisoners, but noted, "If it is intended to raise the black flag against that unfortunate race, they will cheerfully accept." He alleged that the atrocities committed at Fort Pillow had been repeated at Brice's Cross Roads and that, absent any disavowal by the Confederate government, he would assume that the "laudations of the entire southern press of the perpetrators of the massacre," represented official Confederate policy, and the Union general sought clarification in order to respond accordingly. Confederate policy already stood in violation of the laws governing warfare because enemy combatants could be confined, as they were in squalid prisons across the south, but not forced to labor, as captured black soldiers were when returned to their former masters or sold again as slaves.

In a separate correspondence addressed directly to Forrest, Washburn confirmed Forrest's allegations of the oath taken by the black regiments, but noted, "This act of theirs was not influenced by any white officer, but was the result of their own sense of what was due to themselves and their fellows who had been mercilessly slaughtered. I have no doubt that they went into the field, as you allege, in the full belief that they would be murdered if they fell into your hands. The affair at Fort Pillow fully justified that belief." Further,

> You must have learned by this time that the attempt to intimidate the colored troops by indiscriminate slaughter has signally failed, and that instead of a feeling of terror you have aroused a spirit of courage and desperation that will not drown at your bidding. I am left in doubt by your letter as to the course you and the Confederate Government intend to pursue hereafter in regard to colored troops, and I beg you to advise me with as little delay as possible as to your intention. If you intend to treat such of them as fall into your hands as prisoners of war, please so state. If you do not so intend, but contemplate either their slaughter or their return to slavery, please state that, so that we may have no misunderstanding hereafter. If the former is your intention, I shall receive the announcement with pleasure, and shall explain the fact to the colored troops at once, and desire that they recall the oath that they have taken. If the latter is the case, then let the oath stand, and upon those who have aroused this spirit by their atrocities, and upon the Government and the people who sanction it, be the consequences.[60]

As further evidence that Forrest had failed to conduct warfare "on civilized principles," Washburn related an eyewitness account testifying that Major Bradford, who was captured while commanding the Thirteenth Tennessee Cavalry at Fort Pillow, had been murdered while in the custody of Forrest's men.

The exchange, as did many other episodes in his lifetime, provoked Forrest's ire, prompting him to respond personally that Washburn's letter was "discourteous to the commanding officer of this department (Lee) and grossly insulting to myself."[61] He claimed that he was following the policy of his government, and that he would "regard captured negroes as I do other captured property," which left open the question of whether captured "property" could be "destroyed" to prevent its use by the enemy. He claimed, "It is not the policy nor the interest of the South to destroy the negro on the contrary, to preserve and protect him and all who have surrendered to us have received kind and humane treatment," the events of Fort Pillow notwithstanding. He concluded by falsely stating that he deprecated a state of affairs that descended into uncivilized warfare and that he would not be "instrumental in bringing it about," despite the fact that his actions, or the lack thereof, at Fort Pillow had opened the debate in the first place. He denied any knowledge of Bradford's death or the circumstances surrounding it, claiming only the old trope that he "attempted to escape and was shot," and presented, as evidence, against the dozens of sworn statements that a massacre had occurred at Fort Pillow (Washburn had forwarded him a copy of the investigation's results), the testimony of a single Union officer, Capt. John Young of the Sixth US Colored Heavy Artillery (but who was using his former association as a member of the Twenty-Fourth Missouri to disguise his position as an officer in a regiment of black troops), then imprisoned at Cahaba, and which was later admitted to have been coerced from the prisoner under duress, that he had not witnessed any surrendered troops being massacred.[62] Here again, absence of evidence did not provide sufficient evidence of absence.

Lee likewise replied to Washburn, also denying the massacre at Fort Pillow and claiming that the missing troops from Brice's Cross Roads were not slaughtered but were, at the time, "yet wandering over the country, attempting to return to their masters." In his final say on the matter, Washburn again got the best of the exchange, telling Forrest that "of the tone and temper of both I do not complain. The desperate fortunes of a bad cause excuse much irritation of temper, and I pass it by," but that "your attempt to shift from yourself upon me the responsibility of the inauguration of a 'worse than savage warfare' is too strained and far-fetched to require any response." Likewise, he corrected Lee:

> I will close by a reference to your statement that many of our colored soldiers "are yet wandering over the country attempting to return to their masters." If this remark is intended as a joke, it is acknowledged as a good one, but if stated as a fact, permit me to correct your misapprehensions by informing you that most of them have rejoined their respective commands, their search for their late masters having proved

bootless; and I think I do not exaggerate in assuring you that there is not a colored soldier here who does not prefer the fate of his comrades at Fort Pillow to being returned to his "master."[63]

The exchange between Washburn, Lee, and Forrest reinforces the claims of William Freehling that the involvement of Anti-Confederate Southerners increased the level of violence, and of Daniel Sutherland that this descent in violence, often precipitated by guerrilla actions, hastened the move to a "hard war," accelerating the war-winning policies that simultaneously increased the suffering and hastened the war's end. Forrest obviously stood to lose if battles degenerated into bloody slaughter, especially against freedmen and Unionists who refused to be taken alive and fought accordingly.[64]

Even while this exchange of letters between Union and Confederate commanders took place, Washburn equipped and sent yet another expedition deep into Mississippi to keep the raiders there off balance and prevent any interference with Sherman's operations. The next expedition, commanded by A. J. Smith, while Sturgis responded to allegations of drunkenness and incompetence in his handling of the affair at Brice's Cross Roads, included an even larger force of infantry, proceeding along an alternate route and in dryer weather, and achieved its objective of reaching Tupelo, where, as Tom Parson has recently demonstrated, Smith soundly defeated, but failed to destroy Forrest and Lee's forces. Three black regiments, including the Fifty-Ninth, Sixty-First, and Sixty-Eighth USCI, accompanied Smith's expedition and again fought well, despite again being placed at the rear of the formation. Most importantly, Smith kept the rebels in Mississippi and out of northern Alabama, where a far more significant expedition than either Sturgis's or Smith's inflicted exactly the type of damage on Johnston's supply line that both Sturgis and Smith, and their white and black troops, had been laboring to successfully prevent on Sherman's.[65]

Only July 10, Maj. Gen. Lovell Rousseau, a Kentucky native who had served in the Indiana legislature before the war, rode south from Decatur at the head of over 2,500 blue-clad horsemen, unencumbered by foot soldiers or wagons. The men came from three Northern (Eighth Indiana, Ninth Ohio, and Fifth Iowa) and two Southern Unionist (Second Kentucky and Fourth Tennessee) cavalry regiments, the latter of which had recruited heavily in Nashville and had added local Unionists to its ranks while stationed in northern Alabama.[66]

At one point, plans included a liaison with the First Alabama Cavalry some-where in Alabama but, Frank Tupper reported, "he went through without us for some reason or other."[67] Rousseau was, like Forrest, a self-made man with no formal military training, but with a much stronger appreciation of learning and intellectual pursuits, teaching himself French and enough law to pass the Indiana bar exam, before returning to his native Kentucky. Before departing on his raid, he had wired Dodge to contact "R.T. Smith, an Alabamian and ask him to report to me at Decatur at once, to give information touching the country below. This is all important."[68]

In deference to the extremely hot weather of that time of year, the men were in the saddle early and rode until the sun was well up, then took a siesta in the heat of the day to avoid exhausting their mounts. As the sun dipped low, they were back in the saddle, riding through the cooler evening hours until making camp for a few hours' rest around midnight. In this manner, they passed through Somerville and Mt. Alvis, and crossed the path of Streight's raiders of the previous year at Blountsville before reaching Ashville on July 13. Along the way, they levied their needs from the countryside, from both the loyal and rebellious residents of the valleys of the Locust and Mulberry Forks of the Black Warrior River. In Ashville, the command captured large quantities of Confederate stores and fed their horses and refilled their haversacks. They also freed from the jail "four negroes, charged with the crime of seeking their liberty." Several wags took advantage of the abandoned proofs and type of the local newspaper and printed an edition commemorating their visit.[69]

A short distance away, they fought their way across the Coosa at the Ten Islands Ford, scattering a small detachment of home guards under Brig. Gen. James Clanton. On the far side of the river, they captured and destroyed a large foundry making iron for the Confederacy. Upon reaching Talladega, they again found a large quantity of foodstuffs and war material unprotected and put it to the torch before departing on the Montgomery road to throw off any pursuers. More hard riding through Brownsville, Sylacauga, and Dadeville took them to the line of the Western Railway of Alabama at Loachapoka, their objective, on the evening of July 17, narrowly missing out on capturing a train carrying Confederate general Braxton Bragg. Here they went to their work, destroying over thirty miles of that line by prying rails from cross ties and burning them, demolishing packed depots at Auburn, Notasulga, Opelika, and Loachapoka, and defeating another small force of home guards and poorly drilled teenagers sent out from Montgomery to repel them. At one point, a slave warned the commander of the Ninth Ohio Cavalry of a Confederate ambush outside Auburn, allowing the troopers to turn the tables on their would-be attackers.[70] After thoroughly wrecking the line over three days, the command turned north and then east, passing through Bethlehem, Wedowee, and Carrollton, Georgia, before rejoining Sherman's command on the outskirts of Atlanta, bringing in more stock than they had when they departed and "several hundred able-bodied negroes" to fill the new USCT organizations recruiting in the army's rear in Chattanooga. In a raid of just twelve days, Union and Unionist cavalry had wrecked Johnston's main supply line from the west for over six weeks during the critical stages of the Atlanta campaign, when demands for supplies were highest. They had traveled directly through the heart of the state, supplied themselves from the land, and incurred minimal losses, astonishing one wealthy farmer near Talladega who claimed that he had already donated ten of his best mules to the Confederate cause before being informed that his present dust-covered company were not Confederate tax agents but "Yankees." The *Montgomery Advertiser* admitted, "We doubt whether any other raiding party since the commencement of hostilities, comprising no more men, has penetrated as far into the country, done as much damage, and succeeded in escaping with so little loss."[71] The raid had succeeded through sound planning, skilled leadership, and the diversion into Mississippi of Confederate units charged with defending the state, including Forrest's command. The interruption of Johnston's supply line crippled the Confederate forces defending Atlanta and hastened the end of that campaign and with it, the war.[72]

The Atlanta campaign had been unofficially underway since Grant and Sherman had lifted the siege of Chattanooga the previous November, pushing Johnston's Confederate army back into north Georgia. But before Sherman could begin his pursuit and strike through the mountains for Atlanta, he had to refurbish a decrepit logistical system. Union soldiers in Chattanooga were on almost starvation rations during the siege, and the army's animals suffered severely for the want of forage. Simply sustaining the army through the winter months would be a challenge. But Sherman had to do more than that. In order to undertake offensive operations in the spring, he had to accumulate sufficient supplies to sustain his forces, especially during the inevitable interruptions that would come from rehabilitating the line of the Western & Atlantic Railroad between Chattanooga and Atlanta.

At his rear, Sherman had two potential rail lines that could be made capable of sustaining his army and his operations. The Nashville & Chattanooga was largely operational through Middle Tennessee, though it contained steep grades over and through the Cumberland Plateau before reaching the Tennessee River at Stevenson, Alabama. The second route ran from Nashville down to Decatur, Alabama, and then east along the line of the Memphis & Charleston to Stevenson, where it joined the Nashville & Chattanooga in winding along the narrow valley and around Lookout Mountain before reaching the city. But the generally flatter line between Nashville and Decatur had been heavily damaged during the preceding campaigns, and most of the trestles spanning deep valleys burned by Confederates. If he could rehabilitate this line and add additional rolling stock from northern roads, Sherman could run a loop, with full trains coming down the comparatively easier grades to Decatur, and then up the Tennessee Valley to Stevenson, while the lighter empty trains, usually carrying only wounded or sick soldiers, could return directly to Nashville over the plateau, reducing delays caused by waiting for passing trains and increasing both speed and overall efficiency. To put his railroads back in operation, Sherman again reached out to his resident expert, Grenville Dodge, a man with extensive prewar railroad construction experience.

Since leaving his post at Corinth and bringing his troops east to help relieve the siege of Chattanooga, Dodge had been at Pulaski, Tennessee, just north of the Alabama border, where he labored to put the railroad back into commission. In order to protect it from Confederate forays across the Tennessee, he recruited additional regiments of black troops, including the Second, Third, and Fourth Alabama Infantry, African Descent, later redesignated the 110th, 111th, and 106th US Colored Infantry regiments, respectively. These men both labored on the road, building bridges and blockhouses to guard them, and trained as soldiers, in order to successfully defend them against attack. In order to know when these attacks might be coming, Dodge had also sent for his regiment of Alabama Unionists, to collect information from across the river. In addition, he depended, as he had at Corinth, on an extensive network of spies to divine Confederate intentions, including his most trusted agent, Philip Henson, an Alabama native and staunch Unionist familiar with both the surrounding countryside and the inner working of the rebel high command in Mississippi as a result of his prewar residence near Rienzi, just south of Corinth. It was in this capacity that he had first come to Dodge's attention as a man who, by posing as a double agent, could travel freely through the Confederate camps and then report his findings to Dodge.[73]

Adding to his local knowledge of the surrounding area, and focusing on protecting the base of the railroad triangle between Decatur and Stevenson, was the First Alabama and Tennessee Vedette Cavalry, now several hundred strong with recruits from northeast Alabama and the area around Chattanooga. These local auxiliaries served as guides, intelligence sources, and, in emergencies, additional manpower to supplement Federal strength along Sherman's lifelines to the north, and to collect information from deep within the Confederacy. In mid-March, Dodge ordered J. D. Hensal, his chief of scouts, to "send some of his best men south into the mountains, and make arrangements with Union men living there to go to Rome, Atlanta, Selma and Montgomery and see what was going on."[74]

Throughout January and February, troops of the Fifteenth Corps had operated south of the critical junction of Stevenson, breaking up bands of bushwhackers and scouting for Confederate raiders who might threaten the recently reconstructed railroads. On one expedition in late January, Brig. Gen. Morgan Smith reported to Sherman that he took his six regiments south of the river "to carry out your views and capture some of the pickets operating in the valley of the Tennessee, arresting conscripts and intercepting deserters from the army around Dalton." Smith's movements allegedly

caused a general stampede of citizens, negroes, and horses for the other side of the Coosa River. It also enabled men to come out of the fastness of Sand Mountain who had been secreted a great part of the time for two years, several of whom have since raised companies for the First Alabama Cavalry, and some have enlisted in infantry regiments. One man, McCurdy, immediately after our second advance, mustered his company with a pencil on brown paper, christened it, assumed command, ordered an advance on Sand Mountain, and actually made captures of rebel home guards in the same hiding places they had themselves just vacated.

Smith concluded, "These loyal Alabamians are invaluable, and exceed in number and are equal in zeal to anything we discovered in East Tennessee."[75] Pvt. Eugene McWayne of the One Hundred Twenty-Seventh Illinois Infantry wrote from Larkinsville in early February, "We had also some of the Alabama Cavalry raised in this vicinity; they make capital guides, knowing the mountains as we would Kane County," the company's home outside Chicago. One guide was "Moses Morgan, who had been my guide once on a foraging expedition in the vicinity of Pine Island, below here. He is a fine, quiet fellow and knows all the mountain roads, and every man for 20 miles around, I should think." Andrew McCornack, of the same regiment, noted, "There are many of the citizens enlisting and forming into cavalry companies. They will do a great deal of good." These men continued to render important service through February, capturing rebel couriers and forwarding the intercepted dispatches, and keeping Confederate home guards off balance and on the defensive. McWayne even reported, "We found among the hills one fellow of Gen'l Andrew Jackson's Indian war on the Tallapoosa, the Coosa and the Warrior. The old fellow was very bitter against the rebs." Of the rebel population, he found, "They have hunted their neighbors like bloodhounds until the Federal Army came upon them, and then they hurried over to take the oath of allegiance to save their property. The Alabama cavalry in our army know them all and swear vengeance on them as soon as they get armed and equipped."[76]

In order to combine the existing First Alabama Cavalry with the new companies being raised, and to employ it in country they were familiar with, on March 7, Dodge finally secured the regiment's release from the defenses of Memphis. General Grierson reported, "Their horses are in too bad condition to be sent by land, and one-half the regiment is dismounted." Three days earlier, the regiment reported having only 270 horses, despite having an effective strength of five hundred troopers. The men left Memphis on March 27, traveling by steamer up the Mississippi to Cairo, then up the Ohio to Paducah, where Hicks detained them for two days due to concerns for his security with Forrest still prowling in the area. But Hicks quickly released the regiment, allowing them to continue up the Cumberland River, arriving at Nashville on April 3.[77] After a brief stay in the city, the mounted portion of the command drove a herd of beef cattle south for the army's consumption, while the dismounted men rode the newly completed rails to Mooresville, arriving on April 14.

Dodge was already using the forces available to him at Athens to disrupt the Confederate cordon across the river. He reported to McPherson, "There is a cavalry picket line running from Guntersville clear round to Courtland;

this is done to catch the deserters and refugees seeking our lines. The mountains are full of them, and they hold the mountain district in spite of all efforts of the rebels to catch them. I know of several companies of at least 100 men, each led by our scouts and members of the First Alabama Cavalry." On April 27, Bill Looney of Winston County continued his support of the Union war effort by bringing in fourteen deserters who wanted to enlist in the First Alabama.[78] When the regiment finally arrived from Memphis, Dodge ordered a Northern regiment, the Fiftieth Illinois, dismounted, and ordered them to turn over "such stock as the First Regiment Alabama Cavalry Volunteers may need" to facilitate their operations, which included patrolling the river as far as Triana and carrying dispatches.[79] On the scout to Triana, Frank Tupper, now in command of Company K, stopped for dinner at the home of Charley Collier, brother of antebellum governor Henry Watkins Collier, but his men antagonized their hosts by shooting a turkey that belonged to the family. Tupper reported, "I am satisfied I did not make a favorable impression at that place."[80]

Thomas Jefferson Cypert, a Tennessee Unionist and captain in the Second Tennessee Mounted Infantry, provided a firsthand account of the effectiveness of the Confederate cordon south of the river. Cypert had been captured at his home near Waynesboro while attempting to minister to his family, stricken with smallpox.[81] Home guards took Cypert to a camp near Pond Spring, where he suspected he would be executed "while trying to escape," en route to confinement in Tuscaloosa. Cypert managed to elude his captors and spent several weeks hiding out in the countryside, with vital assistance from Unionists and slaves, before returning home safely after a perilous crossing of the river near Florence. On the north bank, Cypert was clothed and fed by a man Cypert described as "my colored friend." In relating their conversation in his memoir, Cypert asked the man, "Well uncle are you a union man?" He replied, "I guess I is, an' so is my wife, and all my boys is too." Cypert responded, "I thank you and your wife and boys for their principles." The man told Cypert, "I allers helps de union peoples for da is my frens." Cypert testified:

> And this is not only my experience, but that of the thousands of hunted union men, and fugitive soldiers from rebel prisons, who have sought aid from our darker brethren. There is scarcely an instance on record of any help being refused which they had the power to give; and equally rare is a case, where they have betrayed the confidence reposed in

them. And has not the Nation a debt of gratitude to liquidate toward these hitherto oppressed people?[82]

After the war, Grenville Dodge seconded Cypert's testimony, reporting, "Negroes were also of great aid to us as messengers and coming into our lines with valuable information and I never heard of a negro giving up a Union soldier, spy, or scout who trusted him."[83]

Many of the "hitherto oppressed people" Cypert argued so eloquently in defense of were increasingly making their way inside Union lines. So many came that Dodge began to have apprehensions about providing for them, or for their security, and demonstrated the depth, or lack thereof, of the Army's concern for the freedpeople. On April 17, he wrote to his detachment commander at Bailey's Springs, near Florence, to "send in no more negro women and children than is absolutely necessary. They are only a burden upon us. We need all able-bodied men you can get. The women and children should stay on the plantations and aid in working them. It is better for them and us both."[84] While Dodge's comments seem callous, they can also be framed in terms of military necessity. Bringing in additional foodstuffs during that time would have further strained army logistics. At the same time, putting a crop in the ground, even for plantation owners who had taken the oath of loyalty, increased the likelihood of the army being able to draw on the countryside for provisions that fall. But it must have made it very difficult for the soldiers of his new African American regiments, then rebuilding and defending the army's railroad, to know that some of their families still suffered under the yoke of slavery, a sentiment even Sherman agreed with.[85]

The First Alabama's stay in the central Tennessee Valley was brief, consisting of a few scouts from Decatur and up the valley, helping Dodge assemble a picture of the Confederate units in the area.[86] Tupper reported that the pontoon bridge connecting the city to the northern shore of the river was "the finest I ever saw, being over half a mile in length and having over 130 boats." Before the war, Decatur had been "a town of considerable importance, having a population of about 1,500 and did have, before General Mitchel burned it last year, a splendid Rail Road bridge across the Tennessee belonging to the Memphis and Charleston R.R." but the town was now "strongly fortified by earthworks."[87] The regiment spent the remainder of the month mounting the dismounted men and practicing battalion drill, and collecting recruits who

continued to come in from the surrounding hills. In April, Capt. Sanford Tramel and a scout of six men stayed in Fayette County with George Cook for two
weeks, and brought Cook's son James in as a recruit. Cook's brother, Charles,
had enlisted the previous fall, but was captured in the skirmish at Vincent's
Crossroads and died (or was murdered) in a Confederate prison. In the fall of
1864, George Cook spent some time in prison in Pikeville for his sentiments
and his son's service, but John Stout, a veteran of the First Alabama Cavalry
who led a Unionist band in Marion County, ran off the guards and released
Cook and other jailed Unionists.[88]

Sherman's operations against Johnston's army kicked off in early May. On
May 1, the 350 mounted men of the regiment left for Stevenson, leaving 200
recruits and unmounted men behind. At Stevenson, much of Dodge's infantry
entrained for Chattanooga, but the First Alabama escorted the wagon trains
and artillery overland into the city.[89] The regiment had been fully equipped,
though Tupper's Company K carried the unreliable Smith's carbine, which was
prone to misfire due to water penetrating the India-rubber cartridge at the
hinged breech, making the men desire Spencer rifles and metallic cartridges.
But Colt and Remington .44-caliber revolvers supplemented the carbines,
and the regiment was well mounted, prepared in all respects for extensive
service in the field. Passing through Huntsville, Tupper recorded, "This is a
very beautiful place. I had often heard it spoken of as such, but now I know
it to be true." In addition to several fine buildings, he was most impressed by
"the numerous mulatto girls and a large number of them are very handsome
and intelligent, they dress neatly."[90] But between Huntsville and Bridgeport,
Francis Dunn remarked, "The farms are barren and uncultivated. A complete
picture of desolation."[91] Tupper, Dunn and their men continued their march
along the railroad in northeast Alabama, reaching Chattanooga on May 9.

In the Atlanta campaign, the First Alabama Cavalry screened the flanks of
Dodge's advance, guarded the wagon train, and again drove beef cattle through
the mountains of north Georgia, grazing their horses in the many ripening
wheat fields when the forage gave out. A detachment escorted a number of
Confederate prisoners back to Dalton, where Tupper observed "a large gallows
where the rebels had hung near a hundred of their deserters as the inhabitants informed us."[92] The regiment briefly held the center of Dodge's widely
separated line along Pumpkin Vine Creek after the battle of Dallas, but after
leading the advance toward Kennesaw Mountain, on June 20 Dodge ordered

the regiment's 382 effectives to Rome, Georgia, where they would protect the railroad lifeline for the rest of the campaign. With the investment of the city of Atlanta, operations had devolved into a siege of the city itself, and the need for cavalry to protect flanks and scout ahead had diminished considerably.[93]

Rome was less than fifteen miles from the Alabama line and only ten miles from the Western & Atlantic Railroad as it swung west of Cartersville, which was then supplying the lifeblood of Sherman's army. It occupied a vulnerable flank, with good roads leading down the Coosa Valley into the portion of Alabama south of Sand Mountain, where Confederate forces could easily concentrate, and which the First Alabama could use to scout toward Gadsden and across Sand Mountain as far as Guntersville, as well as receive new recruits, including deserters from the trapped Confederate army in Atlanta. As James Baggett argues, "Many had deserted from the Confederate army and now sought to survive on what they believed to be the winning side. Through service in the Union army, they felt they could better protect their homes and find food, clothing and shelter as well as enlistment bounties and a salary to support themselves and their families."[94]

The post thus gave the First Alabama Cavalry the opportunity to recruit disaffected Alabamians and northeast Georgians into their ranks, allowing the regiment to fill toward its allotted strength. On July 29, Dodge "asked permission of the War Dep't for Col. Spencer to recruit the 1st Ala. Cav. from refugees and Deserters at Rome, Ga. I raised the Reg't at Corinth. It did good work and has been much reduced."[95] On August 9, Francis Dunn recorded in his diary, "More reports come to the regiment of cruelties practiced upon the relatives of men in the regiment. 8 or nine men killed. One member of the regiment had his leg unjointed, was scalped and castrated. This was in retaliation for the shooting of a conscript officer who was shot for the killing of a brother of one of our men (Bill Sims brother)."[96] Men from the unit continued to recruit inside Alabama's mountain fastness just across the state line, but risked their lives doing so. Alabamians also joined other Federal units during this time, as did Robert, William, and Melvin Carr, who left their home in Cherokee County and traveled to Rome in May. Melvin continued north to Indianapolis, where he enlisted in the Eighth Indiana Cavalry on October 10, helping to replenish the numbers of the veterans of Rousseau's raid.[97]

The First Alabama Cavalry held Rome and scouted the surrounding countryside jointly with the Forty-Fourth USCI, initially organized at the Chattanooga Contraband Camp, "but about the middle of July moved to Rome, Ga., where it was rapidly recruited to the minimum."[98] Tupper described Rome as "a fine flourishing town celebrated for its large manufacturing of iron," but noted that the town now specialized in "some most excellent earthworks of Rebel and Yankee manufacture."[99] His servant, Ben, remained with him and became adept at procuring vegetables for the mess. Tupper reported, "Ben goes out with me on foraging expeditions and picks up a few chickens and a while ago we captured some meal & flour."[100] Otherwise, they subsisted on green corn, plentiful blackberries, peaches, potatoes, and squash, all locally procured.[101]

While garrisoning the railroad was tedious work, which caused the regiment to miss out on Sherman's active cavalry operations during the Atlanta campaign, it was vitally necessary, as demonstrated by Confederate attempts by Joe Wheeler's cavalry to cut the rail line in Sherman's rear in order to force him to retreat from Atlanta. Grant later wrote of Sherman's situation, "He was dependent for the supply of his armies upon a single-track railroad from Nashville to the point where he was operating. This passed the entire distance through a hostile country, and every foot of it had to be protected by troops. The cavalry force of the enemy under Forrest, in northern Mississippi, was evidently waiting for Sherman to advance far enough into the mountains of Georgia to make retreat disastrous, to get upon this line and destroy it."[102]

The regiment also took advantage of its mobility to conduct an active defense of the post and scout and raid well into northern Alabama. In mid-July, Lieutenant Colonel Godfrey took 225 men on an uneventful scout to Centre and Cedar Bluff, reporting, "I found forage and stock very scarce, particularly north of the [Coosa] River."[103] Another expedition later that month encountered few rebels and found forage "very scarce" along the Chattooga River. In August, Major Cramer took two hundred men toward Jacksonville, Alabama, before learning the town was heavily garrisoned, and diverted his march toward Tallapoosa, Georgia, where they "destroyed a quantity of corn and wheat that had been collected for the Confederate Government (and) also burned a steam cotton factory."[104] On one of these scouts, intended to gather beef for the army, John R. Phillips rounded up a herd of cattle, only to later find that some of them belonged to his own uncle, which he endeavored to return. After the war another uncle, whom Phillips described as a "rank secessionist" wrote him and censured him for this "crime."[105] On another scout, a portion of the regiment crossed Sand Mountain near Little River Canyon, with Lieutenant Snelling, a Georgia native, donning the uniform of a captured rebel in order to obtain information from the locals.[106] One of these "locals" turned out to be Judge William Winston of Valley Head, cousin of Governor John Winston, the namesake of Winston County. Judge Winston was one of the fifteen delegates to the 1861 Secession Convention who had refused to sign the ordinance and was then trying to live out the war at his home in remote DeKalb County. According to Francis Dunn, the judge pretended to hold Confederate sympathies when the first few gray-clad Yankees arrived, but quickly revealed his true identity when the rest of the blue-clad troopers rode up. Dunn wrote, "It was amusing to hear the old man and woman come round from Confederate to Union side. . . . He said now that he had to make friends with both sides." Winston was apparently skilled at detecting his interlocutors' allegiances, asking for coffee, which he knew Confederate troops would not have, or tobacco, which was scarce on the Union side. Winston was a committed Unionist who refused to accept the Confederate currency and provided extensive aid to men "lying out" or deserters trying to reach Union lines, advising them the best path to take to a Federal garrison at Trenton, Georgia, or over the mountains to Stevenson in the Tennessee Valley. At the conclusion of his command's visit on August 20, Dunn left Winston a receipt for "75 bushels of corn, 150 pounds of hay for which he will be entitled to pay at the termination of the present war."[107]

In their marches, the men of the Sixteenth Corps benefitted greatly from the efforts of the "Pioneer Corps," which included companies A, B, and C of the 110th USCI, the only black troops to accompany Sherman on his campaign. Pioneers performed important duties, including building bridges and "corduroying" roads by cutting timber and then placing the logs lengthwise across the poor roads of north Georgia, preventing wagon and artillery wheels from cutting into the soft clay, which readily liquefied when wet. They also doubled Sherman's manpower by performing essential entrenching duties for the troops. When units occupied a new position, the pioneers typically labored all night to fortify the position against counterattack with trenches, an abatis, and raised "headlogs" that allowed the troops to fire their weapons underneath with their skulls mostly protected from enemy marksmen. In his memoirs, Sherman acknowledged their valuable contributions, noting, "These pioneer detachments became very useful to us during the rest of the war, for they could work at night while our men slept; they in turn were not expected to fight, and could therefore sleep by day." Dodge's foresight in forming a pioneer corps resulted in the troops being assigned directly to the headquarters of Maj. Gen. James B. McPherson's Army of the Tennessee, where they could be employed in the advance of the army's other corps, meaning Dodge's troops would often have to fend for themselves, but the pioneers' work only increased as a siege demanded entrenchments and the construction of many miles of roads from railheads to the front lines to keep the combat troops supplied.[108] On July 14, Dodge forwarded "thanks to the Pioneer Corps and men engaged on the new bridge over the Chattahoochee River, for the prompt, efficient and speedy manner in which they completed the structure" during July 10–13, and reported on July 29 that they "were employed constantly" on the corps' right, extending the lines to and across the Turner's Ferry road. On August 5, the Pioneer Corps began work on a new line of entrenchments and artillery positions at midnight, and the following day "kept busily at work on the new line in sight of the enemy."[109]

In addition to the three companies of pioneers, men of Companies E and G of the 110th USCI also served as teamsters with the Sixteenth Corps, where "the labor has been very fatiguing a considerable portion of the time during the progress of the campaign as movement of the train has been made during the night." Even at the height of the campaign, including preparations for the Battle of Kennesaw Mountain, Dodge continued to monitor the progress of the regiments he had raised in southern Tennessee and northern Alabama. On June 24 he recorded that there was "one full reg't of colored troops (3rd Ala.) and portions of two reg'ts (2nd & 4th Ala.)," in addition to two regiments of white infantry and ten of cavalry guarding the line of the Nashville & Decatur Railroad between Columbia and Huntsville. On June 28 he asked for "the return of the portion of the Pioneer Corps at Rome, Ga., and the shipment of a company of negroes raised for the 4th Ala. Inf., A. D., to my command, where they belong."[110] But Sherman opposed enrolling new freedmen formally, preferring to employ them as laborers at the reduced rate of ten dollars per day (soldiers received thirteen), although he did allow them to be "fed out of the regular army supplies." Thus, the army became a source of both employment and subsistence for some of the men liberated along the path of Sherman's advance.[111]

By late July, Dodge was feeling the losses suffered in the bloody engagements outside Atlanta, and asked to have the troops left behind guarding the railway added to his command. In addition to the almost 3,000 troops still in northern Alabama, "There are also detached the First Alabama Cavalry at Rome and the Ninth Ohio Cavalry at Decatur, besides some three regiments of colored troops belonging to this command, which makes those absent and without the command fully equal to the present."[112] But the Alabama troops could not be spared from their vital tasks of guarding the railroads. In late August, portions of the First Alabama were following Clanton's Confederate command, the survivors of their brush with Rousseau in June, at Guntersville, while the three black regiments were needed to repel Forrest's belated attempt to cut the Union lines north of the Tennessee. Besides, Sherman had no use for black troops in his department, preferring to use them as paid laborers, if at all. He sparred repeatedly with War Department officials on the subject, and was content to send all freedmen liberated in Georgia to rear areas, especially Chattanooga, to be enlisted. Most significantly for the Alabama units, their mentor, General Dodge, suffered a severe head wound on August 19 while leading his corps. He recuperated in Missouri before continuing his military and professional career in the West, but the regiments he raised felt the loss of their patron keenly. The First Alabama Cavalry likely would have been put to better use in the battles around Nashville and in Wilson's Raid through Alabama in 1865 than they were in the March to the Sea and the Carolinas campaign, but the immediate needs of the army took precedence.

In mid-September, Forrest finally launched his long-deferred raid on Sherman's vulnerable supply lines through Alabama and Tennessee. But it came too late to alter the outcome of the Atlanta campaign, as Gen. John Bell Hood, after relieving Johnston in July and launching several futile and bloody counterattacks against Sherman's forces in July and August, evacuated the city on September 1. Nevertheless, Forrest moved up from Mississippi and crossed the Tennessee River at Florence on September 21, collecting Roddey's command, which gave him over 4,500 effectives supported by eight pieces of artillery. Col. George Spalding, commanding the Tenth and Twelfth Tennessee (US) Cavalry regiments, duly detected and reported these movements to his superior, Brig. Gen. John Starkweather at Pulaski, who was responsible for all the garrisons from that point south to Athens. Spalding overestimated the force to be 8,000 strong, which had an important impact on future events, and reported that they "held all of the mills west of the railroad, and that Forrest's troops were stripping the country of wheat," suggesting an alternative objective for the expedition.[113] On September 23, Forrest sent a detachment to strike the railroad between Athens and Decatur, hoping to isolate the garrison at the latter and prevent it from succoring the troops at the former.

At Athens, Col. Wallace Campbell held the town and a 180- by 450-foot fort just west on Coleman's Hill with 450 soldiers of the 110th, 111th, and 106th USCI and 130 troopers of the Third Tennessee Cavalry. After sending a detachment of his forces on the recently arrived Nashville train south to repel Forrest's detachment at McDonald's station, he found Forrest attacking the city in his rear and quickly backed the train into the city and under the guns of the fort. That evening, a seesaw battle took place in the town, with Confederates briefly taking the depot before being repelled by 300 troops of the Second Tennessee Cavalry, US, sent north from Decatur to support. This small body was insufficient to succor Campbell's command, and it returned to Decatur, where Maj. Gen. Gordon Granger organized a larger body of infantry, including 150 men of the 102nd Ohio and 210 of the Eighteenth Michigan, all under Col. Jonas Elliott, to march to Athens's relief the next morning. Unfortunately for the besieged defenders of Athens, this relief column arrived too late to influence events. Despite fighting their way through successive lines of Forrest's dismounted troopers, they arrived "with musket range" of the fort on Coleman's Hill just as Campbell surrendered the entire garrison.

After refusing an earlier surrender demand, Campbell had agreed to Forrest's offer to inspect his command and determine if it was strong enough to carry the fort. Here Forrest again apparently engaged in subterfuge, exaggerating the size of his command, but, in Campbell's defense, the assembled force was likely strong enough to storm the works which, with its similar "mongrel" garrison of freedmen and Tennessee Unionists, offered an opportunity for a repeat of Fort Pillow, an event Campbell and his men were surely aware of. Campbell had raised the regiment himself and felt he was sparing his men's lives. Afterwards, he claimed, "It is the opinion of officers in my command from conversations held with General Forrest and his officers that had the fort been stormed no lives would have been spared."[114] But most of his subordinates begged to differ, providing sworn testimony from captivity that they disagreed with the colonel's decision and, given that they occupied what they felt was the "strongest work between Nashville and Decatur," were "anxious to try conclusions with General Forrest." They claimed the fort held enough rations for ten days, more than enough to hold out until relief columns arrived, along with 70,000 rounds of ammunition and 120 rounds for each of the two smoothbore howitzers defending the position.[115] Instead, they all went into captivity, with the officers paroled at Meridian, the white prisoners confined at Cahaba, Alabama, and the black soldiers impressed as slaves to serve the Confederacy.

The following month, the *Mobile Advertiser and Register* published a list of 570 former soldiers captured at Athens who were "employed by the Engineer Corps at Mobile Bay. The owners are notified in order to receive the pay due them."[116] In a cruel twist of fate, men who had fled bondage in order to receive the fruits of their own labor were again to have it stripped from them and provided to someone else. The testimony of one of these men, Pvt. Joseph Howard of Company F of the 110th USCI, testifies to the harsh treatment the freedmen received at the hand of their captors. Howard and his compatriots marched over twelve days to Mobile, then threatened by invasion, losing all they possessed along the way, even having their buttons cut off their coats. They were put to work strengthening the city's fortifications, and were "kept at hard labor and inhumanely treated. If we lagged, or faltered, or misunderstood an order, we were whipped and abused—some of our own men being detailed to whip the others. . . . For the slightest causes we were subjected to the lash." After three months of such treatment, Howard made his escape, stealing a skiff and floating down the bay to one of Adm. David Farragut's gunboats, now inside the harbor. In early August, Farragut's fleet ran past the torpedoes blocking the channel between Fort Gaines and Fort Morgan and captured those places. Pvt. Howard rejoined his regiment in Nashville, after a tour around the perimeter of what was left of the Confederacy that included waterborne travel to New Orleans and upriver to Louisville, then by rail to Nashville, where he provided his testimony on January 30.[117] But many of Howard's compatriots still labored on the city's defenses until a Union force including other black troops from the Department of the Gulf liberated them in April 1865.

After capturing both the fort and the survivors of Elliot's command, who had fought their way almost to the fort, Forrest marched north to one of the largest and most significant bridges on the route, over Sulphur Springs Branch, just south of Elkmont, where they camped for the night two miles south of the span. Here, a strong earthen fort defended a 525-foot-long and 73-foot-high wooden trestle that carried the railroad over a tributary of the Elk

River.[118] Inside were three hundred men of the 111th USCI, with two pieces of artillery, and another three hundred troopers of the Ninth Indiana Cavalry, commanded by Maj. Eli Lilly, who would go on to postwar fame as the founder of the pharmaceutical company. Late that evening, Col. John Minnis and his Third Tennessee Cavalry joined the garrison, making it over 1,000 strong. With this force, the garrison's commander, Col. William H. Lathrop of the 111th USCI, determined to make a stand. In late July, Lathrop reported to Dodge that he had completed work on the stockade and blockhouses, and had procured two artillery pieces from Nashville and detailed a crew to work them. During the assault, one of the black gunners, Pvt. William Lee, had an arm broken by a bullet, but when directed to retire to have his wound dressed, responded, "No Lieutenant. I have one hand. I can pull the lanyard yet," and continued to do so.[119] The men were generally well disciplined, though a number had been confined for desertion or sleeping on post, but Lathrop regretted that "owing to our heavy fatigue work there has not been as much time for drill and instruction as I would like."[120]

Unfortunately for Lathrop and his men, the fort had been poorly sited, sitting adjacent to the trestle but below the crests of several commanding hills. Forrest occupied these heights with artillery early on the morning of September 25 and began to shell the garrison, which could not reply to the rifled batteries sited above them. At one point, Pvt. Andrew Hampton of the 111th USCI picked up a cannon ball with a lit fuse and threw it over the parapet, where it exploded.[121] After letting his artillery play on the fort, Forrest sent a flag of truce demanding surrender, again allowing his men to advantageously reposition themselves during the lull. Colonel Lathrop had been killed early in the battle, and Colonel Minnis seriously wounded in the unprotected fort, leaving Major Lilly to surrender the fort's garrison after almost all of their ammunition had been expended, forcing several hundred more black and white soldiers into captivity and enslavement. Lieutenant Nelson's company helped defend the fort, and recorded that men had been whittling down .69-caliber bullets to fit in .58-caliber guns. He also recalled that the garrison received generous terms, with promises that "all black and white were to be treated as 'prisoners of war,'" terms which were later violated by returning the black soldiers to slavery. It came with the usual threat that, if the garrison did not surrender, "the commander of the assaulting force would not be responsible for the conduct of his men." After surrendering, and while attempting to secure care for Private Lee, whose mangled arm still hung limply by his side, Nelson was confronted by a Confederate who put a pistol in his face and accused him of being "one of those G—d— nigger officers." [122] Many of the white prisoners who survived their harsh captivity at Cahaba were killed when the steamer *Sultana* exploded on the Mississippi as it was carrying them back to their homes.[123] Others were even less fortunate, and found themselves at Andersonville for the duration of the war. Nelson gave one former colleague from the Eighty-First Ohio, Sgt. Lyle Adair, a white noncommissioned officer in the 111th USCI, $15, which he used to buy food that sustained him during his captivity.[124]

Forrest pressed north toward the Elk River bridge, capturing blockhouses and scooping up their garrisons in the process. Some held out until cannon fire compelled their surrender; others found discretion the better part of valor and evacuated north to join the growing assemblage of troops at Pulaski, the next major waypoint on the road. Just south of Pulaski at Brown's Plantation, Forest encountered the contraband camp, host to many family members of the now re-enslaved men of the Alabama regiments. Forrest estimated it contained 2,000 old men, women, and children, and claimed in his report, "the negroes were all ragged and dirty and many seemed in absolute want. I ordered them to remove their clothing and bed clothes from the miserable hovels in which they lived and then burnt up this den of wretchedness," without bothering to mention if or how he cared for its residents.[125] In Pulaski, Brig. Gen. John Starkweather received a large additional force hurried south from Nashville and from as far away as Chattanooga, which contested Forrest's advance before falling back on the city. Among them were the Fourteenth USCI, who "inflicted considerable loss on the enemy, suffering but little themselves."[126] Forrest, "fully satisfied that the enemy was strongly posted with a large force . . . determined to make no further assault," and, after building campfires, snuck off to the east toward Fayetteville. Outside of Tullahoma, he again found a strong garrison and learned of additional forces gathering to meet him. He reported, "The severe engagements with the enemy at Athens, Sulphur Springs trestle, and Pulaski had exhausted nearly all my artillery ammunition," and he therefore elected not to risk another engagement.[127]

Instead, he split his force, sending Buford, with 1,500 men and all the artillery pieces and their nearly empty caissons, south to test Granger's defenses at Huntsville and try to damage the Memphis & Charleston Railroad between there and Decatur. Granger foiled their efforts by rushing men from Decatur to bolster the city's defenses. In response to Buford's now customary demand for surrender, Granger impetuously replied, "You can come and take it as soon as you get ready."[128] Buford declined, and, after inflicting only light damage on the railroad west of town and finding the captured but abandoned fort at Athens once again strongly garrisoned, moved on to Florence.

For his part, Forrest sent two small parties of twenty and thirty men to hit the Nashville & Chattanooga north and south of Tullahoma, but these men could only inflict minor damage, which Union forces repaired in several hours, and then retreated west as well. He took a more circuitous route, moving north of Pulaski, capturing a small garrison at Spring Hill and threatening the post at Columbia, again doing minor damage to the Nashville & Decatur Railroad, before also pointing his weary mounts toward Florence and safety below the Tennessee.

The loss of the blockhouses and men along the Nashville & Decatur was a serious blow, but hardly fatal to Union fortunes. Sherman had already taken Atlanta and brushed Hood's men west of the city. After trying Sherman's line below Chattanooga, they eventually moved into Alabama's Tennessee Valley, en route to final defeat and disaster at Franklin and Nashville. Hood's command could easily have inflicted the damage Forrest did on the now superfluous railroad during their movements. Meanwhile, the undamaged Nashville & Chattanooga proved more than adequate for Sherman's armies, who found their logistical requirements decreasing after the end of that campaign and their commissaries filled from the countryside around Atlanta. Indeed, the difficulty of maintaining this vulnerable railroad tether influenced Sherman to move his army from Atlanta and shift his command to a more secure base on the coast. He initially considered a movement southwest through Montgomery toward Mobile but, comfortable that Maj. Gen. Edward Canby had the situation well in hand there, Sherman chose instead to move southeast for Savannah. The valiant defenders of Athens and Sulphur Springs had bought much-needed time, both for the arrival of reinforcements that eventually halted Forrest's raid, and for Sherman, with the Nashville & Chattanooga line intact, to plan, prepare for, and execute his March to the Sea.

In October, the First Alabama Cavalry had its opportunity to push Hood's defeated Confederate army away from Sherman's supply line. As he moved west of Atlanta into Alabama, Hood sent portions of his command against the railroad where it looped to the west between Chattanooga and Atlanta. Sherman's concern was not unfounded. He later recalled, "I had little fear of the enemy's cavalry damaging our roads seriously, for they rarely made a break which could not be repaired in a few days; but it was absolutely necessary to keep General Hood's infantry off our main route of communication and supply."[129] Sherman sent John Corse's division back up the railroad to Rome, where he added the First Alabama to his own Ninth Illinois Mounted Infantry, which "together furnished an excellent mounted brigade for offensive operations and reconnaissances."[130] Corse's troops repelled a strong Confederate thrust at Allatoona on October 5, and Hood bounced northwest off the defenses toward Rome. On October 10, a patrol of the First Alabama under Capt. Henry Peek arrived in Rome with several prisoners from Hood's army, providing confirmation of the units involved and that they were crossing the Coosa downstream and headed for somewhere other than Rome.[131] Additional patrols shadowed the defeated army's movements and provided Sherman and his subordinates near real-time intelligence on Hood's whereabouts as he again probed the railroad near Resaca but, finding that too strongly garrisoned, fell back toward Gadsden. From there the two armies' paths parted as Hood marched north on Nashville and Sherman southeast to the coast.

With Hood off on other pursuits, the First Alabama Cavalry left Rome, their base of operations for the summer and fall of 1864. Upon leaving, the troops had apparently been ordered to destroy the town, which then hosted the families of a number of the regiment's new recruits, as Sherman intended to leave nothing of use to the Confederacy in his wake. Spencer's appeal of this decision provoked a stern rebuke from Sherman, who wrote, "You have known for ten days that Rome was to be evacuated, and have no right to appeal to my humanity. You have neglected to care for those families and I am not going to regulate the movements of an army by your neglect and want of foresight."[132] Before leaving, the army stripped the countryside of forage and sustenance. As Tupper described, it, "We take out the whole reg't with our wagons, stop at a corn field, dismount, in a few minutes the boys have the wagon filled with corn: On the way home they defend themselves as well as they can against hog, fowl, & such."[133] Other Federal troops visited Sarah Espy's nearby farm during this time, killing all her pigs, even the "brood sows," and took all the corn, so that "not one ear remains."[134] Before leaving Rome, the men of the regiment conducted a straw poll for the presidential election, as the Alabama residents were ineligible to vote, with Lincoln carrying the regiment by a margin of 383–24, or 94 percent.[135] The regiment left Rome as ordered on November 10, marching through Cassville, Allatoona, and Kennesaw to the Chattahoochee.

Sherman selected the twenty-one men from Company I to serve as his personal escort on his journey to the coast. A "small company of irregular Alabama cavalry, commanded by Lieutenant Snelling," had served in Sherman's headquarters since April, primarily as "orderlies and couriers."[136] Snelling was a Georgia native, and his knowledge of the physical and human terrain would be of value on the march. Sherman later related an incident where Snelling encountered a former slave who had belonged to Snelling's uncle. On becoming reacquainted, Snelling received Sherman's permission to visit his uncle at his home roughly six miles away. "The uncle was not cordial, by any means, to find his nephew in the ranks of the host that was desolating the land, and Snelling came back, having exchanged his tired horse for a fresher one out of his uncle's stables, explaining that surely one of the 'bummers' would have got the horse had he not."[137] For the rest of the regiment, just being included in the march was recognition of the unit's strength, as many units deemed unfit for the march returned to Nashville with General Thomas.[138]

Gen. Oliver O. Howard's Army of the Tennessee left Atlanta on November 15 with a combined force of infantry, cavalry, and lengthy trains, "the whole preceded by the First Alabama Regiment."[139] They skirmished with rebel home guards and brushed aside resistance for the command, which "found the country full of provisions and forage," enabling it to supply itself almost completely, preserving the rations in the wagons. Howard, in acknowledging some excesses taken by his troops, including the firing of abandoned buildings and the theft of private property, noted, "Having soldiers in the command who have been bitten by bloodhounds, permission has been given to kill them," removing one of the most hated weapons at the hands of both slave patrols and conscription agents hunting deserters. As Margaret Storey found in her study of Alabama Unionists, the frequent use of slave dogs to persecute Union men removed one more distinction between freedmen and loyalists.[140]

By recruiting continually while garrisoning Rome, the regiment now contained a number of Georgians in the ranks, including some from the area now being traversed who had suffered persecution at the hands of their neighbors. Returning now at the head of a conquering army, the opportunity to take revenge on their former oppressors might have been too strong to resist. On November 20, Maj. Gen. Francis Blair, commanding the Seventeenth Corps, sent a pointed letter to Colonel Spencer regarding the activities of the First Alabama on the march. He wrote, "The outrages committed by your command during the march are becoming so common, and are of such an aggravated nature, that they call for some severe and instant mode of correction. Unless the pillaging of houses and wanton destruction of property by your regiment ceases at once, I will place every officer under arrest and recommend them to the department commander for dishonorable dismissal from the service." While Sherman's troops generally behaved well on their "March to the Sea," undoubtedly there were excesses and violations of military discipline that made the march infamous in the eyes of the proponents of the "Lost Cause." The above order suggests that Southern Unionists may have been responsible for a disproportionate number of these and have therefore given the march some of its undeserved reputation.[141]

Despite the admonition, the regiment continued to lead the advance, skirmishing again with Confederates before liberating the town of Gordon on November 21. The regiment also had the honor of capturing the provisional state capitol, when "the mayor of Milledgeville surrendered the town formally to Captain Duncan and a few scouts. Afterward, a company of the 1st Alabama entered the town with Captain Duncan and destroyed the depot and some 75 or 100 boxes of ammunition and (the) telegraph office." They then pushed on to the Oconee River, the last major river obstacle on their route to the coast. Finding the route at Jackson's Ferry impracticable, they pushed south to Ball's Ferry, where, according to Howard, "a detachment of the First Alabama had the day before reconnoitered the ferry. Finding a small force of the enemy, [they] made a raft, crossed the river and drove the enemy back but were subsequently themselves forced to recross the river, with some loss." Once the rest of the army came up, engineers laid a bridge, and the regiment finally traversed the swift-flowing river.[142]

The Sixteenth Corps still contained the three Pioneer companies of the 110th USCI, who labored heavily to keep the army moving. As they moved off the Piedmont and into the coastal plain, the ground became boggy, and one of the rainiest months of the year required that long stretches be corduroyed. In the Seventeenth Corps' Fourth Division alone, the pioneers "constructed seven miles and 300 feet of corduroy road, built 600 feet of bridging, made

150 fascines, built one fort for guns at (the) Oconee River, cut six miles of wagon roads, and removed fallen timber and obstructions from 600 yards of road."[143] Sherman may have been unaware that the pioneer corps contained mustered USCT soldiers, but his decision not to include black combat troops in his command was deliberate. On June 3, 1864, he issued an order from Dallas, Georgia, specifically prohibiting the enlistment of "negroes employed in useful labor on account of the government," and ordering the imprisonment of recruiters who violated the order.[144] Grenville Dodge later recalled that Sherman had told him, "I propose to leave the colored troops to occupy our lines of communication where they can have the protection of entrenchments, and a chance to drill; and I do not propose in this campaign that the rebels shall say it was necessary for me to whip them, to take part of their niggers to do it."[145] His unenlightened racial views notwithstanding, Sherman did require the services of some former slaves to successfully complete his campaign.

Both units pressed on toward Savannah, the pioneers facilitating the army's crossing of the Ogeechee River, and the cavalry brushing aside resistance and investing the city of Savannah. On December 9, several men of the First Alabama, including Francis Tupper, suffered grievous injuries due to Confederate "torpedoes," or land mines, placed on one of the narrow causeways leading to the city. As he described it, "When within seven miles of Savannah, I met with an accident that has made me a cripple for life. The Rebels had planted Torpedoes in the road and our reg't had exploded two of them killing 2 Horses and wounding 2 men. A few yards beyond was a swamp we could not cross. The reg't was halted and I went back to examine the torpedoes. I went to where one had exploded and stooped over with the intention of picking up a piece of that. I saw, as I done so my right foot touched the cap of one that was yet buried and it exploded shattering my leg so bad that it was amputated above the knee." Tupper spent the remainder of the war recuperating from his wound, and was grateful that he wasn't killed, as his clothes were "literally torn in rags."[146] Decades after the war, Tupper, then working as a deputy clerk of court in Denver, was reintroduced to General Sherman during a visit. After a brief glance, Sherman responded, "Why I remember you very well. You are the officer who stepped on a torpedo at a certain point on the way to Fort McAllister," and then proceeded with a detailed description of the incident. Tupper later described the description as accurate, and reported that he had not seen Sherman since he rode up to where he was lying on the ground.[147]

After the city's fall, General Sherman ordered a grand review of the victorious army through the streets of Savannah on December 27. In the order for the Seventeenth Corps, the First Alabama Cavalry was afforded the position of honor, "on the right," leading the unit in its march through the city's streets, in recognition of its role and service throughout the brief campaign.[148]

While in the city, Sherman arranged an audience with Secretary of War Edwin Stanton and twenty local ministers who represented the city's black population. They selected Garrison Frazier as their spokesman, who offered the following answer when asked about the relationship between slavery and freedom: "Slavery is receiving by irresistible power the work of another man, and not by his consent. The freedom, as I understand it, promised by the proclamation, is taking us from under the yoke of bondage and placing us where we can reap the fruit of our own labor, and take care of ourselves and assist the Government in maintaining our freedom." Thus, Savannah's newly freed community offered even further evidence of the central importance of the struggle for their labor, a most valuable resource, in the conflict then raging around them.[149]

While the First Alabama Cavalry and the three companies of the 110th USCI enjoyed a brief repose in Savannah, the reminder of the 110th, as well as the 111th and 106th USCI, again found themselves occupying their old nemesis, Forrest, as well as Hood's entire army on its abortive attack on Nashville. After swinging west into Alabama, Hood's army lingered almost two full months in the Tennessee Valley, attempting to scrape together sufficient food and forage to support an attempt on Thomas's army in Middle Tennessee. The men of the three Alabama USCT regiments who had not been captured in Forrest's earlier raid had been pulled back into Tennessee, there not being much justification for guarding the charred timbers of a railroad that had already served its purpose and, once Sherman reopened communications with the North at Savannah, no longer served Union war aims. But the newly constructed Nashville & Northwestern Railroad, intended to keep the city supplied during periods of low water on the Cumberland River by connecting the city with the Tennessee River, remained an important supply line, and its bridges and trestles were worth guarding.

The railroad's western terminus, at Johnsonville, garrisoned in part by the 110th USCT, came under attack on November 4, when Forrest launched another raid on the Union supply network. This time, finding it too difficult to cross the Tennessee and threaten the railroad directly, he moved down the western bank and focused his artillery on the transports bringing supplies up the river to Johnsonville. After surprising them with artillery masked on the shore, he managed to capture one gunboat and two transports, but lost most of their supplies when a responding flotilla recaptured the transports. Forrest then moved up the river opposite Johnsonville, where he had his batteries shell the town, supply depot, and riverboats moored there. With their vessels disabled, the naval commanders panicked and ordered their ships fired to prevent further capture, and the flames spread quickly to large quantities of supplies stacked along the waterfront, doing an estimated 2.2 million dollars' worth of damage. Content with the havoc he had inflicted, Forrest moved upstream to join Hood. Col. Reuben Mussey, commanding the 110th USCI, reported from its headquarters at Nashville, "The behavior of the colored troops at Johnsonville, Tenn., during the recent attack upon that place was, I am informed by several eyewitnesses, excellent." In addition to manning the post's defenses, two guns manned by the Second U.S. Colored Artillery successfully dueled with Forrest's batteries across the river, forcing them to shift positions several times. Even Forrest admitted, "The rammers were shot from the hands of the cannoneers, some of whom were nearly buried amid the dirt which was thrown upon them by the storm of shell which rained upon them by the enemy's batteries." Mussey concluded, "The affair was slight, but it has gained credit for the colored troops."[150]

Forrest and Hood, having failed to sever Thomas's supply lines leading into Nashville, finally embarked on a campaign for the city itself. They advanced largely up the Nashville & Decatur Railroad, no longer of much use to any army, destroying it through Franklin to the city limits. After a bloody fight at Franklin, Hood's depleted army attempted to besiege Nashville but could only effectively man a small sector on the south side of town, leaving the supply lines on the Cumberland River and the Nashville & Northwestern Railroad open. Thomas patiently waited for the men of Hood's command to weaken, left at the end of a tenuous supply line and shivering in the December cold, before finally launching an attack to repel them on December 15 and 16. In this engagement, he had the benefit of two entire brigades (eight regiments) of black troops under James Steedman, mostly from Tennessee but including men recruited during service in North Alabama. On December 16, these men assaulted the Confederate right on Peach Orchard Hill, forcing Hood to shift reinforcements from his left on Shy's Hill. Subsequent attacks stormed both Shy's and Peach Orchard Hills, putting Hood's entire army to flight. After the battle, an officer recorded, "Black and white lay dead side by side."[151]

Events on the Gulf Coast followed the form of those in northern Alabama, but with even greater threats to the state's wartime infrastructure. Just as growing Federal strength, buttressed by increasing numbers of freedmen and Unionists in the ranks, facilitated major campaigns that severed the state's connections to the east, a long-delayed campaign to close the blockade-running haven of Mobile threatened to further isolate Alabama from the outside world. In August, the two forts protecting the bay's entrance, Fort Gaines and Fort Morgan, fell to a combined ground and naval task force under the command of East Tennessee native David Glasgow Farragut, who had also captured New Orleans in 1862. The city itself remained under Confederate control, protected by earthworks on the eastern side of the bay at Spanish Fort and Blakeley. Pensacola offered easy overland communications with these points, and the city saw increased activity as momentum built for a major campaign to capture Mobile in late 1864.

But 1864 began on the Gulf with continued efforts to break the Confederate cordon around the city, allowing freedmen and Unionists to reach Federal lines. Able-bodied men continued to find employment both as laborers on the docks and in the camps, in addition to serving in the ranks. The Eighty-Second USCI, originally raised in Louisiana as the Tenth Corps d'Afrique Infantry, continued to add bondsmen who had liberated themselves, while the First Florida Cavalry took in white Unionists from the surrounding region. Both units enabled Brigadier General Asboth to weather manpower depletions during furloughs for veteran units, including the Seventh Vermont Infantry, which returned to the Green Mountain State for its long-deferred 30-day furlough in August and did not return to New Orleans until October. In part to offset this loss, the Department of the Gulf transferred two more USCT units: the Twenty-Fifth USCI, a Pennsylvania-raised regiment, and the Eighty-Sixth US Colored Infantry, formerly the Fourteenth Corps d'Afrique Infantry, to Pensacola in April, tripling Asboth's strength in black troops and providing additional units for former slaves desiring military service.

1864 began with Asboth using Pensacola's Northern-raised regiments to facilitate the establishment of the Southern ones. In an operation similar to the one that had rescued Wade Richardson the previous year, on January 27,

Asboth sent Lt. George Ross of Company B, Seventh Vermont Infantry, with seventeen men and the schooner *Sarah Breeze* to Point Washington at the head of Choctawhatchee Bay to push back Confederate pickets and help refugees reach the lines. These included three companies of Confederates who had sent word of their intentions to desert with their entire commands and join the First Florida Cavalry.[152] After traveling over twenty-five miles inland, Ross's small force surprised a rebel camp "stationed there to prevent refugees and deserters escaping to our lines," capturing a number of them. Unfortunately, a force of enemy cavalry overtook Ross's command, forcing him to surrender himself and his captives. In February, Asboth wrote of three companies of Confederate cavalry, "hunting deserters with bloodhounds which have torn to pieces several women and children, creating general indignation among the people."[153] But Asboth's active efforts to push the cordon back from the coast enabled more loyalists to reach his lines, including twenty men who came down Santa Rosa Sound in May. Asboth wrote, "These will fill the sixth company of the First Regiment Florida Cavalry, and yet I have neither arms nor horses for these men, who most anxiously desire to be led against the rebels and avenge the many wrongs inflicted upon them and their families by a barbarous foe."[154]

One of the men who came through in early 1864 was Joseph Sanders, a farmer and millwright from near Newton, in Dale County, Alabama. Sanders enlisted in an Alabama-raised Confederate company that was mustered into the Thirty-First Georgia Infantry, and the men elected Sanders, then a sergeant, to be captain of Company C. After serving with Lee's Army of Northern Virginia in the Antietam and Gettysburg campaigns, and being wounded in the former, Sanders resigned his commission and returned to his home. But constant harassment by conscript agents and home guards led Sanders to travel to Pensacola and offer his services to the Union. As a result of his experience, on June 5, he earned a commission as a second lieutenant in Company F of the First Florida, making him one of the few men to serve as an officer on both sides of the war. After spending most of the summer recruiting, Sanders raised another one hundred men for the First Florida and had his company formally mustered in August.[155]

By July, Asboth reported, "The Florida cavalry, already six companies strong, have no arms and no horses. The men all entered my lines from rebeldom and enlisted in the U.S. Army with the fervent desire to revenge under the Union flag all the wrongs inflicted upon them and their families by the rebels. They are all good horsemen, all good marksmen, and perfectly familiar with the country and people throughout Florida, Alabama and Georgia. Thus their services in the field, if well mounted and armed, would prove more efficient here than of any veteran cavalry regiment."[156] But later that month he felt he had sufficient strength to mount the first of several serious raids on enemy positions in the Florida Panhandle. On July 21, he took almost his entire garrison, including the First Florida and the Eighty-Second and Eighty-Sixth USCI, toward the rail junction at Pollard, Alabama, just north of the Florida line, where the Alabama & Florida Railroad, running between Pensacola and Montgomery, joined a spur of the Mobile & Great Northern, running west to the port of Tensaw at the edge of the river delta above Mobile, and connected to it via steamer. This line carried most of the supplies for Asboth's opponents, as well as providing one of Mobile's two rail links to the interior, along with the Mobile & Ohio, running northwest from the city itself. Asboth had been told to watch for Rousseau's raiding force in the event it had been forced south on its raid through central Alabama.

After a heavy skirmish with three companies of the Confederate Seventh Alabama at Gonzales on July 23, in which Asboth's command captured a rebel fort and a number of its garrison, the general learned from a prisoner of the success of Rousseau's raid farther north, meaning the rail line between Mobile and Sherman's army outside Atlanta had already been severed. The next day he also learned that a much larger Confederate force was moving south from the rail junction, forcing Asboth to curtail the expedition and, protected by a providential rainstorm, elude his would-be captors and return his garrison to their entrenchments in Pensacola. The raid took twenty horses and their equipment, which Asboth turned over to the still unmounted First Florida, and, as Sergeant Ray's detail of the First Florida confirmed on July 28, diverted Col. Henry Maury and the entire Fifteenth Confederate Cavalry away from Mobile at the time Federal forces were investing the forts defending the bay.[157]

Asboth remained active through the summer, including a waterborne raid up Pensacola Bay to Milton on August 29 and a much larger operation to Marianna in September, intended to capture Confederate supplies, raid salt works along the coast, and push Confederate forces farther away from Pensacola. Evidently, this was a truncated version of an earlier plan to raid as far as Columbus, Georgia, after a landing on St. Andrew's Bay, returning via Montgomery. Asboth had learned that "the people on the designated line from Hickory

Hill [near Chipley] to Columbus are tired of rebellion and anxious to return to the Union."[158] On September 19, Asboth again crossed the bay with a battalion of the First Florida Cavalry, two mounted companies of men from the Eighty-Second and Eighty-Sixth USCT, and the Second Maine Cavalry, landing on Santa Rosa Island and marching inland to Eucheeanna, then the county seat of Walton County, just southeast of present-day DeFuniak Springs. Here he surprised a garrison of the Fifteenth Confederate Cavalry, capturing fifteen prisoners and securing sixteen "colored recruits" for his black regiments, all of whom the mounted portion of the First Florida returned to a waiting steamer on Choctawhatchee Bay.

At the next major settlement on the route of march, Marianna in Jackson County, near the junction of Florida, Alabama, and Georgia, their opponents gave Asboth's men a sterner test. Defenders repelled an initial charge on a barricade in the town's streets before a second assault carried the works, but not before Asboth suffered a serious wound. Wade Richardson, an Alabamian with the First Florida, reported, "He would have been captured but for our boys with their sabers who in a hand-to-hand encounter kept the enemy at bay till relief was at hand. . . . From that day the First Florida cavalry wore first honors."[159] After the battle, Asboth's men took eighty prisoners, with "over 200 fine horses and excellent mules, 17 wagons and over 400 head of cattle, already brought within our lines, besides over 600 contrabands who followed us with the greatest enthusiasm." Shot in the face and arm, Asboth turned over command to Col. L. L. Zulavsky of the Eighty-Second USCI, an associate from their days in Hungary, who led the command back to Pensacola.[160]

The Pensacola-based forces followed this expedition up with almost weekly raids. One, on a sawmill near Milton in October, took advantage of waterborne transportation to negate the enemy's advantage in mobility, and benefitted from local knowledge of the Panhandle's waterways. On October 17, the chief engineer at Pensacola provided detailed information on the navigability of the Apalachicola River, and its tributaries, the Chattahoochee, forming the border between Alabama and Georgia, and the Flint, to his superior in New Orleans. He wrote, "I have found three men of the First Florida Cavalry who profess to be able to take boats to the head of navigation on both rivers," which, for the Chattahoochee, was Columbus.[161] The following month, the garrison sortied north toward Confederates encamped at Pine Barren Creek, on the road to Pollard. On November 17 "at sunrise, the advance guard, commanded by Lieutenant Sanders, Company F, First Florida, came upon a rebel picket of three men surprising and capturing them; at a distance of a mile another picket was surprised and captured; and a mile farther on six men, constituting the reserve, were made prisoners." In a skirmish at the bridge over Pine Barren Creek, the raid took thirty-eight more prisoners and forty-seven horses, wiping an entire company off the Fifteenth Confederate Cavalry's order of battle. The men had gained surprise largely through the battle-hardened Sanders's efforts. Lt. Col. A. B. Spurling of the Second Maine Cavalry, who commanded the expedition, wrote of the former Confederate officer, "It would hardly be doing justice did I not make special mention of Lieut. Joseph G. Sanders, Company F, First Florida Cavalry. He is a worthy officer, and deserves high praise for his meritorious conduct. He was at all times in command of the advance guard, and much of the success is due to the prompt and faithful manner in which all orders were executed."[162] Perhaps as a reward for his faithful service, Christmas found Sanders on furlough at home with his family in Dale County, well behind enemy lines.[163]

Like many of his fellow Alabamians in blue, Sanders could look back on a highly successful campaign season in 1864. Freedmen and Unionists from Alabama had prevented Forrest from disrupting Sherman's Atlanta campaign, resulting in the destruction of that city and the presence of Alabama soldiers, black and white, with Sherman's victorious army in Savannah. In the Tennessee Valley, more of Alabama's Union soldiers had chased Hood's army away from Nashville, again extending Federal control into the Tennessee Valley of North Alabama. Only in Mobile, where a number of their former comrades in arms suffered in brutal captivity on the city's defenses, had Confederate forces thus far been able to resist the Union tide. But their day of reckoning was coming. In the following months, another Union army, again containing an entire brigade of black troops, stormed the works at Blakeley, liberating the city and freeing their fellow soldiers from bondage. And Alabama troopers and pioneers escorted Sherman's vengeful army through South Carolina, the seat of the rebellion, to a final reckoning with the last significant Confederate army outside of Virginia. At war's end, after a devastating cavalry raid through the very heart of the state, more Alabamians rode at the head of a liberating army to restore the Stars and Stripes to its rightful place atop the Alabama state capitol in Montgomery, ushering in a too-brief era of freedom, liberty, vindication, and reconstruction.

CHAPTER 5

Victory and Peace, 1865

A s 1865 opened, Alabamians serving in the Union army were making significant contributions to the liberation of their state. In Savannah, the 110th USCI and the First Alabama Cavalry were but a small part of the immense army William Tecumseh Sherman was about to unleash on the Carolinas, prompting the Confederacy to rush the battered remnants of the once-proud Army of Tennessee, again under Joe Johnston's leadership, from the Tennessee Valley on a roundabout journey to North Carolina to oppose him. En route, many Alabama Confederate troops took advantage of the opportunity presented by travel through their home state to quietly slip away and return to their homes, correctly believing that the cause was lost. But Johnston's evacuation of Alabama opened the state to a massive cavalry raid. Launched from the same corner of the state that had first been liberated in 1862, Wilson's Raid devastated Alabama's nascent industrial economy and fledgling manufacturing industry, and brought the last regiments of Alabamians into the Union blue.

Outside Mobile, another Union army sat poised to march inland from the Gulf Coast, sever communications between the port city and the rest of the South, and capture the final major port still in Confederate hands after the fall of Wilmington, North Carolina, in February 1865. Black and white Alabamians supported this effort as well, including a final, triumphant march to Montgomery, where they saw the Stars and Stripes again fluttering above the state capitol. The First Florida Cavalry, and the Eighty-Second and Eighty-Sixth USCI regiments, lent extensive support to the campaign and embarked on the first postwar peacekeeping missions along the Gulf Coast. After a long march, the Alabamians who served with Sherman's army returned to their homes in the Tennessee Valley to support the restoration of order and Federal control there, with black and white Alabamians garrisoning Huntsville together in the latter half of 1865. But against a backdrop of rapid demobilization, these troops ultimately proved inadequate to protect freedpeople and refugees across the state after Lincoln's successor, President Andrew Johnson, enacted a lenient system of Reconstruction that former secessionists used to exert their control over those who had risked their lives for the Union. Many of the battles that had marred the war years continued well afterward, until "redemption" and abandonment by the Federal government forced the state's Union soldiers to either return quietly to their farms, hills and hollows, or flee their native state to escape their persecutors who, despite losing the war, won the ensuing peace.

On the Gulf Coast, 1865 opened with a final Federal effort to capture the port of Mobile, rendered useless to the Confederates as a haven for blockade-runners since the late summer of 1864 after the fall of the forts guarding the bay's mouth. Union campaign plans for 1865 envisioned a continued tightening of the noose around the collapsing Confederacy, with attacks on the remaining ports at Wilmington, North Carolina, and Mobile, coupled with cavalry raids slicing deep into the interior from hard-won bases in eastern Tennessee and northern Alabama, all designed to increase the pressure on Lee's beleaguered forces clinging to their positions in front of Grant's army at Richmond and Petersburg. In order to assemble a sufficient force for the reduction of Mobile, Maj. Gen. Edward R. S. Canby cleaned out his garrison troops along the Mississippi River, enabling him to field an entire division of black troops, most originally from Louisiana. Under the command of Brig. Gen. John Parker Hawkins, this division marched overland from Pensacola and played a significant role in the assault and capture of Fort Blakeley, Alabama, the last position protecting Mobile's eastern approaches.

Although Louisiana was still threatened by Confederate forces west of the Mississippi River, Canby was able to move a large force from the state by replacing them with troops from Memphis and other posts along the Mississippi. The Fifty-Fifth USCI, which had been garrisoning Memphis for over a year, moved by steamer from that city to Morganza, Louisiana, in early March.[1] The regiment's journey was uneventful, but river travel remained dangerous, as evidenced by the loss of the steamer *Autocrat* with five companies of the Sixty-First USCI. Morganza occupied higher ground on the river's west bank, near the confluence of the Mississippi, Red, and Atchafalaya Rivers, and the Fifty-Fifth's service at that post kept Confederates and guerrillas away from the river. In late March, the Fifty-Fifth moved to the squalid camps at Port Hudson, site of a bloody siege in 1863 and now teeming with all of the pathogens that accumulated near the camps of Civil War armies. The Fifty-Fifth held the post throughout the summer of 1865, suffering more from disease than anything else.[2] In August, the unit moved again by steamer to Vidalia, Louisiana, but by the end of the year was in Baton Rouge for their official mustering out. The men were far from their original homes in North Alabama and their loved ones, who were left behind in the contraband camp in Memphis. But many took advantage of the government's offer of transportation to their choice of residence, and by 1866, several veterans were again living in Alabama's Tennessee Valley.[3]

Canby sent Hawkins' division to Pensacola to combine the regiments transferred from Louisiana with the four black regiments, namely the Twenty-Fifth, Eighty-Second, Eighty-Sixth, and Ninety-Seventh USCI, already garrisoning Fort Barrancas and Pensacola itself. Along with the First Florida Cavalry and other white regiments, these units formed a flank column for Canby's primary advance up the eastern shore of Mobile Bay toward Spanish Fort and Blakeley. Under Maj. Gen. Frederick Steele, the "Pensacola Column" headed north from the city toward the Florida & Alabama Railroad junction at Pollard. Once in possession of that place, Steele ensured that reinforcements from the interior of the state could not reach Mobile along the railroad, and also blocked the escape of any Confederates fleeing the city. Protecting Steele's flank, a smaller column of cavalry under Lt. Col. Andrew Spurling, including his own Second Maine Cavalry, the Second Illinois Cavalry, and four companies of the First Florida, who were familiar with the area, left Milton and headed north through Andalusia in order to cut the railroad near Evergreen. Canby had given Steele some latitude to continue toward Montgomery if he was unopposed, but Steele found the countryside so destitute of forage and provisions that he wheeled his blue-clad troops to the left toward Mobile and certain resupply from the ships in the bay.

Before embarking, the Union garrison at Pensacola had to address the potential for a spoiling attack from the Confederates operating east of Mobile. In mid-February, the troops went on alert after reports placed Confederate Brig. Gen. St. John R. Liddell at Perdido Mills, on the Florida–Alabama border, with three regiments of infantry, two battalions of cavalry, and a battery of artillery. A deserter reported, "It was rumored in the rebel camp that it was intended to attack Barrancas and capture the deserters [First Florida Cavalry], obtain provisions, and *destroy* the negro troops" (emphasis added). But freedmen continued to provide valuable intelligence, allaying Union fears. A Federal officer in Pensacola reported, "A colored man who came within our lines on the 4th instant from Blakeley, Ala. reports 2,000 infantry and 100 cavalry at that place," confirming that Liddell had not marched on Pensacola, allowing preparations to continue.[4]

On February 26, Brigadier General Asboth, still commanding at Pensacola, reported the result of a scouting expedition of the First Florida, under Lt. C. B. Pickard, sent to determine the Confederate strength at Perdido Mills. Pickard's men captured two Confederate scouts from the Sixth Alabama who reported that an entire brigade of Alabama troops from Cheatham's division of Hood's army, en route to oppose Sherman in North Carolina, "broke from the train at Montgomery and, dispersing, left for their homes," demonstrating the imminent collapse of discipline and morale among the Confederate troops. Further corroboration came from three enlisted men, Thomas G. Daniels and William Watson of the Fifty-Fourth Alabama and Joseph F. Hicks of the Thirty-Third Alabama, who arrived in Pensacola after deserting from Hood's army in Montgomery. Asboth reported, "They are all veterans, having served in the rebel army from the beginning of the rebellion, and now desire to serve in the Federal army and enlist in the 1st Florida Cavalry. They think that 9,000 of Hood's men have deserted and are now at their homes or in the woods."[5]

By mid-March, all was ready, and the "Pensacola Column," 12,000 strong, set out on its roundabout course for Mobile. Steele reported that he had approximately 5,000 black troops under Hawkins, 5,000 veteran white troops under Brig. Gen. Christopher C. Andrews, and over 2,000 cavalry under Brig. Gen. Thomas J. Lucas. On March 21, Lieutenant Colonel Spurling's column crossed the bay in boats, disembarked near Crigler's Mill at Cedar Grove, south of Milton, and drove rebel pickets through the city and into the piney hills beyond. On March 23, Spurling's column reached Andalusia and found no resistance and very little property belonging to the "rebel government." That evening the fast-moving column reached the railroad just above Evergreen, capturing several pickets in the process, one of whom proved to be "a Lieutenant Watts, of General Clanton's staff, and a son of Governor Watts."[6] After cutting the telegraph and destroying the track, Spurling's men intercepted a northbound train from Pollard and a southbound train from Montgomery containing over one hundred reinforcements for Mobile. The Federal troopers destroyed as much as they could of the railroad, rolling stock, and stores between Evergreen and Pollard, and took ten boxes of tobacco and fifteen barrels of flour from the store of Robert Robb, a loyal Methodist minister in the town.[7] On the 26th, Spurling's men, guided by the Alabamians of the First Florida and now accompanied by one hundred prisoners and "200 negroes" who availed themselves of the opportunity to secure their freedom, passed through Brewton and joined Steele's advance at Pollard.[8] As Canby had predicted in his instructions to Steele, "The Florida cavalry know the country thoroughly and will be particularly valuable to you as scouts."[9] Steele's men had departed Pensacola on the 20th and moved slowly up the railroad, with his advance guard, the First Louisiana Cavalry, a regiment of Unionists raised primarily in New Orleans, dispersing Clanton's rebel cavalry at Bluff Springs, where one of the Louisiana troopers captured the Sixth Alabama's battle flag.[10] His rear now secure from any threat in that quarter, and finding that "the country through which we were passing was almost destitute of supplies," Steele turned the united command west toward Mobile.[11]

Steele's troops skirmished with Confederate defenders en route to Blakeley, which they reached and invested during the first week of April. Along the way they subsisted on cattle driven in from the surrounding countryside and supplies at Canoe Station, where "considerable corn was found at the depot, but the citizens from the surrounding country had made the best use of the time allowed them in carrying off the rebel supplies." Some of the cattle appropriated during the campaign belonged to Unionists in the region, including David and Elisha Nelson, born on the Outer Banks of North Carolina in Carteret County, but wartime residents of Shell Banks, Alabama, who later received reimbursement from the Southern Claims Commission for thirty-nine of their livestock. David Nelson had also helped loyalists evade conscription agents and reach Union lines, and swore that he was "bitterly opposed to secession in 1860, as were almost all my neighbors, but we never were afforded an opportunity to vote against it." He later served as a guide for the troops advancing against Spanish Fort.[12]

On April 1, Spurling's command charged the battered remnants of the Forty-Sixth Mississippi near Holyoke, capturing the command and their battle flag, but according to Spurling, lost "a horse blown to pieces and the rider badly wounded by the explosion of a torpedo [land mine]," which were becoming more common throughout the desperate Confederacy.[13] Along the march, black and white troops apparently got along well, with one chaplain reporting that he had "never witnessed such a friendly feeling between white and colored troops."[14] The march took its toll on the black troops, leaving them hungry for combat, as well as literally. First Sgt. Cassius M. Clay, of the Fiftieth USCI, wrote, "We are only ten days on the siege, and had nothing to eat but Parched Corn. But as luck would have it, I crept out of my hole at night and scared one of the Jonnys so bad that he left his rifle pit, gun and accouterment, also one corn dodger and about one pint of buttermilk, all of which I devoured with a will, and returned to my hole safe and sound."[15]

With the defenders now trapped inside their entrenchments, Union forces settled down to a brief siege. As gunboats in the bay pounded the defenders, Steele and Canby made final preparations for an assault they were certain would overwhelm the undermanned defenders. After Canby's column broke the rebel lines at Spanish Fort on April 8, the surviving defenders of that garrison fled upriver to Blakeley, itself scheduled for assault on April 9, the same day Lee surrendered to Grant at Appomattox Court House. With the nine USCT regiments forming roughly half the investing force, Blakeley offered one final opportunity for black troops to demonstrate their combat ability, as well as an opportunity for the Confederate defenders to experience defeat at the hands of their former slaves. While one Union commander believed "it was time to see if the Niggers would fight," evidently unaware that black soldiers had already conclusively proven that point, Confederate defenders feared retribution for, among other things, the massacre at Fort Pillow, which the black troops remained determined to avenge. As that attack proved, holding a defensive work was fraught with danger for the defenders, as those who had surrendered might face attackers who were unaware and were still fighting.

The assault itself misfired, perhaps after an attempt by the white officers in the black regiments to secure all of the glory for themselves. Taking advantage of an order to drive in the Confederate pickets, the Sixty-Eighth and Seventy-Sixth USCT made a general assault on the right of the rebel lines almost an hour before the scheduled time for the main attack. Unfortunately, this ill-timed assault resulted in heavy casualties, as the defenders shifted troops from unthreatened sectors of the line to easily repel the attackers. But when the main effort kicked off as scheduled, the weakened areas of the Confederate lines were, in turn, easily overwhelmed by Steele's men, and Hawkins' division renewed attempt on their sector likewise carried the lines. According to one account, the routed defenders "ran toward their right to the white troops to avoid capture by the colored soldiers, fearing violence after surrender."[16] In some cases those fears were apparently justified, as Confederate defenders later alleged that their troops had been killed after surrendering by men from the USCT, some of them shouting 'Remember Fort Pillow.'"[17] While a few such instances may have occurred, there was no wholesale or sanctioned slaughter, as there had been at Fort Pillow. The black regiments took large numbers of prisoners, and the defenders' casualty rates were not nearly as high as at Fort Pillow. An officer of a USCT regiment even reported seeing one of his soldiers sharing his canteen with his former master, on the surface an act of humanity but also a powerful image of social leveling, especially given the later practice of maintaining separate drinking fountains for blacks and whites.[18] Despite a few isolated instances of violence, most Confederates survived the assault and passed into a brief captivity. The loss of Blakeley made Mobile untenable, and Confederate forces evacuated the city the following day. On May 4, the Confederate department commander, Lt. Gen. Richard Taylor, surrendered his command to Canby at Citronelle, formally ending the war in Alabama.

The capture of the Confederate forts, and the city itself, finally liberated hundreds of USCT troops captured in the state the previous fall who had been forced to labor on the city's defensive works. But liberation came with one final trial. On May 25, a warehouse storing ammunition on the city's waterfront caught fire and exploded, killing over three hundred, including a number of black soldiers, sank two ships in the river, and heavily damaged the USCT hospital nearby. Lt. Joseph Nelson, of the 111th USCI, had traveled to the city to collect his former soldiers and bring them home. He reported that the Battle House, over a mile from the explosion, had nearly all of its windows blown out, and the next day, "loaded shells were still exploding in the ruins under the heaps of ashes." Nelson also "found our men of the 111th delighted to see us. They had begun to fear that they were abandoned each one to his own resources." He and another officer escorted almost six hundred men from the 106th, 110th, and 111th USCI back to their commands at Nashville.[19] One of these was Pvt. George Allen, of the 110th USCI, captured in Athens in September 1864, who had suffered grievous injuries from the explosion and falling debris and was "considered dead for some hours." In a coma for several days, Allen eventually recovered in Northern hospitals and returned to his unit in the Tennessee Valley, but was a virtual invalid, who, according to a fellow soldier, "did not do any duty after he come back, except he have water for the soldiers and help about cooking." Allen's disability pension and shrewd management enabled him to acquire over 600 acres of land by the time of his death in 1896.[20]

Confederate defenders of Mobile had been deprived of the services of one of their more famous commanders, Lt. Gen. Nathan Bedford Forrest, but given his difficulties in working alongside or under commanders earlier in his career, most notably during the Chickamauga campaign, he may not have been of much help anyway. As it was, Forrest had his hands full defending the large Confederate factories and supply depot at Selma, which were far more important than Mobile if the rebels wanted to continue the struggle. In early March, over 12,000 cavalrymen under Brig. Gen. James H. Wilson left the Tennessee Valley for a raid on Selma, Montgomery, and Columbus, Georgia, as well as on Alabama's nascent iron production at foundries along the way, designed to rip the heart out of the Confederacy. Wilson crossed the same rugged mountains as both Streight and Rousseau had done before him, but angled farther south, reaching Elyton (modern Birmingham) almost unopposed. Along the way, he detached a part of his command under a loyal Kentuckian, Brig. Gen. John T. Croxton, to destroy the war industries in Tuscaloosa and the military college there (now the University of Alabama), which he did, burning most of the important buildings. While "Lost Cause" apologists continued to blame "the Yankees" for the destruction for the next century, the fact that most of the damage was inflicted by fellow Southerners was often omitted from the narrative. Tuscaloosa's slaves, according to one trooper, reveled in their liberation. He wrote, "The negroes flocked into the city in countless numbers," celebrating their day of jubilee.[21] In crossing Sand Mountain, trooper Ebenezer Gilpin of the Third Iowa Cavalry marveled at the rugged scenery. He observed, "This is a country of rivers. The little wriggles of ink down the page of our military map are mountain streams flowing by stately pine woods, through hemlock-bordered ravines; some clear and some colorless, others shaded blue and green, that when falling in sunlit cascades are very beautiful. Clear Creek Falls at the headwaters of the Black Warrior, are the most picturesque imaginable. One would have to be both poet and painter to do them justice in description," but Giplin's efforts are a fair attempt.[22] In his memoirs, Wilson offered his appraisal of the loyal Southerners he observed in this region and throughout the war. He wrote that the typical "po' white man" was "plain, simple-minded, and sensible without sham or pretension; loving the Union because he had been taught to love it; hating the slaveholders rebellion and caring nothing for 'his rights in the territories' because he had no slaves; staying at home when he could and taking no part in the struggle unless he must, because he realized from the first that it was 'the rich man's war and the poor man's fight.' This was the sum of his political philosophy." Wilson's command now passed through the heart of the state, home to many Alabamians who fit this description.[23]

Moving south from Elyton, Wilson destroyed ironworks at Helena, Brier-field, and Shelby before finally meeting Forrest's men south of Montevallo. The depleted Southerners were no match for the well-mounted Union cavalry and their superior Spencer carbines, which easily brushed Forrest aside at Ezra Church, near Maplesville, and invested the defenders inside of the miles of entrenchments around Selma. At this stage of the war, there were simply too few defenders to hold the formidable works, and a frontal assault carried the day, driving Forrest and his men out of the city. Unable to resist the opportunity to inflict one last atrocity, some of Forrest's troopers surprised a camp of the Fourth US Cavalry and took their frustrations out on the isolated command, killing and wounding thirty-five sleeping men before escaping to Mississippi. Wilson observed later that Forrest "appears to have a ruthless temper which impelled him on every occasion where he had a clear advantage to push his success to a bloody end, and yet he always seemed not only to resent but to have a plausible excuse for the cruel excesses which were charged against him."[24]

While at Selma, the commander of Wilson's wagon train, Maj. Martin R. Archer, originally of the Third Ohio Cavalry, recruited the final USCT regiments in the state. Confederates had removed slaves from the surrounding states to the interior of Alabama to prevent their liberation, and then impressed many of them to work on Selma's defenses and in the war industries there. With the town largely destroyed and no prospects for employment or sustenance, many responded to Archer's appeals. Wilson had been authorized to recruit a regiment of colored troops for each of his Cavalry Corps' three divisions, primarily to serve as pioneers and guards, and Archer reported that he had enlisted five hundred men for his regiment on April 8, and had them drilling the next day.[25] By the time the column moved out for Montgomery, the other two regiments had roughly five hundred men as well. Thus, many of Alabama's former slaves were among the first soldiers to enter the capital city as liberators on April 12, four years to the day after the war began at Fort Sumter. Camped near a large plantation, an Iowa cavalryman recalled ex-slaves celebrating their long-awaited freedom: "Tonight is a jubilee in their cabins. We can hear them dancing fiddling, singing and laughing."[26] Rather than attempt to hold the city, Wilson left Montgomery, passing through Tuskegee en route to Columbus, Georgia, where he inflicted significant damage on the war industries there, and procured stocks of gray uniforms for his new black soldiers. Already, many of the men in Northern units also wore gray uniforms captured at Selma to replace their threadbare blue.[27] Wilson continued on to Macon, reaching that place on April 21, where he finally learned of Lee's capitulation. The three new regiments of black troops garrisoned Macon, enabling Wilson to detach a portion of this command to pursue the fleeing president of the Confederacy.[28] Troopers of the First Wisconsin and Fourth Michigan Cavalry captured Jefferson Davis and his entourage on May 10, near Irwinville, Georgia.[29] After mustering the three new regiments in as the 136th, 137th, and 138th US Colored Infantry, the War Department sent the 136th and 138th to Atlanta, where they garrisoned that destroyed city for the remainder of the year, while the 137th remained in Macon. During the summer, Wilson detached Company H of the 137th to assist with establishing a cemetery at Andersonville, site of a notorious Confederate prison, for the remains of over 12,000 Union soldiers interred there, including several from the First Alabama Cavalry. The three-week duty reflected racial stereotypes of the period, which saw many African Americans, including a number of Alabama's black soldiers, relegated to mortuary affairs duties, both at Andersonville and at Murfreesboro, Tennessee.[30]

With Confederate resistance in the state crushed and the road open to Montgomery, Canby hastily assembled a column to permanently occupy the capital and begin the arduous task of restoring Federal authority over the defeated state. On April 13, the same day Wilson left Montgomery for Columbus, Maj. Gen. A. J. Smith's Sixteenth Corps of roughly 15,000 troops left Mobile for Montgomery, arriving on the 25th. On the night of the 17th, a portion of the column camped near the farm of Miles Ryan, a loyal Irish immigrant living in Conecuh County, where they helped themselves to his cattle, sheep, hogs, corn, and bacon.[31] Canby had anticipated this mission, ordering, "Captain Lyons, First Florida Cavalry, to send to General Canby's headquarters six men from his regiment who are best acquainted with the country between the Alabama River and Choctawhatchee, and as far north as Montgomery." Alabamians led the way to the restoration of their flag, and still more Alabamians, namely those enlisted in the USCT regiments of Steele's column, entered the city as liberators.

Arriving at Greenville on April 20, Smith's column scattered a small force of Confederates defending the town, capturing eighty, including several officers. Some members of the command took the liberty of commandeering the press of the *Greenville Observer* and printed a commemorative issue of their arrival. They reported they were encouraged to see that "the Stars and Stripes were unfurled from a neat little cottage," but did not elaborate on whether it represented a long-secreted display by a hidden Unionist, or an opportunistic attempt to deter any potential plunderers, though the soldiers-turned-newspapermen reported that "not a single house has been destroyed and the town is quiet and orderly." While encamped in Greenville, the army learned of Lee's surrender over a week earlier and fired a two-hundred-gun salute on April 22 to commemorate the occasion, in what must be the most impressive military display that small Alabama town has ever seen.[32]

Smith's column traveled overland along the route of the railroad, screened in advance by Maj. Gen. Benjamin H. Grierson's cavalry, while a second, under Steele, including Hawkins' First Division, USCT, moved upriver by steamer, arriving at Selma on April 27. There they found that Wilson had done his work too well, as there was insufficient coal to resupply the ships, delaying their arrival in Montgomery until April 30, when the *Montgomery Daily Mail* reported the arrival of "a large number of the *chasseurs d'Afrique.*"[33] Union soldiers described the black troops' reception from the freedmen in the city: "They would all dance, clap their hands, sing and holler. Then the troops from the boats would cheer."[34] Smith had arrived in Montgomery on April 25, detailing a brigade of Illinois troops to garrison the town and ordering, "This city being in possession of the forces of the United States and, consequently released from the withering grasp of despotism, the inhabitants of the same are invited to resume their several peaceful avocations."[35]

With Smith's forces garrisoning the town, Steele's command returned to Mobile, where specific orders awaited the Eighty-Second USCT. Along with the First Florida Cavalry, they were to sail to Apalachicola, Florida, at the mouth of the river of the same name. Occupation duty highlighted the regiment's extensive postwar service, and kept them in arms until September 1866, making them one of the longest-serving volunteer regiments. On May 31, the regiment, along with the Sixty-First New York, and thirty mounted men of the First Florida, sailed for Apalachicola, arriving the next morning. They found almost 1,000 bales of cotton in the port, which they confiscated and turned over to agents of the Department of the Treasury. General Asboth led the expedition but returned once the Federal forces had been established in the port. Asboth's detailed instructions to the detachment's commander represent one of the earliest efforts at posthostility Reconstruction, but reflect the army's extensive experience in liberated areas, including Pensacola, during the war.

The orders proscribed foraging, except in emergencies, and required that receipts be issued, in accordance with standing instructions. Asboth also insisted that, while Confederate deserters were to be issued pardons, "All deserters of our army within your reach you will endeavor to arrest, including Lieut. J. G. Sanders, First Florida Cavalry, who has been absent without leave for more than three months, and has become, with his armed gang of deserters, a terror to the people of West Florida."[36] Sanders had been ordered back into Alabama in February 1865, with thirty men to recruit for his regiment, but did not return until June, shortly after regarrisoning Apalachicola. Sanders testified that he had been attempting to elude the Confederate Home Guard, which prevented him from returning to Pensacola. Sanders had apparently led his men into an ambush in Newton, Alabama, in March, having been betrayed by one of his own men.[37] Rather than face a court-martial, Sanders tendered his resignation and, after receiving an honorable discharge, attempted to resume his life in Dale County. After killing a former Confederate in self-defense as he tried to enter Sanders' home, the Union veteran fled to Georgia, but was tracked down and murdered in February 1867 as he ate his dinner. Lt. David Snelling, who had commanded Sherman's escort from the First Alabama, also received a hostile reception when he returned to his hometown in Georgia. According to later testimony by the regiment's commanding officer, Col. George Spencer, "The lieutenant commanding that escort was born and raised near Milledgeville, Georgia. After he was mustered out of the service, in August last, he returned to Milledgeville, but was allowed to remain only six hours there. He was mobbed in the streets of Milledgeville, and was charged with being responsible for everything that Sherman's whole army did in Milledgeville. His friends and relations made him leave to save his life."[38]

Even after Sanders' return, deserters reported to be former members of the First Florida continued to terrorize the Wiregrass region. A detachment of the Second Maine Cavalry arrived in Elba on June 23, where local authorities reported, "Deserters from both armies have been lurking about in Coffee County and adjoining counties for over a year, committing depredations upon the property of both loyal and disloyal men . . . more than fifty men, mostly deserters from the First Florida Cavalry, U.S. Army, are engaged in robbing, plundering and committing acts of violence." Given that the testimony came from a "Judge Starke," and "the most influential and respectable citizens," it is not surprising that they blamed the unrest on the "deserters," who were very likely settling scores for the persecution they and their families had suffered. Federal efforts to restore control were initially thwarted by the destitute condition of the country, with one commander reporting: "I could not remain in that locality long enough, being without supplies, and the country being too poor to obtain them." The officer's superior endorsed the report with this bleak assessment: "There is nothing left in the country beyond the actual necessities of the inhabitants."[39]

In addition to combating the lawless bands of guerrillas inhabiting, among other places, a stretch of swamp known today as "Tate's Hell," Federal forces attempted to regulate the former slaves' transition from slavery to freedom. With regard to freedmen, Asboth issued the following instructions:

All persons formerly held as slaves will be treated in every respect as entitled to the rights of freedmen and such as desire their services will be required to pay for them. . . . Freedmen will have to work for their support, but may select their own employers. Persons forcibly retaining or illtreating their former slaves will subject themselves to arrest and trial by military commission.

Thus began one of the most important duties of the Bureau of Refugees, Freedmen and Confiscated Lands (better known as the "Freedmen's Bureau"), namely the regulation of labor agreements between former slaves and former masters. The bureau operated under the auspices of the Army, then, as now, being one of the few instruments of national power capable of such an expansive undertaking as stabilizing a country after war. It is worth noting that the first named constituencies in the bureau's official name was "refugees," acknowledging that many loyal Southerners had been likewise displaced by the war and also required assistance, to include meeting subsistence requirements, at least until crops could be harvested and commerce reestablished. All of Alabama's Federal troops were intimately involved in these activities, at posts across Alabama and in neighboring states. Their efforts to rebuild their state constituted the final service they provided while in uniform.

For the Alabamians who had enlisted in the Eighty-Sixth USCT, most of this service occurred within the borders of their home state. After returning from Montgomery to Mobile, the regiment reported to Fort Morgan, on the sandy spit of land between Mobile Bay and the Gulf of Mexico. For the remainder of 1865 and the first few months of 1866, the regiment provided the garrison for that post and other defenses around Mobile Bay, except for brief service at Bladon Springs, upriver from Mobile, which had been a resort area known as the "Saratoga of the South" before the war. Unfortunately, the locale acquired a less hospitable reputation in the postwar period, at least for freedmen, as it became a hotbed of antigovernment activity. Four companies remained at the former resort through the 1865 election season before returning to their posts along Mobile Bay, where they mustered out in April 1866.[40]

The Alabamians who spent the first days of 1865 in Savannah, Georgia, with Sherman's army also played an extensive role in postwar occupation, most notably in Huntsville, the center of the area where most had lived before the war. But before they returned to reconstruct their home state, they had several more months of hard campaigning through the Carolinas and an arduous journey home over the Appalachians ahead of them. Their efforts, as part of Sherman's force, contributed to the loss of the Confederate ports of Charleston, South Carolina, and Wilmington, North Carolina, and ensured that Lee's army at Richmond and Petersburg could not escape to the south to continue the struggle, even if it could somehow disengage from Grant's besieging army. A final battle, against the hardy veterans of the Army of Tennessee, once again under Joe Johnston, near Bentonville, North Carolina, closed the campaign and ended the fighting in the east.[41]

As Sherman's armies marched farther from Alabama, the Alabama troops found their particular services as guides of less use, and were accordingly incorporated into regular units, proving they could function in that capacity as well as any other regiment in the army. The companies of the 110th USCI remained assigned to Corse's Fourth Division of the Fifteenth Corps, under

Maj. W. C. Hawley, while the First Alabama Cavalry found itself brigaded with fellow Southerners of the Fifth Kentucky Cavalry and one Northern regiment, the Fifth Ohio Cavalry, with now Brigadier General Spencer in command of the entire brigade. Spencer's three regiments comprised the Third Brigade of the cavalry division under Maj. Gen. Hugh Judson Kilpatrick, also known as "Kill Cavalry," for his sometimes wanton disregard for the lives of his men. The loyal Alabamians recovered from the "March to the Sea" but began preparations for an even more difficult journey, as they would now move perpendicular to the deep rivers that cut across the coastal plain from the Piedmont, necessitating miles of "corduroying" by the pioneers and restricting cavalry to the few roads on the high ground between the swamps. In addition, they traveled during the harshest months of the South's comparatively mild winter, when cold, soaking rains and occasional ice, sleet, and snow made them miss the winter quarters armies usually occupied during this time of year, even in the Deep South.[42]

The First Alabama Cavalry spent part of the month of January scouting across the Savannah River into South Carolina, where they found "forage and sweet potatoes in abundance."[43] After getting their mounts in the best condition they could, the regiment's "eighteen officers and 292 men fit for duty" left their permanent camp on the Little Ogeechee River on January 28, and marched to the Savannah River, where delays in assembling the pontoon bridge postponed their crossing until February 3. En route, they assisted with the destruction of the Charleston & Augusta Railroad and skirmished constantly with Confederate cavalry under fellow Alabamian Joe Wheeler, most notably when his command counterattacked them at Williston, South Carolina, on February 8. Confederate troopers charged two companies of the First Alabama on the road to Aiken, but quickly withdrew to a strong position farther from town. When the full regiment arrived, reinforced by the Fifth Kentucky, the loyal Southerners found Col. James Hagan's brigade of six regiments, their opposite number, the Confederate First Alabama Cavalry, as well as the Third, Fifth, Eighth, Twelfth and Fifty-First Alabama Cavalry regiments opposing their advance. Spencer ordered a charge,

> which was done by both commands in the most gallant manner, the enemy stopping to fire but one volley. Then commenced one of the most thorough and complete routs I ever witnessed. The ground was

completely strewn with guns, haversacks, &c. Five battle flags were captured, including the brigade and four regimental flags, and a large number of horses and over thirty prisoners. After a charge of about seven miles from this point the enemy dispersed and went in every direction through woods and swamps.

The result was a far cry from the First Alabama's first engagement at Vincent's Crossroads over two years before, when they had been put to flight, and reflected the reversal of fortune for Alabama cavalrymen on opposing sides. But it was not the last encounter between loyal and disloyal Alabamians in the campaign.[44]

For the remainder of the month, Spencer's men pushed through roads repeatedly described as "almost impassable," "horrible," and "in such a condition that even a mile an hour could not be averaged," across swollen streams until crossing into North Carolina on March 3. Marching on horseback was difficult enough, but the teamster companies of the 110th had to push heavy wagons across the quagmires, frequently dismounting and soliciting assistance to get their charges through. The backbreaking labor often went unappreciated and, far too often, unrecorded, but was essential to the army's success. These men later rejoined their regiment and served alongside the pioneers.[45]

Late on the evening of March 9, Kilpatrick impetuously thrust Spencer's isolated brigade into camp at Monroe's Crossroads on the road to Fayetteville, in an attempt to block the advance of Confederate forces moving toward that town. According to Maj. Sanford Tramel, commanding the First Alabama, "At the sounding of reveille on the morning of the 10th instant, we were aroused from sleep by the whistling of bullets and the fiendish yelling of the enemy, who were charging into our camp."[46] Three full divisions of Confederate cavalry under Wheeler and Wade Hampton surprised the command and drove them to the edge of a swamp. There, aided by two guns of the Tenth Wisconsin Artillery, the blue-clad troopers mounted a counterattack on famished Confederates who had stopped to pilfer the wagon train. The Union troops eventually drove their attackers from the camp, but the First Alabama lost four men killed, twenty-seven wounded, and forty-one captured, including the acting commander, Major Cramer, who was wounded and taken prisoner "while gallantly cheering his men," and Major Tramel, who managed to slip away from his captors five days later and rejoined the regiment.[47] Spencer claimed to have buried over one hundred enemy dead and taken a comparable number of wounded and prisoners, making the affair, like many engagements in the war, a bloody and inconclusive draw.

Kilpatrick's command guarded the Union flank in Johnston's larger scale but equally inconclusive attacks at Averasboro and Bentonville, but the First Alabama, likely due to the losses suffered at Monroe's Crossroads, was not heavily engaged for the remainder of the campaign. Spencer reported that, in fifty-five days, they had marched "over 700 miles, crossing seven large rivers on pontoon bridges and an innumerable number of smaller streams and swamps that under ordinary circumstances would be considered impassible." Along the way, the unit foraged heavily and, Spencer reported, "subsisted almost entirely upon the country for rations for the men and entirely for forage for animals. For fifty days my brigade drew only five days' partial rations from the commissariat."[48] After the Confederate surrender, a humorous mock order, issued by "F. O. RAGE, Chief of Bummers" perhaps a pseudonym for Spencer, dismissed the "bummers" of the Military Division of the Mississippi, "by reason of the promulgation of peace—an event over which they had no control. I need not tell the surviving Bummers of so many thieving expeditions that this unhappy, unthought of, and uncalled for result was brought about by no effort of theirs." The order declined to issue "further orders for your future welfare and discipline . . . feeling assured that each one of you will be eventually cared for in your respective State prisons!"[49] Humor aside, the practice of foraging, especially upon secessionists, proved to be a difficult one to break for the regiment, both in North Carolina and back in Alabama. On April 28, Major Tramel issued strict orders, pointing out that "members of this regiment are in the habit of strolling over the country for many miles around and committing depredations of various kinds upon the citizens." Tramel forbade anyone to leave camp without a pass and instituted a strict regime of roll calls three times daily to ensure accountability. He further stipulated, "No soldier will be allowed to saddle his horse without special permission," and "Horses will not be allowed to pasture on wheat in the vicinity," with violators "punished to the utmost extent of military law."[50]

Following Lee's surrender to Grant, Johnston likewise sought terms from Sherman, ending the war in the east. Most troops, having fulfilled their duty, now sought to return to their homes as quickly as possible. Many Union regiments, formed early in the war, had fulfilled their stated terms of service and were scheduled for an early muster out. In some respects, rapid demo-bilization was justified. Michael Fitzgerald argues the soldiers, "manifested a war-charged hostility to the slaveholding society. They were undisciplined agents of liberation, spreading disorder through the region, much of it unnec-essary or counterproductive."[51] The First Alabama Cavalry, in some respects, fit this description, as one Union soldier reported, "They say they are going back to kill every reb in their country."[52] Having been recruited throughout the war, the regiment contained a number of men with time remaining on their enlistments. While their motivation for revenge would be destabilizing, their knowledge of the physical, cultural and human terrain of northern Alabama continued to make them an indispensable addition to the Union forces sta-tioned there. According to their commander, "many of my men are desirous of going home, having been driven from their state long ago."[53] Accordingly, on May 4, Special Order No. 48 relieved them from duty with Sherman's army and ordered the regiment to "march without delay to Knoxville, Tenn.," where it would report by telegraph to Maj. Gen. George H. Thomas at Nashville for further instructions.[54]

While the First Alabama Cavalry prepared for its journey home, the com-panies of the 110th USCI had a more important duty to fulfill, one that sur-passed even the honor bestowed upon the Alabama cavalrymen in the parade through Savannah. The pioneers of the 110th traveled with Sherman's army to Washington, DC, and were the only USCT unit to participate in the "Grand Review of the Armies" through the capitol.[55] Sherman described his troops as the most magnificent army in existence—65,000 men in splendid *physique*, who had just completed a march of nearly 2,000 miles in a hostile country, in good drill. He reported, "Each division was preceded by its corps of black pi-oneers, armed with picks and spades. These marched abreast in double ranks, keeping perfect dress and step, and added much to the interest of the occa-sion."[56] In his memoirs, Maj. Gen. Joshua Chamberlain, hero of the Twentieth Maine's stand on the Little Round Top at Gettysburg, recalled, "each division is preceded by its corps of black pioneers, shining like polished ebony, armed with pick and spade, proud of their perfect alignment, keeping step to the music with inborn stress."[57] They may not have been identified as soldiers, as the hard work of corduroying roads and building entrenchments had literally worn their old uniforms to shreds, and they likely chose to march with their "picks and shovels," rather than rifles, as badges of honor, as the troops surely knew who had built the roads and bridges they marched over and entrenchments they fought behind continuously for the past twelve months.[58] Equally fitting, behind Sherman's army came the families of freedmen, marching just as they had in the army's wake across the South. Chamberlain recalled, "As a climax, with significance which one might ponder, whole families of freed slaves, as servants, trustfully leading their little ones, obedient to fate, silent, without sign of joy; more touching in some ways than the proud passing column."[59] As William Lloyd Garrison's *Liberator* pointed out the black soldiers and citizens "marched shoulder to shoulder, in the review, with their white comrades, under the same flag."[60]

For the First Alabama Cavalry, their journey across the mountains proved arduous for both men and mounts. Along a route that took them through Salisbury, Lincolnton, Rutherfordton, and Ashville, North Carolina, before crossing the rocky spine of the Smokies into Greenville and Knoxville, Tennessee, troopers reported that, "a large number of our animals gave out for want of forage in crossing the mountains and were abandoned."[61] After arriving at Knoxville on May 28, Thomas ordered the men to proceed by rail to Chattanooga and Huntsville, where they arrived on June 7, after a journey of over seven hundred miles. A week later, they relieved the Sixth Illinois Cavalry and began their efforts to maintain law and order in the area. On June 18, Major Cramer issued Regimental Orders No. 7, which directed that, "when men have permission to go for plumbs [sic] berries or up to town they must walk. The horses must be well groomed and permitted to rest as much as possible." He further enjoined his charges, "The war is over; we are among friends: let us by our dress, conduct and manners show the people that we can be and are good soldiers."[62] The regiment did not remain in Huntsville long before outposting the line of the Memphis & Charleston Railroad south and west of the river between Decatur and Florence, including the towns of Moulton and Pond Spring, which allowed the troopers easy access to their homes while they protected work crews rebuilding this stretch of the railroad. In July, companies I and K proceeded to Nashville to be mustered out, having reached the expiration of their three-year term of service, begun when they were part of the First Middle Tennessee Cavalry. The route retraced the steps those two companies had taken when Buell evacuated the valley in the summer of 1862. The rest of the regiment would have to wait until October 5 for orders authorizing their release from active service.[63]

Affairs in northern Alabama were in a state of disarray, as the Northern regiments remained eager to depart for their homes but Brig. Gen. Robert S. Granger, commanding the post at Huntsville, still had to contend daily with lawless bands of deserters and bushwhackers who threatened citizens and soldiers. Granger reported that Lincoln's assassination had incensed Unionists "who before were in favor of dealing with leniency toward those who sympathized with the South, and would not take the oath of allegiance, now request that all who will not take the oath should leave our lines."[64] Lieutenant Nelson, back in camp at the Sulphur Branch trestle, recalled the day one of his soldiers, Isaac Childs, brought him the news of the assassination, reporting, "Uncle Sam is dead." Nelson believed that this final act of violence "was in accord with the spirit of the rebellion and secession that had actually assassinated scores of patriots, Union men throughout the South."[65]

On May 17, Granger reported that he had met with Brig. Gen. Philip D. Roddey, commanding the Confederate forces across the river, who had agreed to surrender his command the following day. Granger wired his superiors in Nashville:

> He [Roddey] reports to me that there is a band of marauders preying alike upon citizens of all parties and paroled soldiers, murdering and robbing indiscriminately. . . . A party of Texas Rangers, about seventy-five strong, were at Courtland day before yesterday, robbing Union citizens and threatening paroled soldiers. I request that 100 or 200 cavalry be sent to Decatur at once to hunt these outlaws.

The Department of the Cumberland ordered the additional troopers to Granger to "assist him in keeping his district in order until the arrival of the 1st Alabama Cavalry, now on its way there from General Sherman's army."[66] Granger noted the continued presence of the old, prewar affiliations, writing from Decatur on May 12 that "The people of the south side of the river appear much more sincere in their loyalty than on the north, particularly about Huntsville."[67]

On July 17, Granger issued a circular regarding the conduct and treatment of freedmen, duly reprinted in William B. Figures' *Huntsville Advocate*. It specified that freedmen must enter into labor contracts, or report to the contraband camp, where the government would provide work for them. A violation of labor contracts by either party would result in arrest by the Provost Marshal's office or seizure of property necessary to fulfill the contract. The freedmen's government pay at least put money into circulation, and soldiers receiving back pay provided an additional stimulus to the local economy, as the *Advocate* reported soldiers "spending money freely."[68]

Affairs south of the river were generally more peaceful, given the large Unionist population, but the residents also suffered more, given their remoteness. Brig. Gen. Morgan H. Chrysler, commanding at Talladega, reported sufficient forage in the Coosa Valley, and had the railroad and telegraph repaired to Selma by June 1, opening communications with Mobile via the river. Chrysler had a surplus of confiscated military equipment but reported an acute shortage of food, writing: "There are 5,000 poor people in this section that must be fed by the United States Government or they will starve. Any instructions on that point?"[69] But violence continued to mar the area, especially from Unionists out to settle old scores. According to Chrysler, on June 3, "a party of men in disguise, supposed to be from the northern part of the state, made a raid on Columbiana. . . . They hung Mr. Cobb and Mr. Rushing to [from] a tree and left them hanging . . . the men that were hung were actively engaged during the war arresting deserters. The mob may have been actuated by a desire to retaliate."[70] Chrysler's attempts to pursue the men to their mountain hideouts were apparently unsuccessful. But the perpetrators could have been homegrown. By 1864 lawlessness and violence marked Shelby County's experience during the war, as wealthy planters along the Coosa Valley on the county's eastern border sought to protect themselves and their farms from the poorer residents of the rugged hills in the northern, western, and especially southern parts of the county, including the community of Yellow Leaf, in what is now Chilton County. Petitioners begged Governor Watts for assistance, but eventually took matters into their own hands, as a vigilante by the name of Blackwell terrorized families of Unionists and deserters, with the assistance of a Confederate veteran named James Cobb. The latter's efforts in terrorizing the residents of Shelby County in the winter and spring of 1865 purchased his fate in a hangman's noose the following summer.[71]

Several of the men involved may have been from the First Alabama, as eleven troops hailed from Shelby County.[72] On September 16, Maj. Gen. Henry E. Davies, commanding the District of Montgomery, wrote to the department commander at Mobile, reporting that "continued complaints are brought to me of the fact that parties of troops stationed in the District of Huntsville (principally the 1st Ala. Cav'y.) are making excursions into the northern counties of this Distr., taking property from Citizens and committing extensive depredations." Davies requested "that the Commanding Officer of the Dist. of Huntsville may be directed to retain his troops within the limits of his own command."[73] The actions of the loyal Alabama troops mirror those of Jewish soldiers in the British Army at the end of World War II, who used their affiliation and training to hunt down former Nazis across Europe.[74] While it is likely that members of the First Alabama continued to exact revenge on their oppressors, exaggerated complaints to the district commander at Montgomery could also have been a ruse for former rebels to rid themselves of the Unionist army unit, either through reassignment or disbandment, in order to secure their control over the region. The First Alabama Cavalry, being mounted, could patrol widely across the countryside and gave local commanders a powerful deterrent to lawlessness.

The black troops raised in northern Alabama likewise garrisoned their homes, first at the same isolated outposts along the railroad they had held during the war, but eventually as a large combined force in Huntsville. For most of 1865, Col. Lewis Johnson's brigade, consisting of the Eighteenth, Forty-Second, Forty-Fourth, and 110th USCI, held the town with over 2,000 men.[75] The sight of their former slaves, clad in neat blue uniforms and walking the streets armed with rifles, must have been a shock to the former slaveowners of Madison County. Indeed, Maj. Gen. Edward Hatch speculated that former secessionists "would like to have all the troops removed. They might like to have the negro troops removed, because of their antipathy to seeing them carrying muskets."[76] In his book *The Civil War and Reconstruction in Alabama*, Walter L. Fleming alleges, "These negro troops were a source of disorder among the blacks, and were under slack discipline. Outrages and robberies by them were of frequent occurrence. There was ill feeling between the white and the black troops. Even when the freedmen utterly refused to go to work, they behaved well, as a rule, except where negro troops were stationed," but Fleming's flawed account is flatly contradicted by the evidence from Huntsville.[77] Four regiments of black troops brought more order than disorder to the town, probably because white conservatives who might otherwise have oppressed the black community were deterred by the presence of a large number of black troops. And there are no recorded instances of conflict between the black and white troops stationed in Huntsville, despite the racial prejudices of the day. On August 17, the *Huntsville Advocate* reported that "Good order is preserved, the police is rigid day and night, and the city is kept clean. . . . During the entire time we have been under military rule, it has not been milder or more pleasant than it is now."[78]

The loyal troops thus provided an essential service in maintaining law and order. According to a contemporary observer, "Without the aid of the bayonets of the United States Alabama is an anarchy. The best men of Alabama have either shed their blood in the late war, emigrated, or become wholly incapacitated by their former action from now taking part in the government of the State. The more sensible portion of the people tremble at the idea of the military force being eliminated, for, whatever may be their hatred of the United States soldier, in him they find their safety."[79]

Hatch found similar conditions in neighboring Mississippi. In late January 1866, he testified before Congress that public sentiment "grew more bitter than it was immediately after the surrender; . . . The northeastern part of the State had a great many loyal men, and a great many from that portion of the State enlisted in our army. And after the surrender a great many refugees returned there, men who had been driven off from that part of the State. The county of Tishemingo [sic] was a county from which we recruited a great many men for our army. Some went with General Sherman and some went into Tennessee regiments." But these men were entirely dependent on the army for protection. He stated, "I do not believe the Union men could remain there if there were no Federal troops there to protect them. There is a great deal of private enmity and intense personal dislike to them, and I do not think they would be allowed to remain there."[80] The same was true in Alabama: "In the mountain region of Alabama there are a great many loyal people: people poor, but loyal. We recruited two regiments there. Between them and the people of the other portions of Alabama there is a great deal not only of animosity in regard to the question of secession, but of private animosity. The loyal men in that part of the State may be strong enough to protect themselves, as they have gone home with their arms. But their families have suffered everything during the war. I have found a great deal of outlawry in Alabama, and I doubt if the civil authority alone, however much inclined to do so, could control that feeling now."[81]

As further evidence, when Maj. T. M. Goodfellow, chaplain of the 101st

USCT and assistant commissioner of the Huntsville Sub-District of the Freedmen's Bureau, authorized Henry Livingston "to teach school among freedmen at Decatur Ala," on November 22, 1865, he further directed, "the military of the nearest post to where this school is located will furnish any protection necessary," and, if anyone should interfere, "the Provost Marshal will arrest said parties and send them to this officer for trial."[82] Goodfellow's fears were well founded, as residents had burned a freedmen's school in Tullahoma, Tennessee, earlier that month.[83] Some measure of the bureau's success in these endeavors can be found in conservative Provisional Governor Lewis E. Parsons's efforts in lobbying President Johnson to have the bureau "abolished."[84] But by all accounts, the Huntsville bureau and contraband camp were lucky to have Goodfellow's services, as an inspector found that he "was wholly devoted to the care of its inmates."[85]

Under this strong control, Presidential Reconstruction proceeded quickly and relatively peacefully in Huntsville. Elections in August, though open only to white voters, sent delegates for a new constitutional convention in Montgomery, and further elections in November established a provisional, or "Johnson," government under the leadership of Governor Robert M. Patton, a Florence resident and former slaveowner with strong ties to the Huntsville area. Patton opposed secession but later cooperated with the Confederacy, and at least provided a sympathetic ear to freedmen's issues during his tenure, despite his own white supremacist views.[86] His appointment, and those of others who had cooperated with the rebellion, rankled Unionists, one of whom wrote a letter to the *Huntsville Advocate* questioning their loyalty. He complained, "the indelicate inconsistencies of such officials is so apparent—and open to so much observation—but yesterday the sworn enemies of the United States and today kissing the Holy Evangelist in attestation to their devotion to that government whose supremacy was deemed worse than extermination."[87] But statewide those candidates who could take a loyalty oath generally defeated those who had actively supported the Confederate government, especially those who had served in the Confederate army. That so many, including one of Patton's opponents, Col. Michael J. Bulger of Tallapoosa, who had served in the Forty-Seventh Alabama under Lee in Virginia, could appear on a ballot only six months after the end of the war, was a sign of the headway the former traitors were already making in state politics under the Johnson administration.

Only in the former hill counties could Union men participate openly in the political process. According to Col. George Spencer, "No man unless he comes up to the full standard of a secessionist can be elected to any office outside of five counties in Alabama." When asked which five, Spencer replied, "Marion, Winston, Walker, Fayette, and Randolph. They could poll a very good Union vote in some other counties. But in the counties I have named, which were nonslaveholding counties, the Union men have a very large majority. It is respectable to be a Union man there, but in the other counties it is not."[88]

Patton's efforts, and those in Huntsville in general, focused on restoration of business and commerce. In order to forestall famine, Alabamians of whatever loyalty worked to get crops in the ground, in order to have something to eat during the coming winter. Until then, Federal relief would have to feed freedmen, Unionists, and former Confederates alike, and during this time, the Freedmen's Bureau issued almost four million rations.[89] The weather failed to cooperate, with temperatures in the middle part of the state soaring well into triple digits, and the *Montgomery Mail* reporting, "quite a number of sudden deaths have occurred in the previous few weeks and the mortality list has been unusually heavy amongst soldiers and in the negro camps beyond the river."[90] In Huntsville, drought prevailed, with the *Advocate* reporting, "Rain is greatly needed over north Alabama."[91] On September 23, Goodfellow issued a public appeal for relief, as a result of the "small crop put in for the present season, and that has been almost ruined by drouth. So that not more than half subsistence for the next twelve months will be gathered."[92] But the reopening of the Memphis & Charleston Railroad between Huntsville and Memphis in November did much to restore commerce and industry in the city, and alleviate concerns about shortages.

In September, Brig. Gen. Wladimir B. Kryzanowski reported an incident involving the sheriff of Jackson County, a Colonel Snodgrass, "late of the confederate army." According to the report, Snodgrass had arrested fifteen citizens of that county on charges of murder, which they were accused of having "committed while in the service of the United States, under orders from their superiors, in fights with guerrillas." Kryzanowski ordered the prisoners released, but,

a few days afterwards it was reported to me that the sheriff refused to obey the order, and had used the most disrespectful language against the military authorities of the United States. I ordered his arrest, but about the same time I received orders to muster out all white regiments in my district, and my own regiment being among them, I relinquished command of the district. I deem the lives of southern men that have served in the United States army unsafe when they return to their homes. As to the feeling of the people in that section of the country, the majority at this day are as bitter enemies of the United States government as they were during the war.[93]

But the violence and lawlessness was not one-sided, though reports fueled by political and racial animosities have to be taken with a grain of salt. Discipline apparently began to suffer as the months of occupation duty dragged on, with reports reaching Huntsville of the theft of farm produce and animals near Decatur. Citizens lodged complaints against the black soldiers, prompting the new commander, Major General Grierson, to issue an order directing that "citizens in their peaceful vocations and pursuits shall not be molested or interfered with in any manner whatever by the Officers and soldiers of this command, but be treated by them with all due respect." But, recognizing that the soldiers were likely not the cause of the ill feelings, Grierson further ordered, "The General commanding does not desire and will not attempt to exercise an unwarranted control over the actions of those who have heretofore professed so much regard for the negroes as slaves and now manifest such marked dislike for them as Freedmen and soldiers; yet would kindly remind all whom it may concern that harsh or unjust treatment of the colored people, or insults to Officers or Soldiers in the service of the United States will not be tolerated."[94]

Commanders in the USCT units were aware of the existing prejudices and issued orders that attempted to address them. Upon assuming command of the 106th USCI at Stevenson on July 24, Capt. Zene Harlan issued orders directing that "company commanders will see that their companies are efficiently drilled . . . the arms and accoutrements will be kept in the best possible order, the men well-uniformed and kept clean . . . so that we may command the respect of all good soldiers and try to dispel as far as possible all prejudicial feelings by some entertained against this branch of the service."[95] That Harlan had a company to command at all was largely due to the return the previous month of over thirty men from captivity in Mobile, after being taken by Forrest's men the previous September at Athens. The arrival of Company D from North Carolina, where it had served as pioneers with Sherman's army since the previous summer, put the 106th at battalion strength. On August 26, the regiment moved from Stevenson through Chattanooga and Knoxville to President Johnson's hometown of Greenville, Tennessee, where it consolidated with the Fortieth USCT.[96] Their stay there was a brief one, as the following month they were back in northern Alabama, guarding the railroad at Bridgeport. The Fortieth USCT, which now included the four companies of the 106th, mustered out at Nashville in April, 1866.

Events in the department continued to attract attention at the highest levels, as President Johnson remained concerned about affairs in his home state. A proponent of quickly restoring the seceded states to the Union following repeal of the state's secession ordinance and the abolition of slavery by a constitutional convention, Johnson resented what he perceived to be the overzealous efforts of the army officers manning the Freedmen's Bureau. On August 14 he wrote General Thomas that in Nashville, where the 110th and 111th USCT were still serving, and Pulaski, where they had been raised, agents of the bureau were "assuming and exercising powers in taking charge of property and other jurisdiction which is incompatible with the law creating the bureau," and that "the operations of Treasury agents and the Freedmen's Bureau are creating great prejudice to the Government." The latter was true, at least in Pulaski, where white supremacists founded and organized the Ku Klux Klan later that year, and selected Forrest, a native of the region, to lead the new organization. But the bureau's efforts to resettle freedmen on abandoned lands and protect them from abusive employers conflicted with Johnson's vision of an organization intended primarily to help resettle and protect white Unionist refugees. Johnson's efforts undercut the Federal government's close involvement in affairs in the region and ultimately doomed the local bureau's efforts to failure.[97]

The 111th USCI remained in Nashville after the end of hostilities, guarding the Nashville & Northwestern Railroad and reinterring remains in the Stones River National Cemetery near Murfreesboro, until they too were mustered out at the end of April 1866. Lieutenant Nelson, still with the 111th USCI, recalled, "We took up the remains on different parts of the battlefield and buried them side by side on ground purchased by the government," a task he continued supervising after leaving the service, before becoming an agent of the Freedmen's Bureau at Murfreesboro.[98] The 110th USCI had mustered out two months earlier, also in Nashville. One soldier of the 111th, Sgt. William

Holland, captured at Sulphur Branch and held prisoner by Forrest's surgeon, remained as a laborer at the cemetery until his death in 1909, when he was laid to rest near his home on the battlefield.[99] The veterans and their families contributed to a remarkable expansion in the city's African American community. According to a census taken in the summer of 1865, Nashville's black population increased from 4,645 before the war to 10,744 after the close.[100]

But many men returned to their former homes in northern Alabama, and deposited their discharge papers with the bureau office in Huntsville, in hopes of later collecting bounties due them for enlisting. On June 5, 1866, J. Worley Patterson, a bureau agent at Decatur, deposited eighteen such papers from men of the Twelfth, Forty-Second, 106th, 110th, and 111th USCT with the district office in Huntsville. For the rest of the month papers came in from additional members of those regiments from Hartselle and Courtland, demonstrating that many soldiers had returned to Alabama, in search of either missing family members or simply a new life.[101]

In Murfreesboro, Joseph Nelson, now as an agent of the Freedmen's Bureau, likewise worked to obtain bounties of $300 for his former soldiers or their surviving families, but found "a firm of lawyers at Murfreesboro, one of them an ex-Federal Captain, the other an ex-Confederate Lieutenant. They were collecting bounties for the colored ex-soldiers. These bounties were near to $300 to each man. After getting one bounty, they paid the claimant $60, keeping the balance and dividing it between themselves. The law had fixed their pay at $10 for each claim collected." Nelson, upon becoming aware of the fraud, brought the attorneys up on charges and halted the practice, but it was symbolic of how quickly some ex-Union and Confederate soldiers could join together in their efforts to swindle and oppress freedmen.[102]

The men of the black and white Alabama regiments rendered significant service in the restoration and maintenance of Federal control in their home state through the end of 1865. They made the final, victorious campaigns possible and eased the transition from wartime to peacetime. And they actively participated in efforts to remake Southern society. But in the months and years ahead, many found their efforts undermined and eventually undone by their former adversaries in uniform. Without the protection of the blue coats and their comrades in arms, many fell victim to the violence of Southern conservatives and eventually the restoration of Democratic rule in their state. Efforts to divide black and white Republicans, who had served together in the same army and fought for the same cause, formed a centerpiece of Democratic political efforts, resulting in the restoration of white political, economic, and social supremacy that remained unchallenged until the civil rights era of the 1960s. During this "Second Reconstruction," a similar coalition of large numbers of highly motivated and mobilized African Americans and a much smaller number of sympathetic whites—ultimately aided by the Federal government—successfully challenged the segregationist state government and the Jim Crow laws it enacted and enforced. By that time, the memory of black and white Alabamians fighting together against Confederate control of their state had been long suppressed, and largely erased from the collective memory, by proponents of the "Myth of the Lost Cause."[103]

Epilogue and Conclusion

T he mustering out of the regiments of loyal Alabamians in late 1865 and into 1866, coupled with a lenient system of Presidential Reconstruction under President Andrew Johnson, led to significant hardships for veterans of the regiments. At the beginning of 1866, the US Army had 7,832 troops in Alabama, but by year's end, that number had dwindled to only 831.[1] Scattered as they were across the state, they were entirely ineffective in protecting either Unionists from revenge-minded former Confederates or freedmen from planters intent upon swindling newly contracted laborers out of their share of whatever crop they might be able to produce. With much of the state suffering under a second year of drought, provisions became scarce and credit short, adding to a new struggle for life-sustaining resources in the immediate postwar years. While planters sought to regain control over cheap labor, bitter enemies in the Hill Country and Wiregrass again attacked their neighbors' farms and fields in an effort to punish their adversaries and drive them out of the country. As early as June 1865, Union officers in Selma reported that "in the mountainous country toward Talladega acts of lawlessness and violence are not infrequent, originating amongst the poor whites against their rich neighbors who remained at home during the war and were very zealous in returning fugitives to the army."[2] As Margaret Storey points out, "This thirst for justice and retribution, however, would result in a most bitter legacy."[3]

For a brief period from 1867 until 1874, when "Redeemers" used violence and intimidation, as well as racist propaganda, to successfully break up the biracial wartime coalition, a broad-based interracial government prevailed, with strong support from mobilized freedmen, a smaller number of whites, and an interventionist Federal government. With support from all three legs of the stool, Alabama's Reconstruction government provided stability and limited progress within the state. But the Panic of 1873 depressed cotton prices, and famine again threatened Alabama. Northern Republicans, tainted by charges of corruption, with some help from Alabama's Reconstruction state government, gradually lost interest in maintaining this tenuous coalition. Absent the threat of Federal force, the Ku Klux Klan and the Democratic Party regained control of the state and took steps to prevent these three powerful forces from ever again aligning against them, and their interests. The vital tripartite coalition, despite numerous attempts under the flags of "Greenbackers," the Farmer's Alliance, and the Populist Party, struggled unsuccessfully against the "Big Mules" of Alabama's Bourbon Democrats.

By co-opting poor whites with racist rhetoric and disenfranchising blacks at the polls, all while demonizing the Federal government so successfully that deep mistrust lingers to this day, and violently intimidating anyone who dared to raise a voice, much less a firearm, in opposition, a racist coalition of big businesses, interested politicians, Confederate apologists, and white supremacists dictated affairs in Alabama for most of the next one hundred years. Only a reengagement by the Federal government, in support of a civil rights movement begun by Alabama's oppressed black community, and supported by enough white opponents of the segregationists to create a slim majority, eventually overthrew Jim Crow in the state and restored black ballots as well as some measure of self-determination. Despite this second, brief period of limited success, conservatives, now ironically in the Republican Party, quickly regained control of affairs in the state and continue to use race and economic issues to ensure their control of cheap labor and limited involvement by the Federal government. As a result, the state still suffers under many of the same disadvantages that have plagued it since 1874, including a woefully deficient system of public education, extreme levels of black incarceration, and a minimalist and regressive tax structure that generates massive profits for large corporations while keeping a substantial portion of the state's population in poverty. In this unsuccessful struggle for control of the state's abundant resources, including mineral wealth and labor, Alabama's blacks and poor whites have enjoyed only brief periods of limited success, leaving the state in dire need of a third or economic Reconstruction that will reorder the state's economy so that resources are used for a greater public benefit rather than to further line the pockets of an oppressive few. Atlanta, the state's nearest metropolitan neighbor and a near-peer of Birmingham as late as the 1950s, understood the economic repercussions in the 1960s, billing itself as the city "too busy to hate." Birmingham, in contrast, wasn't *that* busy.[4]

For many of the former soldiers, the availability of a support network of fellow anti-Confederates often made the difference in the struggle for survival. While individual Unionists and freedmen might fall victim to violence, communities could band together for mutual protection of lives, farms, and fields. Sharecropping often involved the breaking up of the former slave cabins and removal to separate parcels of rented or share-cropped land on former plantations, but the freedmen's migration toward the Black Belt in general and cities in particular offered at least the protection of numbers. Unfortunately, these same environments were also the unhealthiest, as poor sanitation in the former contraband camps often negated the Freedmen's Bureau's efforts to provide sustenance and protect workers from exploitative contracts. At the same time, groups of veterans or deserters who had banded together for protection continued to do so in the postwar period, especially as former Confederates, often restored to legal power through a simple oath and the votes of their fellow fully restored Confederates, regained control over the legal system and began to use it to prosecute their neighbors for "crimes" committed during the war.[5] While the charges, including theft, arson, and murder, often stemmed from military operations against irregulars or reprisals, they could easily ensnare a Union veteran or anyone else whose loyalty to the former Confederacy had been suspect. With former Confederates in control of relief efforts in the famine-afflicted state, Unionists often found themselves again denied rations, and "questions of access to resources" came to dominate political affairs.[6] For both white and black veterans, the wartime Union League, which had operated in places for years as a refuge for Unionists and freedmen, offered a pre-existing framework for protection as well as a means to petition for redress.

Confronted with this threat to survival, whites and blacks joined protective organizations, most notably the Union League, in order to provide security for themselves and their families. While individual chapters of the Union League remained segregated, the organization represented a continuation of the alliance of black and white Alabamians, aided materially by an interventionist Federal government, most often in the guise of the Freedmen's Bureau, led by officers of the United States Army. As black leagues mobilized, educating freedmen on both the power and the responsibility of the ballot, the secretive society attracted the attention of conservatives and former Confederates.

Through local chapters and assemblies in the protective environment of larger cities, black and white leagues worked to oppose the combined power of former Confederates and helped to strike a fatal blow to Andrew Johnson's lenient program of Reconstruction.[7]

On a tour through the southern states in the summer of 1866, Whitelaw Reid found ready evidence of ex-Confederates who freely expressed their unreconstructed sentiments in front of him. They deplored the conviction and execution of Champ Ferguson, who had brutally persecuted loyal Tennesseans, and lamented that Henry Wirz, the commander of the notorious Andersonville prison, had been hanged. Reid accurately observed that, "they are the ones whose new-born 'loyalty' is sown upon the sand. When the nutriment of the offices is withdrawn, look out for a withering."[8] But at Opelika, Reid confronted the difficulty of overthrowing the rule of ex-Confederates when he questioned a freedman on political affairs and found that he had never heard of President "Andie Johnson." Reid thought the man's responses demonstrated "the lowest degree of intelligence among the class on whom it is proposed to confer the right of suffrage." But when asked, "How much do you suppose you'd sell for?" as a slave, the anonymous freedman demonstrated that he clearly understood that the institution was dead. He poignantly told his questioners, "I's free. Ain't wuf nuffin."[9]

Events in Memphis, where many of Alabama's black troops had served during the war, demonstrated just how difficult it would be to protect freedmen and their families from mobs of racists protected by the reconstructed southern governments. In early May, an altercation between white policemen and black Union veterans led to the wholesale destruction of black homes and the murder of over forty men, women, and children. The pogrom included the arson of black schools and especially black churches, which had occupied a central place in the uplift of the black community. Black churches were so effective in providing encouragement, education, and uplift that they remained a target of racists well into the civil rights era a century later. The Memphis rioters largely achieved their aim, which was to drive many of the newly dignified black veterans and their families out of the city. Similar events occurred in New Orleans the same summer, likely caused by fears of economic competition by poor urban whites and the desire of white planters to restore their labor force on the plantations. The following year urban rioting came to Alabama. On May 14, 1867, a Pennsylvania Republican, William D. Kelley, spoke to a biracial gathering in Mobile, but was heckled and shouted down by conservative white opponents. After protesters fired shots toward the speaker's stand, armed blacks retaliated with shots fired into the air, leading to a violent outbreak, with fatalities on both sides.[10] The increasing violence finally awaked Republicans in Congress to the threats facing freedmen in the Deep South.[11]

At the same time, the service of Alabama's black soldiers, alongside the several hundred thousand free blacks and freedmen who donned the Union blue, spurred change within the US Army. On July 28, 1866, Congress passed the Army Reorganization Act, authorizing the formation of six black regiments within the regular establishment and ensuring that an African American presence would remain in the postwar army. Though Congress later reduced the number to only four regiments, the Ninth and Tenth US Cavalry, and the Twenty-Fourth and Twenty-Fifth US Infantry regiments, they continued the proud tradition of black military service and provided some employment for those hoping to escape the oppressive conditions within the state. The Ninth Cavalry initially recruited heavily in southern Louisiana and concentrated on former soldiers with USCT experience. These efforts may have attracted former the members of the Fifty-Fifth USCI, which had mustered out in New Orleans in December 1865, though the appeal for recruits later expanded across the region.

Though the numbers of soldiers in all four regiments remained small, with just over 4,000 men, compared to the four million former slaves, the African American press followed the exploits of the "Buffalo Soldiers" with great pride in the campaigns to conquer and subjugate the native peoples of the West and open new areas for settlement. Mirroring Jefferson Buford's failed efforts to colonize Kansas with slaveholders during the "Bleeding Kansas" period, many black "Exodusters" likewise embarked for new homes on the plains after Reconstruction's failure, with several communities, including Nicodemus, Kansas, providing refuge and an opportunity for a new life. The Buffalo Soldiers provided security for these communities as they dispossessed the Cheyenne and Arapahoe inhabitants in yet another war for resources.[12] One of the many beneficiaries of these efforts was Lt. Joseph Nelson, of the 111th USCI and Freedmen's Bureau, who purchased 240 acres near Cassoday, in Butler County, Kansas, and lived there until his death in 1917.[13] Within Alabama, two black militia units, Montgomery's Capital City Guards and Mobile's Gilmer Rifles, kept alive the memory of black military service, but mobilization of the black Third Regiment, Alabama Volunteer Infantry, for the Spanish-American War led to racial violence with white units from the upper South while encamped at Anniston, leading to the unit's demobilization after the war and eventual disbandment of black military units in the state.[14]

On the national stage, the plight of Alabama's many Union veterans gained attention thanks largely to the Congressional Joint Committee on Reconstruction, which collected testimony from oppressed Unionists. Alabama's community had several powerful voices, including J. J. Giers, a staunch and well-connected Unionist, and Brig. Gen. George Spencer, former commander of the First Alabama Cavalry. Both men provided testimony on conditions in the state in early 1866 and remained powerful advocates for the constituents. With black enfranchisement, and greater restrictions on those who had so recently engaged in treason, a coalition of black and white Republicans eventually gained political control of the state, putting another former member of the First Alabama Cavalry, William H. Smith, in the governor's mansion, Benjamin Turner, a veteran of the USCT in the House of Representatives, and Spencer, the former commander of the First Alabama Cavalry, in the US Senate.[15] When the new legislature called for a convention to draft a new state constitution, Alabama's Union veterans were well represented among the delegates.[16]

But, without the protections of Congressional—also called Radical—Reconstruction, these men would have been shut out of postwar political life, despite their great sacrifices on behalf of their nation. Smith likely would not have even have carried his home county of Randolph, as Joseph Davis, another veteran of the First Alabama, reported that former Confederates intimidated loyal voters, gathering around the ballot box hurrahing the Confederacy and cursing Unionists, resulting in violence.[17] And even if ballots were cast, they were not guaranteed to be counted. Under Presidential Reconstruction, and for years after the Redeemers had regained control, ballot boxes from heavily Republican precincts often vanished while en route to be counted, and returns from the Black Belt with heavy Democratic majorities provided an easy indication of the level of voter fraud and intimidation taking place.

Smith's election to the governor's office, and the large number of Republican legislators, black and white, seated in Montgomery did not mean a return to security or safety for most of Alabama. Violence returned to the backcountry as a terrorist organization of ex-secessionists claiming to be the ghosts of departed Confederate soldiers turned to "night riding" to intimidate potential voters and punish political opponents. While the Ku Klux Klan had operated in Alabama, especially in the Tennessee Valley, since its founding just across the border in Pulaski, Tennessee, in early 1866, the Republican-controlled government elected in 1868 brought out the organization's worst excesses.[18] Believing they had been illegally disenfranchised and denied their rights at the ballot box, the Klan resorted to extralegal means in a desperate attempt to retain control over local resources. In the Black Belt, this most often meant labor, and Klan activities sought to frighten freedpeople into compliance with the planters' demands, with one Klansman, John Lyons of Lee County, gaining a reputation for mutilating the bodies of his victims.[19] In the upcountry, White Republican "scalawags," in their opponent's parlance, were more often the target, continuing a cycle of violence and retribution that mirrored wartime loyalty. Henry Springfield, a Union veteran from St. Clair County, found his home surrounded by two hundred armed men who literally perforated his home with bullet holes before Springfield surrendered to the mob.

In some cases, the oppressors used "racial shaming" to intimidate whites, much as Barton Myers found in his study of North Carolina Unionists, who were sometimes forced to take their meals alongside blacks, in violation of the racial conventions of the day and in an ironic attempt at racial leveling, or at least an effort to excommunicate disloyal whites from the ranks and privileges of their race.[20] William Anderson of Blount County recalled the harassment of his neighbor, avowed Unionist Thomas Nation, reporting "the Ku Klux went to his house one night and took him out of a sick bed and made him tote a negro girl for some distance." William Mitchell corroborated Anderson's testimony, adding, "the Ku Klux after the war threatened to take him and did take him out at night and carried him away off down in his field some where and I heard they threatened to kill him and throw him in a ditch; they made him carry a negro girl a straddle of his neck[.] Well I heard they would of killed him if his wife had not of went with him and held to him all the time. This happened in 1870 about the close of the year. . . . I hear the Ku Klux got after him because he was a Union man."[21]

To help suppress Klan violence, Isaac Berry, also of Blount County, who served as one of Dodge's spies and had a brother-in-law in the First Alabama Cavalry, apparently "helped organize an armed body of about 100 men who rode in defiance of the Klan dominance in the region. Their group was the anti-Ku Klux. Berry led the group as far as Somerville in Morgan County, stopping at known Ku Klux homes. They called out the Ku Kluxers and threatened to do to them what they were doing to others if they did not stop their night riding."[22] Seeking the cover of legal authority that their opponents had used against them under Presidential Reconstruction, veterans of the First Alabama Cavalry, including J. F. Morton of Fayette County, pleaded with Governor Smith to call out a state militia formed of loyal freedmen and Unionists, but Smith demurred, fearing a race war that might fracture his unstable coalition.[23] Taking matters into their own hands, "Mossybacks" retaliated against Klansmen in a continuation of wartime violence.[24] The name came from their days of "lying out" in the woods to avoid the home guards and conscription agents, which some had done for so long, as the story goes, that moss had grown on their backs.[25]

As a prewar planter and slave owner, Smith offers some insight into the diversity of the Unionist coalition within the First Alabama. Opposing secession, largely on the grounds that a war threatened his slave property, Smith did not share the class animosities of many of his fellow soldiers, or the same threat to his survival and livelihood. In a program that would have appealed to prewar Whigs, many of whom now found common cause as Republicans with the erstwhile antisecession, or "Douglas" Democrats, Smith insisted on rehabilitating the state's dilapidated and destroyed railroads and in using state aid to open up further development, a program that also found favor with northern Republicans and investors.[26] But Smith's sale of bonds to finance both the Alabama & Chattanooga, through the new mineral district around Birmingham, and another line through his home county, proved too tempting for many within the state government, resulting in graft, corruption, and, after the Panic of 1873, bankruptcy and insolvency.

The later economic success of the Alabama Great Southern Railroad, connecting Birmingham and Chattanooga, bore witness to Smith's foresight, but the charges of corruption, much of it engineered by political opponents he sought to mollify, discredited his administration after just one term and opened cleavages with former antitax, antidevelopment Jacksonian Democrats who had found a home in the new Republican Party. Smith feuded constantly with his former commander, Senator George Spencer, whom Smith regarded as an outsider, further endearing him to his former enemies but costing him support with some of the unit's veterans. But his refusal to take action against the Klan at the height of its power cost him support among the freedmen who had put him in office. Smith had noble intentions as a conciliator, but efforts to pull former Confederate and Union soldiers together, not to mention racist white and black Alabamians, proved beyond his capabilities, and perhaps those of any man alive at that time. Ironically, Smith's Democratic successor, Confederate veteran Robert Lindsay, enjoyed greater success in the state's efforts to suppress Klan violence, though his election created the impression that its campaign of violence and intimidation was no longer necessary. His administration proved no less corrupt in the administration of railroads, demonstrating that the charges leveled by future historians, especially Walter Fleming, were not exclusively the fault of Alabama's Republican officeholders during Reconstruction.[27]

The prospect of Republican rule, with a broad coalition of black and white Republicans controlling much of the state government, appeared to be a dire threat to the continued wealth and prosperity of Alabama's planters and disenfranchised former Confederates. Faced with the inability to control government for their own interest, and concerned that a developing economy might provide other employment opportunities for a labor force they could no longer control or exploit, many former Confederates turned to their own secret society and a system of white racial supremacy to facture the coalition aligned against them and regain control of state political, and therefore economic, affairs. The Klan violence of Reconstruction used racial animosities as a lever to exploit divisions in the fragile biracial coalition then ruling the state in order to regain control of resources needed to return cotton-based agriculture to profitability.

The "Redeemers" benefitted greatly from Klan violence that intimidated voters, broke up Republican political meetings, and sowed racial violence across the state. Violence exploded after the Panic of 1873 led to another economic downturn, as Michael Fitzgerald notes, and the increase in violence and economic depression remained closely linked throughout the period.[28] It is worth mentioning that former Confederate Nathan Bedford Forrest's affiliation with the Klan began around the same time he declared bankruptcy, after he faced continuing struggles to recover his fortune lost during the war.[29] As Federal authorities and northern interests tired of the now nearly decade-long struggle to maintain control of the state, the interventionist Federal government, the essential glue in the Republican coalition, began to falter. With only "679 federal troops scattered in thirty locations in twenty-two counties," there was no possible way to ensure the security and integrity of the 1874 elections.[30] One Federal agent with the Justice Department wrote that he would "rather be in the heart of Comanche country than in Sumter County without soldiers."[31] Deep in the Black Belt, USCT veterans in Wilcox County banded together to protect their homes and communities. According to the most recent history of Reconstruction in the state, "The Democrats feared former USCI veterans who had been 'taught that it was right to have military organizations—to drill—be disciplined, and to bear arms,'" which foreshadowed more recent increases in black gun ownership.[32] Not content with a statewide campaign of intimidation, conservative whites resorted to all manners of voter fraud, including illegal ballots from across the state's borders in Mississippi and Georgia, numerous challenges to voter eligibility in heavily Republican areas, personal threats of economic or physical harm to individual voters at the polls, and the ubiquitous "missing ballot boxes" in places where many had demonstrated the courage to vote. Sadly, this successful campaign had long legs, enduring into both the 1901 constitutional convention, which effectively disenfranchised most blacks, along with some poor whites, all the way to the civil rights era, when voter registration drives in the Black Belt prompted the greatest violence, including the famous march from Selma to Montgomery. The assault on legal voting continues to this day, as a recent governor, the now-disgraced Robert Bentley, signed legislation requiring photo identification to vote and then closed many driver's license offices in the Black Belt, while Shelby County, in the Birmingham suburbs, was the first to successfully sue to overturn key provisions of the landmark 1965 Voting Rights Act. It seems William Faulkner's admonitions about the southern past hold especially true in Alabama.

While "New South" boosters touted the region's successful economic recovery, the key to profitability for a select few remained the region's cheap labor. Industrialization led to new opportunities away from the sharecropper's cabin, either in Birmingham's coal mines or steel mills, or in the many textile mills that dotted the Alabama countryside. But these interests aligned naturally to ensure an unbroken supply of inexpensive labor. As the leading history of the state notes, "The mine owner was as determined to hire his labor at the cheapest prices and control his laborer's life as was the Black Belt cotton planter."[33] A statewide system of leasing convict labor, essentially a return to slavery specifically authorized in the "except as punishment for a crime" loophole in the Thirteenth Amendment that ended the institution, kept wages low and provided a ready-made force that mine owners effectively used to break strikes and suppress organization by the United Mineworkers of America, which enrolled both black and white miners. Even today, Alabama's most successful remaining factories, after the collapse of the steel industry, consist of foreign automakers, including Mercedes, Honda, Toyota, and Hyundai, attracted by the cheap labor of nonunionized workers.[34]

Similarly, textile mills exploded across the state in the postwar period, exploiting child labor, especially in "company towns," where a year of hard work could leave a family even deeper in debt, thanks to the legal, and profitable, usury at the company store. In the continuing struggle for resources waged in turn-of-the-century Alabama, the families of the poor whites and freedmen who had fought against the Confederacy continued to come out on the short end, while the heirs of the former slavocracy and their new allies in industry reaped the benefits. Perhaps this is why, as Robin D. G. Kelley argues, Communist organizers found such a fertile recruiting ground in Alabama during the Great Depression, with a constituency not terribly unlike those Alabamians who donned the Union blue, and just as hated by their fellow citizens. As Kelley points out, the Alabama Farmer's Union (AFU) drew its strongest support from the same counties that had provided significant contributions to the Union army, demonstrating the depth of antiplanter sentiment in these regions.[35] But Alabama's Communists found little support from an interventionist Federal government.

The first major revolt against this "new" system in the period after Reconstruction came from the "Greenbackers" of northern Alabama, who needed access to cheap credit to run their small farms. Based in the same Hill Country counties that had provided troopers for the First Alabama Cavalry, the Greenbackers "resented state government run by and in the interest of Black Belt planters and urban industrialists."[36] But with Black Belt planters voting their laborers' ballots by proxy, the small farmers of northern Alabama had little chance to influence economic policy. The next, and most serious threat, came from the Populists in the 1890s. In a statewide revolt of members of white and black Farmers' Alliances, and urban laborers, the state's disenfranchised came closest to overturning the Bourbon Democrats' stranglehold on the state.

Again, electoral improprieties, most notably in Reuben Kolb's 1892 and 1894 gubernatorial campaigns, prevented any substantial reform.

But this challenge had come too close to succeeding. Intent upon preventing any future challenges, the Big Mules gathered in 1901 to rewrite the state constitution, effectively disenfranchising poorer whites and all blacks through a series of poll taxes, literacy tests, and other voting restrictions, with exemptions for those whose "grandfathers" had voted. In the statewide ratification campaign, the strongest opposition came from the same Hill Country and Wiregrass regions that had provided recruits for the First Alabama and First Florida, while the Black Belt—where few blacks could exercise their right to vote, but returns suspiciously exceeded the population in many counties—returned huge majorities for the new constitution.[37] Those who dared to raise their voices in opposition frequently faced a lynch mob's noose. Alabama's trees bore strange fruit indeed.[38]

Using a mix of class-based and racial justifications, Alabama's social and economic elite secured undisputed control of their state's affairs, and its ample resources, for the next fifty years. The Progressive movement, with a misplaced emphasis on Prohibition, did little to improve workers' lives, but did demonstrate that hot-button social issues could be a useful tonic to the electorate to secure their unquestioned support and guarantee economic control that worked against their own self-interest. Modest increases in school funding and a new program of public health did ease some endemic ailments, especially hookworm and pellagra, but relief from malaria awaited the widespread program associated with the war effort in the 1940s. Public education continued to lag, and the state remains rooted in the bottom five nationally, largely from a long-standing belief that a quality education might lead to a refusal to take whatever wages the planters and industrialists, or, today, retail magnates and automakers, offered.

Once blacks were disenfranchised, it became even easier to drive a wedge between white and black Alabamians. As C. Vann Woodward first pointed out, "Jim Crow's" strange career took him from railroad cars to theaters to the ludicrous extremes of water fountains and blood transfusions. Absent a Federal government willing to intervene, and with both black and white Alabamians resigned to legal separation, the racial divide persisted through the 1920s and the rise of the "Second Klan" and into the 1930s, despite the best efforts of Communist organizers to mobilize the black community. But many in Alabama's black communities had already given up on progress ever reaching the state, voting with their feet in the "Great Migration" that began during the First World War and continued through the Second. Only after that war, in which black and white Alabamians served in locations around the globe with more fluid barriers between the races, did the first rumblings of a civil rights era emerge.[39]

The resuscitation of a successful trinity composed of a strong and engaged Federal government, large numbers of courageous and mobilized blacks, and a smaller number of sympathetic whites, successfully challenged control of affairs within Alabama during the civil rights era, but not without the extralegal violence and intimidation that had marked the state for a century. George Wallace's incendiary rhetoric spurred violence, from "Bull" Connor's police dogs and firehoses to the Alabama Highway Patrol's "billy clubs" on the Edmund Pettus Bridge. One of Wallace's key opponents was Frank Minis Johnson Jr., chief judge of the United States District Court for the Middle District of Alabama, an Eisenhower appointee who famously ruled in favor of Rosa Parks, overruled Wallace's prohibition of the march from Selma to Montgomery, and ordered desegregation across the state, battling both Wallace and the Klan. Johnson was a native of Haleyville in Winston County, and his great-grandfather served in the First Alabama Cavalry. Of his Winston County upbringing, he later recalled, "We never did have any racial prejudice, suggestive or overt or any other way, as far as my parents were concerned."[40] While there were substantial cleavages within this "new" coalition, especially with regards to civil rights, politics again made strange bedfellows. As they had a century earlier, blacks and white set aside racial differences and worked together in a common cause.

Today, Alabama in general, and Birmingham in particular, remains racially polarized. A majority white Republican Party easily wins statewide contests against a Democratic Party continually weakened by the continued outmigration or apathy of blacks and progressive whites. Birmingham, in particular, remains one of the most racially divided cities in America, as white flight beginning in the 1960s led to the rise of extremely wealthy, lily-white suburbs such as Mountain Brook, while the inner city remains poor, black, and economically disadvantaged, despite a recent move toward gentrification.[41] Without the tax dollars concentrated in the white suburbs that provide Mountain Brook with the best public school system in the state, Jefferson County's public schools struggle to provide a quality education, leaving even more suburbs to attempt to split away and form their own districts.[42] Birmingham's city government remains divided, with the black-majority inner city struggling to provide effective governance while a string of white-majority suburbs languish economically without a strong central city to sustain them. Effective city-county unions in other Sunbelt cities, such as Charlotte-Mecklenburg in North Carolina, Nashville-Davidson in Tennessee, and Jacksonville-Duval in Florida, have brought growth and prosperity to those cities, while Birmingham, Alabama's leading metropolis, remains mired in its divisive racial past.

Under sustained assault from adherents of the "Myth of the Lost Cause," and the miseducation campaigns propagated by groups such as the United Daughters of the Confederacy, even the memory of the Alabamians who wore the Union blue came under assault. University of Alabama professor William Hoole published a history of the First Alabama Cavalry, under the title *Alabama Tories*, with the Confederate Publishing Company in 1960, complete with three Confederate flags on the book's cover. In Double Springs, the county seat of Winston County, the ubiquitous statue of a Civil War soldier found in virtually every southern, small town courthouse square, is flanked by both an American and a Confederate flag, honoring those who fought for both sides in the war. Typically, the iconic statue faces north, toward the imagined enemy, but Winston County's soldier faces south. While just the presence of such a monument might be welcome in the heart of the Confederacy, one wonders how the many veterans of the First Alabama Cavalry would feel about a Confederate flag still fluttering over Winston County. In the late 1980s, Alabama's Unionists enjoyed a popular revival, as the outdoor drama "The Incident at Looney's Tavern" ran every summer at a specially built park in Winston County.[43] But Alabama's USCT veterans struggled to gain any recognition, with Lawrence County finally erecting a small monument on the courthouse square in Moulton in 2006 to commemorate their service. The community of Dodge City, in Cullman County, which was formed out of Winston County, stands as a tribute to Grenville Dodge's efforts to support and organize loyal Alabamians. Less than five miles away stands Colony, one of Alabama's first postwar settlements of freedmen.[44] While members of the First Alabama Cavalry did hold reunions, these were, as David Blight has pointed out, almost always strictly segregated affairs.[45]

Thus, the Civil War represents not just the bloodiest period in Alabama's, and the nation's history, but also a brief period when the forces of a strong Federal government, large numbers of blacks and smaller numbers of whites combined their energies to bring significant change to the state. By overthrowing the secessionists and helping to militarily defeat the Confederacy, the coalition ended the practice of chattel slavery in the state and opened a path toward greater participation in a new society. Events on the home front had a marked effect on the Confederacy's ability to marshal combat power, but the war did not end, and would not have ended, without a defeat of the Confederate armies in the field. Guerrilla violence raged before the war in Kansas, and after it across the South, but was at its worst during the war, when Hobbes's Leviathan had been slain. It did not end, but diminished significantly, when the war was over.

But history is not linear, and this brief period of cooperation and accommodation extended only until 1874, when Redeemers, by means fair and foul, successfully regained control of state politics and used their influence to keep black and poor whites separated and minimize Federal influence. The second brief period of cooperation, during the civil rights era, overthrew the segregated society that emerged from the Civil War, but it could do little to overcome the economic oppression and struggle for resources that has moved off of Alabama's battlefields and into its courthouses and halls of government. Indeed, the civil rights icon Dr. Martin Luther King Jr. recognized that, after the death of Jim Crow and the establishment of the right to the ballot, economic inequality was the new battleground. In 1967, he wrote, "the real cost lies ahead. The stiffening of white resistance is a recognition of that fact. The discount education given Negroes will in the future have to be purchased at full price if quality education is to be realized. Jobs are harder and costlier to create than voting rolls. The eradication of slums housing millions is complex far beyond integrating buses and lunch counters."[46] While the long view of the state's history is not a positive story, the few bright spots of progress and social change offer hope for the future, when Alabamians can again overcome racial prejudices that divide them and create a society that better functions for the health, security, and prosperity of all its citizens.

Appendix

Detailed Service of Alabama Regiments, 1862–1866

Regiment	Jul	Aug	Sep
1st Alabama Cavalry	2 cos. with 1st Mid. Tenn. Cav. to July 1863		
1st Alabama Colored Heavy Artillery, later 6th, then 7th US CHA, finally 11th US Colored Infantry (New)			
1st Alabama Infantry, African Descent, later 55th US Colored Infantry			
14th Corps d'Afrique Infantry, later 86th US Colored Infantry			
1st Florida Cavalry			
4th Alabama Infantry, African Descent, later 106th US Colored Infantry			
2nd Alabama Infantry, African Descent, later 110th US Colored Infantry			
3rd Alabama Infantry, African Descent, later 111th US Colored Infantry			
136th US Colored Infantry			
137th US Colored Infantry			
138th US Colored Infantry			

Nov   Dec

Oct	Nov	Dec		
	Corinth	Glendale		

1863

Regiment	Jan	Feb	Mar	Apr	May
1st Alabama Cavalry	Glendale	Scouts, 5–13, 18–28	Glendale	15: Tuscumbia	3–12: Pikeville
1st Alabama Colored Heavy Artillery,later 6th, then 7th US CHA, finally 11th US Colored Infantry (New)					
1st Alabama Infantry, African Descent, later 55th US Colored Infantry					
14th Corps d'Afrique Infantry, later 86th US Colored Infantry					
1st Florida Cavalry					
4th Alabama Infantry, African Descent, later 106th US Colored Infantry					
2nd Alabama Infantry, African Descent, later 110th US Colored Infantry					
3rd Alabama Infantry, African Descent, later 111th US Colored Infantry					
136th US Colored Infantry					
137th US Colored Infantry					
138th US Colored Infantry					

Aug→Oct
1863

1ST Ala Cav = Perry, Lt. James
1ST Ala Cav - 1863

Aug

Oct

Jun	Jul	Aug	Sep	Oct	Nov	Dec
Scouts, 5–11, 17–23	Glendale	Glendale	Glendale	Glendale	Camp Davies	Camp Davies
20: Corinth	Corinth	Corinth	Corinth	Corinth	Corinth	Corinth
11: Corinth	Corinth	Corinth	Corinth	Guard RR	Corinth	Corinth
		12: New Orleans	Port Hudson	1–3: Barrancas	Barrancas	Barrancas
						Pulaski, TN
						Pulaski, TN

233

1864

Regiment	Jan	Feb	Mar	Apr	May
1st Alabama Cavalry	15: Memphis	Memphis	27: by Steamer	Mooresville	1: Chattanooga
1st Alabama Colored Heavy Artillery,later 6th, then 7th US CHA, finally 11th US Colored Infantry (New)	15: Memphis	Memphis	28: Fort Pillow	Fort Pillow	redesig. 6th, then 7th USCHA
1st Alabama Infantry, African Descent, later 55th US Colored Infantry	25: Memphis	Memphis	Memphis	redesig. 55th USCI	Memphis
14th Corps d'Afrique Infantry, later 86th US Colored Infantry	Barrancas	Barrancas	Barrancas	Barrancas	Barrancas
1st Florida Cavalry			23: Barrancas	Barrancas	Barrancas
4th Alabama Infantry, African Descent, later 106th US Colored Infantry			3: Decatur	Decatur	23: Athens Co. D Georgia
2nd Alabama Infantry, African Descent, later 110th US Colored Infantry	Pulaski, TN	Pulaski, TN	Pulaski, TN	9: Decatur, redesig. 110th USCI	Athens A–C, E, G Georgia
3rd Alabama Infantry, African Descent, later 111th US Colored Infantry	Sulphur Branch Trestle	Sulphur Branch Trestle	Sulphur Branch Trestle	redesig. 111th USCI	Sulphur Branch Trestle
136th US Colored Infantry					
137th US Colored Infantry					
138th US Colored Infantry					

1864

Jun	Jul	Aug	Sep	Oct	Nov	Dec
Rome, arr. 24	Scout to Cedar Bluff	Rome	Rome	Rome	March to the Sea	Savannah
Memphis	Memphis	3–29: Oxford, MS	Memphis	Memphis	Memphis	Memphis
Brice's Cross Roads	Memphis	3–29: Oxford, MS	Memphis	Memphis	Memphis	Memphis
Redesig. 86th USCI	21–25: Gonzales	13–14: Perdido	16: Marianna	25–28: Pierce's Landing	Barrancas	13–19: Pollard
Barrancas	21–25: Gonzales	13–14: Perdido	18: Marianna	25–28: Vernon	13-17: Pine Barren Creek	13–20: Pollard
Athens Co. D Georgia	Athens Co. D Georgia	Athens Co. D Georgia	Athens Co. D Georgia	Athens Co. D Georgia	Athens Co. D Georgia	Athens Co. D Georgia
Athens A–C, E, G Georgia	Athens A–C, E, G Georgia	Athens A–C, E, G Georgia	Athens A–C, E, G Georgia	Rome, GA	March to the Sea	Savannah, GA
Sulphur Branch Trestle	Sulphur Branch Trestle	Sulphur Branch Trestle	Sulphur Branch Trestle	Pulaski Co. E Swan Crk	Pulaski Co. E Swan Crk	Nashville Co. E Stevenson

1865

Regiment	Jan	Feb	Mar	Apr	May
1st Alabama Cavalry	Carolina Campaign	Aiken	Monroe's Crossroads	Durham, NC	4: March to AL
1st Alabama Colored Heavy Artillery, later 6th, then 7th US CHA, finally 11th US Colored Infantry (New)	Memphis	Memphis	Memphis	Memphis	Memphis
1st Alabama Infantry, African Descent, later 55th US Colored Infantry	Memphis	28: Morganza	29: Port Hudson	Port Hudson	Port Hudson
14th Corps d'Afrique Infantry, later 86th US Colored Infantry	Barrancas	Barrancas	19: Mobile	9: Blakeley, Montgomery	13: Mobile; 23: Fort Morgan
1st Florida Cavalry	Barrancas	Barrancas	19: Mobile	Blakeley, Montgomery	Barrancas
4th Alabama Infantry, African Descent, later 106th US Colored Infantry	Fackler Co. D Carolinas	Fackler Co. D Carolinas	Fackler Co. D Carolinas	Fackler Co. D Carolinas	Fackler & Mud Creek, AL
2nd Alabama Infantry, African Descent, later 110th US Colored Infantry	Carolinas Campaign	Carolinas Campaign	Carolinas Campaign	Carolinas Campaign	Grand Review, Gallatin
3rd Alabama Infantry, African Descent, later 111th US Colored Infantry	Bellevue Co. E Stevenson	Bellevue Co. E Stevenson	Bellevue Co. E Stevenson	Bellevue Co. E Stevenson	Bellevue Co. E Stevenson
136th US Colored Infantry				6: Selma, Macon, GA	Macon, GA
137th US Colored Infantry				6: Selma, Macon, GA	Macon, GA
138th US Colored Infantry				6: Selma, Macon, GA	Macon, GA

1865

Jun	Jul	Aug	Sep	Oct	Nov	Dec
Huntsville	Huntsville	Huntsville	Huntsville	20: mustered out		
Memphis	Memphis	Memphis	Memphis	Memphis	Memphis	Memphis
Port Hudson	Port Hudson	8: Vidalia	Vidalia	Vidalia	Vidalia	31: mustered out
Fort Morgan & Mobile	Fort Morgan & Mobile	Fort Morgan & Mobile	Fort Morgan & Mobile	Fort Morgan & Mobile	Fort Morgan & Mobile	Fort Morgan & Mobile
Barrancas	Barrancas	Tallahassee	Tallahassee	Tallahassee	17: mustered out	
Fackler & Mud Creek, AL	Fackler & Mud Creek, AL	22: Greenville, TN	consol. w/ 40th USCI	Bridgeport and Stevenson	Bridgeport and Stevenson	Bridgeport and Stevenson
Gallatin, TN	Gallatin, TN	Gallatin, TN	Huntsville	Huntsville	Huntsville	Huntsville
Bellevue Co. E Stevenson	18: Murfreesboro	Murfreesboro	Murfreesboro	Murfreesboro	Murfreesboro	Murfreesboro
Atlanta, GA	Atlanta, GA	Atlanta, GA	Atlanta, GA	Atlanta, GA	Atlanta, GA	Atlanta, GA
Macon, GA	Macon, GA	Macon, GA	Macon, GA	Macon, GA	Macon, GA	Macon, GA
Atlanta, GA	Atlanta, GA	Atlanta, GA	Atlanta, GA	Atlanta, GA	Atlanta, GA	Atlanta, GA

1866

Regiment	Jan	Feb	Mar	Apr
1st Alabama Cavalry				
1st Alabama Colored Heavy Artillery, later 6th, then 7th US CHA, finally 11th US Colored Infantry (New)	12: mustered out			
1st Alabama Infantry, African Descent, later 55th US Colored Infantry				
14th Corps d'Afrique Infantry, later 86th US Colored Infantry	Fort Morgan & Mobile	Fort Morgan & Mobile	Fort Morgan & Mobile	10: mustered out
1st Florida Cavalry				
4th Alabama Infantry, African Descent, later 106th US Colored Infantry	Bridgeport and Stevenson	6: mustered out		
2nd Alabama Infantry, African Descent, later 110th US Colored Infantry	Huntsville	6: mustered out		
3rd Alabama Infantry, African Descent, later 111th US Colored Infantry	Murfreesboro	Murfreesboro	Murfreesboro	30: mustered out
136th US Colored Infantry	4: mustered out			
137th US Colored Infantry	15: mustered out			
138th US Colored Infantry	6: mustered out			

Notes

INTRODUCTION

1. The "official" numbers are 4,969 black soldiers and 2,576 white. William A. Gladstone, *United States Colored Troops, 1863–1867* (Gettysburg, PA: Thomas Publications, 1990), 120; Richard Nelson Current, *Lincoln's Loyalists: Union Soldiers from the Confederacy* (New York: Oxford University Press, 1992), 217. Current's numbers include only those who served in units principally raised in Alabama. While Alabamians enlisted in many organizations raised in or credited to other states, prewar residents of neighboring states also enlisted in Alabama-raised or -credited units, so Current's figures are probably an accurate estimate.

2. For a very brief discussion of this historiographical debate, see Kenneth Noe, *Reluctant Rebels: The Confederates Who Joined the Army After 1861* (Chapel Hill: University of North Carolina Press, 2010), 209.

3. For an excellent summary of Forrest's military career, including detailed descriptions of his many shortcomings, see Brian Steel Wills, *The Confederacy's Greatest Cavalryman: Nathan Bedford Forrest* (Lawrence: University Press of Kansas, 1992). For a much briefer assessment, see my review of John R. Scales's *The Battles and Campaigns of Confederate General Nathan Bedford Forrest, 1861–1865, Military Review* (Feb. 2018), accessed March 17, 2018, http://www.armyupress. army.mil/Journals/Military-Review/MR-Book-Reviews/february-2018/Book-Review-010/.

4. William Freehling, *The South vs. the South: How Anti-Confederate Southerners Shaped the Course of the Civil War* (New York: Oxford University Press, 2001).

5. William Thomas, *The Iron Way: Railroads, The Civil War, and the Making of Modern America* (New Haven, CT: Yale University Press, 2011).

6. Freehling, 6, 123.

7. Margaret Storey, *Loyalty and Loss: Alabama's Unionists in the Civil War and Reconstruction* (Baton Rouge: LSU Press, 2004). Storey's work fits well with recent studies of Unionism in the South, including John Inscoe and Robert Kenzer, eds., *Enemies of the Country: New Perspectives on Unionists in the Civil War South* (Athens: University of Georgia Press, 2001); Jon Wakelyn, *Southern Unionist Pamphlets on the Civil War* (Columbia: University of Missouri Press, 1999); Daniel Sutherland, ed., *Guerrillas, Unionists, and Violence on the Confederate Home Front* (Fayetteville: University of Arkansas Press, 1999); Daniel Sutherland, "Sideshow No Longer: A Historiographical Review of the Guerrilla War," *Civil War History* 46 (2000): 5–23; and Barton Myers, *Rebels Against the Confederacy: North Carolina's Unionists* (New York: Cambridge University Press, 2014).

8. George Rable, Review of Margaret Storey, *Loyalty and Loss, Civil War Book Review* (April 2004).

9. William Hoole, *Alabama Tories: The First Alabama Cavalry, U.S.A, 1862–1865* (Tuscaloosa, AL: Confederate Publishing, 1960); Glenda McWhirter Todd, *First Alabama Cavalry, U.S.A.: Homage to Patriotism* (Westminster, MD: Heritage, 2006).

10. Kenneth Noe, ed., *The Yellowhammer War: Civil War and Reconstruction in Alabama* (Tuscaloosa: University of Alabama Press, 2013).

11. Peggy Allen Towns, *Duty Driven: The Plight of North Alabama's African Americans During the Civil War* (Bloomington, IN: Author House, 2012).

12. As just a small example of the excellent recent literature on black military service, see William Dobak, *Freedom by the Sword: The U.S. Colored Troops, 1862–1867* (Washington, DC: Center of Military History, 2011); James Bryant, *The 36th Infantry, United States Colored Troops in the Civil War* (Jefferson, NC: McFarland, 2012); Ian Spurgeon, *Soldiers in the Army of Freedom: The 1st Kansas Colored, the Civil War's First African American Combat Unit* (Norman: University of Oklahoma Press, 2014); Kelly Mezurek, *For Their Own Cause: The 27th United States Colored Troops* (Kent, OH: Kent State University Press, 2016); Stephen Ash, *Firebrand of Liberty: The Story of Two Black Regiments That Changed the Course of the Civil War* (New York: W. W. Norton, 2008); Richard M. Reid, *Freedom for Themselves: North Carolina's Black Soldiers in the Civil War Era* (Chapel Hill: University of North Carolina Press, 2008); and Douglas Egerton, *Thunder at the Gates: The Black Civil War Regiments That Redeemed America* (New York: Basic Books, 2016). These all build upon foundational texts in the field, including George W. Williams, *A History of the Negro Troops in the War of the Rebellion, 1861–1865* (New York: Harper and Brothers, 1888); Joseph T. Wilson, *The Black Phalanx* (Hartford: American Publishing, 1890); Benjamin Quarles, *The Negro in the Civil War* (Boston: Little, Brown, 1953); Dudley T. Cornish, *The Sable Arm: Negro Troops in the Union Army, 1861–1865* (Lawrence: University Press of Kansas, 1987); Joseph Glatthaar, *Forged in Battle: The Civil War Alliance of Black Soldiers and White Officers* (New York: The Free Press, 1990); James Hollandsworth Jr., *The Native Guards* (Baton Rouge: LSU Press, 1995); Ira Berlin, Joseph Reidy, and Leslie Rowland, eds., *Freedom's Soldiers: The Black Military Experience in the Civil War* (New York: Cambridge University Press, 1998); Edward Miller, *The Black Civil War Soldiers of Illinois* (Columbia: University of South Carolina Press, 1998); and John David Smith, ed., *Black Soldiers in Blue: African American Troops in the Civil War Era* (Chapel Hill: University of North Carolina Press, 2002).

13. The US Army's official historians allege that it is easier to locate any given regiment during the Civil War than a unit that served in Iraq or Afghanistan, largely due to the transient nature of digital sources.

14. There are two diaries by Northern-born officers of the First Alabama Cavalry: Francis Tupper's, of Minooka, Illinois, housed at the Lincoln Library in Springfield, Illinois, and Francis Wayland Dunn's, also of Illinois, housed at the Bentley Historical Library at the University of Michigan. Two Alabama natives published memoirs: John R. Phillips, *The Story of My Life*, in 1923, and Wade Richardson, *How I Reached the Union Lines*, in 1905. In 1909, Joseph Kibler Nelson penned his memoir of his service in the 111th USCT as "Recollections of My Early Life." A white noncommissioned officer of the 111th, Sgt. Lyle Adair, kept a diary of his time as a prisoner at Andersonville, but it has comparatively less to say about his time in the USCT regiment.

15. Microfilm M2062, Approved Claims, 1871–1880, Alabama; Settled Case Files for Claims Approved by the Southern Claims Commission, 1871–1880; RG 217, Records of the Accounting

Officers of the Department of the Treasury, 1775–1978, National Archives and Records Administration, Washington, DC. Hereafter SCC. Almost half (45%) of the submitted claims come from counties along the Tennessee River, while another half (44%) are from the Hill Counties of North Alabama, with most of the rest following the routes of the various raids (Streight's, Rousseau's, and Wilson's) across the state. Less than 1 percent are from the Wiregrass.

16. As a recent example, see Andrew Masich, *Civil War in the Southwest Borderlands, 1861–1867* (Norman: University of Oklahoma Press, 2017).

17. See Daniel Sutherland, *A Savage Conflict: The Decisive Role of Guerrillas in the American Civil War* (Chapel Hill: University of North Carolina Press, 2009); Brian McKnight and Barton Myers, eds., *The Guerrilla Hunters: Irregular Conflicts during the Civil War* (Baton Rouge: LSU Press, 2017); Robert Mackey, *The Uncivil War: Irregular Warfare in the Upper South, 1861–1865* (Norman: University of Oklahoma Press, 2004); Clay Mountcastle, *Punitive War: Confederate Guerrillas and Union Reprisals* (Lawrence: University Press of Kansas, 2009); Joseph Beilein, *Bushwhackers: Guerrilla Warfare, Manhood, and the Household in Civil War Missouri* (Kent, OH: Kent State University Press, 2016); and Matthew Stith, *Extreme Civil War: Guerrilla Warfare, Environment, and Race on the Trans-Mississippi Frontier* (Baton Rouge: LSU Press, 2016).

18. For a recent discussion of this concept, see Ethan Rafuse, "'Little Phil,' a 'Bad Old Man,' and the 'Gray Ghost': Hybrid Warfare and the Fight for the Shenandoah Valley, August–November 1864," *Journal of Military History* 81, no. 3 (July 2017): 775–801.

19. See R. Douglas Hurt, *Agriculture and the Confederacy: Policy, Productivity, and Power in the Civil War South* (Chapel Hill: University of North Carolina Press, 2015).

20. See Victoria Bynum, *The Free State of Jones: Mississippi's Longest Civil War* (Chapel Hill: University of North Carolina Press, 2003).

21. See, for example, Lisa Brady, *War Upon the Land: Military Strategy and the Transformation of Southern Landscapes during the American Civil War* (Athens: University of Georgia Press, 2012); Kathryn Shively Meier, *Nature's Civil War: Common Soldiers and the Environment in 1862 Virginia* (Chapel Hill: University of North Carolina Press, 2013); Brian Drake, *The Blue, the Gray, and the Green: Toward an Environmental History of the Civil War* (Athens: University of Georgia Press, 2015); and Megan Kate Nelson, *Ruin Nation: Destruction and the American Civil War* (Athens: University of Georgia Press, 2012).

22. Stephen Ash, *When the Yankees Came: Conflict and Chaos in the Occupied South, 1861–1865* (Chapel Hill: University of North Carolina Press, 1995), 77.

23. At the time of preparation of this manuscript, Joan Cashin's work *War Stuff: The Struggle for Human and Environmental Resources in the American Civil War* (New York: Cambridge University Press, 2018) had not yet been released, and I did not have the benefit of consulting what is sure to be a pathbreaking work. See also David Williams, *Rich Man's War: Class, Caste, and Confederate Defeat in the Lower Chattahoochee Valley* (Athens: University of Georgia Press, 1998).

24. Noe, *Reluctant Rebels*, 106; Russell Johnson, *Warriors into Workers: The Civil War and the Formation of Urban-Industrial Society in a Northern City* (New York: Fordham University Press, 2003). For the prevailing interpretation of Civil War soldiers' motivations, see James McPherson, *For Cause and Comrades: Why Men Fought in the Civil War* (Oxford, UK: Oxford University Press, 1997).

25. Walter Fleming, *Civil War and Reconstruction in Alabama* (New York: Columbia University Press, 1905).

26. For the model revised history of the period, see Eric Foner, *Reconstruction: America's Unfinished Revolution, 1863–1877* (New York: Harper Collins, 1988).

27. Robert Reid, Review of Walter L. Fleming, *Civil War and Reconstruction in Alabama*, *Journal of Negro History* 35, no. 4 (Oct. 1950): 453–56.

28. Christopher McIlwain, *Civil War Alabama* (Tuscaloosa: University of Alabama Press, 2016), and *1865 Alabama* (Tuscaloosa: University of Alabama Press, 2017).

29. Michael Fitzgerald, *Reconstruction in Alabama: From Civil War to Redemption in the Cotton South* (Baton Rouge: LSU Press, 2017).

30. Joseph W. Danielson, *War's Desolating Scourge: The Union's Occupation of North Alabama* (Lawrence: University Press of Kansas, 2012); Anthony Carey, *Sold Down the River: Slavery in the Lower Chattahoochee Valley of Alabama and Georgia* (Tuscaloosa: University of Alabama Press, 2011); David Williams, *I Freed Myself: African American Self-Emancipation in the Civil War Era* (Cambridge, UK: Cambridge University Press, 2014).

31. Noe, ed., *Yellowhammer War*.

32. Earl Hess, *The Civil War in the West: Victory and Defeat from the Appalachians to the Mississippi* (Chapel Hill: University of North Carolina Press, 2012).

CHAPTER ONE

1. For an excellent summary of the southern environment, see Albert Cowdrey, *This Land, This South: An Environmental History* (Lexington: University Press of Kentucky, 1996).

2. "Water Resources in Alabama," *Encyclopedia of Alabama*, accessed June 16, 2018, http://www.encyclopediaofalabama.org/article/h-1645.

3. "Physiographic Sections of Alabama," *Encyclopedia of Alabama*, accessed July 31, 2017, http://www.encyclopediaofalabama.org/article/h-1362 .

4. See Kathryn Braund, *Deerskins and Duffels: The Creek Indian Trade with Anglo-America, 1685–1815* (Lincoln: University of Nebraska Press, 1993).

5. See Lenny Wells, *Pecan: America's Native Nut Tree* (Tuscaloosa: University of Alabama Press, 2017).

6. See Dan Flores, *American Serengeti: The Last Big Animals of the Great Plains* (Lawrence: University Press of Kansas, 2016), 14.

7. Lawrence Keeley, *War Before Civilization* (New York: Oxford University Press, 1996), viii.

8. Keeley, *War Before Civilization*, 139.

9. Keeley, *War Before Civilization*, 140–41.

10. See Vernon Knight, ed., *The Search for Mabila: The Decisive Battle between Hernando de Soto and Chief Tascalusa* (Tuscaloosa: University of Alabama Press, 2009).

11. William Rogers, Robert Ward, Leah Atkins, and Wayne Flynt, *Alabama: The History of a Deep South State* (Tuscaloosa: University of Alabama Press, 1994), 31; Daniel H. Thomas, *Fort Toulouse: The French Outpost at the Alabamas on the Coosa* (Tuscaloosa: University of Alabama Press, 1989), 1–10.

12. See Alfred Crosby, *Ecological Imperialism: The Biological Expansion of Europe, 900–1900* (Cambridge, UK: Cambridge University Press, 1986).

13. See Steven Hahn, *The Invention of the Creek Nation, 1670–1763* (Lincoln: University of Nebraska Press, 2004).

14. See Paul Kelton, *Epidemics and Enslavement: Biological Catastrophe in the Native Southeast, 1492–1715* (Lincoln: University of Nebraska Press, 2007).

15. See Christina Snyder, *Slavery in Indian Country: The Changing Face of Captivity in Early America* (Cambridge: Harvard University Press, 2010).

16. James Benson Sellers, *Slavery in Alabama* (Tuscaloosa: University of Alabama Press, 1950; repr., 1994), 3–4.

17. Rogers et al., *Alabama*, 30, 94.

18. See Fred Anderson, *Crucible of War: The Seven Years' War and the Fate of Empire in British North America, 1754–1766* (New York: Knopf, 2000).

19. Rogers et al., *Alabama*, 36.

20. William Bartram, *Travels Through North & South Carolina, Georgia, East and West Florida, the Cherokee Country, the Extensive Territories of the Muscogulges, or Creek Confederacy, and the Country of the Chactaws; containing an Account of the Soil and Natural Productions of those Regions, together with Observations on the Manners of the Indians* (Philadelphia: James & Johnson, 1791); Gregory Waselkov and Kathryn Braund, eds., *William Bartram on the Southeastern Indians* (Lincoln: University of Nebraska Press, 1995).

21. Bartram, *Travels*, 54–55.

22. Rogers et al., *Alabama*, 9.

23. Bartram, *Travels*, 257–58.

24. "Federal Road in Alabama," *Encyclopedia of Alabama*, accessed July 31, 2017, http://www.encyclopediaofalabama.org/article/h-2999. See also Angela Hudson, *Creek Paths and Federal Roads: Indians, Settlers, and Slaves and the Making of the American South* (Chapel Hill: University of North Carolina Press, 2010).

25. Gregory A. Waselkov, *Conquering Spirit: Fort Mims and the Redstick War of 1813–14* (Tuscaloosa: University of Alabama Press, 2006).

26. Frank Owsley Jr., *Struggle for the Gulf Borderlands: The Creek War and the Battle of New Orleans, 1812–1815* (Tuscaloosa: University of Alabama Press, 1981); Kathryn Braund, ed., *Tohopeka: Rethinking the Creek War and the War of 1812* (Tuscaloosa: University of Alabama Press, 2012).

27. Virginia Van der Veer Hamilton, *Alabama: A History* (New York: Norton, 1977), 8; "The Saga of William Bauck "Bill" Looney," accessed July 31, 2017, http://www.swannco.net/1st_Ala_Cav/biographies/looney.html. Henry's "dogtrot" home still stands near Asheville, Alabama.

28. Rogers et al., *Alabama*, 62.

29. Rogers et al., *Alabama*, 69.

30. Hamilton, *Alabama: A History*, 12.

31. Rogers et al., *Alabama*, 57.

32. Rogers et al., *Alabama*, 55.

33. "Alabama Fever," *Encyclopedia of Alabama*, accessed July 31, 2017, http://www.encyclopediaofalabama.org/article/h-3155.

34. Jeffrey Benton, ed., *The Very Worst Road: Travelers' Accounts of Crossing Alabama's Old Creek Indian Territory, 1820–1847* (Tuscaloosa: University of Alabama Press, 2009).

35. Herbert Lewis, *Clearing the Thickets: A History of Antebellum Alabama* (New Orleans: Quid Pro Books, 2013).

36. Rogers et al., *Alabama*, 55.

37. Rogers et al., *Alabama*, 77.

38. Reprinted in Shelly McWhorter Wright, *Some Descendants of David McWhorter (McWhirter) and his wife Mary Poston (Posten) McWhorter* (Longview, TX: McWhorter, 1978), 111–12. Original in author's possession.

39. "Alabama History Timeline," accessed July 31, 2017, http://www.archives.alabama.gov/timeline/a11801.html.

40. See Angela Lakwete, *Inventing the Cotton Gin: Machine and Myth in Antebellum America* (Baltimore: Johns Hopkins University Press, 2003).

41. Joseph Kibler Nelson, "Recollections of My Early Life" (unpublished manuscript, 1909), 5, 8. Copy at the Army Heritage and Education Center, Carlisle, PA.

42. Arthur P. Bagby et al., eds., *The Code of Alabama* (Montgomery, AL: Brittain and De Wold, 1852), 234–42.

43. Bagby et al., *The Code of Alabama*, 234–42.

44. William Thomas, *The Iron Way: Railroads, the Civil War, and the Making of Modern America* (New Haven, CT: Yale University Press, 2011).

45. Michael W. Fitzgerald, *Reconstruction in Alabama: From Civil War to Redemption in the Cotton South* (Baton Rouge: LSU Press, 2017), 17.

46. Michael Dubin, *United States Gubernatorial Elections, 1776–1860: The Official Results by State and County* (Jefferson, NC: McFarland, 2003), 7–8.

47. Dubin, *United States Presidential Elections, 1788–1860: The Official Results by County and State* (Jefferson, NC: McFarland, 2002).

48. See Kristin Epps, *Slavery on the Periphery: The Kansas-Missouri Border in the Antebellum and Civil War Eras* (Athens: University of Georgia Press, 2016).

49. "Jefferson Buford, Proslavery Colonizer, 1807–1861," *Kansaspedia*, Kansas Historical Society, accessed July 14, 2017, https://www.kshs.org/kansapedia/jefferson-buford/15130. See also Nicole Etchison, *Bleeding Kansas: Contested Liberty in the Civil War Era* (Lawrence: University Press of Kansas, 2004).

50. Dubin, *United States Presidential Elections*. Winston Country was then known as Hancock. It changed its name to honor the popular two-term Democratic governor the following year.

51. Rogers et al., *Alabama*, 173–79; "Alabama Railroads," *Encyclopedia of Alabama*, accessed July 17, 2017, http://www.encyclopediaofalabama.org/article/h-2390.

52. "Andrew B. Moore (1857–1861)," *Encyclopedia of Alabama*, accessed 22 July 2017, http://www.encyclopediaofalabama.org/article/h-1454.

53. Roy Basler, ed., *The Collected Works of Abraham Lincoln*, 8 vols. (New Brunswick, NJ: Rutgers University Press, 1953), 3:249.

54. Thomas Nation Claim, 36837, SCC.

55. Dubin, *United States Presidential Elections*, 159–60.

56. Rogers et al., *Alabama*, 173.

CHAPTER TWO

1. For a detailed accounting of slave resistance, see David Williams, *I Freed Myself: African American Self-Emancipation in the Civil War Era* (Cambridge, UK: Cambridge University Press, 2014), 54–56.

2. Even Fleming pointed out this irony. Walter Fleming, *Civil War and Reconstruction in Alabama* (New York: Columbia University Press, 1905), 49.

3. See Edmund Morgan, *American Slavery, American Freedom* (New York: Norton, 1975).

4. Fleming, *Civil War and Reconstruction*, 38, 40.

5. It is on the basis of this argument that Fleming falsely asserts that the delegates were united in their agreement for secession, but simply disagreed on the timing. Fleming, *Civil War and Reconstruction*, 30.

6. For an excellent discussion of the convention and its constituencies, see Christopher Mcllwain, *Civil War Alabama* (Tuscaloosa: University of Alabama Press, 2016), 34–44.

7. See Fleming, *Civil War and Reconstruction*, 31; Mcllwain, *Civil War Alabama*, 28.

8. William Smith, *The History and Debates of the Convention of the People of Alabama, Begun and Held in the City of Montgomery, on the Seventh Day of January, 1861 in which is Preserved the Speeches of the Secret Sessions, and Many Valuable State Papers* (Montgomery, AL: White, Pfister, 1861), 69, accessed July 15, 2017, http://docsouth.unc.edu/imls/smithwr/smith.html#p116.

9. Smith, *History and Debates*, 73, 74.

10. Smith, *History and Debates*, 84.

11. Smith, *History and Debates*, 104.

12. Fleming, *Civil War and Reconstruction*, 55.

13. Wesley Thompson, *The Free State of Winston: A History of Winston County, Alabama* (Winfield, AL: Pareil Press, 1968), 25.

14. Thompson, *Free State of Winston*, 120.

15. *Moulton (Ala.) Democrat*, March 1, 1861, reprinted in the *Athens (Tenn.) Post*, March 8, 1861, 2.

16. Mcllwain, *Civil War Alabama*, 51.

17. See Fitzgerald, *Reconstruction in Alabama: From Civil War to Redemption in the Cotton State* (Baton Rouge: LSU Press, 2017), 21–22.

18. John Bell to Henry Bell, April 11, 1861, Moore Papers, ADAH, quoted in Hugh C. Bailey, "Disloyalty in Early Confederate Alabama," *Journal of Southern History* 23 (Nov. 1957): 522–28.

19. *The War of the Rebellion: A Compilation of the Official Records of the Union and Confederate Armies* (Washington, DC: Government Printing Office, 1880–1901), Series 1, 1:327. (Hereafter OR, all Series 1 unless noted).

20. See Kathryn Braund, *Deerskins and Duffels: The Creek Indian Trade with Anglo-America, 1685–1815* (Lincoln: University of Nebraska Press, 1993); Jeanne and David Heidler, *Old Hickory's War: Andrew Jackson and the Quest for Empire* (Baton Rouge: LSU Press, 2003); and Matthew J. Clavin, *Aiming for Pensacola: Fugitive Slaves on the Atlantic and Southern Frontiers* (Cambridge, MA: Harvard University Press, 2015).

21. OR, 1:444.

22. OR, 1:448.

23. OR, 1:451.

24. OR, 1:467.

25. Troy (Ala.) *Independent American*, May 22, 1861, 3.

26. Troy (Ala.) *Advocate and American*, July 18, 1961, 3; Clavin, *Aiming for Pensacola*.

27. OR, 6:666.

28. David Williams, "The 'Faithful Slave' Is About Played Out: Civil War Slave Resistance in the Lower Chattahoochee Valley," *Alabama Review* 52 (April 1999): 95.

29. Williams, *I Freed Myself*, 66.

30. *Montgomery Advertiser*, Dec. 30, 1860.

31. David Williams, *I Freed Myself*, 67.

32. Daniel Hundley Diary, ADAH, quoted in McIlwain, *Civil War Alabama*, 57.

33. Abbeville (Ala.) *United South*, May 25, 1861, 3.

34. See Winthrop Jordan, *Tumult and Silence at Second Creek: An Inquiry into a Civil War Slave Conspiracy* (Baton Rouge: LSU Press, 1993); and David Williams, *Rich Man's War: Class, Caste, and Confederate Defeat in the Lower Chattahoochee Valley* (Athens: University of Georgia Press, 1998).

35. Margaret Storey. *Loyalty and Loss: Alabama's Unionists in the Civil War and Reconstruction* (Baton Rouge: LSU Press, 2004), 52–53.

36. Williams, "The 'Faithful Slave,'" 88–89.

37. Hall later affirmed, "When the war began I did not understand the questions involved as I was a slave, but I soon learned and believed that if the Union cause was successful I would gain my liberty. I then talked in private among the colored people in favor of the Union cause." Hall later worked as a cook for the Ninth Minnesota in Selma in the summer of 1865. Henry Hall, SCC Claim 41006, Dallas County.

38. Storey, *Loyalty and Loss*, 54; Henry Hall, SCC Claim 41006, Dallas County.

39. William Winston SCC Claim 3984, DeKalb County.

40. OR, 1:447.

41. Braxton Dunlavy Claim 9101, Winston County.

42. Green Haley Claim 2177, Winston County.

43. Andrew McCollum Claim 8987, Winston County.

44. Buckner Walker Claim 18032, Winston County.

45. William Winston SCC Claim 3984, DeKalb County.

46. Zacharia White Claim 16847, Winston County.

47. Thompson, *Free State of Winston*, 5.

48. William Hoole, *Alabama Tories: The First Alabama Cavalry, U.S.A., 1862–1865* (Tuscaloosa, AL: Confederate Publishing, 1960), 96.

49. Thompson, *Free State of Winston*, 4, 6.

50. See Victoria Bynum, *The Free State of Jones: Mississippi's Longest Civil War* (Chapel Hill: University of North Carolina Press, 2001).

51. W. Hunsgrove to Andrew Moore, July 16, 1861, quoted in Malcolm McMillan, *The Disintegration of a Confederate State: Three Governors and Alabama's Wartime Home Front, 1861–1865* (Macon, GA: Mercer University Press, 1986), 22.

52. Storey, *Loyalty and Loss*, 107.

53. Nathan Montgomery Claim 43897, Winston County.

54. Thomas Sawyer Claim 48165, SCC.

55. Thompson, *Free State of Winston*, 31, 41, 44.

56. In his testimony before the Southern Claims Commission, Thomas Nation of Blount County claimed it "got so hot he had to play shut mouth," Nation Claim 36837, SCC; Storey, *Loyalty and Loss*, 52.

57. McIlwain, *Civil War Alabama*, 65.

58. Andrew Ingle SCC Claim 2178, Winston County.

59. Bailey, "Disloyalty in Early Confederate Alabama," 527.

60. Smith, *History and Debates*, 86.

61. OR, 16:1, 474.

62. OR, 16:1, 32.

63. John R. Phillips, *The Story of My Life* (Tuscaloosa, AL: John Phillips, 1923), 39.

64. Storey, *Loyalty and Loss*, 57.

65. McIlwain, *Civil War Alabama*, 96.

66. OR, 10:2, 431.

67. OR, 16:1, 729.

68. See Michael W. Fitzgerald, "He Was Always Preaching the Union: The Wartime Origins of White Republicanism during Reconstruction," in Kenneth Noe, ed., *Yellowhammer War: Civil War and Reconstruction in Alabama* (Tuscaloosa: University of Alabama Press, 2013), 228–29.

69. Storey, *Loyalty and Loss*, 109.

70. Storey, *Loyalty and Loss*, 79.

71. James Baggett, *Homegrown Yankees: Tennessee's Union Cavalry in the Civil War* (Baton Rouge: LSU Press, 2009), 126.

72. Storey, *Loyalty and Loss*, 88, 97.

73. The best account of Turchin's life and the affair at Athens are found in Stephen Chicoine's *John Basil Turchin and the Fight to Free the Slaves* (Westport, CT: Praeger, 2003). Much of the following account comes from Chicoine's work, as well as the OR.

74. Joseph W. Danielson, *War's Desolating Scourge: The Union's Occupation of North Alabama* (Lawrence: University Press of Kansas, 2012).

75. Mark Grimsley, *The Hard Hand of War: Union Military Policy towards Southern Civilians, 1861–1865* (Cambridge, UK: Cambridge University Press, 1995).

76. Chicoine, *John Basil Turchin*, 49.

77. OR, 10:2, 619.

78. Chicoine, *John Basil Turchin*, 67.

79. Fleming, *Civil War and Reconstruction*, 63.

80. Chicoine, *John Basil Turchin*, 90–91.

81. Chicoine, *John Basil Turchin*, 93, 101.

82. OR, 16:2, 588.

83. Benjamin Turner SCC Claim (No Number), Dallas County. Turner owned a livery stable in Selma in 1865 and lost substantial property when Wilson's raiders arrived, for which he was later generously reimbursed.

84. OR, 16:2, 44.

85. Danielson, *War's Desolating Scourge,* 108–9.

86. Danielson, *War's Desolating Scourge,* 110–11.

87. OR, 10:2, 102.

88. OR, 10:2, 103.

89. OR, 10:2, 105, 166.

90. Storey, *Loyalty and Loss,* 113.

91. William Dobak, *Freedom by the Sword: The U.S. Colored Troops, 1862–1863* (Washington, DC: Center of Military History, 2011), 173, 263.

92. Earl Hess, *The Civil War in the West: Victory and Defeat from the Appalachians to the Mississippi* (Chapel Hill: University of North Carolina Press, 2012), 89; Meriwether quoted in McIlwain, *Civil War Alabama,* 249.

93. Levi Coffin, *Reminiscences of Levi Coffin, the Reputed President of the Underground Railroad; Being a Brief History of the Labors of a Lifetime in Behalf of the Slave, with the Stories of Numerous Fugitives, who Gained their Freedom through his Instrumentality, and Many Other Incidents* (Cincinnati: Freedom Tract Society, 1876), 619.

94. Danielson, *War's Desolating Scourge,* 113; Dobak, *Freedom by the Sword,* 263.

95. Danielson, *War's Desolating Scourge,* 93–94.

96. U.S., *Statutes at Large, Treaties, and Proclamations of the United States of America* (Boston, 1863), 12:589–92, Section 1.

97. See Ian Spurgeon, *Soldiers in the Army of Freedom: The 1st Kansas Colored, the Civil War's First African American Combat Unit* (Norman: University of Oklahoma Press, 2014), and James Hollandsworth, *The Louisiana Native Guards: The Black Military Experience During the Civil War* (Baton Rouge: LSU Press, 1995).

98. Emancipation Proclamation, Sept. 22, 1862.

99. OR, 20:2, 403.

100. William Curtis SCC Claim 10339, Winston County; Peter Gossett, "Free State Civil War Events and the Jasper Raid," accessed March 11, 2018, https://www.freestateofwinston.org/jasperraid.htm. Conscription agents under Stoke Roberts murdered Curtis after he lingered too long near his home, hoping to see and hug his first grandchild.

101. See Robin Sterling, *Winston County, Alabama Files from the Southern Claims Commission,* p. 126.

102. Green Haley SCC Claim 2177, Winston County.

103. Thomas Martin SCC Claim 2231, Winston County; see Peter Gossett, "Free State Civil War Events and the Jasper Raid," accessed March 11, 2018, https://www.freestateofwinston.org/jasperraid.htm.

104. See Daniel Sutherland, *A Savage Conflict: The Decisive Role of Guerrillas in the American Civil War* (Chapel Hill: University of North Carolina Press, 2009).

105. OR, 16:1, 786.

106. OR, 16:1, 789.

107. OR, 16:1, 790.

108. Frank Moore, *The Civil War in Song and Story* (New York: P. F. Collier, 1889), 216.

109. John Smith SCC Claim 51296, Allen Smith Service Record, CSR. Enlistment records show three other Smiths (Henry, John, and Matthew) enlisting on the same date and at the

same place as the elder Smith, but it is unclear who was his son and who were nephews or other relatives.

110. Storey, 109.

111. Moore, *Civil War in Song and Story*, 216–17.

112. "Christopher Sheats," *Encyclopedia of Alabama*, accessed Aug. 25, 2017, http://www.encyclopediaofalabama.org/article/h-1868.

113. OR, 16:2, 118.

114. OR, 16:2, 182.

115. OR, 16:2, 193.

116. OR, 16:2, 288.

117. OR, 10:1, 891.

118. OR, 10:2, 162, 167.

119. OR, 16:2, 37.

120. OR, 16:1, 202.

121. John Beatty, *The Citizen-Soldier; or, Memoirs of a Volunteer, 1861–1863* (1879; repr., New York: Norton, 1946), 85.

122. Danielson, *War's Desolating Scourge*, 69.

123. OR, 16:2, 309.

124. Henry Slaughter SCC Claim 48164, Morgan County.

125. OR, 16:2, 123.

126. OR, 16:2, 165, 198.

127. OR, 16:1, 602.

128. OR, 16:1, 633.

129. OR, 16:1, 834.

130. See Megan Kate Nelson, *Ruin Nation: Destruction and the American Civil War* (Athens: University of Georgia Press, 2012).

131. OR, 16:2, 14.

132. Leslie Anders, *The Eighteenth Missouri* (Indianapolis: Bobbs-Merrill, 1968), 100.

133. OR, 16:2, 24.

134. OR, 16:2, 225.

135. OR, 16:1, 485, 496.

136. OR, 16:2, 183.

137. OR, 16:2, 383.

138. OR, 16:2, 461, 477.

139. OR, 16:2, 391.

140. Record of Events, Companies I and K, 1st Alabama Cavalry, Microfilm M594 and Compiled Service Records of Volunteer Union Soldiers from the State of Alabama, Microfilm M263, Record Group 94, Records of the Adjutant General's Office, National Archives and Records Administration, Washington, DC.

141. OR, 20:1, 7, 618.

142. On July 7, 1862, Sarah Rousseau Espy wrote in her diary at Cherokee, Alabama, "Warm and dry—we need rain so much now," on July 17, "We are needing rain badly," on July 19, "The crops will soon be ruined if rain does not come," and on July 25, "Still dry. We are suffering

badly for rain. The garden is burnt up nearly." The Espy farm was on the Coosa River in eastern Alabama, near Centre, sixty miles southeast of Huntsville. Espy Diary, Alabama Department of Archives and History, ADAH, Montgomery, AL.

143. William Rogers, Robert Ward William, Leah Atkins, and Wayne Flynt, *Alabama: The History of a Deep South State* (Tuscaloosa: University of Alabama Press, 1994), 209.

144. OR, 16:1, 474–75.

145. R. Douglas Hurt, *Food and Agriculture during the Civil War* (Santa Barbara, CA: ABC-CLIO, 2016), 36.

146. Phillips, *The Story of My Life.*

147. OR, 17:2, 191.

CHAPTER THREE

1. For detailed coverage of Perryville, see Kenneth Noe, *Perryville* (Lexington: University of Kentucky Press, 2001). Thomas Connelly argues, "in the total production of corn, hogs, cattle, mules, and horses, the lower Middle Tennessee zone was one of the richest areas in the *entire Confederacy*" (emphasis in original). Connelly, *Civil War Tennessee: Battles and Leaders* (Knoxville: University of Tennessee Press, 1990), 13.

2. Grenville Dodge to Nathan Dodge, Sept. 28, 1862, Box 2, File 4:2, Dodge Papers, State Historical Society of Iowa (SHSI), Des Moines.

3. Margaret Storey, *Loyalty and Loss: Alabama's Unionists in the Civil War and Reconstruction* (Baton Rouge: LSU Press, 2004), 69.

4. Storey, *Loyalty and Loss,* 99.

5. See Peter Cozzens, *The Darkest Days of the War: The Battles of Iuka & Corinth* (Chapel Hill: University of North Carolina Press, 1997).

6. Leslie Anders, *The Eighteenth Missouri* (Indianapolis: Bobbs-Merrill, 1968), 106.

7. Rikard testified, "I had one brother, one brother in law and six or seven cousins in the Union Army, all but two were in Company F 64th Regiment Illinois Infantry. The other two were in the 1st Alabama Cavalry." Henry Rikard, SCC Claim 43912, Franklin County.

8. Christopher Tompkins SCC Claim (No Number), Franklin County.

9. US War Department, *The War of the Rebellion: A Compilation of the Official Records of the Union and Confederate Armies* (Washington, DC: GPO, 1880–1901), Series I, Vol. 17, Part 1, 377, 541 (hereafter OR).

10. OR, 23:1, 11.

11. Dennis Cantrell, SCC Claim 18014, Winston County.

12. "Order No. 1," 1st Alabama Cavalry, Regimental Order and Detail Book, Book Records of Volunteer Union Organizations, RG 94, Records of the Adjutant General's Office, National Archives and Records Administration, Washington, DC.

13. "James C Cameron," 1st Alabama Cavalry Searchable Roster, accessed Aug. 23, 2017, http://www.1stalabamacavalryusv.com/Roster/Troopers.aspx?trooperid=331.

14. George Spencer to Grenville Dodge, Sept. 7, 1863, Box 2, File 5:3, Dodge Papers, SHSI.

15. James Baggett, *Homegrown Yankees: Tennessee's Union Cavalry in the Civil War* (Baton Rouge: LSU Press, 2009), 168.

Margaret Storey
Loyalty + Loss

Margaret Storey
Corinth
Blk Area.

16. Grenville Dodge, "The Secret Service in the Civil War," p. 3, Box 43, File 99:2, Dodge Papers, SHSI. For a full accounting of Union intelligence gathering during the war, see William Feis, *Grant's Secret Service: The Intelligence War from Belmont to Appomattox* (Lincoln: University of Nebraska Press, 2004), and Brent Ponsford, "Major-General Grenville M. Dodge's Military Intelligence Operations During the Civil War," unpublished MA thesis, Iowa State University, Ames, IA, 1976. For a memoir of one of Dodge's best spies, see George Johns, *Philip Henson, the Southern Union Spy* (St. Louis: Nixon-Jones, 1887). Henson was an Alabama native but lived in Tishomingo, MS before the war. He frequently gained the confidence of Confederate interlocutors by carrying letters from members of the First Alabama to their families, including from "Colonel" W. H. Smith from Randolph County, who served as a Republican governor of Alabama during Reconstruction.

17. John Nesmith Claim 41034, Blount County. After the war, Berry apparently "helped organize an armed body of about 100 men who rode in defiance of the Klan dominance in the region. Their group was the anti-Ku Klux. Berry led the group as far as Somerville in Morgan County, stopping at known Ku Klux homes. They called out the Ku Kluxers and threatened to do to them what they were doing to others if they did not stop their night riding." Robin Sterling, *Blount County, Alabama Confederate Soldiers: Vol. 3, Miscellaneous* (Owens Cross Roads, AL: Robin Sterling, 2013), 38.

18. Phoebe Bennett, SCC Claim 6087 (Disallowed), Winston County.

19. William Dodd, SCC Claim 17325, Winston County.

20. Green Haley, SCC Claim 2177, Winston County.

21. Stephen Ash, *When the Yankees Came: Conflict and Chaos in the Occupied South, 1861–1865* (Chapel Hill: University of North Carolina Press, 1995), 63.

22. Spencer quoted in Dodge, "The Secret Service in the Civil War," p. 11, Box 43, File 99:2, Dodge Papers, SHSI.

23. Stanley Hirshson, *Grenville M. Dodge: Soldier, Politician, Railroad Pioneer* (Bloomington: University of Indiana Press, 1967), 74. Henson's pay records reveal a trip to Columbus, MS, March 1–17; Okolona, MS, May 1–17; and again to Okolona, May 27–June 3, for which Henson received the sum of $350. "Secret Service Records," No. 22, Box 63, File 148:1, Dodge Papers, SHSI.

24. Dodge, "The Secret Service in the Civil War," p. 10, Box 43, File 99:2, Dodge Papers, SHSI.

25. Oates to Dodge, April 3, 1895, Box 59, File 140:1, Dodge Papers, SHSI.

26. Daniel Sutherland, *A Savage Conflict: The Decisive Role of Guerrillas in the American Civil War* (Chapel Hill: University of North Carolina Press, 2009), 175.

27. See Ben H. Severance, "Confederate Alabama's Finest Hour: The Battle of Salem Church, May 3, 1863," pp. 55–70 in Kenneth Noe, ed., *The Yellowhammer War: The Civil War and Reconstruction in Alabama* (Tuscaloosa: University of Alabama Press, 2013).

28. See Lisa Brady, *War Upon the Land: Military Strategy and the Transformation of Southern Landscapes During the American Civil War* (Athens: University of Georgia Press, 2012), for a description of the term and an effective argument for the use of these raids in the Civil War.

29. See F. W. Weatherbee, *Fifth (First Middle) Tennessee Cavalry, USA* (Carrollton, MS: Pioneer, 1992), 6–9; War Department, Special Orders No. 287, June 25, 1863, copy in Box 58, File

Vincent's CrossRoads ☆   get   Co. E

137:5, Dodge Papers, SHSI; Regimental Order No. 14, Headquarters, 1st Alabama Cavalry, Glendale, MS, Sept. 24, 1863, Regimental Order Books, RG 94, NARA, Washington, DC. On Stones River, see Peter Cozzens, *No Better Place to Die: The Battle of Stones River* (Urbana: University of Illinois Press, 1990).

30. See Joseph Wheelan, *Libby Prison Breakout: The Daring Escape from the Notorious Civil War Prison* (New York: PublicAffairs, 2010).

31. OR, 23:1, 292.

32. OR, 23:1, 293.

33. For a full account of Grierson's historic raid, see Stephen Starr, *The Union Cavalry in the Civil War*: Vol. 3, *The War in the West, 1861–1865* (Baton Rouge: LSU Press, 1985), 189–95.

34. OR, 23:1, 250.

35. OR, 23:1, 251.

36. OR, 23:1, 247.

37. OR, 23:1, 245–50; Hirshson, *Grenville M. Dodge*, 73.

38. OR, 23:1, 287.

39. Henry Breidenthal, "Col Streights's Expedition: Journal of H. Breidenthal, Sergeant, Co. A, Third Ohio Vol. Infantry," in Frank Moore, ed., *The Rebellion Record: A Diary of American Events, with Documents, Narrative, Illustrative Incidents, Poetry, Etc.*, 11 vols. (New York: Putnam, 1864),1:340 (hereafter Breidenthal Diary).

40. Baggett, *Homegrown Yankees*, 193.

41. Breidenthal Diary, 341. Lawrence County's two delegates to the convention were David P. Lewis and James S. Clarke, both of whom were cooperationists at the convention but reversed themselves after the vote and signed the ordinance. The description from Breidenthal's Diary fits Lewis, who was a judge in Moulton in 1863 but later went north to Nashville. From 1872 to 1874 he served as Republican governor of Alabama during Reconstruction.

42. Robert Willett, *The Lightning Mule Brigade: Abel Streight's 1863 Raid into Alabama* (Carmel, IN: Guild Press, 1999), 98.   1st Ala Co. K.

43. OR, 23:1, 287. David Smith, who commanded Company E, 5th Middle Tennessee Cavalry (later Company K, 1st Alabama) was a prewar resident of Marion County, Alabama, who traveled to Huntsville shortly after its liberation in April 1862 and enlisted in the 21st Ohio Infantry. On July 25 he earned a commission as captain of the Alabama troops organizing in Huntsville under General Buell's orders. Smith recruited an associate in the 21st Ohio, Joseph Hornbeck of Wood Co. Ohio, to serve as his first lieutenant. Hornbeck was captured twice, first at Stones River, Tennessee, and again across the Mississippi River from Memphis in March 1864, but returned to command his company both times. He survived the engagements at Vincent's Crossroads and at the Oconee Bridge, was wounded at Monroe's Crossroads, but mustered out with his company in July 1865. Details in 1st Alabama Cavalry Descriptive Book, Cos. G–M, Book Records of Volunteer Union Organizations, Record Group 94, Records of the Adjutant General's Office, National Archives and Records Administration, Washington, DC.

☆ *Vincent*   David Smith   Commanded   Co. Ⅲ K 1st Ala   get ☆

44. Breidenthal Diary, 338.

45. OR, 23:1, 287; Willett, *Lightning Mule Brigade*, 128.

46. Breidenthal Diary, 341.

47. Breidenthal Diary, 343.

Vincent's CrossRoads = Hornbeck, Joseph   David Smith   Co. K.

48. OR, 23:1, 290.

49. Breidenthal Diary, 343; Ben Severance, *Portraits of Conflict: A Photographic History of Alabama in the Civil War* (Fayetteville: University of Arkansas Press, 2012), 234.

50. Willet, *Lightning Mule Brigade*, 196; First Alabama Cavalry Descriptive Book, Cos. G–M, Book Records of Volunteer Union Organizations, Record Group 94, Records of the Adjutant General's Office, National Archives and Records Administration, Washington, DC.

51. Robert Mackey, *The Uncivil War: Irregular Warfare in the Upper South, 1861–1865* (Norman: University of Oklahoma Press, 2004), 175.

52. For an excellent discussion of the Corinth Contraband Camp, see Chandra Manning, *Troubled Refuge: Struggling for Freedom in the Civil War* (New York: Vintage, 2016), 114–18.

53. For a full discussion of the Corinth Contraband Camp and the units raised there, see Joseph E. Brent, *Occupied Corinth: The Contraband Camp and the First Regiment of African Descent, 1862–1864* (Washington, DC: American Battlefield Protection Program, 1995).

54. Letter, Maj. Edward Wiley, 61st USCT, Aug. 6, 1864, in James Alexander Service Record, Compiled Service Records of Union Volunteers in the US Colored Troops, Fifty-Fifth U.S. Colored Infantry, Microfilm M2000, Roll 162, NARA, Washington, DC (hereafter Fifty-Fifth USCT CSR).

55. For a description of the camp itself, see Cam Walker, "Corinth: The Story of a Contraband Camp," *Civil War History* 20, no. 1 (March 1974): 5–22.

56. "Condition and Treatment of Colored Refugees," 38th Congress, 2nd session, S. Ex. Doc. 28, p. 20. Quoted in William Dobak, *Freedom by the Sword: The U.S. Colored Troops, 1862–1867* (Washington, DC: Center of Military History, 2011), 295.

57. Headquarters, District of Corinth, General Order No. 31, Feb. 23, 1863, Box 58, File 137:1, Dodge Papers, SHSI.

58. Headquarters, District of Corinth, General Order No. 42, March 7, 1863, Box 58, File 137:1, Dodge Papers, SHSI.

59. Brent, *Occupied Corinth*, 18.

60. Corinth *Chanticleer*, June 12, 1863.

61. *Slave Narratives: A Folk History of Slavery in the United States from Interviews with Former Slaves*, Arkansas Narratives, Vol. II, Part 6 (Washington, DC: GPO, 1941), 212.

62. Dodge, untitled manuscript, p. 20, Box 43, File 99:3, Dodge Papers, SHSI.

63. Alexander to Dodge, Oct. 19, 1863, Box 2, File 5:5, Dodge Papers, SHSI.

64. Michael Fitzgerald, *Reconstruction in Alabama: From Civil War to Redemption in the Cotton South* (Baton Rouge: LSU Press, 2017), 39.

65. Levi Coffin, *Reminiscences of Levi Coffin, the Reputed President of the Underground Railroad . . .* (Cincinnati: Freedom Tract Society, 1876), 636.

66. Stephen Starr, *Jennison's Jayhawkers: A Civil War Cavalry Regiment and Its Commander* (Baton Rouge: LSU Press, 1974).

67. Joseph Kibler Nelson, "Recollections of My Early Life" (unpublished manuscript, 1909), Army Heritage and Education Center, Carlisle Barracks, PA, 32.

68. Brent, *Occupied Corinth*, 19.

69. Timothy Smith, *Corinth 1862: Siege, Battle, Occupation* (Lawrence: University Press of Kansas, 2012), 292.

70. Record of Events, Company A, 55th U.S. Colored Troops, Microfilm M594, Roll 211, RG 94, National Archives and Records Administration, Washington, DC.

71. Coffin, *Reminiscences*, 636–37.

72. Description in Paul S. Pardue, "In Search of the 1st Regiment of African Descent and the Contraband Camp of Corinth Mississippi," Sept. 2000, in file, "Contraband Camp," Corinth Battlefield Unit, Shiloh National Military Park, Corinth, MS.

73. Cincinnati *Daily Gazette*, July 16, 1863, quoted in Pardue, "In Search of the 1st Regiment…"

74. Dobak, *Freedom by the Sword*, 194.

75. J. W. Barnes to Grenville Dodge, Aug. 27, 1863, Box 2, File 5:2, Dodge Papers, SHSI, Des Moines; Nelson, "Recollections," 34.

76. Col. James Alexander to Grenville Dodge, Oct. 19, 1863, Box 3, File 5:5, Dodge Papers, SHSI, Des Moines.

77. Charles O. Dewey to Dodge, April 19, 1863, Box 2, File 4:6, Dodge Papers, SHSI, Des Moines.

78. Record of Events, First Alabama Siege Artillery, African Descent, Microfilm M594, Roll 206, RG 94, NARA.

79. Letter, Major McCord to Gen. Lorenzo Thomas, June 28, 1865 in Alexander Service Record, 55th USCT CSR.

80. See Jennifer Mittelstadt, *The Rise of the Military Welfare State* (Cambridge, MA: Harvard University Press, 2015).

81. Letter, Officers of the First Alabama Infantry, A. D., Fort Pickering, Tennessee, March 25, 1863, in Alexander Service Record, 55th USCT CSR.

82. Augustus Norton, *History of the Presbyterian Church in the State of Illinois* (St. Louis: W. S. Bryan, 1879), 1:481.

83. Nelson, "Recollections," 32.

84. War Department, Special Orders No. 63, Sept. 29, 1863, Vicksburg, MS. Copy in Box 58, File 138:2, Dodge Papers, SHSI, Des Moines.

85. Hirshson, *Grenville M. Dodge*, 75.

86. Hirshson, *Grenville M. Dodge*, 61. For accounts of the Battles of Chickamauga and Chattanooga, see Peter Cozzens, *This Terrible Sound: The Battle of Chickamauga* (Urbana: University of Illinois Press, 1992), and *The Shipwreck of Their Hopes: The Battles for Chattanooga* (Urbana: University of Illinois Press, 1994).

87. Letter, Alexander to A. A. G., Corinth District, Nov. 19, 1863 in Regimental Letter, Endorsement and Order Book, 55th USCT Infantry, Book Records of Volunteer Union Organizations, Record Group 94, Records of the Adjutant General's Office, National Archives and Records Administration, Washington, DC.

88. Headquarters, 16th Army Corps, General Order No. 173, Dec. 17, 1863, Memphis, TN. Copy in Box 60, File 141:2, Dodge Papers, SHSI.

89. Brent, *Occupied Corinth*, 20.

90. Hirshson, *Grenville M. Dodge*, 77.

91. Dunn Diary, July 23, 1863, Francis W. Dunn Papers, Bentley Historical Library, University of Michigan, Ann Arbor.

91. July 23, 1863 Dunn Diary

92. Spencer to Dodge, Sept. 7, 1863, Box 2, File 5:3, Dodge Papers, SHSI, Des Moines.

93. J. W. Barnes to Dodge, Sept. 10, 1863; Spencer to Dodge, Sept. 30, 1863, Box 2, File 5:3, Dodge Papers, SHSI, Des Moines.

94. See Johnny L. T. N. Potter, *First Tennessee & Alabama Independent Vidette Cavalry Roster, 1863–1864: Companies A, B, C, D, E, F, G, H* (Chattanooga, TN: Mountain Press, 1995).

95. John Barnes, SCC Claim 43820, DeKalb County.

96. Bowman Claim 43825, Cherokee County.

97. Bowman Claim 43825, Cherokee County.

98. Baggett, *Homegrown Yankees.*

99. OR, 30:3, 179.

100. OR, 30:3, 343.

101. See Carl von Clausewitz, *On War*, trans. and ed. by Michael Howard (1832; repr., Princeton, NJ: Princeton University Press, 1984).

102. OR, 30:3, 529.

103. OR, 30:4, 380.

104. OR, 30:4, 118.

105. *Perrysburg (Ohio) Journal*, Sept. 28, 1863. Full text, accessed Aug. 24, 2017, http://www.1stalabamacavalryusv.com/Fights/hornbeck2.aspx.

106. Timothy Smith, *Corinth 1862*, 297.

107. Thomas Files SCC Claim 7537, Winston County.

108. *Perrysburg (Ohio) Journal*, Dec. 30, 1863. Full text, accessed Aug. 24, 2017, http://www.1stalabamacavalryusv.com/Fights/hornbeck3.aspx.

109. John R. Phillips, *The Story of My Life* (Tuscaloosa, AL: John Phillips, 1923), 43.

110. Phillips, *Story of My Life*, 50.

111. John R. Phillips Service Record, Compiled Service Records of Union Volunteers from the State of Alabama, 1st Alabama Cavalry, Microfilm M276, RG 94, NARA, Washington, DC.

112. See Seip, "Of Ambition and Enterprise: The Making of Carpetbagger George E. Spencer," in Noe, ed., *The Yellowhammer War*, 191–219; Dodge to George Thomas, Sept. 25, 1862, File 4:1, Box 2, Grenville Mellen Dodge Papers, SHSI, Des Moines.

113. Regimental Order, No. 22, Headquarters, 1st Alabama Cavalry, Glendale, MS, Nov. 1, 1863, Regimental Order and Record Book, Book Records of Volunteer Union Organizations, Record Group 94, Records of the Adjutant General's Office, NARA.

114. Regimental Order No. 26, Headquarters, 1st Alabama Cavalry, Glendale, MS, Nov. 7, 1863, Regimental Order and Record Book, Book Records of Volunteer Union Organizations, Record Group 94, Records of the Adjutant General's Office, NARA.

115. Francis Dunn Diary, Nov. 7, 1863, Bentley Historical Library, University of Michigan, Ann Arbor.

116. Phillips, *Story of My Life*, 53.

117. Seip, 203–4; OR, 31:1, 37–38, 579–80; Francis Dunn Diary, October 26, 1863, Bentley Historical Library, University of Michigan, Ann Arbor.

118. Spencer to Dodge, Dec. 10, 1863, Box 3, File 5:7, Dodge Papers, SHSI, Des Moines; 1st Alabama Cavalry Descriptive Book, Cos. G–M, Book Records of Volunteer Union Organizations, Record Group 94, Records of the Adjutant General's Office, National Archives and Records Ad-

ministration, Washington, DC; "Death in the 1st Alabama Cavalry, USV," accessed Aug. 24, 2017, http://www.1stalabamacavalryusv.com/Fights/death.aspx.

119. Francis Tupper to "My Dear Parents," Nov. 17, 1863, Francis W. Tupper Papers, Abraham Lincoln Presidential Library (ALPL), Springfield, IL.

120. Tupper to Ma, December 27, 1863, Tupper Papers, ALPL, Springfield, IL.

121. Chetlain to Dodge, Dec. 10, 1863, Box 3, File 5:7, Dodge Papers, SHSI, Des Moines.

122. Headquarters, Left Wing, 16th Army Corps, Special Orders No. 35, Special Orders No. 45, Dec. 11, 1863, Pulaski, Tenn. Copy in Box 53, File 137:3, Dodge Papers, SHSI, Des Moines.

123. Nelson, "Recollections," 39.

124. Matthew J. Clavin, *Aiming for Pensacola: Fugitive Slaves on the Atlantic and Southern Frontiers* (Cambridge, MA: Harvard University Press, 2015).

125. Harriet Ryan, ed., "The Letters of Harden Perkins Cochrane, 1862–1864, Part 1," *Alabama Review* 7 (Oct. 1954): 292–93.

126. Wade Richardson, *How I Reached the Union Lines* (Milwaukee: Meyer-Rotier, 1905), 12.

127. Richardson, *How I Reached*, 17.

128. Richardson, *How I Reached*, 19.

129. Richardson, *How I Reached*, 22.

130. Alexander Bodiford SCC Claim 43874, Crenshaw County.

131. Celinda Hood, SCC Claim 43868, Crenshaw County; Randall Taylor, SCC Claim 43935, Crenshaw County.

132. Banks instead elected to please his political connections in the cotton mills of Massachusetts by liberating all the cotton in Texas in the failed Red River expedition in the spring of 1864, meaning Mobile would hold out until the last days of the war and was unable to play the role of refuge that Pensacola did for Alabama's freedmen and Unionists.

133. OR, 26:1, 780.

134. David Hartman and David Coles, *Biographical Rosters of Florida's Confederate and Union Soldiers, 1861–65*, 6 vols. (Wilmington, NC: Broadfoot Publishing, 1995), 4:1725–81. Three additional southeastern Alabama counties, Escambia, Geneva, and Houston, were carved out of the aforementioned counties after the war. See Map 3.

135. Richardson, *How I Reached*, 24.

136. Williams, *I Freed Myself: African American Self-Emancipation in the Civil War Era* (Cambridge, UK: Cambridge University Press, 2014), 163, 167.

137. OR, 26:1, 818.

138. Richardson, *How I Reached*, 25–26.

139. Matthew J. Clavin, "Interracialism and Revolution on the Southern Frontier: Pensacola in the Civil War," *Journal of Southern History* 80, no. 4 (Nov. 2014): 816.

140. OR, 26:1, 834.

141. OR, 26:1, 886.

CHAPTER FOUR

1. War Department, Orders No. 23, June 25, 1864, Nashville, TN. Copy in Dodge Diary, Box 58, File 137:5, Dodge Papers, SHSI, Des Moines.

2. In January 1864, several state officials, including Robert Jemison Jr., William Russell Smith, and C. C. Clay Jr., appealed to the Confederate secretary of war for additional protection, arguing that the Tennessee River had become the de facto northern border of the Confederacy, and, in a moment of prescience, that if an enemy crossed the river, "there is no natural barrier to prevent him from sweeping as low down the country as the Alabama River, penetrating that region of the State in which are located the mining and manufacturing establishments now getting into successful operation, and which it is believed are and will continue to be of great benefit to our cause." The facilities included "the cotton mills at Tuscaloosa, Scottsville and Prattville, the iron and coal works in Bibb and Shelby Counties and the foundry and Government works at Selma and Montgomery." Further, if successful in crossing the Tennessee, Federal forces "will not find it difficult to extend [their] line to the Warrior, and perhaps to the Alabama River, without meeting with serious opposition, but would on the contrary receive great encouragement in the mountain regions in our State, where there is unfortunately in some parts a disaffected population" (OR, 32:2, 515, 561).

3. James Alexander to Grenville Dodge, Jan. 16, 1864, Box 3, File 6:1, Dodge Papers, SHSI, Des Moines.

4. OR, 32:2, 15, 514.

5. Francis Tupper to William R. Tupper, Jan. 25, 1864, Tupper Papers, ALPL, Springfield, IL.

6. Francis Tupper to William R. Tupper, Feb. 2, 1864, Tupper Papers, ALPL, Springfield, IL.

7. John R. Phillips, *The Story of My Life* (Tuscaloosa, AL: John Phillips, 1923), 59.

8. Headquarters, Left Wing, 16th Army Corps, Jan. 26, 1864, Special Orders No. 26, Box 58, File 137:5, Dodge Papers, SHSI, Des Moines. Dodge's orders were in accordance with Gen. U. S. Grant's instructions, issued at Chattanooga on Nov. 5, 1863, requiring that "Wealthy secession citizens will be assessed in money and provisions for the support of Union refugees, who have and may be driven from their homes, and into our lines, by the acts of those with whom such secession citizens are in sympathy." Headquarters, Military Division of the Mississippi, General Orders No. 4, Box 58, File 138:4, Dodge Papers, SHSI, Des Moines.

9. Headquarters, Left Wing, 16th Army Corps, Jan. 30, 1864, Special Orders No. 30, Box 58, File 137:5, Dodge Papers, SHSI, Des Moines.

10. Dodge to Lt. Col. T. S. Bowers, Jan. 29, 1864, Box 3, File 6:1, Dodge Papers, SHSI, Des Moines; Thomas Vincent to Dodge, March 1, 1864, Box 3, File 6:3, Dodge Papers, SHSI, Des Moines.

11. Headquarters, Left Wing, 16th Army Corps, Special Orders No. 15, Nov. 18, 1863, Pulaski, Tenn., Copy in Box 58, File 137:2, Dodge Papers, SHSI, Des Moines.

12. Nelson "Recollections of My Early Life" (unpublished manuscript, 1909), Army Heritage and Education Center, Carlisle Barracks, PA, 42.

13. Henry Mizner to Grenville Dodge, Jan. 22, 1864, Box 3, File 6:1, Dodge Papers, SHSI, Des Moines.

14. Lorenzo Thomas to Dodge, Feb. 3, 1864, Box 3, File 6:2, Dodge Papers, SHSI, Des Moines.

15. Grant to Dodge, Jan. 30, 1864, Dodge Papers, SHSI, Des Moines.

16. OR, 32:2, 74, 76, 255–56; OR, 32:3, 111.

17. Dodge Diary, July 2, 1864, Box 61, File 141:4, Dodge Papers, SHSI, Des Moines.

18. Trial of Private Henry Brown, Company D, Third Regiment, Alabama Infantry Volunteers, March 22, 1864. Copy in Box 58, File 137:1, Dodge Papers, SHSI, Des Moines.

19. Nelson, "Recollections," 42–45.

20. J. W. Harris to J. B. Weaver, May 1, 1864, Box 61, File 144:2, Dodge Papers, SHSI, Des Moines.

21. Dodge Diary, April 17, 1864, Box 61, File 142:4, Dodge Papers, SHSI, Des Moines.

22. J. W. Harris to J. D. Haggard, June 2, 1864, Box 62, File 145:1, Dodge Papers, SHSI, Des Moines.

23. Robert Cowden, *A Brief Sketch of the Organization and Services of the Fifty-Ninth Regiment of United States Colored Infantry and Biographical Sketches* (Dayton, OH: United Brethren Publishing House, 1883), 51–52.

24. "Local Garrisons in 16th Army Corps," Jan. 25, 1864, Box 61, File 141:5, Dodge Papers, SHSI, Des Moines.

25. Francis Tupper to William Tupper, Feb. 19, 1864, Tupper Papers, ALPL, Springfield, IL.

26. Francis Tupper to William Tupper, Feb. 10, 1864, Tupper Papers, ALPL, Springfield, IL.

27. Francis Tupper to William Tupper, Feb. 19, 1864, Tupper Papers, ALPL, Springfield, IL.

28. Francis Tupper to William Tupper, March 10, 1864, Tupper Papers, ALPL, Springfield, IL.

29. Francis Tupper to William Tupper, March 23, 1864, Tupper Papers, ALPL, Springfield, IL.

30. OR, 32:2, 328; 32:3, 132.

31. See James Baggett, *Homegrown Yankees: Tennessee's Union Cavalry in the Civil War* (Baton Rouge: LSU Press, 2009), 199–204.

32. OR, 32:1, 548–49.

33. OR, 32:1, 553.

34. OR, 32:1, 611–12.

35. Brian Steel Wills, *The Confederacy's Greatest Cavalryman: Nathan Bedford Forrest* (Lawrence: University Press of Kansas, 1992), 143. For more on the Fort Pillow Massacre, see John Cimprich, *Fort Pillow, a Civil War Massacre and Public Memory* (Baton Rouge: LSU Press, 2005), and Brian Steele Wills, *The River Was Dyed with Blood: Nathan Bedford Forrest and Fort Pillow* (Norman: University of Oklahoma Press, 2014).

36. OR, 32:1, 556–57.

37. *Charleston Mercury*, March 10, 1864, quoted in Christopher McIlwain, *Civil War Alabama* (Tuscaloosa: University of Alabama Press, 2016), 166.

38. Dudley Cornish, *The Sable Arm: Negro Troops in the Union Army, 1861–1865* (New York: Longmans, Green, 1956), 175.

39. OR, 32:1, 623, 562; Joint Committee on the Conduct of the War, *Fort Pillow Massacre*, 38th Congress, 1st Session, 1864, H. Rep. No. 65, p. 42; OR, 39:1, 229.

40. OR, 32:1, 511.

41. OR, 32:1, 555.

42. Joint Committee, *Fort Pillow Massacre*, p. 66. For a detailed account of operations in northern Mississippi during the summer of 1864, see Thomas E. Parson, *Work for Giants: The Campaign and Battle of Tupelo/Harrisburg, Mississippi, June–July 1864* (Kent, OH: Kent State University Press, 2014).

43. OR, 39:1, 222.

44. OR, 39:1, 97.

45. OR, 39:1, 100.

46. OR, 39:1, 87, 96, 100.

47. OR, 39:1, 218.

48. Cowden, *Brief Sketch*, 69.

49. OR, 39:1, 215.

50. OR, 39:1, 105.

51. OR, 39:1, 181.

52. Jenkins Pension Application, RG 15, Records of the Veterans Administration, NARA, Washington, DC, quoted in Dobak, *Freedom by the Sword*, 212.

53. For example, each company had the following men available for duty on May 31 (before leaving), June 10 (after the battle), and June 30 (after returning and several weeks after the battle):

Co.	May 31	June 10	June 30
A	95	61	75
B	89	58	77
C	98	75	88
D	89	64	73
E	95	63	74
F	87	63	66
G	94	63	81
H	91	66	75
I	96	57	75
K	90	60	75
Totals	924	630	759

Thus, despite losing over 30 percent of its men in the battle, in less than a month the unit regained its strength to over 80 percent of its original complement. Numbers from Book Records of Volunteer Union Organizations, 55th USCI, Regimental Letters, Endorsements and Order Books (8 vols.), vol. 6 (Morning Reports, Companies A–E) and Vol. 7 (Morning Reports, Companies F–K), Record Group 94, Records of the Adjutant General's Office, NARA, Washington, DC.

54. OR, 39:1, 87.

55. OR, 39:1, 93.

56. OR, 39:1, 106.

57. OR, 39:1, 109.

58. OR, 39:1, 219.

59. OR, 32:1, 586.

60. OR, 32:1, 589.

61. OR, 32:1, 590.

62. OR, 32:1, 605.

63. OR, 21:1, 604.

64. See William Freehling, *The South vs. the South: How Anti-Confederate Southerners Shaped the Course of the Civil War* (New York: Oxford University Press, 2001), and Daniel Sutherland, *A Savage Conflict: The Decisive Role of Guerrillas in the American Civil War* (Chapel Hill: University of North Carolina Press, 2009).

65. For an excellent and detailed accounting of this campaign, see Parson, *Work for Giants.*

66. The Fourth Tennessee also included in its ranks Pvt. John Henry Ball, a resident of Jackson County, AL, who is buried under a marker commemorating his Union service in the Davistown Cemetery. "Some Civil War Union Soldiers Buried in North Alabama," *Alabama Genealogical Society Magazine*, vol. 49, Spring/Summer 2016, 50.

67. Francis Tupper to William Tupper, Aug. 3, 1864, Tupper Papers, ALPL, Springfield, IL.

68. David Evans, *Sherman's Horsemen: Union Cavalry Operations in the Atlanta Campaign* (Bloomington: Indiana University Press, 1996), 32, 37.

69. From just one loyal planter, Thomas Nation, who lived three miles northeast of Blountsville along Blue Springs Creek, the raiders took a horse, four mules, three hundred pounds of bacon, two sacks of salt, two gallons of sorghum syrup, two demijohns of molasses, ten bushels of wheat, and two hundred bundles of oats, which they fed to their horses on the spot, for which he was later reimbursed $596.00, with two of his former slaves, George Nations and Julia Robinson, testifying on his behalf. Nation was a native of East Tennessee and may have offered the goods to the troopers of the Fourth Tennessee, raised in his native region, or had relatives in the unit, as twenty-three of them under Captain Gray returned a week later and again had their horses fed. Nation reported, "I had some nephews in the federal army who went in from East Tennessee, I have a large connection up there, and they were powerful Union folks." After the war, Nation reported that he served as a deputy US marshal and in 1870 was "Ku Kluxed" on account of his Union sentiments. Thomas Nation, SCC Claim 36837, Blount County.

70. William Hamilton, *Recollections of a Cavalryman of the Civil War After Fifty Years, 1861–1865* (Columbus, OH: F. J. Heer Printing, 1915), 137.

71. *Montgomery Weekly Advertiser*, Aug. 10, 1864.

72. For detailed accounts of the raid, see Rousseau's official report in OR, 38:2, 904–9; Mark Fretwell, "Rousseau's Alabama Raid," *Alabama Historical Quarterly* 18 (Winter 1956): 526–51; "General Rousseau's Raid," *New York Times*, Aug. 3, 1864, http://www.nytimes.com/1864/08/03/news/gen-rousseau-s-raid-highly-interesting-particulars-expedition-departure-decatur.html?pagewanted=all, accessed July 1, 2016. By far, the most detailed account can be found in Evans, *Sherman's Horsemen*, 98–174. For a first-person account by one of the Tennessee troopers, see James W. Godwin, "Diary of the 4th Regiment Tennessee Cavalry, Volunteers," accessed July 1, 2016, http://www.rootsweb.ancestry.com/~tn4cav/diary1.html.

73. See George Sibley Johns, *Philip Henson, the Southern Union Spy* (St. Louis: Nixon-Jones Printing, 1887).

74. Daily Diary, Box 61, File 142:2, Dodge Papers, SHSI, Des Moines.

75. OR, 32:1, 128–29.

76. OR, 32:1, 393–94, 486–87; Eugene McWayne to "My loved, my honored, much respected friends," February 4, 1864, and Andrew McCornack to "Parents and Sisters," January 31, 1864,

both in Wiley Sword Collection, Army Heritage and Education Center, Carlisle Barracks, PA. Thanks to Eric Burke for identifying this source.

77. OR, 32:3, 132, 205, 216; Tupper Diary, March 27, 30, 31, April 3, Francis Tupper Papers, ALPL, Springfield, IL.

78. Dodge Diary, April 17, 1864, Box 61, File 142:4, Dodge Papers, SHSI, Des Moines. On March 21, Looney had received $50 from Dodge's "Secret Service" account, paid to spies in the interior. "List of Monies Expended for Secret Service," Box 63, File 148:3, Dodge Papers, SHSI, Des Moines.

79. OR, 32:3, 274, 312, 370.

80. Tupper Diary, April 16, 1864, Tupper Papers, ALPL, Springfield, IL.

81. On March 20, 1864, Dodge recorded in his diary that "Cypert has a reg't. of loyal Tennesseans at Clifton," who were watching the Tennessee River for a crossing by Forrest on the raid that eventually led him to Paducah and Fort Pillow. Dodge Diary, Box 61, File 142:2, Dodge Papers, SHSI, Des Moines.

82. Thomas Cypert, with Margaret Storey, *Tried Men and True, or Union Life in Dixie* (Tuscaloosa: University of Alabama Press, 2011), 101, 103.

83. Dodge, "The Secret Service in the Civil War," 32, Box 43, File 99:2, Dodge Papers, SHSI, Des Moines.

84. OR, 2:3, 391.

85. Sherman wrote his wife that he didn't want freedmen "hunted and badgered to make a soldier of when his family is left back on the plantations." Quoted in Anne Bailey, "The USCT in the Confederate Heartland, 1864," in John David Smith, ed., *Black Soldiers in Blue: African American Troops in the Civil War Era* (Chapel Hill: University of North Carolina Press, 2002), 228.

86. Dodge Diary, April 18, 1864, Box 61, File 142:4, Dodge Papers, SHSI, Des Moines.

87. Tupper Diary, April 17 & 18, 1864, Tupper Papers, ALPL, Springfield, IL.

88. George Cook Claim 47904, Fayette County; Charles Cook, CSR, 1st Alabama Cavalry.

89. OR, 38:3, 483, Francis Tupper to William Tupper, May 7 and May 9, 1864, Tupper Papers, ALPL, Springfield, IL.

90. Tupper Diary, May 1, 2, 1864; Ordnance Returns, Company K, 1st Alabama Cavalry, June 30, 1864, Tupper Papers, ALPL, Springfield, IL.

91. Francis Dunn Diary, May 5, 1864, Bentley Historical Library, University of Michigan, Ann Arbor, MI.

92. Tupper Diary, May 17, 1864, Tupper Papers, ALPL, Springfield, IL.

93. Dodge Diary, May 23 & 24, June 20, 1864, Box 61, File 142:4, Dodge Papers, SHSI, Des Moines.

94. Baggett, *Homegrown Yankees*, 160.

95. Dodge Diary, July 29, 1864, Box 61, File 142:5, Dodge Papers, SHSI, Des Moines.

96. Francis Dunn Diary, Aug. 5, 1864, Bentley Historical Library, University of Michigan, Ann Arbor, MI.

97. Melvin Carr, SCC Claim 36588, Cherokee County.

98. OR, Series III, 4, 765. The Forty-Fourth went on to see combat at Dalton during the fall campaign, where Hood captured most of the regiment and his men murdered a number of sol-

diers in cold blood. One of its soldiers, Pvt. Hubbard Pryor of Polk County, Georgia, became the subject of one of the most popular "before and after" photos of a member of the USCT, dramatically illustrating the transformation from slave to soldier.

99. Francis Tupper to William Tupper, June 24, 1864, Tupper Papers, ALPL, Springfield, IL.

100. Francis Tupper to William Tupper, July 15, 1864, Tupper Papers, ALPL, Springfield, IL.

101. Francis Tupper to William Tupper, July 23, 1864, Tupper Papers, ALPL, Springfield, IL.

102. OR, 34:1, 31.

103. OR, 52:1, 105.

104. OR, 52:1, 106.

105. Phillips, *Story of My Life*, 69-70.

106. Francis Tupper to William Tupper, Aug. 27, 1864, Tupper Papers, ALPL, Springfield, IL.

107. Francis Dunn Diary, Aug. 20, 1864, Bentley Historical Library, University of Michigan, Ann Arbor, MI; William Winston, SCC Claim 3984, DeKalb County. Winston was successful in his efforts to spare his home, built in the 1830s, from destruction, as it still stands in Valley Head, AL, and his estate received reimbursement for the fodder taken; accessed Aug. 26, 2017, http://focus.nps.gov/pdfhost/docs/NRHP/Text/87000476.pdf.

108. Dodge Diary, June 22, 1864, Box 61, File 142:5, Dodge Papers, SHSI, Des Moines.

109. Dodge Diary, July 15, 29, and Aug. 5, 1864, Box 61, File 142:5, Dodge Papers, SHSI, Des Moines.

110. Dodge Diary, June 24 and 28, 1864, Box 61, File 142:5, Dodge Papers, SHSI, Des Moines.

111. Record of Events, 110th US Colored Infantry, Microfilm M 594, Roll 216, NARA, Washington, DC; William T. Sherman, *Memoirs of Gen. W. T. Sherman, Written by Himself* (New York: Charles Webster, 1891), 2:55-56. Sherman was apparently unaware that some of his pioneers, whom he regarded as contracted laborers, were actually mustered soldiers. On September 14, in an exchange over his conduct toward the civilians of Atlanta with Confederate general John Bell Hood, he wrote, "We have no 'negro allies' in this army; not a single negro soldier left Chattanooga with this army, or is with it now," which is clearly in error. Sherman, *Memoirs*, 2:127.

112. OR, 38:5, 244.

113. OR, 39:1, 536.

114. OR, 39:1, 523.

115. OR, 39:1, 524.

116. *Mobile Advertiser and Register*, Oct. 6, 1864. Full list reproduced in Robert Dunnavant, *The Railroad War: N. B. Forrest's 1864 Raid through Northern Alabama and Middle Tennessee* (Athens, AL: Pea Ridge Press, 1994), 153-65, and Peggy Allen Towns, *Duty Driven: The Plight of North Alabama's African Americans During the Civil War* (Bloomington, IN: Author House, 2012), 88-101. The listing provides the county of residence of the owners, demonstrating that over half the men came from the Tennessee Valley counties of northern Alabama, with most of the remainder from adjoining counties in Tennessee, especially Giles County, where the regiment was formally mustered in.

117. Entry 238, "Affidavit by an Alabama Black Soldier," in Ira Berlin, ed., *Freedom: A Documentary History of Emancipation, 1861-1867; Series II: The Black Military Experience* (Cambridge: University Press, 1982), 594-95.

118. "Memoranda of Number and Dimensions of Bridges and Trestles on Tenn. & Ala. R.Rd. between Nashville and Decatur," Box 62, File 145:1, Dodge Papers, SHSI, Des Moines.

119. Nelson, "Recollections," 47.

120. Lathrop to Dodge, July 21, 1864, Box 61, File 144:3, Dodge Papers, SHSI, Des Moines.

121. Nelson, "Recollections," 47.

122. Nelson, "Recollections," 46–47.

123. Baggett, *Homegrown Yankees,* 367–69.

124. Nelson, "Recollections," 50. Adair, also originally of the Eighty-First Ohio, kept a diary of his time in captivity, which was edited by Glenn Robins and published in 2011 by Kent State University Press as *"They Have Left Us Here to Die": The Civil War Prison Diary of Sgt. Lyle G. Adair, 111th U.S. Colored Infantry* (Kent, OH: Kent State University Press, 2011).

125. OR, 39:1, 545.

126. Entry 218, "Commander of a Tennessee Black Regiment to the Commissioner for the Organization of Black Troops in Middle and East Tennessee," in Berlin, ed., *Freedom: A Documentary History of Emancipation, 1861–1867; Series II: The Black Military Experience,* 556–57.

127. OR, 39:1, 546.

128. OR, 39:1, 516.

129. Sherman, *Memoirs,* 2:146.

130. OR, 39:1, 761.

131. OR, 39:1, 768.

132. OR, 39:3, 730.

133. Francis Tupper to William Tupper, Nov. 1, 1864. Tupper Papers, ALPL, Springfield, IL.

134. Sarah Espy Diary, Oct. 24, 1864, ADAH.

135. Joseph Glatthaar, The *March to the Sea and Beyond: Sherman's Troops in the Savannah and Carolinas Campaigns* (Baton Rouge: LSU Press, 1985), 202.

136. Civil War commanders often selected a company of cavalry to serve as a personal escort for them and their staffs. In an emergency, the escort was large enough to engage any body of attacking troops, buying time for the commander to escape. But mostly the escort served as couriers, delivering messages to subordinate commanders and posts. To be selected as an escort was a high honor, and the First Alabama's selection demonstrated the appreciation Sherman had for their activities during his very successful campaign. Sherman, *Memoirs,* 2:31.

137. Sherman, *Memoirs,* 2:186–87.

138. See Glatthaar, *March to the Sea and Beyond,* 20.

139. OR, 44, 66.

140. Margaret Storey, *Loyalty and Loss: Alabama's Unionism in the Civil War and Reconstruction* (Baton Rouge: LSU Press, 2004), 69, 78, 222.

141. OR, 44, 504. See also Glatthaar, *March to the Sea and Beyond,* 147, 149.

142. OR, 44, 68, 509.

143. OR, 44, 154.

144. Headquarters, Military Division of the Mississippi, Special Field Order #16, June 3, 1864. Copy in Box 58, File 136:1, Dodge Papers, SHSI, Des Moines.

145. Grenville Dodge, "Recollections of Sherman," p. 13, Box 43, File 98:5, Dodge Papers, SHSI, Des Moines.

146. Tupper to "My Dear Parents," Dec. 24, 1864, Tupper Papers, ALPL, Springfield, IL.

147. Undated newspaper clipping, Tupper Papers, ALPL, Springfield, IL.

148. OR, 44, 815.

149. Sherman, *Memoirs*, 2:246.

150. OR, 39:1, 868, 872.

151. Col. Reuben Mussey to Capt. C. P. Brown, Dec. 21, 1864, in Berlin et al., *Black Military Experience*, 560–62.

152. OR, 35:2, 7.

153. OR, 35:1, 471.

154. William Holbrook, *A Narrative of the Services of the Officers and Enlisted Men of the Seventh Regiment of Vermont Volunteers (Veterans) from 1862 to 1866* (New York: American Bank Note Co., 1882), 140–41; OR, 35:1, 399.

155. Val L. McGee, "The Confederate Who Switched Sides: The Saga of Captain Joseph G. Sanders," *Alabama Review* 47 (Jan. 1994): 20–28.

156. OR, 35:2, 166.

157. Holbrook, *Narrative of the Services*, 144–46; OR, 35:1, 413–14, 419.

158. OR, 35:2, 165–66.

159. Wade Richardson, *How I Reached the Union Lines* (Milwaukee: Meyer-Rotier, 1905), 26–27.

160. OR, 35:1, 443, 144; Holbrook, *Narrative of the Services*, 154–55.

161. OR, 41:4, 26.

162. OR, 44, 418–19.

163. McGee, "Confederate Who Switched Sides," 23–24.

CHAPTER FIVE

1. OR, 48:1, 1158.

2. For a detailed account of one USCT regiment's suffering from disease at Port Hudson, see Christopher M. Rein, "Louisiana: The First Corps d'Afrique Cavalry," in "Trans-Mississippi Southerners in the Union Army, 1862–1865" (Master's thesis, Louisiana State University, 2001), https://digitalcommons.lsu.edu/gradschool_theses/748/.

3. In June 1866, Jesse Robb and Jordan Harris, both of Company G, Fifty-Fifth USCT, deposited their discharge papers with the Freedmen's Bureau agent in Courtland, Alabama. Copies of Contracts, Microfilm M1900, Roll 15, RG 105, Records of the Bureau of Refugees, Freedmen and Abandoned Lands, NARA, Washington, DC.

4. OR, 48:1, 508.

5. OR, 49:1, 71, 906.

6. OR, 49:1, 310.

7. Robert Robb, SCC Claim 41855, Conecuh County.

8. Ned Smith, *The 2nd Maine Cavalry in the Civil War: A History and Roster* (Jefferson, NC: McFarland, 2014), 130.

9. OR, 49:2, 8.

10. OR, 49:1, 280. For a full discussion of the First Louisiana's origins and service, see Chris-

topher M. Rein, "Trans-Mississippi Southerners in the Union Army, 1862–1865" (Master's thesis, Louisiana State University, 2001), http://etd.lsu.edu/docs/available/etd-08152004-142832/.

11. OR, 49:1, 281.

12. OR, 49:1, 281; David Nelson Claim 51275; Elisha Nelson Claim 51276, SCC. For more on the Unionist community on Bon Secour Bay, see Storey, *Loyalty and Loss: Alabama's Unionists in the Civil War and Reconstruction* (Baton Rouge: LSU Press, 2004), 27.

13. OR, 49:1, 281.

14. Report of C. W. Buckley, April 1, 1865, RG 94, NARA, quoted in Michael W. Fitzgerald, "Another Kind of Glory: Black Participation and Its Consequences in the Campaign for Confederate Mobile," *Alabama Review* (Oct. 2001), 252.

15. Cassius Clay Alexander to New York *Weekly African American*, Nov. 18, 1865, quoted in Edwin Redkey, ed., *A Grand Army of Black Men: Letters from African-American Soldiers in the Union Army, 1861–1865* (Cambridge, UK: Cambridge University Press, 1992), 157.

16. OR, 49:1, 289–90.

17. Fitzgerald, "Another Kind of Glory," 260.

18. Fitzgerald, "Another Kind of Glory," 267.

19. Nelson, "Recollections of My Early Life" (unpublished manuscript, 1909), Army Heritage and Education Center, Carlisle Barracks, PA, 53.

20. Peggy Allen Towns, *Duty Driven: The Plight of Alabama's African Americans During the Civil War* (Bloomington, IN: Author House, 2012), 45–46. Towns is a descendant of George Allen.

21. McIlwain, *Civil War Alabama,* 255.

22. E. N. Gilpin, *The Last Campaign: A Cavalryman's Journal* (Leavenworth, KS: Press of Ketcheson Printing, 1908), 629.

23. James H. Wilson, *Under the Old Flag; Recollections of Military Operations in the War for the Union, the Spanish War, the Boxer Rebellion, etc.* (New York: D. Appleton, 1912), 2:287.

24. Quoted in Wills, *The Confederacy's Greatest Cavalryman,* 310–11.

25. OR, 49:2, 818–20.

26. Gilpin, *Last Campaign,* 650.

27. Gilpin, *Last Campaign,* 643, 645.

28. OR, 49:2, 816.

29. For a full account of Wilson's raid, see James Pickett Jones, *Yankee Blitzkrieg: Wilson's Raid Through Alabama and Georgia* (Lexington: University Press of Kentucky, 1976). A historical marker commemorating Wilson and his efforts in 1865 had to be removed from downtown Montgomery to the safety of nearby Maxwell Air Force Base due to frequent and repeated vandalization, where its daily passage by the author provided inspiration for this study.

30. OR, Series III, 5:319–22, "Records of the Colored Troops Division, 1865," University of Georgia Library, Athens, GA; Compiled Records Showing Service of Military Units in Volunteer Union Organizations, Microfilm M594, Roll 217, RG 94, NARA, Washington, DC.

31. Miles Ryan SCC Claim 54849, Conecuh County.

32. *Greenville Observer,* April 21, 1865.

33. "Arrival of the Fleet," *Montgomery Daily Mail,* May 1, 1865, 1.

34. Fitzgerald, *Reconstruction in Alabama,* 43.

35. "General Orders No. 2," *Montgomery Daily Mail,* May 1, 1865, 2.

36. OR, 49:1, 571.

37. Val McGee, "The Confederate who Switched Sides: The Saga of Captain Joseph G. Sanders," *Alabama Review* 47, no. 1 (Jan. 1994): 26.

38. Testimony of George Spencer, Jan. 26, 1866, in US Congress, "Report of the Joint Committee on Reconstruction," 39th Congress, 1st Session, Part II, pp. 8–9.

39. OR, 49:2, 1045.

40. Compiled Records Showing Service of Military Units in Volunteer Union Organizations, Microfilm M594, Roll 213, RG 94, NARA, Washington, DC, Microfilm M594, NARA, Washington, DC; Ray Granade, "Violence: An Instrument of Policy in Reconstruction Alabama," *Alabama Historical Review* (Fall–Winter 1968): 181–202.

41. See Mark L. Bradley, *The Battle of Bentonville: Last Stand in the Carolinas* (El Dorado Hills, CA: Savas Beatie, 1996); and Nathaniel Hughes, *Bentonville: The Final Battle of Sherman and Johnston* (Chapel Hill: University of North Carolina Press, 1996).

42. OR, 47:1, 48, 55. For a full discussion of the campaign, see Charles Royster, *The Destructive War: William Tecumseh Sherman, Stonewall Jackson, and the Americans* (New York: Knopf, 1991); and John G. Barnett, *Sherman's March Through the Carolinas* (Chapel Hill: University of North Carolina Press, 1956).

43. OR, 47:2, 10.

44. OR, 47:1, 892, 896.

45. OR, 47:1, 893–95; 47:3, 154.

46. OR, 47:1, 897.

47. OR, 47:1, 897.

48. OR, 47:1, 895.

49. Headquarters, Chief of Bummers, General Orders No. 1865, Raleigh, NC, April 27, 1865. Copy in Box 61, File 144:4, Dodge Papers, SHSI, Des Moines.

50. Headquarters, 1st Alabama Cavalry, Regimental Orders No. 4, Durham Station, NC, April 28, 1865, Book Records of Volunteer Union Organizations, 1st Alabama Cavalry, Regimental Order and Detail Book, RG 94, NARA.

51. Fitzgerald, *Reconstruction in Alabama*, 54.

52. Fitzgerald, *Reconstruction in Alabama*, 58.

53. OR, 49:2, 924.

54. OR, 47:3, 397.

55. Sherman's Order of Battle clearly shows the 110th USCI as part of the Third Brigade, Fourth Division, Fifteenth Army Corps (Sherman, *Memoirs of Gen. W. T. Sherman, Written by Himself* [New York: Charles L. Webster, 1891], 2:335), and the Regimental Returns of the 110th USCI for May 1865 give the location as "near Washington, DC" (Record of Events, 110th USCI, Microfilm M594, Roll 216, RG 94, NARA, Washington, DC).

56. Sherman, *Memoirs*, 2:377–78. The Washington, DC *Daily National Intelligencer* at least reported the equipment correctly as "spades and axes," as axes were essential for felling trees and crossed axes were the symbol of the pioneer corps. Gary Gallagher, *The Union War* (Cambridge, MA: Harvard University Press, 2011), 20.

57. Joshua L. Chamberlain, *The Passing of the Armies: An Account of the Final Campaign of the*

Army of the Potomac, Based Upon Personal Reminiscences of the Fifth Army Corps (New York: G. P. Putnam's Sons, 1915), 365.

58. Despite receiving new uniforms for the occasion, many troops of the western army chose to march barefoot and in ragged uniforms, as they had fought, in contrast to the eastern Army of the Potomac, which had paraded the day before in full "spit and polish." The westerners wore their haggard appearance as a badge of honor, believing how any army *fought* was far more important than how it *looked*. See Joseph Glatthaar, *The March to the Sea and Beyond: Sherman's Troops in the Savannah and Carolinas Campaigns* (Baton Rouge: LSU Press, 1985), 180–81.

59. Chamberlain, *Passing of the Armies*, 367.

60. Quoted in Gallagher, *The Union War*, 21.

61. Compiled Records Showing Service of Military Units in Volunteer Union Organizations, First Alabama Cavalry, Microfilm M594, Roll 1, RG 94, NARA, Washington, DC.

62. First Alabama Cavalry, Regimental Order and Detail Book, RG 94, NARA.

63. First Alabama Cavalry, Special Orders No. 22, July 11, 1865, and Special Orders No. 37, Oct. 5, 1865, Regimental Order and Detail Book, RG 94, NARA.

64. OR, 49:2, 380.

65. Nelson, "Recollections," 54.

66. OR, 49:2, 820.

67. OR, 49:2, 735.

68. *Huntsville Advocate,* July 26, 1865.

69. OR, 49:2, 947.

70. OR, 49:2, 963.

71. Alan J. Pitts, "Violence and Confederate Recruiting Efforts: Shelby County, Alabama, 1863–1865," Presentation at the Alabama Historical Association Annual Meeting, 1994. Full text accessed April 12, 2018, https://www.alagenealogy.com/Patriarchs/Cobb,%20Alexander.htm.

72. William Hoole, *Alabama Tories: The First Alabama Cavalry, U.S.A., 1862–1865* (Tuscaloosa, AL: Confederate Publishing, 1960), 16.

73. Vol. 2, Letters Sent and Endorsements Sent, Department of Alabama, Records of Continental Army Commands, Record Group 393, Entry 2318, National Archives and Records Administration, Washington, DC.

74. See Howard Blum, *The Brigade: An Epic Story of Vengeance, Salvation and WWII* (New York: Harper, 2001).

75. Returns from Huntsville, Alabama, September to December 1865, Returns from US Military Posts, 1800–1916, Microfilm M617, Roll 501, RG 94, NARA.

76. Testimony of Maj. Gen. Edward Hatch, Jan. 25, 1866, "Report of the Joint Committee on Reconstruction," 39th Congress, 1st Session, Part II, p. 7.

77. Walter Fleming, *Civil War and Reconstruction in Alabama* (New York: Columbia University Press, 1905), 417.

78. *Huntsville Advocate*, Aug. 17, 1865.

79. Statement of General Thomas Kilby Smith, New Orleans, Sept. 14, 1865, in Carl Schurz, Report on Reconstruction, Senate Ex. Doc. 2, 39th Congress, 1st Session.

80. Testimony of Maj. Gen. Edward Hatch, Jan. 25, 1866, "Report of the Joint Committee on Reconstruction," Part II, p. 5.

81. Testimony of Maj. Gen. Edward Hatch, Jan 25, 1866, "Report of the Joint Committee on Reconstruction," Part II, p. 5.

82. Records of the Bureau of Refugees, Freedmen and Abandoned Lands, Subdistrict of Huntsville, Endorsements Sent, Microfilm M1900, Roll 14, RG 105, NARA.

83. *Huntsville Advocate,* Nov. 16, 1865.

84. *Advocate,* Nov. 9, 1865.

85. William Dobak, *Freedom by the Sword: The U.S. Colored Troops, 1862–1867* (Washington, DC: Center of Military History, 2011), 295.

86. Rogers et al., 231–32.

87. *Huntsville Advocate,* July 26, 1865.

88. Testimony of George Spencer, Jan 26, 1866, "Report of the Joint Committee on Reconstruction," Thirty-Ninth Congress, First Session, Part II, p. 9.

89. Fleming, *Civil War and Reconstruction in Alabama,* 282.

90. *Montgomery Mail,* July 27, 1865.

91. *Huntsville Advocate,* Aug. 17, 1865.

92. *Huntsville Advocate,* Oct. 12, 1865.

93. Statement of W. Kryzanowski, Nashville, Tenn., Sept. 29, 1865, in Carl Schurz, Report on Reconstruction, Senate Ex. Doc. 2, Thirty-Ninth Congress, First Session.

94. *Huntsville Advocate,* Oct. 12, 1865.

95. Order Book, Company B, 106th US Colored Infantry, Book Records of Volunteer Union Organizations, RG 94, Records of the Adjutant General's Office, NARA, Washington, DC.

96. Order Book, Company B, 106th US Colored Infantry, Book Records of Volunteer Union Organizations, RG 94, Records of the Adjutant General's Office, NARA, Washington, DC.

97. OR, 49:2, 1100; Elaine Parsons, *Ku-Klux: The Birth of the Klan during Reconstruction* (Chapel Hill: University of North Carolina Press, 2016).

98. Nelson, "Recollections," 55–56.

99. Michael Thomas Gavin, "A History of the 110th and 111th Regiments United States Colored Troops (USCT)," 2004, accessed May 4, 2017, https://www.nps.gov/stri/learn/historyculture/upload/History_110_111_regiments-2.pdf.

100. *Huntsville Advocate,* Aug. 17, 1865.

101. Copies of Contracts, Microfilm M1900, Roll 15, RG 105, NARA, Washington, DC.

102. Nelson, "Recollections," 56–57. See David Blight, *Race and Reunion: The Civil War in American Memory* (Cambridge, MA: Harvard University Press, 2001).

103. See, among others, Gaines M. Foster, *Ghosts of the Confederacy: Defeat, the Lost Cause, and the Emergence of the New South, 1865–1913* (Oxford, UK: Oxford University Press, 1988).

EPILOGUE AND CONCLUSION

1. Michael W. Fitzgerald, *Reconstruction in Alabama: From Civil War to Redemption in the Cotton South* (Baton Rouge: LSU Press, 2017), 123.

2. OR, 49:2, 976.

3. Margaret Storey, *Loyalty and Loss: Alabama's Unionists in the Civil War and Reconstruction* (Baton Rouge: LSU Press, 2004), 169.

4. In 1950, Birmingham had a population of 326,037, thirty-fourth largest in the nation, while Atlanta numbered 331,314, thirty-third largest. By 2010, the Atlanta MSA ranked ninth, Birmingham forty-ninth. Census of the United States, 1950, 2010. See Kevin Kruse, *White Flight: Atlanta and the Making of Modern Conservatism* (Princeton, NJ: Princeton University Press, 2005).

5. Fitzgerald, *Reconstruction in Alabama*, 76. For a full discussion, see Fitzgerald, "Wartime Origins of White Republicanism," in Kenneth Noe, ed., *The Yellowhammer War: Civil War and Reconstruction in Alabama* (Tuscaloosa: University of Alabama Press, 2013).

6. Storey, *Loyalty and Loss*, 184.

7. Michael W. Fitzgerald, *The Union League Movement in the Deep South: Politics and Agricultural Change During Reconstruction* (Baton Rouge: LSU Press, 1989).

8. Whitelaw Reid, *After the War: A Southern Tour, May 1, 1865, to May 1, 1866* (New York: Moore, Wilstach & Baldwin, 1866), 367.

9. Reid, *Southern Tour,* 370–71.

10. Sarah Woolfolk Wiggins, "The 'Pig Iron' Kelley Riot in Mobile, May 14, 1867," *Alabama Review* 23 (1970): 45–55.

11. See Stephen Ash, *A Massacre in Memphis: The Race Riot That Shook the Nation One Year after the Civil War* (New York: Hill and Wang, 2013).

12. On the Buffalo Soldiers, see William Leckie, *The Buffalo Soldiers, A Narrative of the Negro Cavalry in the West* (Norman: University of Oklahoma Press, 1984); Debra Sheffer, *The Buffalo Soldiers: Their Epic Story and Major Campaigns* (Westport, CT: Praeger, 2015); and Harry E. Johnson, "Buffalo Soldiers: The Formation of the Ninth Cavalry Regiment; July 1866–March 1867" (Master's thesis, Command and General Staff College, Fort Leavenworth, KS, 1991). On the Exodusters, see Nell Painter, *Exodusters: Black Migration to Kansas after Reconstruction* (New York: Knopf, 1977).

13. Nelson, "Recollections of My Early Life" (unpublished manuscript, 1909), Army Heritage and Education Center, Carlisle Barracks, PA, 58.

14. William Rogers, Robert Ward, Leah Atkins, and Wayne Flynt, *Alabama: The History of a Deep South State* (Tuscaloosa: University of Alabama Press, 1994). 338–42.

15. While Turner's name does not appear on the muster rolls of any of the USCT regiments recruited in Selma, his affidavit before the Southern Claims Commission claims that he was a "Captain" of Company A of the "11th Alabama," which may have been a postwar militia organization. His claim suggests that it was with one of the USCT raised in Selma during Wilson's Raid, as he followed Wilson as far as Atlanta, where two of the regiments mustered out, and one of Turner's employees testified that he saw him in a blue suit carrying a sword and carbine. See Fitzgerald, *Reconstruction in Alabama*, 110; Benjamin Turner SCC Claim (No Number), Dallas County.

16. Storey found at least six Union veterans as delegates, most from the First Alabama Cavalry. Storey, *Loyalty and Loss*, 206.

17. Storey, *Loyalty and Loss*, 172.

18. See Elaine Frantz Parsons, *Ku-Klux: The Birth of the Klan During Reconstruction* (Chapel Hill: University of North Carolina Press, 2016).

19. David Williams, *I Freed Myself: African American Self-Emancipation in the Civil War Era* (Cambridge, UK: Cambridge University Press, 2014), 225.

20. Barton Myers, *Rebels Against the Confederacy: North Carolina's Unionists* (New York: Cambridge University Press, 2014), 70.

21. Thomas Nation SCC Claim 36837, Blount County.

22. Robin Sterling, *Blount County, Alabama Confederate Soldiers,* Vol. 3: *Miscellaneous* (Owens Cross Roads, AL: Robin Sterling, 2013), 38; Robin Sterling, *Tales of Old Blount County* (Owens Cross Roads, AL: Robin Sterling, 2013), 158.

23. Storey, *Loyalty and Loss,* 225–26.

24. Fitzgerald, *Reconstruction in Alabama,* 195.

25. Storey, *Loyalty and Loss,* 133; Myers, *Rebels Against the Confederacy,* 82.

26. See Mark W. Summers, *Railroads, Reconstruction, and the Gospel of Prosperity: Aid Under the Radical Republicans, 1865–1877* (Princeton, NJ: Princeton University Press, 1984).

27. For a complete discussion of the Smith administration, see Sarah Woolfolk Wiggins, *The Scalawag in Alabama Politics, 1865–1881* (Tuscaloosa: University of Alabama Press, 1977). Fleming's caustic and biased *Civil War and Reconstruction in Alabama* remained the standard account of the period in the state until finally overturned during the civil rights era.

28. Fitzgerald, *Reconstruction in Alabama,* 5, 281.

29. See Brian Steel Wills, *The Confederacy's Greatest Cavalryman: Nathan Bedford Forrest* (Lawrence: University Press of Kansas, 1992), 337, 345.

30. Rogers et al., *History of a Deep South State,* 263.

31. Ray Granade, "Violence: An Instrument of Policy in Reconstruction Alabama," *Alabama Historical Quarterly* (Fall–Winter 1968), 199.

32. Fitzgerald, *Reconstruction in Alabama,* 259.

33. Rogers et al., *History of a Deep South State,* 288.

34. See "Inside Alabama's Auto Jobs Boom: Cheap Wages, Little Training, Crushed Limbs," accessed Jan. 22, 2018, https://www.bloomberg.com/news/features/2017–03–23/inside-alabama-s-auto-jobs-boom-cheap-wages-little-training-crushed-limbs.

35. Robin D. G. Kelley, *Hammer and Hoe: Alabama Communists During the Great Depression* (Chapel Hill: University of North Carolina Press, 1990). Kelley notes Socialists and Communists in the AFU were active in "Winston, Walker and Greene counties" in North Alabama during the Depression, and that small farmers in "Baldwin, Covington and Escambia counties" resented the establishment of corporate-style plantations in that region that undercut their efforts (170). Sadly, deeply engrained racism in many of these communities prevented more effective cooperation with the largely black Sharecroppers Union (SCU) (47). But urbanization, unleashed by southern industrialization, provided more fertile recruiting grounds for biracial political cooperation, however temporal, especially in the mines and mills around Birmingham (28).

36. Rogers et al., *History of a Deep South State,* 291.

37. Rogers et al., *History of a Deep South State,* 353.

38. Abel Meeropol, "Strange Fruit," performed by Billie Holiday (1939). Meeropol's song, and Holiday's performance, remain perhaps the most visible legacy of the interracial Communist collaboration of the 1930s.

39. See C. Vann Woodward, *The Strange Career of Jim Crow* (New York: Oxford University Press, 1955).

40. Jack Bass, *Taming the Storm: The Life and Times of Judge Frank M. Johnson, Jr., and the South's Fight over Civil Rights* (Athens: University of Georgia Press, 2003), 8, 15, 17. Bass claims that it was two of Judge Johnson's great-uncles who served in the First Alabama, but Dan Carter believes it was his great-grandfather. See Carter, *The Politics of Rage: George Wallace, the Origins of the New Conservatism, and the Transformation of American Politics* (Baton Rouge: LSU Press, 2000), 48. Special thanks to Matt White for these tips.

41. "The 9 Most Segregated Cities in America," accessed Aug. 29, 2017, http://www.huffingtonpost.com/entry/the-9-most-segregated-cities-in-america_us_55df53e9e4b0e7117ba92d7f. On white flight, again see Kevin Kruse, *White Flight*.

42. In 2017, the NAACP successfully filed suit against the middle-class but white-majority city of Gardendale when it attempted to break away from Jefferson County to form its own school district. Why it did not file suit to require Mountain Brook to rejoin the Jefferson County system is unclear. See, accessed Aug. 29, 2017, https://www.washingtonpost.com/local/education/judge-says-mostly-white-southern-city-may-secede-from-its-school-district—even-though-the-effort-has-attacked-dignity-of-black-school-children/2017/04/26/4d654232–2a89–11e7-b605–33413c691853_story.html?utm_term=.9c0607b1f82d.

43. "Incident at Looney's Tavern," *Encyclopedia of Alabama*, accessed Aug. 10, 2017, http://www.encyclopediaofalabama.org/article/h-3864.

44. "Colony," *Encyclopedia of Alabama*, accessed Aug. 18, 2017, http://www.encyclopediaofalabama.org/article/h-3432.

45. David Blight, *Race and Reunion: The Civil War in American Memory* (Cambridge, MA: Harvard University Press, 2001).

46. Martin Luther King Jr., *Where Do We Go From Here: Chaos or Community?* (New York: Harper and Row, 1967), 6.

Bibliography

UNPUBLISHED PRIMARY SOURCES

Alabama Department of Archives and History, Montgomery, AL
  Sarah Espy Diary
  Andrew Barry Moore Papers
  Lewis Parsons Papers
  John Gill Shorter Papers
  Thomas Hill Watts Papers
Bentley Historical Library, Ann Arbor, Michigan
  Francis Wayland Dunn Papers
  Ransom Dunn Papers
Lincoln Library, Springfield, Illinois
  Francis Tupper Diary
National Archives and Records Administration, Washington, DC
  RG 94, Records of the Adjutant General's Office
    Book Records of Volunteer Union Organizations
        1st Alabama Cavalry
        55th US Colored Infantry
        106th US Colored Infantry
        110th US Colored Infantry
        111th US Colored Infantry
    Records of the Colored Troops Division
    Compiled Records Showing the Service of Volunteer Union Organizations,
        Microfilm M594
    Compiled Military Service Records of Volunteer Union Soldiers Who Served
        in Organizations from the State of Alabama, Microfilm M276
    Compiled Military Service Records of Volunteer Union Soldiers Who Served
        in the US Colored Troops: 1st through 55th Regiments
  RG 105, Records of the Bureau of Refugees, Freedmen and Abandoned Lands
    Records of the Department of Alabama, Microfilm M1900
  RG 217, Records of the Accounting Officers of the Department of the Treasury,
    1775–1978

Settled Case Files for Claims Approved by the Southern Claims
Commission, 1871–1880; Microfilm M2062, Approved Claims,
1871–1880, Alabama
RG 233, Records of the US House of Representatives, Microfilm M1407, Barred
and Disallowed Case Files of the Southern Claims Commission, 1871–1880
RG 393, Records of Continental Commands
Returns of Posts
Department of Alabama
District of Huntsville
Newberry Library, Chicago, Illinois
Edgar McLean Papers
Norwich University Archives, Northfield, VT
Grenville Dodge Papers
State Historical Society of Iowa, Des Moines, IA
Grenville Mellen Dodge Papers
University of Georgia, Athens, GA
Records of the Colored Troops Division, 1865 (137th USCT, Co. D)
University of Tennessee–Martin
John Reed Papers
US Army Heritage and Education Center, Carlisle, Pennsylvania
Joseph Kibler Nelson, "Recollections of My Early Life." Unpublished manuscript,
Wiley Sword Collection

NEWSPAPERS

Athens, TN *Post*
Greenville, AL *Southern Messenger*
Huntsville, AL *Advocate*
Montgomery, AL *Advertiser*
Moulton, AL *Democrat*
Perrysburg, OH *Journal*
Troy, AL *Southern Advertiser*

PUBLISHED PRIMARY SOURCES

Bagby, Arthur P., et al., eds. *The Code of Alabama*. Montgomery, AL: Brittain and De
Wold, 1852.
Bartram, William. *Travels Through North & South Carolina, Georgia, East and West Florida, the Cherokee Country, the Extensive Territories of the Muscogulges, or Creek Confederacy, and the Country of the Chactaws; containing an Account of the Soil and Nat-*

ural *Productions of those Regions, together with Observations on the Manners of the Indians.* Philadelphia: James & Johnson, 1791.

Basler, Roy, ed. *The Collected Works of Abraham Lincoln,* 8 vols. New Brunswick, NJ: Rutgers University Press, 1953.

Beatty, John. *The Citizen-Soldier; or, Memoirs of a Volunteer.* Cincinnati: Wilstack, Baldwin & Co., 1879.

Berlin, Ira, Joseph Reidy, and Leslie Rowland, eds. *Freedom's Soldiers: The Black Military Experience in the Civil War.* New York: Cambridge University Press, 1998.

Chamberlain, Joshua L. *The Passing of the Armies: An Account of the Final Campaign of the Army of the Potomac, Based Upon Personal Reminiscences of the Fifth Army Corps.* New York: G. P. Putnam's Sons, 1915.

Clemens, Jeremiah. *Tobias Wilson: A Tale of the Great Rebellion.* Philadelphia: Lippincott, 1865.

Coffin, Levi. *Reminiscences of Levi Coffin, the Reputed President of the Underground Railroad; Being a Brief History of the Labors of a Lifetime in Behalf of the Slave, with the Stories of Numerous Fugitives, who Gained their Freedom through his Instrumentality, and Many Other Incidents.* Cincinnati: Freedom Tract Society, 1876.

Cowden, Robert. *A Brief Sketch of the Organization and Services of the Fifty-Ninth Regiment of United States Colored Infantry and Biographical Sketches.* Dayton, OH: United Brethren Publishing House, 1883.

Cypert, Thomas Jefferson, with Margaret Storey. *Tried Men and True, or Union Life in Dixie.* Tuscaloosa: University of Alabama Press, 2011.

Dodge, Grenville. *Battle of Atlanta and Other Campaigns.* Council Bluffs, IA: Monarch Printing, 1910.

Eaton, John. *Grant, Lincoln and the Freedmen: Reminiscences of the Civil War with Special Reference to the Work for the Contrabands and Freedmen of the Mississippi Valley.* New York: Longmans, Green, 1907.

Eckel, Alexander. *History of the Fourth Tennessee Cavalry, USA, War of the Rebellion, 1861–65.* Johnson County, TN: Overmountain Press, 1929; repr., 2001.

Gilpin, E. N. *The Last Campaign: A Cavalryman's Journal.* Leavenworth, KS: Press of Ketchison Printing, 1908.

Hamilton, William. *Recollections of a Cavalryman of the Civil War After Fifty Years, 1861–1865.* Columbus, OH: The F. J. Heer Printing, 1915.

Holbrook, William. *A Narrative of the Services of the Officers and Enlisted Men of the Seventh Regiment of Vermont Volunteers (Veterans) from 1862 to 1866.* New York: American Bank Note Company, 1882.

Johns, George. *Philip Henson, the Southern Union Spy.* St. Louis: Nixon-Jones, 1887.

McGee, B. F. *History of the 72d Indiana Volunteer Infantry of the Mounted Lightning Brigade.* Lafayette, IN: S. Vater, 1882.

Moore, Frank, *The Civil War in Song and Story.* New York: P. F. Collier, 1889.

———, ed. *Rebellion Record: A Diary of American Events, with Documents, Narrative, Illustrative Incidents, Poetry, Etc.* 11 vols. New York: Putnam, 1864.

Phillips, John R. *The Story of My Life.* Tuscaloosa, AL: John Phillips, 1923.

Redkey, Edwin, ed. *A Grand Army of Black Men: Letters from African-American Soldiers in the Union Army, 1861–1865.* Cambridge, UK: Cambridge University Press, 1992.

Reid, Whitelaw. *After the War: A Southern Tour: May 1, 1865, to May 1, 1866.* New York: Moore, Wilstach & Baldwin, 1866.

Richardson, Wade. *How I Reached the Union Lines.* Milwaukee: Meyer-Rotier, 1905.

Robins, Glenn, ed. *"They Have Left Us Here to Die": The Civil War Prison Diary of Sgt. Lyle G. Adair, 111th US Colored Infantry.* Kent, OH: Kent State University Press, 2011.

Rohr, Nancy, ed. *Incidents of the War: The Civil War Journal of Mary Jane Chadick.* Huntsville, AL: Silver Threads Publishing, 2005.

Ryan, Patricia, ed. *Cease Not to Think of Me: The Steele Family Letters.* Huntsville, AL: Huntsville Planning Department, 1979.

Sherman, William. *Memoirs of Gen. W. T. Sherman, Written by Himself.* New York: Charles L. Webster, 1891.

Smith, William. *The History and Debates of the Convention of the People of Alabama, Begun and Held in the City of Montgomery, on the Seventh Day of January, 1861 in which is Preserved the Speeches of the Secret Sessions, and Many Valuable State Papers.* Atlanta: Rice, 1861.

Tharin, Robert. *Arbitrary Arrests in the South; Or, Scenes from the Experience of an Alabama Unionist, by R. S. Tharin, A.M., a Native of Charleston, S.C.; For Thirty Years a resident of the Cotton States and Commonly Known in the West as "The Alabama Refugee."* New York: John Bradburn, 1863.

United States War Department. *The War of the Rebellion: A Compilation of the Official Records of the Union and Confederate Armies.* Washington, DC: GPO, 1880–1901.

US Congress. "Fort Pillow Massacre." 8th Congress, 1st Session, Rep. No. 65.

———. "Report of the Joint Committee on Reconstruction at the First Session, Thirty-Ninth Congress." Washington, DC: GPO, 1866.

Wilson, James H. *Under the Old Flag; Recollections of Military Operations in the War for the Union, the Spanish War, the Boxer Rebellion, etc.* 2 vols. New York: D. Appleton, 1912.

BOOKS

Anders, Leslie. *The Eighteenth Missouri.* Indianapolis: Bobbs-Merrill, 1968.

Ash, Stephen. *Firebrand of Liberty: The Story of Two Black Regiments That Changed the Course of the Civil War.* New York: W. W. Norton, 2008.

———. *A Massacre in Memphis: The Race Riot That Shook the Nation One Year After the Civil War.* New York: Hill and Wang, 2013.

———. *When the Yankees Came: Conflict and Chaos in the Occupied South, 1861–1865.* Chapel Hill: University of North Carolina Press, 1995.

Baggett, James. *Homegrown Yankees: Tennessee's Union Cavalry in the Civil War.* Baton Rouge: LSU Press, 2009.

———. *The Scalawags: Southern Dissenters in the Civil War and Reconstruction.* Baton Rouge: LSU Press, 2003.

Bailey, Richard. *Neither Carpetbaggers Nor Scalawags: Black Officeholders during the Reconstruction of Alabama.* Montgomery, AL: R. L. Bailey, 1991.

Bass, Jack. *Taming the Storm: The Life and Times of Judge Frank M. Johnson, Jr., and the South's Fight over Civil Rights.* Athens: University of Georgia Press, 2003.

Beilein, Joseph. *Bushwhackers: Guerrilla Warfare, Manhood, and the Household in Civil War Missouri.* Kent, OH: Kent State University Press, 2016.

Benton, Jeffrey, ed. *The Very Worst Road: Travelers' Accounts of Crossing Alabama's Old Creek Indian Territory, 1820–1847.* Tuscaloosa: University of Alabama Press, 2009.

Berlin, Ira, Joseph Reidy, and Leslie Rowland, eds. *Freedom's Soldiers: The Black Military Experience in the Civil War.* New York: Cambridge University Press, 1998.

Blair, William. *With Malice Toward Some: Treason and Loyalty in the Civil War Era.* Chapel Hill: University of North Carolina Press, 2014.

Bledsoe, Andrew. *Citizen-Officers: The Union and Confederate Junior Officer Corps in the American Civil War.* Baton Rouge: LSU Press, 2015.

Blight, David. *Race and Reunion: The Civil War in American Memory.* Cambridge, MA: Harvard University Press, 2001.

Bradley, George, and Richard Dahlen. *From Conciliation to Conquest: The Sack of Athens and the Court Martial of Colonel John B. Turchin.* Tuscaloosa: University of Alabama Press, 2006.

Bradley, Mark L. *The Battle of Bentonville: Last Stand in the Carolinas.* El Dorado Hills, CA: Savas Beatie, 1996.

Brady, Lisa. *War Upon the Land: Military Strategy and the Transformation of Southern Landscapes During the American Civil War.* Athens: University of Georgia Press, 2012.

Braund, Kathryn. *Deerskins and Duffels: The Creek Indian Trade with Anglo-America, 1685–1815.* Lincoln: University of Nebraska Press, 1993.

———, ed. *Tohopeka: Rethinking the Creek War and the War of 1812.* Tuscaloosa: University of Alabama Press, 2012.

Brent, Joseph. *Occupied Corinth: The Contraband Camp and the First Alabama Regiment of African Descent 1862–1864.* Washington, DC: American Battlefield Protection Program, 1995.

Bryant, James. *The 36th Infantry, United States Colored Troops in the Civil War.* Jefferson, NC: McFarland, 2012.

Buker, George. *Blockaders, Refugees, and Contrabands: Civil War on Florida's Gulf Coast.* Tuscaloosa: University of Alabama Press, 1993.

Bynum, Victoria. *The Free State of Jones: Mississippi's Longest Civil War.* Chapel Hill: University of North Carolina Press, 2001.

Carey, Anthony. *Sold Down the River: Slavery in the Lower Chattahoochee Valley of Alabama and Georgia.* Tuscaloosa: University of Alabama Press, 2011.

Carter, Dan. *The Politics of Rage: George Wallace, the Origins of the New Conservatism, and the Transformation of American Politics.* Baton Rouge: LSU Press, 2000.

Cashin, Joan. *War Stuff: The Struggle for Human and Environmental Resources in the American Civil War.* New York: Cambridge University Press, 2018.

Castel, Albert. *Decision in the West: The Atlanta Campaign of 1864.* Lawrence: University Press of Kansas, 1992.

Chicoine, Stephen. *John Basil Turchin and the Fight to Free the Slaves.* Westport, CT: Praeger, 2003.

Cimprich, John. *Fort Pillow, a Civil War Massacre and Public Memory.* Baton Rouge: LSU Press, 2005.

Clavin, Matthew J. *Aiming for Pensacola: Fugitive Slaves on the Atlantic and Southern Frontiers.* Cambridge, MA: Harvard University Press, 2015.

Cooling, Benjamin F. *Fort Donelson's Legacy: War and Society in Kentucky and Tennessee, 1862–1863.* Knoxville: University of Tennessee Press, 1997.

———. *To the Battles of Franklin and Nashville and Beyond: Stabilization and Reconstruction in Tennessee and Kentucky, 1864–1866.* Knoxville: University of Tennessee Press, 2011.

Cooper, William. *Liberty and Slavery: Southern Politics to 1860.* New York: Knopf, 1983.

Cooper, William, and James McPherson, *Writing the Civil War: The Quest to Understand.* Columbia: University of South Carolina Press, 1998.

Cornish, Dudley. *The Sable Arm: Negro Troops in the Union Army, 1861–1865.* Lawrence: University Press of Kansas, 1987.

Cowdrey, Albert. *This Land, This South: An Environmental History.* Lexington: University of Kentucky Press, 1996.

Cozzens, Peter. *The Darkest Days of the War: The Battles of Iuka and Corinth.* Chapel Hill: University of North Carolina Press, 1997.

———. *No Better Place to Die: The Battle of Stones River.* Urbana: University of Illinois Press, 1990.

———. *The Shipwreck of Their Hopes: The Battles for Chattanooga.* Urbana: University of Illinois Press, 1994.

———. *This Terrible Sound: The Battle of Chickamauga.* Urbana: University of Illinois Press, 1992.

Crosby, Alfred. *Ecological Imperialism: The Biological Expansion of Europe, 900–1900.* Cambridge, UK: Cambridge University Press, 1986.

Current, Richard Nelson. *Lincoln's Loyalists: Union Soldiers from the Confederacy.* New York: Oxford University Press, 1992.

Danielson, Joseph W. *War's Desolating Scourge: The Union's Occupation of North Alabama.* Lawrence: University Press of Kansas, 2012.

Degler, Carl. *The Other South: Southern Dissenters in the Nineteenth Century.* Boston: Northeastern University Press, 1982.

Dobak, William. *Freedom by the Sword: The U.S. Colored Troops, 1862–1867.* Washington, DC: Center of Military History, 2011.

Dodd, Donald, and Amy Bartlett-Dodd. *The Free State of Winston.* Charleston, SC: Arcadia Publishing, 2000.

Dodd, Donald, and Wynelle Dodd. *Winston: An Antebellum and Civil War History of a Hill County of North Alabama.* Jasper, AL: Elliot, 1972.

Dorman, Lewy. *Party Politics in Alabama from 1850 through 1860.* 1935; repr., Tuscaloosa: University of Alabama Press, 1995.

Drake, Brian Allen, ed. *The Blue, the Gray, and the Green: Toward an Environmental History of the Civil War.* Athens: University of Georgia Press, 2015.

Dunnavant, Robert. *Decatur, Alabama: Yankee Foothold in Dixie, 1861–1865.* Athens, AL: Pea Ridge Press, 1995.

———. *The Railroad War: N. B. Forrest's 1864 Raid through Northern Alabama and Middle Tennessee.* Athens, AL: Pea Ridge Press, 1994.

Egerton, Douglas. *Thunder at the Gates: The Black Civil War Regiments That Redeemed America.* New York: Basic Books, 2016.

Evans, David. *Sherman's Horsemen: Union Cavalry Operations in the Atlanta Campaign.* Bloomington: Indiana University Press, 1996.

Evans, E. Raymond. *Contributions by United States Colored Troops (USCT) of Chattanooga & North Georgia during the American Civil War, Reconstruction and Formation of Chattanooga.* Chickamauga, GA: B. C. M. Foster, 2003.

Feis, William. *Grant's Secret Service: The Intelligence War from Belmont to Appomattox.* Lincoln: University of Nebraska Press, 2004.

Fitzgerald, Michael. *Reconstruction in Alabama: From Civil War to Redemption in the Cotton South.* Baton Rouge: LSU Press, 2017.

———. *The Union League Movement in the Deep South: Politics and Agricultural Change During Reconstruction.* Baton Rouge: LSU Press, 1989.

Fleming, Walter. *Civil War and Reconstruction in Alabama.* New York: Columbia University Press, 1905.

Foner, Eric. *Reconstruction: America's Unfinished Revolution, 1863–1877.* New York: Harper Collins, 1988.

Foster, Gaines. *Ghosts of the Confederacy: Defeat, the Lost Cause, and the Emergence of the New South, 1865–1913.* Oxford, UK: Oxford University Press, 1988.

Freehling, William. *The Road to Disunion.* 2 vols. New York: Oxford University Press, 1991, 2007.

——. *The South vs. the South: How Anti-Confederate Southerners Shaped the Course of the Civil War.* New York: Oxford University Press, 2001.

Fuchs, Richard. *An Unerring Fire: The Massacre at Fort Pillow.* Cranbury, NJ: Associated University Presses, 1994.

Gallagher, Gary. *The Union War.* Cambridge, MA: Harvard University Press, 2011.

Gladstone, William A. *United States Colored Troops, 1863–1867.* Gettysburg, PA: Thomas Publications, 1990.

Glatthaar, Joseph. *Forged in Battle: The Civil War Alliance of Black Soldiers and White Officers.* New York: The Free Press, 1990.

——. *The March to the Sea and Beyond: Sherman's Troops in the Savannah and Carolinas Campaigns.* Baton Rouge: LSU Press, 1985.

Goodrich, Thomas. *Black Flag: Guerrilla Warfare on the Western Border, 1861–1865.* Bloomington: University of Indiana Press, 1995.

Grimsley, Mark. *The Hard Hand of War: Union Military Policy towards Southern Civilians, 1861–1865.* Cambridge, UK: Cambridge University Press, 1995.

Hahn, Steven. *The Invention of the Creek Nation, 1670–1763.* Lincoln: University of Nebraska Press, 2004.

——. *A Nation Under Our Feet: Black Political Struggles in the Rural South from Slavery to the Great Migration.* Cambridge, MA: Harvard University Press, 2003.

Hamilton, Virginia. *Alabama: A History.* New York, Norton, 1977.

Hartman, David, and David Coles. *Biographical Rosters of Florida's Confederate and Union Soldiers, 1861–65.* 6 vols. Wilmington, NC: Broadfoot Publishing, 1995.

Hearn, Chester. *Mobile Bay and the Mobile Campaign: The Last Great Battles of the Civil War.* Jefferson, NC: McFarland, 1998.

Heidler, Jeanne, and David Heidler. *Old Hickory's War: Andrew Jackson and the Quest for Empire.* Baton Rouge: LSU Press, 2003.

Hess, Earl. *The Civil War in the West: Victory and Defeat from the Appalachians to the Mississippi.* Chapel Hill: University of North Carolina Press, 2012.

——. *Civil War Logistics: A Study in Military Transportation.* Baton Rouge: LSU Press, 2017.

Hirshson, Stanley. *Grenville M. Dodge: Soldier, Politician, Railroad Pioneer.* Bloomington: Indiana University Press, 1967.

Hollandsworth, James G. Jr. *The Louisiana Native Guards: The Black Military Experience During the Civil War.* Baton Rouge: LSU Press, 1995.

Hoole, William. *Alabama Tories: The First Alabama Cavalry, U.S.A., 1862–1865.* Tuscaloosa, AL: Confederate Publishing, 1960.

Hoole, William, and Elizabeth Hoole McArthur. *The Yankee Invasion of West Alabama, March to April, 1865, Including the Battle of Trion (Vance), the Battle of Tuscaloosa, the Burning of the University, and the Battle of Romulus.* University, AL: Confederate Publishing, 1985.

Horn, Stanley. *The Decisive Battle of Nashville.* Baton Rouge: LSU Press, 1956.

Hudson, Angela. *Creek Paths and Federal Roads: Indians, Settlers, and Slaves and the Making of the American South.* Chapel Hill: University of North Carolina Press, 2010.

Hughes, Nathaniel. *Bentonville: The Final Battle of Sherman and Johnston.* Chapel Hill: University of North Carolina Press, 1996.

Hurt, R. Douglas. *Agriculture and the Confederacy: Policy, Productivity, and Power in the Civil War South.* Chapel Hill: University of North Carolina Press, 2015.

Inscoe, John, and Robert Kenzer, eds. *Enemies of the Country: New Perspectives on Unionists in the Civil War South.* Athens: University of Georgia Press, 2001.

Johnson, Russell. *Warriors into Workers: The Civil War and the Formation of Urban-Industrial Society in a Northern City.* New York: Fordham University Press, 2003.

Jones, James Pickett. *Yankee Blitzkrieg: Wilson's Raid Through Alabama and Georgia.* Lexington: University Press of Kentucky, 1976.

Jordan, Winthrop. *Tumult and Silence at Second Creek: An Inquiry into a Civil War Slave Conspiracy.* Baton Rouge: LSU Press, 1993.

Keeley, Lawrence. *War Before Civilization.* New York: Oxford University Press, 1996.

Kelley, Robin D. G. *Hammer and Hoe: Alabama Communists During the Great Depression.* Chapel Hill: University of North Carolina Press, 1990.

Kelton, Paul. *Epidemics and Enslavement: Biological Catastrophe in the Native Southeast, 1492–1715.* Lincoln: University of Nebraska Press, 2007.

Kirby, Jack Temple. *Mockingbird Song: Ecological Landscapes of the South.* Chapel Hill: University of North Carolina Press, 2006.

Klingberg, Frank. *The Southern Claims Commission.* Milwood, NY: Kraus, 1980.

Knight, Vernon, ed. *The Search for Mabila: The Decisive Battle between Hernando de Soto and Chief Tascalusa.* Tuscaloosa: University of Alabama Press, 2009.

Kolchin, Peter. *First Freedom: The Responses of Alabama's Blacks to Emancipation and Reconstruction.* Westport, CT: Greenwood, 1972.

Kruse, Kevin. *White Flight: Atlanta and the Making of Modern Conservatism.* Princeton, NJ: Princeton University Press, 2005.

Lang, Andrew. *In the Wake of War: Military Occupation, Emancipation, and Civil War America.* Baton Rouge: LSU Press, 2017.

Lewis, Herbert. *Clearing the Thickets: A History of Antebellum Alabama.* New Orleans: Quid Pro Books, 2013.

Mackey, Robert. *The Uncivil War: Irregular Warfare in the Upper South, 1861–1865.* Norman: University of Oklahoma Press, 2004.

Manning, Chandra. *Troubled Refuge: Struggling for Freedom in the Civil War.* New York: Vintage, 2016.

Marsh, Sharon. *The 1st Florida Cavalry Union Volunteers in the Civil War: The Men and Regimental History; and What That Tells Us About the Area During the War.* N.p.: Sharon D. Marsh, 2016.

Martin, Bessie. *A Rich Man's War, A Poor Man's Fight: Desertion of Alabama Troops from the Confederate Army.* New York: Columbia University Press, 1932.

Masich, Andrew. *Civil War in the Southwest Borderlands, 1861–1867.* Norman: University of Oklahoma Press, 2017.

Massey, Mary Elizabeth. *Refugee Life in the Confederacy.* Baton Rouge: LSU Press, 1964.

Mays, Joe. *Black Americans and Their Contributions toward Union Victory in the American Civil War, 1861–1865.* Lanham, MD: University Press of America, 1984.

McCaslin, Richard. *Tainted Breeze: The Great Hanging at Gainesville, Texas, 1862.* Baton Rouge: LSU Press, 1994.

McGregory, Jerrilyn. *Wiregrass Country.* Jackson: University Press of Mississippi, 1997.

McIlwain, Christopher. *Civil War Alabama.* Tuscaloosa: University of Alabama Press, 2016.

———. *1865 Alabama.* Tuscaloosa: University of Alabama Press, 2017.

McKenzie, Robert. *One South or Many: Plantation Belt and Upcountry in Civil War–Era Tennessee.* New York: Cambridge, 1994.

McKnight, Brian, and Barton Myers, eds. *The Guerrilla Hunters: Irregular Conflicts during the Civil War.* Baton Rouge: LSU Press, 2017.

McMillan, Malcolm, ed. *The Alabama Confederate Reader.* Tuscaloosa: University of Alabama Press, 1963.

———. *The Disintegration of a Confederate State: Three Governors and Alabama's Wartime Home Front, 1861–1865.* Macon, GA: Mercer University Press, 1986.

McPherson, James. *For Cause and Comrades: Why Men Fought in the Civil War.* Oxford, UK: Oxford University Press, 1997.

———. *The Negro's Civil War: How American Negroes Felt and Acted During the War for the Union.* New York: Pantheon, 1965.

Meier, Kathryn Shively. *Nature's Civil War: Common Soldiers and the Environment in 1862 Virginia.* Chapel Hill: University of North Carolina Press, 2013.

Mezurek, Kelly. *For Their Own Cause: The 27th United States Colored Troops.* Kent, OH: Kent State University Press, 2016.

Miller, Edward. *The Black Civil War Soldiers of Illinois.* Columbia: University of South Carolina Press, 1998.

Mills, Gary. *Southern Loyalists in the Civil War: The Southern Claims Commission.* Baltimore: Genealogical Publishing, 1994.

Mitchell, Reid. *Civil War Soldiers: Their Expectations and Their Experiences.* New York: Viking, 1988.

Mittelstadt, Jennifer. *The Rise of the Military Welfare State.* Cambridge, MA: Harvard University Press, 2015.

Mize, Joel. *Unionists of the Warrior Mountains of Alabama.* Lakewood, CO: Dixie Historical Research, 2004.

Morgans, James Patrick. *Grenville Mellen Dodge in the Civil War: Union Spymaster, Railroad Builder and Organizer of the Fourth Iowa Volunteer Infantry.* Jefferson, NC: McFarland, 2016.

Mountcastle, Clay. *Punitive War: Confederate Guerrillas and Union Reprisals.* Lawrence: University Press of Kansas, 2009.

Murray, Williamson, and Wayne Wei-Siang Hsieh. *A Savage War: A Military History of the Civil War.* Princeton, NJ: Princeton University Press, 2016.

Myers, Barton A. *Rebels Against the Confederacy: North Carolina's Unionists.* New York: Cambridge University Press, 2014.

Nelson, Megan Kate. *Ruin Nation: Destruction and the American Civil War.* Athens: University of Georgia Press, 2012.

Noe, Kenneth. *Reluctant Rebels: The Confederates Who Joined the Army after 1861.* Chapel Hill: University of North Carolina Press, 2010.

———, ed. *The Yellowhammer War: Civil War and Reconstruction in Alabama.* Tuscaloosa: University of Alabama Press, 2013.

O'Brien, Michael. *Mountain Partisans: Guerrilla Warfare in the Southern Appalachians, 1861–1865.* Westport, CT: Praeger, 1999.

Otto, John. *Southern Agriculture during the Civil War Era, 1860–1880.* Westport, CT: Greenwood, 1994.

Parson, Thomas. *Work for Giants: The Campaign and Battle of Tupelo/Harrisburg, Mississippi, June–July 1864.* Kent, OH: Kent State University Press, 2014.

Parsons, Elaine. *Ku-Klux: The Birth of the Klan during Reconstruction.* Chapel Hill: University of North Carolina Press, 2016.

Potter, Johnny. *First Tennessee & Alabama Independent Vidette Cavalry Roster, 1863–1864: Companies A, B, C, D, E, F, G, H.* Chattanooga, TN: Mountain Press, 1995.

Quarles, Benjamin. *The Negro in the Civil War.* Boston: Little, Brown, 1953.

Rable, George. *But There Was No Peace: The Role of Violence in the Politics of Reconstruction.* Athens: University of Georgia Press, 2007.

Redkey, Edwin, ed. *A Grand Army of Black Men: Letters from African-American Soldiers in the Union Army, 1861–1865.* Cambridge, UK: Cambridge University Press, 1992.

Reid, Richard. *Freedom for Themselves: North Carolina's Black Soldiers in the Civil War Era,* Chapel Hill: University of North Carolina Press, 2008.

Rogers, William, Robert Ward, Leah Atkins, and Wayne Flynt. *Alabama: The History of a Deep South State.* Tuscaloosa: University of Alabama Press, 1994.

Royster, Charles. *The Destructive War. William Tecumseh Sherman, Stonewall Jackson, and the Americans.* New York: Knopf, 1991.

Sanders, Charles W. Jr. *In the Hands of the Enemy: Military Prisons of the Civil War*. Baton Rouge: LSU Press, 2005.

Sefton, James. *The United States Army and Reconstruction, 1865–1877*. Baton Rouge: LSU Press, 1967.

Sellers, James. *Slavery in Alabama*. Tuscaloosa: University of Alabama Press, 1994.

Severance, Ben. *Portraits of Conflict: A Photographic History of Alabama in the Civil War*. Fayetteville: University of Arkansas Press, 2012.

Shaffer, Donald R. *After the Glory: The Struggles of Black Civil War Veterans*. Lawrence: University Press of Kansas, 2004.

Silver, Timothy. *A New Face on the Countryside: Indians, Colonists and Slaves in South Atlantic Forests, 1500–1800*. Cambridge, UK: Cambridge University Press, 1990.

Smith, John David, ed. *Black Soldiers in Blue: African American Troops in the Civil War Era*. Chapel Hill: University of North Carolina Press, 2002.

Smith, Ned. *The 2nd Maine Cavalry in the Civil War: A History and Roster*. Jefferson, NC: McFarland, 2014.

Smith, Timothy. *Corinth 1862: Siege, Battle, Occupation*. Lawrence: University Press of Kansas, 2012.

Spurgeon, Ian. *Soldiers in the Army of Freedom: The 1st Kansas Colored, the Civil War's First African American Combat Unit*. Norman: University of Oklahoma Press, 2014.

Starr, Stephen. *Jennison's Jayhawkers: A Civil War Cavalry Regiment and Its Commander*. Baton Rouge: LSU Press, 1974.

——. *The Union Cavalry in the Civil War*. Vol. 3, *The War in the West, 1861–1865*. Baton Rouge: LSU Press, 1985.

Sterling, Robin. *Tales of Old Blount County*. Owens Cross Roads, AL: Robin Sterling, 2013.

——. *Winston County, Alabama Files from the Southern Claims Commission*. Owens Cross Roads, AL: Robin Sterling, 2013.

Stith, Matthew. *Extreme Civil War: Guerrilla Warfare, Environment, and Race on the Trans-Mississippi Frontier*. Baton Rouge: LSU Press, 2016.

Storey, Margaret. *Loyalty and Loss: Alabama's Unionists in the Civil War and Reconstruction*. Baton Rouge: LSU Press, 2004.

Sutherland, Daniel. *A Savage Conflict: The Decisive Role of Guerrillas in the American Civil War*. Chapel Hill: University of North Carolina Press, 2009.

——, ed. *Guerrillas, Unionists, and Violence on the Confederate Home Front*. Fayetteville: University of Arkansas Press, 1999.

Tatum, Georgia. *Disloyalty in the Confederacy*. Lincoln: University of Nebraska Press, 2000.

Thomas, Daniel. *Fort Toulouse: The French Outpost at the Alabamas on the Coosa*. Tuscaloosa: University of Alabama Press, 1989.

Thomas, William. *The Iron Way: Railroads, the Civil War, and the Making of Modern America*. New Haven: Yale University Press, 2011.

Thompson, Wesley. *The Free State of Winston: A History of Winston County, Alabama*. Winfield, AL.: Pareil Press, 1968.

Thornton, J. Mills. *Politics and Power in a Slave Society: Alabama, 1800–1860*. Baton Rouge: LSU Press, 1978.

Todd, Glenda McWhirter. *First Alabama Cavalry, U.S.A.: Homage to Patriotism*. Westminster, MD: Heritage, 2006.

Towns, Peggy Allen. *Duty Driven: The Plight of North Alabama's African Americans During the Civil War*. Bloomington, IN: Author House, 2012.

Urwin, Gregory. *Black Flag over Dixie: Racial Atrocities and Reprisals in the Civil War*. Carbondale: Southern Illinois University Press, 2004.

Wakelyn, Jon L. *Confederates against the Confederacy: Essays on Leadership and Loyalty*. Westport, CT: Praeger, 2002.

———. *Southern Unionist Pamphlets on the Civil War*. Columbia: University of Missouri Press, 1999.

Walther, Eric. *William Lowndes Yancey and the Coming of the Civil War*. Chapel Hill: University of North Carolina Press, 2006.

Waselkov, Gregory. *Conquering Spirit: Fort Mims and the Redstick War of 1813–14*. Tuscaloosa: University of Alabama Press, 2006.

Weinfeld, Daniel. *The Jackson County War: Reconstruction and Resistance in Post–Civil War Florida*. Tuscaloosa: University of Alabama Press, 2012.

Wheelan, Joseph. *Libby Prison Breakout: The Daring Escape from the Notorious Civil War Prison*. New York: PublicAffairs, 2010.

Wiggins, Sarah Woolfolk. *The Scalawag in Alabama Politics, 1865–1881*. Tuscaloosa: University of Alabama Press, 1977.

Wiley, Bell I. *The Life of Billy Yank: The Common Soldier of the Union*. Indianapolis: Bobbs-Merrill, 1952.

Willett, Robert. *The Lightning Mule Brigade: Abel Streight's 1863 Raid into Alabama*. Carmel, IN: Guild Press, 1999.

Williams, David. *Bitterly Divided: The South's Inner Civil War*. New York: New Press, 2008.

———. *I Freed Myself: African American Self-Emancipation in the Civil War Era*. Cambridge, UK: Cambridge University Press, 2014.

———. *Rich Man's War: Class, Caste, and Confederate Defeat in the Lower Chattahoochee Valley*. Athens: University of Georgia Press, 1998.

Williams, George. *A History of the Negro Troops in the War of the Rebellion, 1861–1865*. New York: Harper and Brothers, 1888.

Williams, Horace Randall, ed. *Weren't No Good Times: Personal Accounts of Slavery in Alabama*. Winston-Salem, NC: John F. Blair, 2004.

Wills, Brian Steel. *The Confederacy's Greatest Cavalryman: Nathan Bedford Forrest.* Lawrence: University Press of Kansas, 1992.

———. *The River Was Dyed with Blood: Nathan Bedford Forrest and Fort Pillow.* Norman: University of Oklahoma Press, 2014.

Wilson, Joseph. *The Black Phalanx.* Hartford: American Publishing, 1890.

Woodward, C. Vann. *Origins of the New South.* Baton Rouge: LSU Press, 1951.

———. *The Strange Career of Jim Crow.* Oxford, UK: Oxford University Press, 1955.

Woodworth, Steven. *Six Armies in Tennessee: The Chickamauga and Chattanooga Campaign.* Lincoln: University of Nebraska Press, 1998.

ARTICLES

Bailey, Hugh. "Disloyalty in Early Confederate Alabama." *Journal of Southern History* 23 (Nov. 1957): 522–28.

Bailey, Joe. "Union Lifeline in Tennessee: A Military History of the Nashville and Northwestern Railroad." *Tennessee Historical Quarterly* 67 (Summer 2008): 106–23.

Bearss, Edwin. "Rousseau's Raid on the Montgomery and West Point Railroad." *Alabama Historical Quarterly* 25 (Spring–Summer 1963): 7–48.

Bethel, Elizabeth. "The Freedman's Bureau in Alabama." *Journal of Southern History* 14 (Feb. 1948): 49–92.

Cimprich, John, and Robert Mainfort Jr. "The Fort Pillow Massacre: A Statistical Note." *Journal of American History* 76 (Dec. 1989): 830–37.

Clavin, Matthew J. "Interracialism and Revolution on the Southern Frontier: Pensacola in the Civil War." *Journal of Southern History* 80 (Nov. 2014): 791–826.

Dee, Christine. "Trying James Hickman: The Politics of Loyalty in a Civil War Community." *Alabama Review* 58 (April 2005): 83–112.

Dodd, Donald. "The Free State of Winston." *Alabama Heritage* 28 (Spring 1993): 8–19.

Fitzgerald, Michael. "Alabama's Class Politics through the Civil War Crisis and its Echoes." *Civil War Book Review* (Winter 2018).

———. "Another Kind of Glory: Black Participation and Its Consequences in the Campaign for Confederate Mobile." *Alabama Review* 54 (Oct. 2001): 243–73.

———. "From Unionists to Scalawags: Elite Dissent in Civil War Mobile." *Alabama Review* 55 (April 2002): 106–21.

———. "Wager Swayne, the Freedmen's Bureau, and the Politics of Reconstruction in Alabama." *Alabama Review* 48 (July 1995): 188–232.

Fretwell, Mark. "Rousseau's Alabama Raid." *Alabama Historical Quarterly* 18 (Winter 1956): 526–51.

Gabel, Martha. "General O. M. Mitchel's Occupation of Huntsville." *Huntsville Historical Review* 1 (July 1971): 12–28.

Gavin, Michael. "A History of the 110th and 111th Regiments United States Colored Troops (USCT)." N.p., 2004.

Granade, Ray. "Violence: An Instrument of Policy in Reconstruction Alabama." *Alabama Historical Review* (Fall–Winter 1968): 181–202.

Horton, Paul. "Lightning Rod Scalawag: The Unlikely Political Career of Thomas Minott Peters." *Alabama Review* 64 (April 2011): 35–48.

———. "Submitting to the 'Shadow of Slavery': The Secession Crisis and Civil War in Alabama's Lawrence County." *Civil War History* 44 (1998).

Jones, Allen. "Unionism and Disaffection in South Alabama: The Case of Alfred Holley." *Alabama Review* 24 (April 1971): 114–32.

Long, Durwood. "Unanimity and Disloyalty in Secessionist Alabama." *Civil War History* 11 (Sept. 1965): 257–73.

McGee, Val. "The Confederate Who Switched Sides: The Saga of Captain Joseph G. Sanders." *Alabama Review* 47 (Jan. 1994): 20–28.

McKenzie, Robert. "The Economic Impact of Federal Operations in Alabama during the Civil War." *Alabama Historical Quarterly* 38 (1976): 51–68.

Owens, Scott. "The Federal Invasion of Pickens County, April 5–7, 1865: Croxton's Sipsey River Campaign." *Alabama Review* 62 (April 2009): 83–112.

Purcell, Douglas. "Military Conscription in Alabama during the Civil War." *Alabama Review* 34 (1981): 94–106.

Rafuse, Ethan. "'Little Phil,' a 'Bad Old Man,' and the 'Gray Ghost': Hybrid Warfare and the Fight for the Shenandoah Valley, August–November 1864." *Journal of Military History* 81 (July 2017): 775–801.

Ryan, Harriet, ed. "The Letters of Harden Perkins Cochrane, 1862–1864, Part 1." *Alabama Review* 7 (Oct. 1954): 277–94.

Shapiro, Norman. "Invasion and Occupancy of Huntsville, Alabama by the Federals, April 11 to August 31, 1862." *Huntsville Historical Review* 27 (Winter–Spring 2000): 1–24.

Storey, Margaret. "Civil War Unionists and the Political Culture of Loyalty in Alabama, 1860–1861." *Journal of Southern History* 69 (Feb. 2003): 71–106.

Sutherland, Daniel. "Sideshow No Longer: A Historiographical Review of the Guerrilla War." *Civil War History* 46 (2000): 5–23.

Tumlin, Mary. "Criminal Justice in Madison County, Alabama, April 1865 to December 1974." *Huntsville Historical Review* 19 (Summer–Fall 1992): 3–10.

Walker, Cam. "Corinth: The Story of a Contraband Camp." *Civil War History* 20, no. 1 (March 1974): 5–22.

Watson, Elbert. "The Story of Nickajack." *Alabama Review* 20 (Jan. 1967): 17–26.

Wiggins, Sarah Woolfork. "The 'Pig Iron' Kelley Riot in Mobile, May 14, 1867." *Alabama Review* 23 (1970): 45–55.

Williams, David. "The 'Faithful Slave' Is About Played Out: Civil War Slave Resistance in the Lower Chattahoochee Valley." *Alabama Review* 52 (April 1999): 84–104.

Woolfolk, Sarah. "George E. Spencer: A Carpetbagger in Alabama." *Alabama Review* 19 (Jan. 1966): 41–52.

THESES AND DISSERTATIONS

Dodd, Donald. "Unionism in Confederate Alabama." PhD diss., University of Georgia, 1969.

Evans, William. "Rousseau's Raid, July 10–July 22, 1864." PhD diss., University of Georgia, 1982.

Newhall, Caroline Wood. "'This Is The Point On Which The Whole Matter Hinges': Locating Black Voices In Civil War Prisons." MA thesis, University of North Carolina, 2016.

Ponsford, Brent. "Major-General Grenville M. Dodge's Military Intelligence Operations During the Civil War." Unpublished MA thesis, Iowa State University, 1976.

Rein, Christopher M. "Trans-Mississippi Southerners in the Union Army, 1862–1865." MA thesis, Louisiana State University, 2001.

WEBSITES

http://www.1stalabamacavalryusv.com
http://www.encyclopediaofalabama.org/
http://www.freestateofwinston.org/

Index